The Economist

AMERICA
1843–1993

The Economist

AMERICA
1843–1993

150 YEARS OF REPORTING
THE AMERICAN CONNECTION

ALASTAIR BURNET

The
Economist
Books

First published in Great Britain by

The Economist Books Ltd
25 St James's Street
London SW1A 1 HG

The greatest care has been taken in compiling this book. However,
no responsibility can be accepted by the publishers or contributors
for the accuracy of the information presented. Where opinion is
expressed it is that of the author and does not necessarily coincide
with the editorial views of *The Economist* Newspaper.

Any correspondence regarding this publication should be addressed
to: The Editorial Director, The Economist Books Ltd,
25 St James's Street, London SW1A 1HG.

A catalogue record for this book is available from the British Library.

ISBN 0 241 00182 X

*Endpaper picture: New York, 1858. The city of half a million
people, much the largest in the Union, symbolised to the paper
the commercial America that lived by the North Atlantic trade
with industrial Britain. The United States, it believed then,
must become the world's greatest country.*

Printed in Great Britain by The Bath Press, Avon

CONTENTS

INTRODUCTION

THAT RELATIONSHIP

The Economist, for 150 years, has thought of itself as being at the centre of the Anglo-American connection, and for much of the time it has been right. From the start it looked upon America and Americans as the best hope for the future, an American future that it believed was destined to dominate the twentieth century as Britain dominated the nineteenth. The paper was designed by its founder, James Wilson, financial secretary to the treasury, in 1843 to be an independent supporter of the free trade cause orchestrated by the radicals, Richard Cobden and John Bright. So it identified itself with the young republic whose conversion, it supposed, would be the embodiment of the cause's universal success.

When Cobden declared that "the superiority of the United States to England is ultimately as certain as the next eclipse" it agreed with him. British policies that presumed otherwise had no realism. Any threat to the security and wellbeing of Victorian Britain did not come from the supposed enmity or impoverishing armaments of a France or a Russia but from the silent and peaceful rivalry of American commerce. This was beyond conventional politics and politicians.

In essence, the paper's ideal of progress was the unexpected arrival in Liverpool docks in April 1845 of the *Muskingham*, a small 350-ton American ship, built on the Ohio River above Cincinnati, which had sailed 1,700 miles down to the Gulf of Mexico and then across the Atlantic with a cargo of oil cake and Ohio provisions. To *The Economist* it was as if it had revealed the human capability to overleap customs houses and protectionist laws, as trade should, and as it did between the opposite banks of the River Thames. The paper never thought Americans lived on a different planet.

It was fascinated by America and Americans from the beginning. It was captivated by the potential of the country, the energy of the people, their intellectual vigour, and by the very difference between their society and manners and British ways. It believed it had a commercial purpose to explain and interpret one country to the other, and to use its experience to write with authority for both. In turn this became a political function, defining what it saw as an inherent common interest in the crises of the two centuries. It has been an extraordinary achievement.

The paper's consistent policy has been to encourage the Anglo-American connection as the first foreign policy requirement of both countries. It has regretted whenever, in the past 50 years, this has seemed less intrinsic to American interests than British, but even when the connection has been at its least effective and most distrustful, the paper has seen it as the most singular relationship between two considerable powers in history. Exceptionally, the political and economic superiority, and hence the liberal democratic responsibility, was passed from one to the other almost by consent and almost without confrontation.

In this the paper's influence has, of necessity, been targeted. The authority it has had has come from the authority of its readers. These have been on both sides of the Atlantic from the early days. The outbreak of the American civil war in 1861 was a bad blow to its slender circulation (then of some 3,000 a week in all) and to its new editor, Walter Bagehot. When in 1870–71 a united Germany destroyed the French army and besieged Paris, the paper was the first advocate of settling all Britain's disputes with the United States. They were settled. The British foreign secretary, Lord Granville, who considered Bagehot a valued friend, declared that whenever he felt uncertain he liked to wait to see what the next *Economist* had to say. Woodrow Wilson, president from 1913 to 1921, was a Bagehot admirer too; he epitomised the ideals and the illusions of his generation of *Economist* readers.

The paper, and especially its American Survey, has been necessary reading in all modern American administrations, and not only in the State Department and the National Security Council. John Kennedy, Lyndon Johnson and Richard Nixon were three presidents who valued it personally. Its weekly circulation in the United States has risen to 215,000 (1992 figure), an unprecedented influence for a non-American publication. It has been in its way a part, and even a reflection, of the relationship itself.

Things have not always gone *The Economist*'s way, which may have been just as well. An emergent America run by the free-trading (and slave-trading) south would not have survived long. Bagehot himself would not have minded if North America had been divided into several competing countries; but a Europe in the new world would not have had the ability to redress the errors and horrors of the old Europe when needed. It suited the paper to encourage American imperialism at the turn of the century; it was the isolationist United States that decided to limit that instinct, not the liberal one.

The paper's own self-confidence in pursuing its policy has sometimes been patchy. America-firsters have always disturbed it, probably too much. American demands in the western alliance have worried it less than being ignored by America altogether. It condemned Churchill for appeasing the Americans too much and too often; it believed it knew better, but its efforts at independence were not always prescient.

It has, however, got most things right on the decisions that have mattered over the years. This has been not so much because of its own preferences and even less because of what happened to be the popular British opinion of the time, but because it normally understood what to expect of Americans. Its conceit has been that it was regarded, and regarded itself, as a "spare chancellor" in determining British economic policy, but its more important function has probably been as a reliable alternative British embassy in Washington, judging American interests by different criteria from those of British state or party machines. An independent eye has mattered.

Thus the paper never saw Canada as an essential British interest to be defended; it was never preoccupied with the idea that Canada was somehow a permanent hostage for British good behaviour. It never supposed that the United States would exactly desert Britain in the crises of the two world wars, but did so without sentiment; it never counted on direct American intervention in either, except to ensure what were manifestly American interests.

It never sought, and always opposed, the concept of an exclusive Anglo-American alliance, even when occasional American moods and opinions favoured it. Sensibly, it doubted if everyone else would allow it. It utterly opposed any notion of a naval race with the United States in the 1920s, whatever the admirals wanted, even though it was the last time that the Royal Navy still appeared to give Britain a world superpower's authority. It grasped very early on how far a dependent state can safely expect to go to influence or divert the policies of a related military and commercial mega-state. In the years of Britain's further decline it has never pretended, even to itself, that the United States would allow Britain a refuge in a North American economic community: Europe has been the only path.

If this adds up to understanding the art of the possible, it accounts for a sound enough record on the 15 primary issues in Anglo-American relations over the 150 years of *The Economist*'s life and commentary. On these tests of attitude the paper proves to have been reliable on American actions on all but one (on which the Macmillan government was almost as shaky): Cuba and the missile crisis in 1962. The 15 issues are:

1. Economic predominance.
2. Intervention in the civil war.
3. The *Alabama* arbitration treaty, 1871.
4. The Spanish-American War.
5. Neutrality, 1914–17.
6. Isolationism and its consequences.
7. Naval rivalry, 1927–30.
8. Neutrality again, 1939–41.
9. The strains of alliance, 1941–45.
10. Cold war policies.
11. The bomb.
12. Suez, 1956.
13. The Cuban missile crisis.
14. Vietnam.
15. The Reagan programme.

THE PROMISING LAND

The paper grasped, at its outset, that the United States would be the most important country by the end of the century. Immigration would give America a population of 100m, far ahead of Britain and France (Germany was not yet united; Matthew Perry only anchored in Tokyo Bay in 1853). These would be "intelligent people", with "railroads, telegraphs and other still more wonderful inventions", having a vast influence over the world's life and trade. It would be a free country, like Britain, and unlike Europe which was menaced by anarchy and despotism. The paper never forgot this; it motivated its approach to America and its patience towards Americans it disagreed with.

The economies of the two countries were then complementary. Britain was the great manufacturing country of the world, America "the great field for the production of much of the food and the raw material on which our industry can alone thrive". Nearly half American exports went to Britain; 40% of American imports came from Britain. The paper believed that free trade between them was irresistible; there would be reciprocal benefits that even politicians would understand. It was wrong. But it did not stop believing, and it was not going to make life difficult for the backward and evasive partner. Every Democrat from James K. Polk to Woodrow Wilson was looked to, hopefully. The rise of American industry, especially in New England and Pennsylvania, backed by superior education and driven by "an energy absolutely unknown in any other part of the world", was a challenge that the paper refused to view with the "narrow jealousy" of the outmoded.

It believed that the world was a market, that American ingenuity and skill would prosper there, as would British. Cotton, tobacco and wheat had to be sold. Yankee clipper ships might excite admiration, but the chief trading routes, and especially the North Atlantic, were being dominated by British steam. American machinery had surprised the Great Exhibition of 1851, but the exhibition itself was a consequence of free trade. This was not the voice of comfortable Britain, unaware that it would be overtaken, but the contrary; it was a voice from a country rich enough and confident enough to see ahead and refuse to let essentially minor disagreements stand in the way of a beneficial design.

So the paper did not like the American annexation of Texas, which Britain had recognised as an independent country, chiefly because it was annexed by the wrong Americans, the "reckless and lawless land-jobbers" anxious to accommodate the interests of the slave-breeding states. It suspected that a defence of Texas might be easily converted into aggression on Mexico, which duly followed. It did not suggest British intervention when California fell to American conquest in 1846. It saw no reason why Britain should dispute "so worthless a possession" as Oregon or why the United States should risk the destruction of New York by British bombardment for territory "requiring a five months' voyage to reach it". Two populations amounting to 46m with splendid prospects ought not to be wasting their time.

Its view of Canada, the fixed British obligation on the continent, was central to this detachment. European statesmen, it thought, should have no interest in territory which could not be other than a charge and an encumbrance; Canada was not going to become a manufacturing country for years and perhaps never would; but Canadians were not silly enough to pay import duties of up to 40% in a United States committed to protecting manufacturing corporations in New England. The Canadian border was so long as to be undefendable. But as long as Canadians wished to be part of the empire, they should be defended. This was a deflation of American, or chiefly American-Irish, claims that Canada was an imperial anomaly in the western hemisphere and so susceptible to invasion. It was no longer to be allowed to be a major distraction in Anglo-American relations.

It was the paper's belief that the United States should be treated seriously as an international power, brought into ever closer touch with Europe by the steamship and the annihilation of distance, not isolated from it. The Americans had no military force; they and their Monroe doctrine were protected not just by distance but by the Royal Navy, whatever they chose to think of it. But the Americans had moral force, and the power of trade to back it up. When, after the Battle of Inkerman in the Crimean war, the House of Representatives' foreign affairs committee suggested to President Franklin Pierce that he should offer to mediate, British opinion was dismissive. The paper quickly took it up when it realised that mediation was strongly supported by the mercantile community of New York.

Here was the country that, "in all probability", was going to become "the most powerful nation that ever existed on the earth" suggesting a policy that might be in European interests. It should not be slighted. The merchants of New York actually spoke a universal language. War destroyed trade, but all nations "are now traders, even the most barbarous". It would not necessarily be right, but the voice would be increasingly heard.

CIVIL WAR ILLUSIONS

The paper was cautious over the civil war. It abominated slavery, but it believed the South had rights and it thought war, and especially any encouragement of black insurrection, was the wrong way to get abolition. It vastly underestimated Abraham Lincoln. It did not seek or support European intervention and when there were difficulties with the North its advice was temperate. Walter Bagehot, the editor, did not think the South had the strength to win: a wealthy 20m whites must conquer 7m poor ones. But his fallacy was to suppose that as the South's territory was too extensive to be occupied so the North would not succeed conclusively, either.

This argued for diplomatic prudence. So the paper shared neither the pro-southern sympathies of much of the British middle class nor the pro-union ones of much of the working class. That the North would be beaten at first it thought "exceedingly probable". That the South itself withheld its cotton and tried relatively little blockade-running was unexpected. It averted much of the danger of British clashes with Federal cruisers and concentrated the paper's attention on financial relief for the cotton trades in the north of England and on new sources of cotton supply.

The two Confederate diplomats, James Mason and John Slidell, taken off the British mail packet *Trent* in 1861, were an explosive cargo, but the paper believed the "insane outrage" was prompted more by bitterness against the South than "insolence to us". Lincoln, it thought, acted wisely in handing them back, whatever the grounds. It advised the Foreign Office to ask "courteously but peremptorily" when there was future trouble.

That arrived with the Confederate commerce-destroyer *Alabama*, built on the Mersey, which Lord Palmerston's government failed to arrest in time. The paper's instinct was to insist that Britain had behaved legally, but news of the mercantile panic in New York and Boston changed its mind: if ever there were 20 French, Russian and American *Alabamas* preying on

British shipping the cost would be "fearful". The paper accepted, after the war, that damages were due from the British taxpayer. The diplomatic reality was that both London and Washington knew neither could afford to go to war against the other. Lancashire had to manage with little or inferior cotton, but hefty British shipments of arms and material to the North and northern ones of wheat to Britain crossed the Atlantic almost unscathed.

The paper adhered to Palmerston's policy of acknowledging the Confederacy as a belligerent, but not giving it full recognition. It rebuked the youthful William Gladstone for his speech in which he "led the world to expect it". It had nothing to do with notions of mediating, which would have required recognition, preferring that to be left to Napoleon III. It had no objection (as the Foreign Office had none) to the French expedition that took Mexico City in 1863 and installed the luckless Maximilian of Austria as emperor.

That was not Britain's business. British military resources were committed to Canada, where anything might happen: Confederate raids south across the border, Fenian raids the other way. There had been threatening talk in Washington after the North's early defeats that it would recompense itself in Canada; and after 1865 General Ulysses S. Grant's victorious army would have been formidable to stop.

In Bagehot's own eyes there was an argument for redrawing the map of America to the United States' disadvantage. European minds saw no difficulty in a division between four or more American nation states, of which one might be a beaten Confederacy, economically feeble and confined east of the Mississippi, where slavery would die out in time. This satisfied a wish to stifle American conceit rather than create new alliances and opportunities for Europe to exploit. It came, certainly, from a mind that did not understand Lincoln's.

It was a lapse in the paper's grasp of reality. By 1864 it had come to see Lincoln's purpose in the Union as well as the Union's growing military ability, and it much preferred him to a General McClellan who would accept slavery to preserve the Union. When Lincoln was shot his virtues, it seemed, became even easier to understand. It was enough for the paper's reputation that it had read the civil war badly but not fatally wrong. Britain and the United States had looked each other in the eye, and both had blinked.

THE NEW IMPERIALIST

With the war over, the paper was concerned to get the pieces picked up, to get, if it could be got, a "hearty understanding" with the Americans again, even to think of an America that could become a free-trade ally one day. It wanted the *Alabama* damages settled by arbitration. If the Americans would not do the same for Fenian damage in Canada that was acceptable; the essential was to restore "cordial relations" with the United States which were the best way of ensuring that future Fenian enterprises would not succeed.

The United States was an important power and market. A strong president (it expected Grant to be elected) could be relied on, especially when not dependent on Irish and anti-English votes. No country was less likely to tolerate the communist International or the works of "Dr Karl Marx". It was safely liberal: married women controlled their own property without the family suffering. It had just bought Alaska from the Russians but the paper did not expect it to buy or invade Cuba; if it did, there was "no good reason why this country should object", although some Americans might.

The decisive factor was the Prussian success in the 1870 war. To those who wished Britain to stay neutral in Europe the paper argued that, as the United States was now so dominant in North America, it was right to settle all disagreements with it. To those who wanted future intervention in Europe on the side of "self-government and freedom", any embroilment with the Americans would be fatal. Britain would be "paralysed". In any event, no war with the United States was ever likely to leave Americans "more just, or happy, or free". This policy on Germany was to be permanent. But the paper was not looking for an Anglo-American alliance. When W.E. Forster, a potential successor to Gladstone, suggested the idea to the Union League Club of New York in 1874, the paper called it "grandiose", doubted if it were practicable between a protectionist country and free-trading Britain; anyway, it was "most perilous" even to aim at it.

The right way was to settle differences as they arose, and to keep a careful eye on the American psyche. Grant was playing it that way too, at the cost of being called pro-British. The United States depended on active British investment and trade. Even the expansionist James G. Blaine, running for the presidency in 1884, was not anxious about Canada; Americans would rather settle for Nicaragua, where a canal could be cut joining Atlantic and Pacific. The Senate, the paper recognised, would always baulk at an arrangement with Canada in a close election, chiefly just to twist the lion's tail. Once the election was over the hostility was forgotten and "the most friendly intimacy" that the paper desired could be resumed.

What mattered was that the protectionist Republicans, unwilling to lower tariffs, began to spend the Treasury surplus on a big navy; it would not be big enough to challenge the Royal Navy but it showed nascent imperial ambitions. To Britain it was something to be encouraged. If the United States insisted on controlling any canal across the Panama isthmus or spend money annexing Hawaii, the paper could not see Britain taking exception. Step by step the United States was doing what the Foreign Office was content to see it do.

Even when Grover Cleveland, coming up to a difficult election year in 1896, berated Britain over a boundary dispute with Venezuela, the paper could not believe he was serious. The Monroe doctrine, as enunciated by James Monroe, actually protected Canada and the West Indies as much as the United States; when Cleveland seemed to deny this it doubted if he wanted "a white elephant" as a resistant Canada would be or add to his black population if he took over Jamaica. Cleveland was best faced with patience and good temper; there must be a "total absence of passion" in London. The paper praised both Lord Salisbury for his "courtesy, friendliness and good feeling" towards the Americans and the "graver sections of Americans", including the clergy, who spoke out for peace during the "Venezuela craze". In 1902 Britain gave up what the paper called the "mess" and "folly" of joining the Germans to go debt collecting in Venezuela and so antagonising the White House.

The Spanish-American war duly made the United States an imperial power. Popular opinion in Britain, the paper said, was "always inclined to sympathise with Americans" but, it turned out, continental European governments did not. Americans had been under "the perfectly honest illusion" that they were popular on the continent. But the attack on Spain had been resented; so was American protection against European trade and the "dog-in-a-manger policy" over South America. The one country that was friendly turned out to be Britain. The Americans were being initiated into the animosity that imperialists had to grow accustomed to.

The odium fell on Britain again over the Boers. American feeling had not shared Kaiser Wilhelm II's sense of outrage; Boer emissaries were popular chiefly in the German mid-west; and, when the Boer war came, "thousands of empty cans which have contained American beef are strewn throughout the entire route to Pretoria". It was not an alliance but a business partnership: "the distance between them is not very far".

The paper had no doubt of what was happening to Americans. A people once possessed of a powerful fleet and a mobile army "finds its horizon imperceptibly expand, and with it its ambition". If there had been a British trap, it had closed. While the republic had been "a middle-class state" no one had cared; its managers could isolate its policy. Now they were a nation watched by all eyes, one "whose alliance is sought by all governments".

All governments that was, except Canada's. Its prime minister had called the United States "a mass of foreign ignorance and vice", and a Canada bitter at being "vivisected" in the British wooing of Washington was going to reject a trade reciprocity treaty with the United States. For Americans there were now more distant and inspiring objectives.

There were the Philippines, which Germany had coveted, to occupy and govern. There was China to rescue from hopelessness. Suddenly, "the Union is the greatest of all the Pacific powers". China's market had to be kept open, with British support, against predatory powers. The British understood then, and would not forget, that although Americans were consistently reluctant to do anything in Europe, nothing was too demanding or difficult for China, except defending it.

The paper believed that the Americans were not ready yet to take full responsibility for their "wish to be great throughout the world" and so dealings with them would not be easy. But they would learn. They would join the rest of the world "in recognising that Russia's word is never her bond". They would find that although Japan believed it would be the long-sought link between east and west, "there is something of the wasp about her, which should be borne in mind". And they would recognise the percipience in the warning of Elihu Root, the secretary of war, that the United States must either give up the Monroe doctrine or be pre-

pared to fight for it. America was no longer seen by the other powers to be "a sort of separate planet". The armaments race would eventually decide its future.

AMERICA INTERVENES

America was determinedly neutral when the Great War began and intended to stay that way. Woodrow Wilson was a "model of correctness". (*The Economist* could hardly berate Americans for what it had initially sought for Britain. It had declared instinctively on August 1st 1914: "Every British interest points irresistibly to the maintenance of strict neutrality.") Wilson had brought a new "moral tone" to American diplomacy, had refrained from a full-scale invasion of Mexico, and believed in keeping his word. When he stood out for neutral rights against the Royal Navy's searches for contraband the paper thought British complaints were "absurd". It understood how American merchants were irritated if they could not take advantage of the war.

It even joined American criticism that Winston Churchill had failed to provide protection for the *Lusitania*. There was reason to have a strong neutral power, one that could be activated to bring about a just peace when the opportunity came. Francis Hirst, the editor up to 1916, disliked even Liberal imperialists and opposed conscription. To him, the United States was simply behaving as Britain did whenever it was neutral.

Even when the war was going badly the paper felt that, rather than carping at Wilson, Britain should be grateful for what it called his "friendly neutrality", allowing the allies to raise credit and loans and buy munitions, food and raw materials in the United States. The war would be ended by negotiation one day and Wilson was the man to secure a charter of "liberty, law and peace" for Europe. The paper did not reprimand Americans; neither did it appeal to them to help. Wilson was driven to war by the Germans' resumption of unrestricted U-boat warfare. It was a turning-point in twentieth-century Europe.

In the war and after it Wilson had the paper's entire confidence, especially in comparison with European politicians. He dealt in economic realities. His aims were to protect small nations and international law. The paper backed his League of Nations and his Fourteen Points. Its only substantial worry had been the arrival of the American army in time; it took American shipbuilding to win the sea war. It recognised that allied war orders had already turned the United States from a debtor into a creditor nation. By 1919 the paper's chief aim was not to let American influence be lost.

That was more easily said than done. America was having nothing to do with Wilson or his league, or with, as the paper put it, the "struggling Old World" or the "mouldy old hemisphere". The paper had four priorities: to clear up the war debts issue; to settle in Ireland; to get the Americans committed to disarmament or any other diplomacy even though they were not in the League of Nations; and to avoid anything the Americans would not like.

Much of the time these were British policies. To clear the debts the paper thought Britain should pay its debt in full, provided it could be funded over 50 years or so, and, however quixotic it seemed, to forget what the allies owed Britain. It wanted to restore certainty, without which trade would not recover. It thought Britain could afford it. It also expected America to reverse its high-tariff policy if the money really were to be found. America did not. In 100 years, the paper thought, world policing, such as the Great War, would be paid for "by the nations on the basis of their respective wealth", so that America would be the biggest contributor. But not yet.

The reparable British attitudes which Americans most disliked were over Ireland and Japan. The attempt to quell the Irish nationalist revolt in 1919–21 was, the paper said after the peace, "the most disastrous and discreditable chapter in the history of British rule", though it did not comment at the time. What became clear was that many Irish-Americans deserted Wilson (because he was Britain's friend) and made it clear to Warren Harding that, if Britain could fight an imperial war in Ireland, it could start paying its war debt to America. The advent of the Irish Free State was, the paper said, "a genuine and signal effort" to close the chapter. The Anglo-Japanese treaty, although entailing no British commitment against the United States, was deeply distrusted by Americans (and Canadians) who suspected there were secret clauses.

The paper thought naval disarmament a good thing anyway, especially as the Americans were content with parity, and the British and Americans were together in refusing it to the Japanese. If the Japanese did not like it, the Americans could always outbuild them three to one. Britain was entirely happy to drop the Anglo-Japanese alliance.

When the British and Americans quarrelled over cruiser sizes, it emerged that the Americans were trying to match the Japanese; the paper was appalled to find that the British admiralty was still engaged in the "futility" of not ruling out war against the United States. Even though the Americans continued to argue for neutral rights in international law and the British for blockade rights, the paper had recognised by the end of 1928 that the United States, "when her day comes", would make the sovereignty of the seas its own. It agreed, though with doubts, that Britain should sign the Kellogg-Briand Pact wordily outlawing war solely because it was an American initiative.

The paper had regularly propounded the view that the Americans would never look at Europe, and the British would never give the Far East priority. It was right. So it had regular complaints to make. Naturally it welcomed the American offer to support the league against Japanese aggression in Manchuria. It thought it "an event of first-class importance" and so found British reluctance to act "perilously near to British collusion" with Japanese policy. When the Japanese reached Shanghai it forecast that Australia and New Zealand would look to Washington, not London, for support. It told the Americans they should not think of clearing out of the Philippines. Franklin D. Roosevelt's recognition of the Soviet Union in 1933 allowed it to say the Americans and British should get together with China and Russia, and it commended the Pacific manoeuvres of 1935 taking American aircraft within striking distance of Japan.

It was not wholly sure of Roosevelt. He condemned the dictators of Europe, but the paper suspected him of "contracting out" of doing anything more. The United States and its oil firms ignored the league's attempted sanctions against Italy over the invasion of Abyssinia. It did not blame the United States altogether. Europe, it saw, was on the verge of a "prospective suicide" so the Americans would need to keep their hands free for "when Japan gets to mischief". The sinking of the American gunboat *Panay* by Japanese bombers in 1937 added point to that: the Pacific Ocean and China Sea were to the United States what the Mediterranean and Indian Ocean were to the British. It saw no hope of ending these priorities.

The Munich deal in 1938 encouraged America's isolationists, but it prompted Roosevelt to start to remove America's neutrality legislation if Britain and France needed to buy arms. The paper thought hard about what America, in reality, could be expected to do. It decided half of all Americans would be allied partisans, especially if it were a hard war, and especially if it were against Germany. Heavy air raids would bring a "strong and violent" American reaction. There was no question of soliciting, far less expecting, American intervention.

When war came in 1939 Britain could assume nothing more than "cash and carry" for American arms; the phoney war encouraged American suspicions that a deal was being done with Adolf Hitler. When France fell the paper told America what was needed first was not planes but machinery, machine tools and steel. It never had any doubt that the United States was the "most powerful economic unit" in the world and so ultimate success was ensured.

It was equally sure that, even when things were worst, appealing to the United States to enter the war did "rather less than no good at all". That was important. It helped the paper's authority when specific comment could be influential. It stuck to the belief that the destroyers-for-bases deal in 1940 was "practical evidence" that Britain and America complemented each other's defences. The lend-lease arrangement meant that a non-intervening America was committed to only one outcome.

When America was duly brought into the war it was by the Japanese in the Pacific. As in 1917–18 the paper had no doubt that American productivity would win, as American shipbuilding again won the battle of the Atlantic. It saw only two problems. First, the British defeats at Singapore and Tobruk prompted loud American disillusionment with British military capabilities; Congress nosed suspiciously among lend-lease arrangements. Second, the American disparagement of the British Empire, and especially doubts over the future of India, "simplified as an issue between light and darkness", was harder to answer; the paper normally just accused the American press of irresponsibility. It was not at all happy about the decisions at Yalta. Its doubts prompted two unusual grumbles. It accused the Americans of indecision, "their unwillingness or inability to make their general commitments specific". And it accused Churchill of "deference" to the Americans, of "appeasement" of them, which had not been necessary since Pearl Harbor.

There actually were what it called "legitimate British interests"; the next issue was how they would fare, if they fared at all, in a post-war world in which the essential British interest was to keep the Americans in Europe this time.

COLD WAR CALCULATIONS

Erosion in the Anglo-American relationship in the years after the second world war was consistent with the decline of British political influence, economic importance and self-confidence. The value of the relationship to the United States rose and fell by turns but proceeded inexorably, for the British, from pretended equality to evident dependence. Things went wrong, on both sides, when this was not understood.

Dwight Eisenhower and John Foster Dulles, the paper believed, had simply taken Britain for granted over Suez, thinking it "too loyal to go off on a violent diversionary action of its own". Lyndon Johnson and Dean Rusk could not understand why Britain would not even send a token force, a battalion of the Black Watch, to Vietnam. Jimmy Carter, engrossed with Iran and the hostages, took it for granted that Margaret Thatcher would agree to go along with full economic sanctions; she did not.

The reality, however, had been plain as early as 1943 when the paper, contemplating a future war, saw no option: "We shall need American support to avoid defeat". So it followed, in 1946, that agreement with the United States on fundamental issues had to be "a first commandment of British policy", but with the British view expressed with clarity and "as little apology as possible". By 1950, despite differences, it could say that "no imperial power has ever been so fortunate in its successor"; and Geoffrey Crowther, in his last article as editor in April 1956, believed that the important change in the world was that, for the first time in modern history, "the defending powers are virtually as strong, and as ready, as the potential aggressors".

The British hand had to be careful and restrained. Its prime role was to "nudge the Americans back on course" when needed. Clement Attlee had done this in helping to dissuade the Americans from a war against China in 1950, Harold Macmillan had persuaded them towards detente with the Soviet Union, and even

Harold Wilson had stopped the absurdity of a NATO nuclear fleet in 1964.

The paper was fastidious in not claiming too much. It saw Anglo-American relations as "a straight international bargain". What was real in the relationship apart from that was "beyond the power of governments to prevent" and the common language was "no more escapable than a common cold". It thought there was little in seeing the British as the Greeks in another Roman empire: it feared the idea of them "sitting like Diogenes in his barrel" lecturing the more affluent passers-by. By the 1970s it had accepted that Germany was the most important country in Europe, although the special German relationship with the United States might not be "quite like the one Britain used to have". Swallowing false pride had to become a regular diet.

Britain's first post-war necessity was to cut its commitments. As the conditions for the American loan in 1945 were misconceived, the paper saw no options to this. So the responsibilities for Greece and Palestine were dumped; India and Pakistan were going anyway. The last semblance of Pax Britannica went unlamented. The first duty Britain had to take up was persuading the Europeans to get into a state where the Americans thought they were worth rescuing. After all, Roosevelt had only got lend-lease through Congress after the Battle of Britain had been won.

Marshall aid was "enlightened self-interest", but "the generosity and the grand sweep" of the plan would have been inconceivable only a year before. It was right, in return, that Britain joined the Berlin airlift and helped to end European reluctance to join NATO. The crucial factor was that while the American neutrality laws had given Hitler the certainty of not being stopped in 1939, NATO removed that certainty from Joseph Stalin. The paper saw no use in talking to the Russians about the bomb; while their ingrained hostility to democratic life remained, any arrangement would bring "only lazy and false security" to the West.

The test that mattered was South Korea. The paper warned in February 1950 that it was essential to put a stop-line around China if a landslide of border states to communism was to be averted. When Harry S Truman decided to bar the North Koreans pushing south in June the alternative would have meant that no one would have been stopped anywhere. Now the failures of the 1930s were being repaired.

It was also the first war managed with self-restraint:

wisdom for the West was "to exercise a strict economy of resources in continental adventures". When the French were in hopeless trouble in Vietnam in 1954 and the Americans thought of intervention, the paper was disappointed that because, unlike in Korea, there were no British forces in Indo-China there was no British influence. That was not to change through the 1960s and 1970s.

The critical British misjudgment was the attempt at independent action at Suez in 1956. The paper was deeply unhappy. The West had been caught unprepared; the best policy seemed to be to go along with Dulles's idea of undermining Gamal Abdal Nasser by a lengthy boycott of the canal, but that was chiefly because it was an American policy. The paper agreed with Americans who thought the Anglo-French case "rather weak". The ensuing flop, the collapse of what it called "splenetic isolation", left the paper humiliated at Britain's failure. Against advice, Anthony Eden had thrown away the country's remaining concept of itself: "We are not the Americans' equals now, and cannot be". It was some time since they had been, but the bluff had been called: "There is not, and cannot be, anything exclusive now in the relationship".

That, as it happened, was not strictly true, as Eisenhower and John Kennedy thought it worth showing. But now it was back to common sense. When the Russians were thought to be ahead in intercontinental missiles in 1958 the paper had no doubts: Britain was "the most sensible place" for medium-range missiles pointed at Moscow. When the U-2 spy plane was shot down in 1961 the enterprise was "nothing to be ashamed of, but a necessity if a nuclear Pearl Harbor is to be avoided". It never equated American society with Russian society or American aims with Russian aims.

But over Cuba in 1962 it faltered. When Nikita Khrushchev was found to be shipping missiles to Fidel Castro the paper seemed to doubt the evidence ("the military aid Russia has been sending ... brings no change in the situation"), opposed the use of force and expected communist retaliation in Berlin and Vietnam. In its way it was no more than a mild anti-American reaction among the alarmed British media and politicians. The paper's proposal was that Cuba might be left with enough weapons to deter an invasion but not to devastate the United States.

Kennedy's success brought immediate amends. It

praised him not just for securing the Russian retreat, but for statesmanship in doing so: "He knew not only how far to go, but precisely where to stop". It had been an unusual deviation in *Economist* policy.

The American intervention in Vietnam, which Kennedy had begun, did not prompt another. The paper agreed with the aim of making it possible for South Vietnam to keep down insurgency in its territory and stop infiltration of men and arms from the North. Its own expectations were low: "something short of victory would do". Adding to American forces might "turn out to be mistaken". When Johnson justified himself to Congress it thought it "vastly odd" that the Vietnamese navy should have dared to attack the Seventh Fleet in the Gulf of Tonkin. However, the basic Johnson argument was essentially its own. It was the discouragement of aggression. The paper had consistently supported the British effort to defeat the communist guerrillas in Malaya and the Indonesians trying to take over Borneo. The United States was fighting the same war in South Vietnam and its presence there was essential to the British and Malaysian success further south.

The paper had no time for South Vietnam's politicians; it did not respect its soldiers; it doubted the success of the invasions of Cambodia and Laos; it understood the cost in lives and wasted opportunities; it recognised the alienation of a substantial part of America's intelligentsia. It still believed the war was worth fighting, that the media misunderstood the lesson of the Tet offensive. It supported Richard Nixon's policy of stopping a slide, not towards negotiation, but towards isolationism. When Vietnam was finally lost in 1975 it told Americans Vietnam was a "bungled and lost war" but it was "not in its origins a purposeless war". It was over "what people still hope the United States can do in the world".

MAKING DO WITH EUROPE

The Economist faced no dilemma in advocating British entry to the European Community in the 1960s and 1970s. It was confident that United States policy wanted Britain inside Europe's political structure, whatever the disadvantages to American trade. It had believed since the Messina conference in June 1955 that British interest was to join a tariff-cutting Europe, despite Commonwealth preferences, because its exclusion would be fatal when West German industry was in.

Conservative government opinion was then still strongly opposed. In November 1955 the paper said: "It will find that it has missed a bus that it will wish it had caught." It saw that the working alliance between France and West Germany had made Britain "a marginal, even a negligible, factor in European politics". To those who declared Britain would be better off as the 51st state of the United States, it replied that "the new common market colossus ... being forged under our eyes at this moment" was forming a relationship with America that was "possibly even closer and more 'special' than the Anglo-American alliance".

It saw in this no diminution in western defence against the Soviet Union because a Britain-in-Europe would continue its essential role: "The American alliance is, and must continue to be, the iron framework of British policy." With this reliance it declared in June 1960: "We believe that Britain would be wise to make an offer of full-scale participation in the European common market and community."

The paper judged that for a decade wholehearted American support for the Six had been "an essential, perhaps a decisive, factor in their success". So when Macmillan decided to apply to join in August 1961 it thought Kennedy would induce General de Gaulle to make the essential concessions on both farming and the Commonwealth. It was even optimistic enough to suppose that "an Atlantic union no longer smacks of fantasy". That would be, it thought, the vindication of "the long-held and sometimes lonely opinion of this newspaper".

To de Gaulle, of course, the American anxiety for British membership meant raising his terms. Britain had become "an American Trojan horse". The paper did not mind this: "In a sense it is, and quite rightly; it is a pity a Trojan horse cannot be more nimble sometimes." It was as sure as it had ever been that western Europe and North America were going to share the same future, good or bad.

So the paper had a ready answer for Dean Acheson when he said at West Point in December 1962 that Britain's hope of performing "a separate power role, apart from Europe", was about played out. Britain's function, it held, was precisely to keep on insisting that the unity of western Europe must "be used to unite, not divide, the Atlantic world". In contrast to de Gaulle's Eurocentric vision, it asserted that the divided European world "stretches from the Urals on one side to the Cascade mountains in the western United States on the other".

The expensive debacle of Skybolt, the air-launched missile that would have kept the British V-bomber force effective in the 1970s, prompted the Macmillan government to throw itself on American mercy to get the nuclear Polaris. The paper did not agree. The Americans should not be inveigled into providing "face-savers, flag-wavers and evanescent expedients". De Gaulle thought the same and vetoed the British application.

That was a blow, but the paper persisted in the European cause. A Britain standing alone, it estimated, would need to devalue the pound by 10–20% and even then the free trade gamble would be "hazardous". As for trying to join the Americans, Congress would never "come within shouting distance" of enacting the legislation that would be needed for including Britain "in a preferential Atlantic trading area".

What the paper depended on in the bleak years after the Gaullist veto was the potential British contribution to a "science-based" European system that could match American efforts in computers, aircraft and rockets. Harold Wilson bought it in 1966; no one else did. When in the early 1970s Edward Heath persuaded himself to pay Georges Pompidou's price for entry, it was done almost without evident consideration for American predilections. Heath himself was not impressed with either Nixon or the Vietnam war. But the paper felt that joining Europe was still the reverse of opting out of the American connection.

Whatever the American impulse to forget about an ungrateful world, or whatever European politicians chose to think, the paper saw constant evidence of growing Atlantic interdependence in hard reality, and in Henry Kissinger a tactician unwilling to accept European neutrality or an alliance ready to fall apart. For the paper "the iron framework" of its own convictions, and of Britain's function, could persist.

A SUPERPOWER'S PAINS

The Reagan-Thatcher relationship in the 1980s did not mean that the American connection with Britain lived through placid years. They were squally. Unity of purpose was sustained on the big issues: opposition to communism, strong defence, toughness on terrorism. However, the paper found Margaret Thatcher dubious of the status of the strategic defence initiative (SDI) under existing defence treaties and "unnerved" that Ronald Reagan might have thought of giving too much away at Reykjavik. She did not consult the Americans before sending the Falklands task force and was piqued that the Americans did not consult her over Grenada. There was thus much British rumination about the standing of the connection. The paper felt that the American interest in the Falklands lay, from the start, "overwhelmingly in preventing British failure". It thought Reagan's backing arrived "tardily", so that the British recovery of the islands was essentially a political victory for Caspar Weinberger, the defence secretary, and the US navy. Britain was not exactly like Israel, a "dependent who will die if deprived of support", but the United States had been "trapped by the obligations of superpower status". Allies could readily involve the Americans in conflicts not of their own choosing.

The allies the Americans involved in the invasion of Grenada were the small east Caribbean states; it was an exercise in overwhelming American power. The paper concluded that "superpowers do not need allies, only cheer-leaders". It was the fate of medium-sized powers to need superpowers. This was only a small exaggeration. The American bombing of Libya from British bases was agreed to by a reluctant Thatcher for the alliance's sake. The paper thought it would be "right to use more force" if needed. Since the remainder of western Europe refused even over-flying rights, her agreement compensated for the Falklands support and for her cavalier attitude to European unity. The British commitment to the retaking of Kuwait was usefully early and substantial.

The paper was satisfied that the British part in the connection was never subservient; it thought this "alternately annoys and pleases the Americans". At bottom there were only three exclusive ties remaining from the past: nuclear defence, the navies and intelligence.

The paper was enthusiastic about Reagan's strategy on the Soviet Union from the outset. Leonid Brezhnev was shown that America now questioned "the whole concept of what came to be called detente"; it sent a chill through Moscow. The rearming of America had changed the whole argument. First, the arrival of the first cruise missile in Europe—for which the paper had campaigned over the years—made Europe "a slightly safer place as a result". Second, the SDI showed Reagan's ability "to cut through the worst-looking complications and come up with something attractively simple". There was "nothing wicked" about the project, and it had brought the Russians back to the negotiating table. The paper told Europeans not to be "panicked" by the apparent failure of the Reykjavik summit. But it would not have given arms control the superpower priority it was getting. Other issues—Afghanistan, the Gulf, Nicaragua, human rights—should be the horse in the policy: "arms control is the cart".

The incipient weakness of the Soviet economy had been apparent in the Brezhnev years so its precipitate collapse under Mikhail Gorbachev left the paper neither confused nor disconcerted. It was not a Gorbachev admirer; either he had not understood, or lacked the ability to adopt, the market system. When peace was adjudged to have broken out in 1990, the paper looked back on the cold war without remorse but reckoned it had, in fact, been the "most stable and least lethal balance of power" in the century.

The Gulf war emphasised again the reanimated issue of Islam; the growing American fixation on Japanese trade methods, an impending confrontation which the paper thought needless between two powers whose capital interest should be in multilateral free trade. There was no prospect of a Marshall Plan for the constituents of the new Commonwealth of Independent States. The Soviet Union had not had a workable economic system; it had excluded itself from world trade; it never had world-class industries. Unlike western Europe, there was nothing to revive. Anyway, unlike in Truman's day, a decade of Republican economics had left the United States with deficits which made serious money for the CIS "unthinkable".

American policy in Central America, especially Nicaragua and El Salvador, earned the paper's initial support for stopping "the export of revolution" from Cuba. It thought the United States should agree to live beside a neighbour whose people had chosen socialism but it need not let communists help any "election-rejecting minority impose its will". It approved of much American intervention, even when free elections went wrong, as they often did in El Salvador, and returned the "unsavoury far right". It thought the Contras, disliked in Congress and fighting in the dirtiest of

wars, were at least trying to hold the Sandinists to their 1979 promise of making Nicaragua "a pluralist democracy". This sympathy was unusual in Europe. By the 1990s the paper was glad to find Nicaragua rejecting Sandinism, "a mutant of communism", although El Salvador was still showing "mixed results" for America's investment of $6 billion. Both outcomes had been decided by the collapse in Moscow. In the Philippines, it was comforted to see America "edging away" from Ferdinand Marcos in 1983 and was sure his resistance would end in the storming of the Malacanang palace.

Reagan's costly exercise in Lebanon in 1982 failed because, the paper thought, the president "needs a clearer idea of what he is trying to achieve". It also thought Americans should be told by a "European newspaper" that they should not turn "a punch on the nose into the end of the world". It occasionally reminded them that, "yes, you are the superpower" when things went wrong. It was sceptical of the first reflagging of Gulf tankers but thought it would be "culpable weakness" if the West turned tail after the cruiser *Vincennes* shot down an Iranian airliner, killing 290 passengers, in 1988.

It had suspected that Iraq's Saddam Hussein had come to rely on the Americans to get him out of his war with Iran, but by April 1990 it was suggesting that a "mad Iraqi president" might try to take over the Gulf. By that August it was clear that, faced with a choice, "Mr Bush should go to war", and he should not listen to the western "weasel chorus". Before the fighting began it thought it right that Saddam Hussein should be allowed to stay in power in Baghdad afterwards. It "may stick in the throat, but it would be a lesser evil" than having to subjugate the whole of Iraq. When the land war began in February 1991 it observed: "It all seems horribly one-sided, which is excellent".

It drew two morals from Kuwait. First, to defeat a country with the national product of Portugal had taken 75% of America's tactical aircraft and 40% of its tanks. Second, Americans ought to have been reminded that "not all foreign entanglements end in disaster"; not all allies were perfidious nor all enemies resilient; television pictures did not always lose wars; and the Soviet Union, on its last legs, "does not always stand in the way of what needs doing". Still, it doubted if omnipotence would persist.

The remaining superpower, the paper thought, began to run a capable post-cold war policy under

George Bush. It told the Clinton administration to continue it. It was a diminished role for the slayer of communism but American readiness to intervene in starving Somalia and to try to restrain the Serbs in Bosnia appeared to show that the United States was not yet wholly preoccupied with its own uncertainties.

The Europe that America had recreated was still divided, self-interested and essentially dependent. It felt comfortable only if America remained global, asserting itself to operate in the cause of liberal democracy. History had not ended. To *The Economist*, the moral of 150 years in an imperfect world remained: the transatlantic connection had to persist.

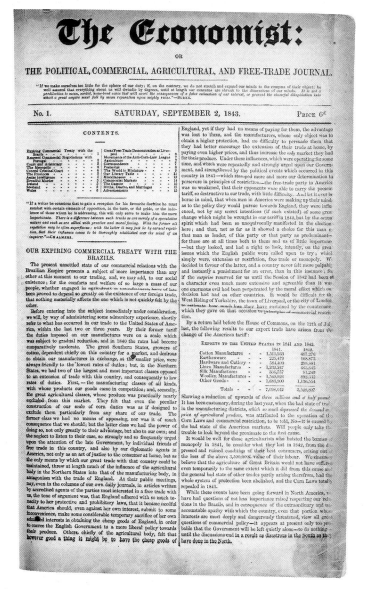

The first issue of The Economist *was published on September 2nd 1843 by James Wilson, a London businessman and aspiring Liberal politician, to further the cause of free trade independently among influential readers. The paper was never disabused of this ambition.*

Daniel Webster, twice US secretary of state, long-time senator from Massachusetts. Caught between two worlds: opposed the 1812 war, aspired to be US minister in London, 1843, but a diehard protectionist of New England industry.

1

THE MOST IMPORTANT COUNTRY

1843–1860

EXTINGUISHING DISTANCE

The delight, and the ambition, of the early Economist *and its readers was the rapid narrowing of transatlantic times and exchanges*

Many of the hopes, much of the basic optimism, of the early *Economist* were pinned across the Atlantic in the United States. The pulse of the world was quickening, mileage was shrinking, intelligence, reason and trade were imposing themselves on the community of the North Atlantic. The freer the trade, the better America's prospects. In October 1843, the paper's second month, it quoted Daniel Webster, then secretary of state,

approvingly: "The great power of steam has extinguished distance. England lies close to New York. Twelve or thirteen days only make the communication. We measure things by time. England is not more than half as distant from us, for every purpose of international intercourse, as she was thirty years ago."

Webster the protectionist would not often get the paper's praise, but it relished that growing nearness. It believed in America's resources and potentialities, in its future as the century's most important country. It had small regard for American boasts and aggressiveness, far less for American politicians and their pretensions. It despised most of the prejudices of American democratic opinion, as it did of English. But

---

CHRONOLOGY

1843	John C. Frémont reconnoitres (Mexican) California		Bay to open trade with Japan
1845	James K. Polk becomes president	1854	Crimean war begins: Britain and France against
	US annexes Texas		Russia
1846	US declares war on Mexico; California conquered	1856	Republican Party's first convention
	US and Britain agree on the Oregon boundary		Gail Borden takes out first patent for condensed
	Britain repeals its corn laws, aiding American		milk
	farmers	1857	James Buchanan becomes president
1847	Cyrus McCormick sets up his reaper factory in	1858	First Atlantic cable completed; insulation fails
	Chicago		Debates on slavery between Stephen Douglas and
1848	Gold discovered in California		Abraham Lincoln
	Revolutions in Austria, France, Italy and Prussia	1859	John Brown raids the Federal armoury at Harper's
	Communist manifesto published		Ferry
1849	Zachary Taylor becomes president		France defeats Austria in Italy
1850	Millard Fillmore becomes president		Charles Darwin publishes *Origin of Species*
	Henry Clay's compromise legislation, continuing the	1860	Guiseppe Garibaldi lands in the Kingdom of the Two
	union, passed		Sicilies
1851	Louis Napoleon stages a coup d'état in Paris		Abraham Lincoln elected president
1853	Franklin Pierce becomes president		South Carolina leads the secession of southern
	Commodore Matthew Perry's squadron in Tokyo		states

---

it admired America's energy and its education, and it faced facts.

The two Anglo-Saxon populations were rising by the mid-1840s to some 25m apiece, but the paper expected immigration to take the United States to 100m by the year 1900. (It actually happened by 1915.) Nearly 50% of United States exports went to Britain, the bulk of them raw cotton to Lancashire; in return 40% of United States imports came from Britain. Interdependence seemed self-evident.

The paper believed that even the political interests of the two countries were not far apart. They spoke the same language, shared much of their law and literature. It saw, unlike most of the press on either side of the Atlantic, no good reason why they should go to war again. They were as near as Webster made out in distance, and in more than distance. This mattered, especially to its readers, when every day, and eventually even every hour, could be cut in their intercommunication.

So there was great excitement in September 1843 over the race between the *Great Western* from New York and the *Hibernia* from Boston, which the *Hibernia* won: 11 days from Boston to Liverpool, a mere nine from Halifax, Nova Scotia. The paper echoed the enthusiasm of the reformer, John Bright, at getting a letter mailed in Halifax only 25 days after the sender had sailed from the Mersey. It was a wonder on a par with getting from London to Boulogne in six hours by train and steam packet. From Boston to New York, 250 miles, took 7 hours, 25 minutes.

As distance was almost annihilated, so, the paper thought, the differences between Britain and the United States, the corn laws, the shipping discrimination, the American protective tariffs, must diminish. With James K. Polk the president in Washington and Sir Robert Peel the prime minister in London the principles of Adam Smith must at last be applied.

The electric telegraph was the miracle of the decade. It replaced rumour with instant fact, and at a profit to private investors. Polk's nomination by the Democratic convention in Baltimore in May 1844 was the first to be transmitted directly to Washington. By November 1848 the telegraph was transmitting news of General Zachary Taylor's success in recovering the presidency for the Whig Party: "Putting an end to doubt, and leaving no opportunity for promoting mischief by sinister reports.... The owners of the magnetic

telegraphs throughout the Union are said to obtain from 10 to 14 per cent on their outlay."

This was a characteristically American enthusiasm. In January 1852 the paper recognised that in Britain the telegraph was still confined largely to the stock exchange and the rich. In North America there were already 11,000 miles of wire from Quebec to New Orleans, from New York to Wisconsin; ordinary mothers, travelling on the railroad, had got used to wiring their families ahead with their progress. More than that, the telegraph was creating an American appetite for news, not just political opinion, in newspapers.

Even so, plain words, plain print, still had limitations, useful or otherwise, for the supposedly important. The paper reported blandly in March 1853 that President Franklin Pierce had reached Washington by train for his inaugural: "His person being generally unknown, he was enabled to take refuge at his hotel without being recognised. He ... was devoting himself entirely to the formation of his Cabinet."

The Atlantic cable was to be the ultimate achievement in communications. Unhappily, "we confess we should look with much more hope to the success of the achievement if it had been undertaken by a private firm". When it had been laid it was, naturally, "the greatest and most marvellous enterprise which science has suggested to our modern world". But from the outset the paper was leery of what it might mean in instant diplomacy: "It must be remembered that the United States are the only real democracy with which we have any close connection.... The pride of a democracy is easily hurt."

What the paper called "this climax of subaqueous correspondence" was to be delayed. The technical doubts were justified. The cable could not be repaired until after the civil war.

British money drove railway construction on both sides of the Atlantic, in both boom and slump. *The Economist* was generally gratified at all news of investment responding to demand, not least the railroads driven west into the new corn states beyond Ohio. It was triumphant that private enterprise was doing it: "In the main these gigantic works, both here and in the United States, have been achieved by private men for the sake of profit. We are not acquainted with any public work of equal magnitude executed by the Government of any nation, either of ancient or modern times, in an equally short period."

The paper was visionary about development from coast to coast, even grasping at the Mormons' application to form a state or territorial government in distant Utah: "A new centre of civilisation, thus established and expanding, more than half way on the route to the Pacific, must help forward with great rapidity the peopling and the civilisation of the vast wastes that lie between Missouri and San Francisco."

It needed only 60,000 free inhabitants to qualify for recognition, but the paper saw no virtue in caution: "Our youth will live to see the growth, in the new world, of an empire which will far overshadow and shame all the enfeebled and degraded sovereignties of continental Europe. Nor will it be otherwise than strange should the hitherto despised Mormons practically teach some of the most enlightened nations of the world how to solve the perplexing problems of emigration and colonisation."

The premature project of a railroad from St Louis to San Francisco, floated in November 1849, made the paper reflect ruefully on Britain's own imperial record: "Such a vast project makes us reflect with some shame on the little in making railways that has yet been done in our Indian Empire."

Distances would be beaten in America first. "The journey across the continent, that now requires, if performed with waggons, five or six months, will be performed in ten days." Tariff reform had in six years encouraged the sale of 12m acres of land by the Federal government; 1.5m immigrants, largely still engaged on the land, had been settled; six railroads now connected the Atlantic ports with what was then thought of as the west: "The whole continent of America is becoming, in fact, more accessible to the commerce and people of Europe than is the interior of Spain or of France, and its produce is more easily distributed over Europe than is the wine of these countries. The prospect which this opens for the future is brilliant and is of great practical importance."

Even the age of the common man might be in sight: "The continual communication of intelligence, opinions, and sentiments between nations by railways, telegraphs, and journals, and the continual interchange of good offices or mutual services by trade, now render special communication between the Governments of comparatively little utility, and more likely to beget strife than preserve peace."

Cyrus McCormick's reaper. Farm mechanisation began in the 1840s, helping to expand exports to Britain. The labour shortage in the civil war forced almost all northern farms to use machinery.

BRITAIN: SET TO BE JUNIOR PARTNER
*American industry, ingenuity and education
in the 1850s worried the world's richest nation*

Having accepted that the United States must become, one day, the senior partner in the relationship, the paper, like the country, was disturbed to find that Britain's own day might be closing faster than it had supposed. American farm implements and machinery were on display at the Great Exhibition in London in 1851. It was at once apparent that they were designed for an agriculture unknown in Europe. The paper was patronising: "There we see agricultural produce in great variety, and of very good quality; but their implements prove to demonstration that such produce must be obtained from the soil with little labour, for they have no tools capable of compelling the unwilling soil to yield even such returns as we are accustomed in this country to regard as very moderate."

But it saw the essential difference. In America every farm was, literally, up for sale if the price were right. There was little evidence of adherence to local ties or even to family possession: neither landlord nor peasant thought like that in the old world.

In the summer of 1851 the clipper *America* beat all British yachts in the challenge series that was to begin the America's Cup. She sailed a whole point nearer the wind than any competitor. This was utterly serious: the performance of the United States frigates had surprised the Royal Navy in the war of 1812: "The *America*, by beating the very best of our craft, has at once alarmed and convinced us.... We rejoice in the success of the *America* because we believe it is likely to ensure us against defeat on matters of much greater moment than yacht sailing."

Naval sensitivity was to survive the century and long after. The two countries were not, in fact, to go to war with each other again, but that was far from received opinion. Historians were to write long after that it was the Royal Navy that actually enforced the Monroe doctrine, but that was not apparent then. What was increasingly visible was the technological challenge the United States was mounting: "It is not only in building and managing ships that the Americans surpass us. They have picked our patent unpickable locks, have taught us how to sew clothes and reap corn by machinery, and by their revolvers to protect or destroy life. For all these manifestations we

are indebted to Free Trade and the Exhibition, which is itself a consequence of Free Trade."

And the British merchant marine seemed increasingly vulnerable: "American ships make quicker passages, and deliver their cargoes in better condition, than English ... there is no drunkenness on board American ships."

When the New York industrial exhibition opened in 1854, the two British commissioners, Joseph Whitworth and George Wallis, found disconcerting evidence: "They are more industrious than we are; they work longer and more continuously; English artisans come away from the States because they find the work too much for them; and American factories are regulated with as much care as the best factories of England."

The impression was dawning that it was not just the tariff that was nurturing American manufactures but the discipline and, even more, the education of much of the New England workforce. That was where Manchester and Rochdale could be caught: "The bulk of the people are sober, steady, methodical and energetic. Unless we direct all our energies to the work of self-improvement, the Americans will surpass us as much in ingenuity and skill, in intelligence and power, as they are certain to surpass us in numbers."

The paper reported on the American schools systems, envious of local control, interest and initiative. It found in some states that the teachers were nearly all females, most of them under 20, and with as many as 70 children in their charge ("40 being about the right number"). There was a want of classrooms. Even so, it was far superior to working-class schooling in England, and there was no prospect of England putting its mind to catching up.

The paper, like so much of British society, still saw America as an unsophisticated place, the victim of democracy and its shortcomings. Social equality meant the wife and daughter of an operative carpenter would be "decked out as fashionably as the lady of a governor or a judge". But nothing, of course, could be of the quality or style required by *The Economist* that was manufactured behind a tariff. Even language was being cheapened by American democracy, and by the claims of democracy in Britain. President Pierce's inaugural in 1853 was, it happened, a sign of the times. Pierce had abandoned his notes and delivered his speech as an oration. The paper did not appreciate the feat: "There the style of Emerson or of Mrs Beecher is taking the place of that of Franklin; just as here the style of Mr Dickens, Mr Carlyle, and similar writers, is superseding that of Locke and Addison and Smith."

Perhaps it could not be helped: "Mr Pierce, a man of the people, conforms in his language, as in his ideas, to the public taste; and the floweriness of his address, in contrast to addresses of his predecessors, is a symptom and a proof of the general change. He means, we believe, no evil."

So, by the end of the 1840s and 1850s, the two North Atlantic countries, each by then of about 28m people, speaking much the same language and recognising much the same intellectual roots, divided by two past wars and by regularly discovered disputes and distrusts, yet locked into the most demanding, successful and potential trading system the world had seen, settled down to watch each other suspiciously and profitably.

To the paper, and to those that thought like it, the merits of the argument, in mind and in purse, were such that there could be only one conclusion. And yet, when the paper did envisage, as in September 1854, what might be ineluctable, as the United States grew with a rapidity and to a strength that the world had not experienced before, it saw starkly in the American coal and iron figures a still distant relationship that no politician had yet entertained: "Our trade with the States may perhaps become to them what the Russian trade is at present to us, desirable enough while continued, but not of sufficient importance to stand in the way of considerations of national honour; and, though the loss may be somewhat regretted, scarcely worth a sigh."

That was more than depressive talk prompted by the problems of the Crimean war. It was the reality of a relationship in which the population of one state was increasing three times as quickly as in the other. In *The Economist's* first 20 years things were shaping up decisively in the North Atlantic community. The paper itself was the creation of free traders. It existed to propagate the cause, to foster discussion, trounce critics, report the great meetings and debates, and ensure that no argument missed its mark. From the first article of the first issue on September 2nd 1843, the Anglo-American market, restricted by high tariffs, corn laws, navigation acts and the like, was at the centre of its thinking.

THE VISION OF FREE TRADE
The radical thinkers' ideal: free trade between English factory and American field

It was the South, anxious to sell its cotton and tobacco and with few nascent manufactures of its own, which was "always friendly to the lowest rates of duties". New England, with its growing factories, could not be propitiated; the first issue of the paper reported new plant, double the previous size, going up in Manchester, New Hampshire, and in Albany, New York. But the agricultural interest, which should have been a potential market for British goods, had been neglected when it might have been appeased.

The corn laws, resolutely defended by the landowners of Britain and only partially mitigated by a sliding scale that allowed intermittent imports when prices peaked, were resented by the American producers who saw themselves increasingly locked into the United States's own high-tariff system. British exports to America halved between 1841 and 1842.

A campaigning *Economist* could declare at once: "A country never felt more palpably and instantly a punishment for an error." The corn laws were simply protecting an oligarchic class at the expense of high food prices paid by the poor and handicapping the growth of markets for the manufacturers of the north of England (half of Britain's manufactured exports were cotton goods) and the traders and investors of the City of London. This was unreasonable and even irrational. The principles of free trade had made evident progress in both Britain and the United States: it was now the responsibility of the prime minister, Peel, and Henry Clay (who was expected to be the next president) to recognise the mutual advantages of lower tariffs: "It is quite melancholy to think of the great mutual benefits which are wasted between that great producing continent and ourselves, by a silly and absurd system of restriction on intercourse."

However, the mood of Clay's party, the Whigs, was still highly protectionist and hard to alter. *The Economist* argued purposefully that retaliation against higher American duties would only make things worse: "Cheapness and not dearness is the true weapon to combat commercial hostilities, and cheapness can only be secured by freedom and not restriction."

It took some comfort from the signs that the high

James K. Polk: president 1845–49. Reduced the protectionist tariff:
manufacturing still flourished and revenue increased.
Took Texas and California into the Union.

tariffs were bringing American trade "to a dead lock". Goods were not being imported, customs revenue was not being collected, and an unfunded national debt was being created "at a time of profound peace". And this was not even helping the 250,000 or so who relied on the protection of manufactures because trade was falling: they could not take up what the farmers could produce.

Customs duties in the port of New York were down by 11.7% in the first three quarters of 1843; agricultural prices in Boston market were badly down; and there were said to be 100 farms for sale within a circle of 15 miles from Lowell, Massachusetts. There had to be a better way. The paper summed up the argument in January 1844: "On the one hand we exclude the chief produce by high and prohibitory duties; on the other hand they exclude our manufactures by an increased tariff. We for the purpose of protecting our home land produce—they for the purpose of protecting their own

dear manufactures. Both fail in effecting the advantages they contemplated to the producers; they only succeed in producing misery and suffering among the consumers in each country.... On both sides of the ocean the best interests of the community are sacrificed to the selfish objects, but ignorant and mistaken views, of the dormant classes."

What was worse, the United States had got itself into the grip of a banking crisis. States had even begun to repudiate their public debt. Pennsylvania, the "Bankrupt State", had already done so; Maryland and Ohio were suspect. In March the paper recorded the death of "Mr Nicholas Biddle, of Pennsylvania, the great banker, and, as we may say, swindler". In April came word of a tariff-cutting commercial treaty between the United States and the German customs union, the Zollverein: "The most striking and important fact is this—that America should go to Germany to contract a treaty, in apparent hostility to this country, or at least, to the preference of the goods of another country, when we consider that there are so few ways in which Germany can be useful to America compared with our own country."

Reason, though, was not winning. America faced the presidential election; the German states resented the corn laws too, and the arrogance that Germans normally identified with Englishmen. If the North Atlantic free trade community was to come about it would need much more than the supposed benevolence of Henry Clay or oratorical meetings in Manchester. Two things then happened within a year; the emergence of Polk, the almost unknown governor of Tennessee, and the arrival of the potato blight in England and Ireland.

Polk's nomination "was entirely unexpected.... The effect of this nomination is to sever all the old bonds of party union ... Polk is against the present tariff."

Polk was a very considerable president: he brought both Texas and California into the union. What might have been just as important for America's future was that he began the demolition of the high tariff which threatened to confirm the isolation of the United States and could have condemned it, whatever happened to the South, to regular separatist crises. Polk's victory contributed a cause, an argument, to modern America. The economics of it seemed plain enough: "Mr Polk has secured the support of all those whose intercourse with this country is rendered possible by the state of our laws. Mr Polk, by his advocacy of a free commercial policy, essentially represents the feelings of the great Southern states—the producers of cotton, rice, and of tobacco. He has also secured large majorities in the states of Pennsylvania and New York, by which it is evident that the great mercantile interests of those states are superior to the manufacturing and agricultural interests which combined in support of Mr Clay."

Again, however, Britain was losing its chance. The states Polk did not take were the non-cotton South; the growing factory towns of Massachusetts, Connecticut and New Jersey; and Ohio. Ohio was then the third most populous and the biggest farm state; it was the biggest wheat-growing state of the union. It needed to keep the British market and it needed cheap British manufactures, but the corn laws kept it a supporter of Clay. This had to be changed. Polk himself had shown the way: "Public opinion in America, as expressed in favour of protection, as long as our Corn Laws exist, is no criterion whatever of what it would be if those laws were relaxed."

Free trade was becoming patently urgent for Britain: "On all hands it is admitted that, with our increasing population, we require a larger permanent field for the supply of food and the consumption of our manufactures. America presents both."

That was in September 1845. A month later the inexorable starvation of Ireland began to force Peel's hand in London. Potato blight had been first reported from the Kent coast: "Since then it has spread in every direction, and has become almost universal, not only in England but in Ireland.... Wheat is everywhere defective in quality, and in many places deficient in quantity."

How were people to be fed? The old agricultural interest in Peel's Conservative Party would not countenance any substantial change to the corn laws, far less the opening of the ports. But in Ireland and the Scottish Highlands, the potato was the staple diet. Their plight induced disbelief; and exclamation points: "Seven millions of people ... are threatened with absolute want and starvation, while enormous duties are permitted to remain upon all kinds of grain; and the only suggestion on their behalf is an appeal to charity!!"

Continental Europe, however, was short of grain too, everywhere west of Odessa and the Black Sea. There could be only one recourse: "Our chief reliance must be upon the United States. Their crop of Indian corn has been good and that of wheat, taken altogether, has been an average one.... With a removal of all restrictions, we may hope for considerable supplies of flour and Indian corn; for the latter of which the poor Irish are now craving."

The potato failure was worldwide and included the northern states and Canada, but the American wheat and corn supplies were enough for everyone except "the poor settlers in the mountains" who depended on the potato. Now it was apparent both to the Peelites and the Liberal opposition that the corn laws had to go. Peel repealed them, divided his party, and was then driven from office. *The Economist* was satisfied that the right tariff policies were now practicable on both sides of the Atlantic, to the general improvement of Anglo-American relations: "We feel quite easy in placing Mr Polk's tariff reform on the one hand, and the repeal of the Corn Laws on the other hand, if honestly carried out, as a set off against all the dangers of an interruption to friendly relations between England and the United States." The New York correspondent was frank: "The news appeared to be altogether too good to be true."

It was some years, in fact, before America could become a regular and substantial supplier. American farm wages were relatively high, the extremes of climate made bulk storage difficult, and the Atlantic ports were increasingly distant from the new wheat lands. But a principle had been established. By August 1847 the paper reported confidently how the tariff cuts had brought prosperity to American farmers. New lands were being cultivated, canals and railroads were being completed, the demand for British manufactures was rising and even states like Pennsylvania and Ohio had started to pay off their debt. For good free traders there was "no other country which possesses the same amount of internal resources of every description calculated to minister to national wealth and to individual prosperity".

THE GOLD RUSH
California's boom meant monetary worries,
but growth and wealth too

The discovery of gold in California in 1848 prompted the celebrated rush to the territory (which became a

California gold: the rush began near Sacramento in January 1848. The trek west was in full force within a
year, the gold encouraging US trade and economic growth.

state two years later), and ensured, in *The Economist's* view, another shrinking of the world: "It must hasten, to an incalculable degree, the communication with all the distant parts of the globe. A railroad across the Isthmus of Panama is to be commenced, or a road of some kind."

Initially, however, the paper looked severely on the economic costs of exaggerated hopes: "Great losses, great misery, we are afraid, and numerous crimes, will be the consequence of the delusion. From there, too, the evils will spread to the Atlantic coasts and to Europe.... The history of California will supply another painful chapter to the work on 'Popular Delusions'."

Month by month through 1849 it kept up a jeremiad: "A great loss must ultimately arise, and there is reason to believe that we shall suffer in common with the Americans. Their imports from Europe have been increased on their anticipations of gold from the diggings; their exportations to California, including large supplies of European goods, have been forwarded on the same delusion; and much of their losses, which seem certain, will fall on their creditors in Europe."

By 1851 the paper found it had fewer worries, especially about the effect on the price of gold itself: "The effective demand for the precious metals will increase at least as fast as the supply; and should that be the case, though they may, in common with all the products of labour and skill, be obtained at less and less cost, they will not decline in relative value, nor will prices rise, as after the discovery of America, in relation to the precious metals."

The positive signs were now showing through, to everyone's advantage: "They ... indicate the increased trade with Europe which has been created by the discovery of California, which has not only created a new market for our goods, but has also furnished a new product, so far as the United States are concerned, for the payment of their increased imports."

And by now, too, other players were developing in the game. California was by far the star with an estimated annual production worth £15m, but Russia with £4m and Australia with £1m were increasingly important: "The real question then is, will California, Russia and Bathurst, in their increased production of gold, outstrip the remarkable agencies which are now at work for an increased production of all other commodities?"

The paper felt the balance was being maintained;

optimism was justified: "All the productive classes in the world, but especially in this country, will be greatly benefited and much enriched."

By 1853 the paper was prepared to give its formal blessing to at least California and Australia because their mineral wealth was contributing to the general good: "Diffusing much desired wealth more equally than heretofore, the gold discoveries will help more than political revolutions to promote and secure liberty. Stimulating honest industry and leading to abundance, they will give additional security to property and lessen crime, while they extend freedom."

Doubt and scepticism were thus banished. History had taken a beneficent turn again in the favoured country. The gold rush would be, it felt: "The forerunner of rapid and extensive social improvements, such as, but far greater than, those which ensued after the first discovery of America."

TESTING TRUST

Border disputes grew with the expansion of the United States westwards, without disturbing London unduly

In 1849 the remainder of the British navigation laws that still applied to American shipping were repealed. So ended such anomalous restrictions as those preventing American shipping carrying flour, from wheat taken to Europe to be ground, being allowed into Britain. By August 1851 the paper was gratified to acknowledge that "all that we gave to them on the 1st of January, 1850, the day on which the repeal of our Navigation Laws took effect, they on the same day gave us". The satisfaction was the greater in that, a year later, Britain provided 80% of the foreign shipping in the United States trade, the United States only 18% of the foreign trade to Britain.

There would be further high-tariff scares (especially in the Millard Fillmore presidency) but by then the paper had decided to discount them. It relied on the American character: "The Americans are more impatient of taxation than the larger and heavier taxed Europeans, and they will never consent to a scheme which, under the pretence of raising a revenue that is not wanted, restricts and perverts their industry, and takes from them a much larger sum than finds its way into the coffers of the state."

That was not taking what was to be the crippling cost of a civil war into account, but it affirmed the basic instinct of the paper and its mercantile readers: "Beyond all comparison the country which presents the deepest interest, whether present or future, to the English mind, is the United States of America. Of all the great foreign nations of the world, it alone exhibits symptoms of vitality and progress worthy of the century in which we live."

This trust was being repeatedly tested, but usually, until the civil war, in quite small matters. *The Economist* had been suspicious of President Tyler's efforts to annex Texas, not so much because it entertained specific British ambitions there but because it disliked the lawless southern land-jobbers whose aim, it believed, was entirely predatory: "To give increased value to land, by the introduction of slave-labour, and thus affording a demand and an outlet for the population of the slave-breeding states, which will perpetuate slavery and the internal slave traffic of America for an indefinite period."

So it saw the brief period of Texan independence as "a mere hypocritical parenthesis". The European powers had been gulled: "France and England have both recognised the independence of Texas, and we have made with that state not only a treaty of commerce, but also, in our simplicity, one for the suppression of the African slave trade."

As even the Mexicans had decreed that no one could be born, or introduced into, Mexico as a slave, that left the United States in moral deficit. Still, facts were facts, especially when Polk accepted them. By 1845 the paper was resigned to them: "Were we to look only to the future political and material consequences of the union, without referring to the means by which it has been brought about, we should see little in it to regret." Since Texas had been recognised it was, legally, "at liberty to adopt any form of government, or any alliance with the States, she pleases."

When, at the end of 1846, Commodore Robert F. Stockton had annexed California "by right of conquest", the paper was scarcely affronted. It was concerned, not with the American presence on the west coast of the continent, but with Mexico's own future: "We can well understand that the American Government will be satisfied to leave Mexico with what remains of her original territory for a few years."

The issue that was really raising hackles was the future of Oregon. The paper felt this was to be taken seriously only by governments, retired military men in their clubs, and the American settlers who were moving in, in ten times the numbers from Canada, with the full support of the Irish-American press. It felt simply that it would be "a terrible disgrace to the age in which we live, if it shall unhappily be recorded in history that two nations, each containing upwards of 20,000,000 of people, more or less dependent on each other—the one containing a London, a Liverpool, a Manchester and a Lancashire, with its millions of population dependent upon, and living by, the American cotton and American commerce—and the other a Boston, a New York, and a New Orleans, with their commerce and their interests so closely associated with ours—were plunged into hostilities about a distant and barren speck of territory, and a rugged piece of coast, which in themselves possess little or no intrinsic value to either country".

The paper suspected that the free-trading South would not allow a war anyway. John C. Calhoun, the South's intellectual mentor, voted to block one. In any event, Britain could move a fleet and troops from the China seas to occupy Oregon in six weeks; any American forces could take six months to struggle round Cape Horn or cross the Indian territory west from Missouri.

President Polk, it was sure, would realise this: "We have every confidence that the question will finally be settled by peaceful means, without any reflection upon the honour of either country."

Polk, of course, had been elected on slogans like "Fifty-two Forty or Fight", the northerly latitude that American popular opinion insisted on. Britain was reluctant to concede much north of the Columbia River. But what good would a war do? "If England destroyed New York, or bombarded New Orleans, and ultimately obtained possession of the whole of Oregon, after American frigates had taken or destroyed some score of English merchantmen, what would it all prove? Certainly not the title of England to Oregon."

When Polk offered the 49th parallel, plus the whole of Vancouver island, to Britain, the paper thought it was worth accepting. The Columbia was a river that soon became unnavigable; the Hudson's Bay company was not even making much of its trading posts. What was much more important, war with America was almost unthinkable: "We should shrink with horror from a war with Scotland or Ireland, and a war with the United States is not less unnatural and revolting." So one more outstanding territorial boundary was settled.

Mexico and the American intentions towards it were a continuing worry. The campaign of 1847 had brought General Winfield Scott and his troops to Mexico City, but the war had not been ended. The paper's American correspondent, writing from Boston, was impatient: "If the silly, impotent, ignorant Mexicans do not speedily come to terms and make peace, Brother Jonathan will lay his greedy paws upon the entire republic, annex it, endow it with slavery, and appropriate the mines to his own special use, no matter to whom they belong."

Brother Jonathan was the predecessor of Uncle Sam and not, perhaps, quite so likeable a character. The paper was sure that American eyes were on Cuba, and on Canada. The Canadians should always beware of offers: "There is no chance of Canada becoming a manufacturing country for many centuries, if ever. But were she to ally herself to the United States, she would be called upon to pay import duties of 20, 30 and 40 per cent for the protection of manufacturing corporations in New England."

Polk had not delivered the miracle yet. Even so, the best way to avoid confrontations was to solve the small problems without anyone getting too worked up about them. The paper sided with the Americans in opposing the double postage Britain charged on mail carried by American steamers (to protect the Cunard company). It favoured a quick end to the fisheries dispute of 1852 by "a friendly communication to the American Government, not a hostile attack on industrious, if mistaken, fishermen". When the Crimean war began it was even prepared to consider the suggestion by the Foreign Affairs Committee of the House of Representatives that President Pierce should mediate: "It is not for the English to be insensible to the wishes, or even to slight in the smallest degree, the just and kindly opinions of the great people who are fast filling the broad land between the Atlantic and Pacific Oceans, and who, in all probability, before the end of the century, will be the most powerful nation that ever existed on earth."

Of course, it was not yet Lord Palmerston's war, but the more pliable Lord Aberdeen's. The paper judged American opinion with a certain insight: "The Americans, too, have a strong opinion that we are haughty and dictatorial, and they would not be sorry to see us humbled ... who would grieve indeed to see us seriously injured or disabled, but would rejoice at any smart rap on the knuckles that did not compromise our safety or our liberties."

So when Sir John Crampton, the British minister in Washington, was implicated in trying to recruit a British legion to serve in the Crimea there was only one way out: Crampton was sent home, but George M. Dallas, the American minister in London, was not: "It is plain now, and we have both in words and by actions distinctly admitted, that our endeavour to recruit volunteers from the United States was a blunder."

The paper was far from happy about American adventurers in the Caribbean even farther afield than Cuba: it totally opposed any claim on the small, struggling British possession at Belize. But, almost invariably, it found American enthusiasm hard to resist: "You cannot for ever uphold the semi-civilised, semi-Spanish, degenerate Mexicans or Nicaraguans—with their incurable indolence and their eternal petty squabbles—with their effeminate habits and their enfeebled powers—against the hasting, rushing, unresting, inexhaustible energies of the Anglo-Saxon Americans. Criminal, coarse, violent as they often are, it cannot be denied that they rule and conquer by virtue of superior manhood."

IN THE SHADOW OF SLAVERY
The argument for restraint in dealing with the South and its peculiar institution

The Economist did not sympathise with lesser breeds, but it was not racist. From the beginning it was deeply opposed to slavery and wished for its extinction from the continent. In May 1847 its American correspondent watched black children being taught in Philadelphia and found them perfectly capable of advancing into algebra: "I did not discover any natural incapacity for learning, or want of aptness.... If phrenologists, physiologists, or keepumdownologists would assert the contrary, I would simply answer that experience is better than assertion."

Slavery was growing, however, and dangerously so. In June 1848: "Sixty years ago there were only half a

John Brown: dedicated anti-slavery agitator. Planned to terrorise slave-owners from a mountain stronghold.
Attacked federal armoury at Harper's Ferry, Virginia, 1859. Captured by Col. Robert E. Lee and hanged.

million slaves in the United States; now they are estimated at three millions and a half, with every prospect of a rapid and continued increase, both in slaves and slave states."

Still, gradualism was the only recommended policy. There was cotton to think of, and more than cotton: "It is probable that the people of the States will outgrow slavery, as the people of Europe, without any positive decrees for abolishing it, have outgrown the serfdom that once prevailed amongst them; and the process is scarcely worth hastening, supposing it would not be retarded, while evils infinitely greater than slavery would be inflicted on humanity by the breaking up of the Union and the wars which would certainly ensue."

Calhoun, the South's advocate, had spoken threateningly about the growth of population in the North and the increasing number of northern states. The paper stood by the union: "To the Union the South is indebted for its peace; and for its power to make any use of those newly acquired territories, which it dreads will add to the preponderance of the North. It must recognise that as the element of its own safety, and acquiesce in an aggrandisement it can only temporarily retard by its own total ruin."

So it saw some virtues in the series of measures that amounted to the Compromise of 1850, among them California's entry into the union, although its preference was not for the measures the South had insisted on. The pro-slavery party was "headstrong, domineering, insolent and cruel".

John Brown's insurrection at Harper's Ferry in 1859 was, it thought, a "great miscalculation ... or fanatical enthusiasm of a truly boyish kind". Slavery was detestable in principle; its enforcement was "monstrous and inhuman;" but the paper did not support

religious zeal as the best instrument of removing it. Equally, it thought the recovery of fugitive slaves in the North "one of the most fatally injudicious moves" that the slave states had made: "Let the conviction that the Fugitive Slave Bill is a logical and inevitable sequence of the institution of slavery, stimulate the zeal of the North and awaken the conscience of the South."

To the end the paper could not bring itself to desert the South and the Democrats totally, because they were the champions of free trade. But its heart was heavy: "They include the most wild and ignorant of the population. It is among them that the opposers and defiers of established authority are principally found. They are the chief favourers and executors of Lynch law."

The old order, the balance and the blind eyes by which the union had survived so long were reaching the point of breakdown. Clay, the great compromiser, had died in 1852; Pierce's favouritism and negligence had morally damaged him and the southern cause; and by the end of 1856 James Buchanan, "a grey-headed statesman, of some European experience", was about to take over to try what diplomacy could do. The European feeling was now increasingly against slavery: the pressure was to stop and search suspected slave ships.

The paper still counselled restraint: "Nothing could be more injudicious, more thoroughly and recklessly culpable, than to precipitate the present unhealthy tendencies of American politics by irritating their national pride, and so placing the Anti-Slavery party among them at a disadvantage. We have no right to do this."

The time was at hand when America would have to decide for itself.

Abraham Lincoln: president 1861–65. Campaign portrait 1860 by Mathew Brady, the great civil war photographer. Lincoln averred: "This portrait made me President of the United States."

2

THE CIVIL WAR DILEMMA

1861–1865

DIVIDING AMERICA

Walter Bagehot, the paper's best-known editor, saw advantages in the civil war if it led to two or more separate American nations

The American civil war impaled *The Economist*, like much British opinion, on a succession of dilemmas. The North, the Federal states, stood for much of what *The Economist* and Walter Bagehot, the editor, admired and hoped for in the United States; not least in the growing north-western states that had so much of the potential and space for the future. However many North American countries there might ultimately be, they would be great powers in the world.

The North was plainly right, too, about anti-slavery. The transatlantic brotherhood and sisterhood of liberal reform encompassed much the same sort of middle-class sympathisers. But then the North, though it had the enthusiasts, had long allowed itself politically to be locked in with the slave-owning South and had shown no aptitude and little wish to get out. Further, the North was protectionist, anathema to the cause of free trade, while the South, whatever its faults, had to sell its cotton.

What, probably, was even worse for *The Economist* was that it found the North arrogant, self-confident and almost incorrigibly anti-British. Bagehot and his contributors puzzled long and hard about how this could be and, being of an intellectual disposition, put it down to the fallacies of the written American constitution. To any British constitutional expert, especially when expressly opposed to the concept of universal manhood suffrage, the temptation was all too irresistible to point out to the Americans the basic error of their ways.

The paper was clear that the American colonies had had the right to choose Washington against George III. It was just as clear that the South, or any combination of states, had the right to go their own way. It had no doubt that what it characterised as English virtues were the essential Anglo-Saxon virtues of even a divided and warring America. But Bagehot himself, who knew the British constitution (as he personally interpreted it for ensuing generations), was intellectually unable to see that the Americans had faced the democratic future and he had not.

From the start he had underestimated the abilities and the potential of Abraham Lincoln. *The Economist*,

---

CHRONOLOGY

1861	Abraham Lincoln becomes president		Battle of Gettysburg; fall of Vicksburg
	Confederate attack on Fort Sumter, South Carolina	1864	Prussia and Austria invade Denmark
	Battle of Bull Run		Confederate raider, *Alabama*, built in Britain, sunk
	Union navy takes Confederate agents from the British steamer *Trent*		William T. Sherman captures Atlanta
1862	Otto von Bismarck prime minister of Prussia	1865	Robert E. Lee surrenders to Ulysses S. Grant at Appomattox
	Lincoln's proclamation emancipating the slaves		Lincoln shot at Ford's Theatre, Washington, DC
1863	Revolution in (Russian) Poland put down		Andrew Johnson becomes president
	French troops occupy Mexico		Thirteenth amendment abolishes slavery

---

initially, was happy enough with Lincoln's election: "It would be a great mistake to suppose that Mr Abraham Lincoln is an extreme man."

He was not. He proposed to continue a modified Fugitive Slave Law, do nothing about the internal slave trade, and only gradually abolish slavery in the District of Columbia itself. Lincoln was "obnoxious" to the South, yet he appeared reluctant to take up "the high ground" against the spread of slavery. He, like his colleagues in the cabinet, seemed too small a man to respond to the crisis of the union: "Mr Lincoln is a nearly unknown man—who has been but little heard of—who has had little experience—who may have nerve and judgment or may not have them—whose character, both moral and intellectual, is an unknown quantity—who must, from his previous life and defective education, be wanting in the liberal acquirements and mental training which are principal elements of an enlarged statesmanship."

For the United States, with all its boasts and its pretensions, to have come sufficiently unstuck to seem to be about to become decisively unstuck as a single nation was too much for Victorian Britain to ignore. It raised many questions: in particular, was the superior American theory of one-continent, one-nation at all correct?

To Americans of a Federal persuasion it went without saying. There were ministers in Lincoln's cabinet who thought the North could redress something of what it might lose in the South by a judicious attempt on Canada. To Europeans, though, there was no difficulty in thinking of a North America beneficially divided into four or more countries, as Europe was. And, without question, such an accepted or even an enforced division would very probably not be against British national or trade interests.

Like most English politicians and papers, *The Economist* was contemptuous of American politicians. In January 1860, before the break, it concluded: "Passion, spite, petty personality, small wit, the spirit of compromise, and, as the best and highest of all, the spirit of short-sighted, unstatesmanlike anger against the slave states, mark the tone of the debates in Congress."

The South had appeared to know, all along, what it was doing. Inferior in population and enormously inferior in wealth, it had regularly elected a president of its own way of thinking: now that strategy had failed. For the decades in which it had worked the

North had been in enforced subordination. But the North still seemed set on further embarrassment: "The Northern states, especially the Atlantic ones, which are comparatively wealthy, populous and powerful, and which for a quarter of a century have been dragged through every species of moral and political mire by their slaveholding associates—to whom at first sight it would seem as if severance would be liberation from a galling and dishonourable servitude—are temperate, conciliating, and rational, and would fain dissipate the danger, if they could see their way to doing so."

So it was necessary for a candid friend to assure the Americans that, however mortified they might be, the change must be for the better: "It is true their republic will be less vast, but it will be their own fault if it be less great. Their national life will be purer, more consistent, less incessantly lowered and stained by disreputable compromises. They may be less feared by Europe, but assuredly they will be more respected."

It was not the sort of consolation that would ever appeal to a Lincoln. It sounded even less plausible when set beside the practical advantages to Britain itself, to whom "it may not indirectly be rather beneficial than otherwise". Or to be specific: "We may expect that America will be somewhat less aggressive, less insolent, and less irritable than she has been. Instead of one vast state ... we shall have two, with different objects and interests, and by no means always disposed to act in concert or in cordiality. Instead of one, showing an encroaching and somewhat bullying front to the rest of the world, we shall have two, showing something of the same front to each other."

And for the North, besides its redeemed reputation, a glimpse of how economic forces must inevitably bring their own rewards. Commerce would find a way: "The North will soon renew in one form or another its old transactions with the South. It will still supply the Southerners with ships; it will still advance them money; it will still discount their bills—more cautiously, no doubt, at perhaps higher interest, with perhaps stricter security. It will still send them provisions, and receive their cotton in return.... So long as there is mercantile honesty and productive industry, there will be mercantile transactions and brisk interchange."

If this patronised the North, there was no redemption for the South, and least of all for those there emboldened to argue that slavery was, in fact, a blessing to both races: "The only excuse for the men who adopt it is that they appear to be men of narrow minds and small passions, who prefer challenging or caning an antagonist to overcoming him in debate."

The paper never faltered in the abolitionist cause, although it never favoured the war and still less a black uprising to ensure the cause's success. It would need patience and persistence to keep the newly independent slave states isolated. The South, it seemed plain, would lose power. It could not hope to expand in Cuba or elsewhere in the Gulf: "They can scarcely hope to be permitted in their severed condition to renew the African slave trade, in defiance of the general outcry of the civilised world, and the active, persistent, because morally-based and almost fanatic opposition both of England and of the Northern Federation."

All they could hope for was what faced other pariahs: "They may hope ... to keep down their slaves, as Austria keeps down Venice, by incessant vigilance, by increased severity, by organising a large and impermanent force of whites."

The poor whites, who had the controlling vote, were the most contemptible: "Perhaps the most degraded, ignorant, brutal, drunken, violent class that ever swarmed in a civilised country."

The South, it had to be conceded (as most of English political society readily conceded), had the right to be recognised as a belligerent. But the fundamental issue would remain unresolved: "We confess we see no daylight through this appalling picture. When the dissolution of the Union is consummated without provision being made for ultimate emancipation and abandonment of slavery, we greatly fear that security for life and property must henceforth be at an end for the South."

As the differences widened and the drift to Fort Sumter and war gathered pace, all that an Englishman could see was that Lincoln was doing nothing, perhaps could do nothing. The very choice of a president was a much less remediable action than the choice of a prime minister. The president could not be stopped by parliamentary doubt or opposition for four years. The president was personally responsible for his policy and could not modify it, with credit, as a prime minister could regularly do: "The Government is almost in as little direct contact with the people as the Russian Government, and yet it has to guide itself by the wishes of the people, which the Russian Government does not pretend to do."

It had little contact even with the Congress. Congress never saw the president; the House of Commons saw Lord Palmerston every day.

CANADA AND COTTON

The paper doubted if Canada could be defended against a northern attack, but the market would replace southern cotton

Properly, Britain's own interests were very prominent in The Economist's thinking from the start. There was the rivalry with the Americans, stoked up by repeated quarrels. British governments, particularly those headed by Palmerston and Lord John Russell, remembered vividly the war of 1812–15, the continuing disputes over the Canadian border in the east from the 1820s to the 1840s, American expansion in the south and west (where Britain had actually turned down the offer of California by Mexico's Antonio Lopez de Santa Anna), the Canadian rebellion in 1837, and the arrest and near lynching of Alexander McLeod in New York in 1841.

Canada was a worry in more ways than one: "If the people of the Canadas universally wish to throw off the yoke of England and annex themselves to the United States, no obstacle will be interposed on the part of Great Britain. To us Canada is, from a military point of view, expensive; and to defend for her so long a frontier line is no little responsibility in case of war with the United States." Although the Guards were sent, Whitehall doubted if there could be a defence west of Montreal.

In practice, British governments were prepared to foot the bill for sending reinforcements across (making sure they were not Irish regiments), entirely for the Canadians' own good. If Canada were absorbed by the United States "it would reduce her to a position of insignificance and virtual dependence.... She would then at best form only two States out of twenty or twenty-five, and have not as many votes in Congress as New York".

By 1864 the answer was found under the war's pressure: the advance towards the hitherto unthinkable scheme of federation between English and French Canada.

More important was trade, and most important of all was the transatlantic trade in cotton on which Lancashire and Cheshire depended. A Federal blockade to cut the Confederacy off from Liverpool was generally expected, although it was thought some Federal cruisers might turn a blind eye to consignments intended for the mill towns of Massachusetts. What was not expected was that the Confederacy decided not to ship cotton at all, not even from the plantations to its own ports, a stratagem to force the British and French governments to intervene on its side to stop distress among their textile operatives.

The Economist was as clear about a world shortage of cotton as it has been about world shortages of anything. New suppliers would be developed, especially in India. Substitutes would be found by land and sea, among them a development of flax by the Chevalier Claussen, "who we regret to learn is now in a lunatic asylum". Scarcity would bring greater efficiency. Even so, by 1864 it had to admit to other effects. Liverpool was destitute of the American staple it needed, and of short staple: "Owing to the enormous prices obtainable, an immense quantity of rubbish has been shipped under the name of cotton, for which in ordinary years no one would have thought it worth while to incur the cost of freight."

Back in 1848 the paper's American correspondent, reporting the South's efforts to industrialise by using slave labour to manufacture cotton goods, had advised Britain to cultivate raw cotton in the colonies. It had not happened.

There certainly was distress in Lancashire: since cotton goods and yarn accounted for one-third of all exports of British manufactures before the war, it could not have been avoided. The market did work, however, in its own time. The 1859 crop had been a bumper one, and it had been expeditiously shipped across the Atlantic. There was work for Lancashire for the next two years, even if not enough. For once *The Economist* was ready for hands to be dipped in the local public purse: "We would rather sacrifice some money to undue leniency than impair the self-respect or offend the real delicacy of the highest of our working classes by too suspicious watchfulness or over-precise suspicions."

For these were, for once, the worthy, Smilesian poor. They had used their savings, credit, energy and resourcefulness before ever appealing to the system: "The really grievous results of this crisis will be, not the temporary reduction of a whole population to scanty earnings and charitable aid, but the destruction and waste of the laborious hoardings of many years, and the reduction to actual poverty of thousands whom a long course of frugality and forethought had raised from the position of daily labourers almost into that of small capitalists."

Lancashire's workers continued to support the North, even when the owners of small houses or people who had something in the savings bank were bankrupted. When the bite was really on, in the winter of 1862–63, the paper did not blink at a modest public bill: "No one fancies that England or Lancashire cannot maintain the unemployed operatives and those dependent upon them for a year or two years if necessary even although these should swell to double their present number. Four or five millions, if properly levied and adjusted, will not sink a ship like ours."

In the end both Lancashire and Massachusetts lasted out. By 1865 high English prices diverted most Indian cotton Liverpool's way. Mill owners with cotton stocks of any kind were sitting on gold, and the inferior staple needed more hands and more machinery to spin and weave. There were hopes of returning to full employment even before Richmond fell.

That the cotton workers and their unions consistently refused to agitate for intervention in the war to save their jobs was a major factor in lowering the political temperature whenever the North and Britain fell out, and so in negating Confederate policy.

RIVAL FORCES

The Federal forces ought to win, but the South would fight hard and it would be impossible to occupy

The paper, and especially Bagehot in his own articles, knew that the North, with all its resources, should win the war. What it doubted was that the North had the organisation and resolution to do so. It doubted wholeheartedly if the North could ever subdue the South; and it quickly persuaded itself of this certainty after the North's early reverses, especially what it called "the panic at Manassas Gap". The recurrent theme became: "The South can never again expect to dominate the North. The North cannot seriously expect to subjugate the South."

This miscalculation was widespread in Britain.

Andrew Jackson's victory at New Orleans in 1815 still rankled; the United States's other wars had merely been against "naked Indians and degenerate and undisciplined Mexicans". Still, facts were facts: "A wealthy and free population of twenty millions cannot but conquer in the long run in a contest with a poor free population of the same race, numbering at most seven millions even if we give the South the whole of the border states. That the North may be beaten at first, we regard as exceedingly probable.... In the long run, no doubt wealth and numbers must decide this fatal strife."

The South did have three advantages. First, in European eyes, it was vast: "A traveller marches for days, and meets only occasional shanties and log-houses. Flying columns might march for days and meet no foe, and no shelter. The largest army would be a mere speck in such a desert." Second, the southern troops were predominantly Anglo-Saxons, and so were fierce, obstinate and untamable: "Does anyone acquainted with the temper of the Southerner—who unites all the fiery pride of a Frenchman with all the stubborn pride of an Englishman –believe that defeat and privation will do more than envenom and exasperate the strife?" Third, the paper was deeply sceptical of the North: "We are strongly impressed with the conviction that there is no degree of incapacity, confusion, feebleness, mismanagement and thorough imbecility on the part of the Government at Washington, which is not upon the cards. We should deeply grieve, for the honour of our common ancestry, to see it. But it would not surprise us."

Such was cousinly confidence. And by October 1861 the paper had taken the unusual step for it of employing "a Gentleman of great intelligence, practically acquainted with the Cotton Trade, who is now on his voyage to America to learn, as far as possible, the real facts from personal observation". The paper would have read events the better had it taken this correspondent's initial finding in New York to heart:

Union troops on parade. The early federal forces were ill-trained and ill-led and met repeated defeats by the Confederates. They needed time to develop tactics in a railway age and make use of modern firepower.

"Republicans, Democrats, Abolitionists—all, so far as I have yet been able to discover, are united on one point—that whatever the sacrifices to the present generation, the Union must be preserved. Tell them it will produce national bankruptcy—that the grass will grow in Broadway—that army after army will be annihilated by starvation and disease, if not by battle, before eight millions of men as brave as themselves will be conquered by a race they detest as they do the Yankees—and still you can get no concession."

THE TRENT AFFAIR

Both Lincoln and Palmerston acted wisely in defusing the crisis

Yankee self-confidence got British politicians (and editors) badly worried when in November 1861 Captain Charles Wilkes took the two Confederate envoys to Europe, James Mason and John Slidell, off the British packet *Trent*. Bagehot (like Palmerston) was outraged: "As we should not permit the Austrian Government to take Mazzini from the packet between Dover and Calais—as we should not permit the French Emperor to harm Louis Blanc between Dublin and Holyhead—so we must protect those so-called American rebels on our ship between St Thomas and the Havana."

If hotter heads were ready to go to war the paper was not, as yet. Of course the American captain was wrong: "The captain of a man-of-war has no power to adjudicate on such questions as the present. Naval officers on remote stations, with passions and without books, are not fit to adjudicate on important and anxious questions."

On balance, however, it believed the American authorities intended no insult: "The highest authorities in this country we understand hope not. They believe that this insane outrage was caused rather by enmity to the South than by insolence to us."

Of course it was absurd to suppose that the North would take on Britain: that would ensure the independence of the South if nothing else did. Still, Britain was dealing with Americans: "America is a very extraordinary nation; and the time is a very extraordinary time. Nothing is impossible to a democracy in revolution. The President is unequal to the situation."

Lincoln delayed; it was his instinct. That was hopeful. But there was "an utter madness among a very large part of the American nation, fostered by long prosperity and assiduous adulation". They were not much given to paying apologies and compensation: "We must bear in mind that the Northern Americans are, in several of our most ineradicable qualities, alarmingly like ourselves. They do not know any better than we do, nor so well, how to give in when beaten."

So it might end badly. There might be nothing else for it: "Unless substantial reparation be offered, war, with all its contingencies—nay, with all its certainties—must be cheerfully accepted."

Whether it was Prince Albert's dying rewrite of the government's note or not, the good news was already on its way: "At last we are relieved from the uncertainty which, for the last few weeks, has been hanging over us. The American Government has decided—not very logically, perhaps, but very wisely—to release on our demand the commissioners whom it had previously detained and imprisoned.... An old proverb tells us not to scrutinise gifts too closely, and under the circumstances we will consider the act of Mr Lincoln a free gift."

Captain Wilkes, it was decided, had acted without authority. He had actually done to the *Trent* no more than the Royal Navy had done to American shipping before the 1812 war. Delay had helped. The Atlantic cable was out of operation. It was back to five weeks for letters to cross and return. But Bagehot drew a firmer conclusion: "In all future dealings with the American Government, we must ask for what we want, courteously but peremptorily.... The effect of the Palmerstonian policy is evident.... An aged statesman will seldom be able to the extremity of his life to confer so signal and characteristic a benefit on his country."

WAR AND STALEMATE

Northern incompetence brought it regular defeat. The paper thought it legally right, but unwise, to let the commerce raider Alabama *escape*

The northern armies made little progress, apart from capturing New Orleans in May 1862, a place that the paper dismissed as "a pestilential Capua" which the North would only hold at the point of the bayonet "as France holds Rome". There were those, now, who thought they saw a chance for mediation. Napoleon III was keen on it. The paper did not think then that Britain should try. It would merely antagonise the North: "Let France mediate alone, with our full sanction and goodwill. Let her do all the service and reap all the credit. So that peace is restored, we need not care much who is the peacemaker."

What it thought practicable was to confirm the Confederacy in its diehard states east of the Mississippi. It thus awarded West Virginia, Kentucky, the main portion of Tennessee, Missouri and Texas to the North. Only the "most slave" parts of Arkansas and Louisiana west of the Mississippi would remain with the South. The 500,000 slaves this would give to the North would either be purchased and set free or would be allowed to move to the independent South with their masters. It supposed the South would be content with an area of land "nearly equal to France, England and Austria combined".

But whatever the Confederacy might or might not settle for, the North would have nothing of it, even though by that August the northern armies were again in full retreat from before Richmond: "The Federal army has abandoned its principal attempt; our Crimean army never, even at its worst and most suffering moment, abandoned ours. Yet the state of American opinion is wholly different from what ours then was.... If we had known whom to hang, we should have hanged someone. But the Americans feel no rage and no anger. We are assured by recent observers that they hardly know that they have been materially defeated."

There were three immediate explanations. First, Britain had a more watchful public opinion. Second, the American public, "inferior as it is", had not been trained as the naturally superior English public had been trained: by Parliament. Third, there were no good

Lincoln with his stylish but indecisive commander, General George B. McClellan (right), whom he had to dismiss for lack of aggression. McClellan contested the presidency against Lincoln and failed in 1864.

American political newspapers. *The Economist* worried repeatedly about the American press and its perversely anti-British attitudes. By October 1863 it felt able to pronounce judgment: "It is cheap and is on the whole addressed to the most numerous and the least-educated part of the community; it does not, as a rule, yield any large profits, and the writers, therefore, belong to a very third-rate order of literary men; and partly on this account and partly from accident, it has fallen to a great extent into the hands of Irishmen, who usually hate England, which they have fled from, and were brought up from the cradle to abuse."

From the start, Bagehot had correctly identified the chief source of trouble between the North and Britain as the blockade. He had expected more significant blockade-running than the South managed; the Federal navy made it a dangerous sport for outsiders, too. The five-hour fight between the *Merrimac* and the *Monitor* in Hampton Roads in March 1862 showed the Royal Navy that it must take ironclad ships seriously. The paper was clear—on one condition: "To maintain the relative naval power of England, we must, as quickly as our means will permit, transform our wooden fleet into an iron fleet—always conditioning, however, that this fleet shall in the first place be in every respect seaworthy, and only in the second place as shot-proof as a seaworthy fleet can be.... We want something with which we can threaten a distant coast." Both the *Merrimac* and the *Monitor* were homemade for coastal waters.

It came as no surprise to all except the British authorities that the Confederacy was building a powerful ocean commerce-raider at Laird's yard in Birkenhead in July 1862. Charles Adams, the American minister in London, warned Palmerston, but orders to stop the ship arrived after it had sailed. International law allowed neutrals to build ships for belligerents, but they could not be armed. The *Alabama* was to prey on Federal shipping for two years. London and Washington were at loggerheads again. *The Economist* had no doubts: "The vessel left the Mersey, a simple unfreighted ship, without a single gun or a single bag of powder on board. She cleared out for Nassau, but went to Terceira (we believe) where she was ordered to be delivered to the purchasers, and there, in the dominions of the King of Portugal and not of Queen Victoria, she took in her armament and all her warlike stores."

There were some second thoughts when reports arrived of the panic in New York and Boston. Britain had just built the sort of cruiser British men of business most dreaded: "Fancy the effect if we were at war with France or Russia, of a score of *Alabamas* (whether French or Russian steam cruisers or American privateers) infesting the seas in any part of the world—for every sea swarms with British ships—and looking out for the British flag.... The harvest they would reap would be enormous, the injury they would inflict would be fearful."

Palmerston did act in 1863 (after Gettysburg) to stop two further Confederate raiders being built by Laird, and told the Commons the law was on the Federal side. The paper saw the eventual end of the *Alabama* with truculent relief: "The *Alabama* was well-manned, well-armed and commanded by a hero; yet as soon as the United States, instead of whining about the English reluctance to alter municipal laws, sent out a vessel of equal burden, equal audacity, greater speed, and heavier guns, the *Alabama*'s career was closed."

The paper was still adamant that British neutrality at sea had been almost entirely to the North's advantage: "For one vessel laden with arms and warlike stores that has entered a Southern port twenty have entered Northern ports. Nine-tenths of the Federal forces have been clothed and armed with British imports. Nine-tenths of the Confederate soldiers who have fallen have been slain by guns made in the United Kingdom." Eight years later the United States was awarded $15.5m damages against Britain.

On land, Federal progress was still slow. The paper saw a chance for mediation in August 1862. It decided, to its own satisfaction, that popular feeling in the North would accept a rational settlement: "The Americans, having chosen their rulers, leave more to the action of their rulers, and acquiesce in that action much more readily and conclusively, than we do. The *Trent* affair showed this very remarkably. If, therefore, the Government can be persuaded ... that European mediation offers the easiest and most dignified mode in which such accommodation can be inaugurated, we do not much fear that the popular voice will repudiate the proceedings of the Government."

Mediation meant full recognition, and the South was pressing for it militarily and politically. The paper was becoming impressed: "The Confederates appear to have crossed the Potomac; by this time they are probably in full possession of Maryland, and are in a position to attack Washington from the North and Philadelphia from the South." There followed the appropriate rhetoric: "Who can say that the Confederates have not made good their claim to be considered as a People who have fairly won their independence and are able to maintain it, and deserve to have it recognised?"

have been to give the North, and especially William H. Seward, secretary of state and no friend of Britain, the pretext that Britain had actually done what he continually complained about and had intervened directly in the war. Whatever Palmerston thought about it privately, he was much too old a hand to be pushed before he was ready.

Robert E. Lee: the dominant Confederate commander, a master of defensive strategy who failed in his two attempts to invade the North.

Gladstone, chancellor of the exchequer, was immediately prepared to be just as rhetorical, affirming at a dinner in Newcastle that the Confederates "had succeeded in making an army, in making a navy—nay, more, in making a nation". This was strong stuff, even for after dinner. The paper was not quite ready for it: "We are scarcely prepared to recommend immediate recognition, and we incline to regret that Mr Gladstone should, by implication, have sanctioned it, and led the world to expect it."

This was common sense. The worst outcome would

LINCOLN'S INITIATIVE
Bagehot believed the emancipation of the slaves merely encouraged false hope

Lincoln now took his decisive initiative. Or, rather, that was what the future came to decide he did. Bagehot saw it as nothing of the sort. That October there were two proclamations: one emancipated all slaves in rebel states or belonging to rebels, the other suspended the writ of habeas corpus and declared martial law on anyone helping the South or hindering the draft. *The Econ-*

omist thought that both epitomised Lincoln's "absence of statesmanship, and indeed of ordinary political sagacity". Emancipation, it insisted, merely encouraged false hope: "To emancipate slaves whom your proclamation cannot reach or rouse is futile and foolish. To rouse a population whom you could neither aid or protect, merely that they may create a diversion in your favour, is iniquitously unkind and selfish."

The paper recognised Lincoln was aiming for Europe's moral support, but it thought it knew better. It was no encouragement to the anti-slavery party in either America or Britain to find that the slaves belonging to masters who still supported the North were not to be freed: "He proclaims emancipation to the slaves whom he cannot liberate, and he retains in slavery those whose fate lies within his power.... He enacts that in future the negroes in the slave states shall be free, and that the negroes in the free states shall be slaves. The North henceforth is to be the only slave portion of the Union."

As for suspending habeas corpus, called a "pseudo-vigorous decree", the president had no right to do it, but if he persisted in it he would merely make it harder to enforce conscription wherever it was unpopular: "If Mr Lincoln endeavours to enforce his decree, the tyranny will exasperate many of his Northern supporters. If he recalls it, the weakness displayed in the whole transaction will disgust them even more."

The paper's view in late October was that the declaration of emancipation would do less than Lincoln expected: "We do not believe it will at all facilitate the subjugation of the South. We do not believe it will emancipate many Negroes. Nor do we believe it will tend to the massacre of many Whites." It thought that Lincoln's aim was acceptable: "To cripple your adversaries by depriving them of the services of their labouring population would, as a military expedient, be perfectly warrantable and exceedingly effective."

The unacceptable part was that if it was to work it would put the blacks who did respond at risk: "How can a humane man, a thoughtful man, and a just man—and we believe Mr Lincoln to be naturally all three—have ventured to urge a multitude of ignorant, helpless, excitable Negroes to revolt against their masters when perfectly aware that he can afford them neither aid nor protection in their outbreak, and that he has been preparing for them only certain discomforture and cruel punishment?"

FROM GETTYSBURG TO THE END
The paper wanted slavery to be confined east of the Mississippi. It welcomed Vicksburg but not Gettysburg; and then Sherman surprised it

By the summer of 1863 it was plain that it would be the soldiers who decided the war, or at least who decided what Europe would or would not do about the war. Recognition of the Confederacy, mediation, intervention were repeatedly canvassed by all those who could not see the North's strategy succeed and who did see the cotton industry suffering in both Britain and France. What the Confederacy's friends in Europe wanted was the demonstration that the South could advance into the North and even take Washington. Robert E. Lee had failed the previous summer at Antietam in Maryland. Lee's push into southern Pennsylvania was what Palmerston, Russell and Napoleon III (and *The Economist*) had been waiting for.

Gettysburg was fought on July 1st–3rd 1863, and on July 4th Lee withdrew south of the Potomac again. None of this was known in London, so it was sensible for Bagehot that he set no store on second-guessing what the military might do: "That amateur generalship which excels in anticipation has never been permitted to *The Economist*." What was permitted, apparently, was wishful thinking: "The Federal states seem to look on, we do not say placidly or calmly, but still without zeal, without an excess of military enthusiasm, without passion, while their capital is in danger, and the soil of their country is polluted. When first Fort Sumter was attacked, a nerve of exquisite feeling thrilled through the country; there is nothing like that now."

While Lee was loose there was the chance of peace by stalemate. Once the invasion had failed there had to be another reappraisal of the war aims. Bagehot kept to three. First, the South should be independent. This was for the moral good of both sides: "We wish to save the North from the danger of military pre-eminence, as well as the South from the disgrace and pain of military subjugation." Second, the South, though independent, should be weak: "We wish that the area of slavery should be so small that, by the sure operation of economic causes, and especially by the inevitable exhaustion of the soil which it always produces, slavery should, within a reasonable time, be gradually extinguished." Third, the war should cease as soon as possible.

So the paper was pleased with General Ulysses S. Grant's efforts in the west, not so pleased with General George G. Meade in the east: "We shall rejoice at the reduction of Vicksburg and of Port Hudson by the Federal armies. The best mode of confining slavery within fixed limits is the conquest by the North of the line of the Mississippi.... But we must regret the defeat of General Lee's invasion of the North."

Now the war would go on, and not even the anti-conscription riots in New York would bring its end any nearer: "They do not prove Mr Lincoln to be unable to raise for a considerable time many men and some money. In New York he may not enforce the conscription, but elsewhere he can and will; and while a war government has sufficient men, sufficient money, and plausible hope, any peace is beyond probability."

So too, of course, was recognition of the South: "We do not consider that the independence of the South is much less likely than it formerly was. Their run of luck is over, and they must look for the natural consequences which all thinking people predicted at the outset of these events. Their real strength is their vast area, which has not been and cannot be curtailed."

It remained the paper's conviction, almost to the end, that the South could not be occupied and so could not be defeated. Every southern defeat, from New Orleans onwards, was no more than a reverse. The fighting would still go on. At the end of 1863 the paper even came up with fresh cannon fodder: "They may themselves liberate and arm their slaves.... If they are thoroughly reduced to submission, negro slavery is at an end—and to their utter ruin. May it not, as the last resort, become wise for them to take the initiative in the inevitable course, and end negro slavery, by their own enactment, and to their own profit and salvation?" President Jefferson Davis did tell Europe he was prepared to offer abolition for recognition in January 1865; but it was far too late.

By May 1864 the paper had to admit that the Federal armies were making progress: "The Northerners, though always losing battles, are nearly always gaining ground." But the end was still not visible. The advance of the election season and the campaigning of the northern Democrats, even the resignation of Salmon P. Chase, the secretary of the treasury who had raised the war loans for Lincoln, led Bagehot back to hope for peace by stalemate: "Already some such conception has been dimly shadowed out in the shape of two separate republics, or it may be three, united in a federal bond."

People were at least beginning to talk about peace. People, "the more thoughtful spirits of the North, both in the east and in the west", were weary of the war: "The repeated failures of successive generals and armies to penetrate to Richmond; the small effect produced on the resolution or strength of their antagonists by even the most decided federal successes, such as those of Vicksburg and New Orleans; the unflinching determination of the South in spite of the disappointment of all their hopes of foreign assistance—even the most indirect; and the increasing cost and difficulty of finding recruits to fill up the vacancies in their ranks caused by unprecedented slaughter, disease, and desertion—these things have slowly forced on the minds of all who are not too passionate either to observe or think, the conviction that they are engaged in a hopeless task, and that the South cannot and will not be conquered."

To those who accepted that argument anything, apparently, was possible for peace: the secession of New England, two republics with one federal foreign policy, even "the reconsecration of slavery". It was Bagehot himself who sounded war-weary.

Lincoln's re-election was a mild relief to the paper. As an American politician he had his merits: "In Europe, and merely considering the bare choice between the two candidates, the election of Mr Lincoln will unquestionably give general satisfaction ... Mr Lincoln said: 'I wish to maintain the Union by destroying slavery.' General McClellan said: 'I wish to maintain the Union by retaining slavery.'"

Even though the war was plainly going the Federal way, the paper still could not bring itself to accept or understand that Lincoln had been able to use the presidency and the constitution to organise a highly effective military machine. More than that: "Mr Lincoln has been honest, but he has been vulgar; and there is no greater external misfortune ... than for a great nation to be exclusively represented at a crisis far beyond previous, and perhaps beyond future, example, by a person whose words are mean even when his actions are important." The Gettysburg speech had been delivered a year before.

The evidence of Federal success grew. The Confederate Treasury now had to confess that it had an utterly depreciated currency, approaching worthlessness. It had been only 18 months since the paper had recommended a Confederate loan in Europe, despite the possibility that the South might be reannexed. "This danger, however, as our readers know, we should be inclined to estimate very lightly." Now things were rather different: "The masterly and daring march of Sherman across Georgia, his capture of Savannah, his commander, and that another severe blow and heavy discouragement is hanging over the Confederate cause."

Even so, *The Economist*, if not the South, would not give up. The South still had large armies in the field; it still had "the ablest generals of the Republic in their

Ulysses S. Grant: the Union commander who brought the Confederacy to its knees by sheer attrition. Lincoln said of him: "I can't spare this man. He fights."

reported and very probable intention of fighting his way up through the Carolinas to join Grant, and the great likelihood, in case of his success, of the capture of Richmond, all seem to intimate both that the Federals have at length found a really competent ranks"; and the very depredations of the war had made the two sides "pretty nearly irreconcilable".

One of the Confederates' last throws was to raid from Canada into Vermont (simply robbing banks) and across Lake Erie. This was stopped, but it was an uncomfortable business. The new reputation of the Federal armies was such that the thought crossed some minds in London: what would happen if Grant and his men were ordered north to settle scores with Canada?

The paper appeared to have no such worries about British military capability: "With a superior navy, with the power of throwing 50,000 men into Canada, and all the help the British Americans themselves could give us, which, from a population of 3,000,000 should be at least equivalent to a force of 20,000 men, and with the advantage—always great—of acting on the defensive, we do not see that the contest, if ever provoked, need be so unequal."

At last, in April 1865, Richmond fell. There could be no illusions about that: "The fall of Richmond is one of the most striking events in modern history." For this, credit had to be given where credit was due: "Every Englishman at least will feel a kind of personal sympathy with the victory of the Federals. They have won, as an Englishman would have won, by obstinacy."

What mattered was that this was final: whatever the paper had said before, it was now the end of the southern resistance: "Without organised armies, can the Confederates be defended by loose insurgents and guerrilla warfare, acting alone and without support? We believe that history affords no countenance to such an idea."

In the relief that it was all over, there was a businesslike relief that Richmond had not fallen before, when the price of cotton was astronomical and the fortunes of those who then held it would have promptly disintegrated: "It is undeniable that the fall of Richmond, such as we have ascertained it to be, would have been of disastrous consequences to several branches of English commerce if it had happened six months ago."

So business, normal service, could be resumed with a clear conscience. But peace, the paper thought, might not immediately be worth all that much. The North had spent and borrowed recklessly; that was going to make further protection seem a necessity while the debt began to be paid off.

So much for the confident morning of free trade. The North, of course, still had vast resources, but the South was bankrupt and exhausted, nor would it buy again as it had done before the war. Financially, peace had been discounted.

A GREAT MAN PASSES
In his death The Economist *discovered his virtue*

Lincoln was shot at Ford's Theatre in Washington on the night of April 14th 1865 (and Seward, the secretary of state, was shot and wounded at his home the same evening). *The Economist* saw fit to lead its next issue with its views of Gladstone's budget, but its second article recognised the greatness in the man it had consistently undervalued. His murder, it said, was a very great and very lamentable event, perhaps the greatest since Waterloo: "It is not merely that a great man has passed away, but he has disappeared at the very time when his special greatness seemed almost essential to the world, when his death would work the widest conceivable evil, when the chances of replacing him, even partially, approached nearest to zero."

All at once, his undiscovered virtues were apparent: "Mr Lincoln, by a rare combination of qualities—patience, sagacity and honesty—by a still more rare sympathy, not with the best of his nation, but with the best average of his nation, and by a moderation rarest of all, had attained such vast moral authority that he could make all the hundred wheels of the constitution move in one direction without exerting any physical force."

The defective education, the poor way with words, the lack of sagacity and the vulgarity were now as if they had never been. Even the execrable constitution, which compounded the presidential weaknesses, could actually be made to work by the paragon himself. As a retraction it was well done. As an explanation for the years of failing to recognise his abilities, it was not entirely wide of the mark. Lincoln had grown in office from an unknown into a statesman: "We do not know in history such an example of the growth of a ruler in wisdom as was exhibited by Mr Lincoln. Power and responsibility visibly widened his mind and elevated his character. Difficulties, instead of irritating him as they do most men, only increased his reliance on patience; opposition, instead of ulcerating, only made him more tolerant and determined."

Bagehot never met Lincoln; he never even visited America. He did not conceive of extending outside London, Paris and essentially European affairs the ready access to the powerful and the illuminating around the world which editors use today. London was the centre of the globe: America, even in the crisis of its existence, was too far away, its affairs were too anomalous and unpredictable, its national character too uncertain and unexplained, for an English gentleman, however percipient, to read it convincingly let alone successfully. What may be said of Bagehot is that he read it better than most Englishmen.

It is pertinent that although Bagehot himself wrote frequently, as new editors tend to do, about the early stages of the war, the paper became less and less interested in what was actually happening on the North American continent from Gettysburg until the concluding weeks of the fighting. It was increasingly as if it was only when the war impinged directly on Europe, as it did with commerce raiding, markets, finance and fears over Canada, that it was thought to be worthy of comment. Appreciably more space was given to what Napoleon III was up to in Mexico ("nothing with which Englishmen have any reason to quarrel"), and the complicated and confusing dispute over the Danish duchies, with the emergence of an unpredictable new character, Otto von Bismarck. Such was life without the Atlantic cable.

The paper allowed the closing stages of the war a dying fall. When William T. Sherman gave too lenient terms to Joseph E. Johnson, which had to be countermanded, it was robust in its condemnation: "The truth is that unless this disastrous war initiates a revolution, and a great revolution, at the South, it will have failed of all its effect; and neither the Union, for which the North have fought so bravely, can be preserved—nor the Slavery, for the extinction of which we all hope, be destroyed." Whatever the advocate of reconstruction proposed, the white South had its own ideas.

There remained what to do with the man for, or over, whom many thought the war had been fought: the slave. The paper wished "to abolish all distinctions of colour summarily, to declare the negro a citizen, entitled to all the advantages of one, including a vote, which will practically give him possession of the balance of power. This plan has the advantages of finality."

It thought there would be only "a short spasm of conflict". It was certainly visionary for 1865. However, politics apart, what was really to be done for the millions of freed slaves without schooling or skills or even belongings? The answer was pat: "The easiest way to deal with the irrepressible negro is to leave him alone, and permit the strong compulsion of hunger to act upon him as upon all other human beings."

It was the voice Bagehot's world respected.

Grover Cleveland, twice Democratic president, giving his first inaugural speech in 1885, with (left) the outgoing Republican Chester A. Arthur. Cleveland made modest tariff cuts and challenged Britain over Venezuela.

3

IN PURSUIT OF WEALTH

1866–1895

AMERICA THE RIVAL

The threat to Britain came from the industrial power of America and Germany, not the ambitions of France or Russia

Post-bellum America was more than ever *The Economist's* country of the future. True, it still insisted on running its economy wrongly, and it now had to build something from the embittered and ruined south. Nevertheless it had its unbounded energy and resources, and commendably, almost created by the war, the north had developed a bedrock public opinion of its own which could be relied on. For decades the north had been manipulated by the south; it had no settled mind of its own; its political leaders were influential only in their own states; and anyway, unlike in England, scant deference was paid to leaders' opinions. The paper found the new northern mind active and curious: "It is open to almost any proposition at first; is amused at hearing the discussion; listens with the utmost nonchalance to all sorts of novelties; rather enjoys suspending its judgment; and does not, to use Mr Lincoln's expressive phrase, 'put its foot down' on any definite conclusion till the time has actually come

---

CHRONOLOGY

1866	Austro-Prussian war
1867	US buys Alaska from Russia
	Federation of Canada
	Karl Marx's *Das Kapital* published
1869	Ulysses S. Grant becomes president
	Pacific railroads joined at Promontory, Utah
1870	Franco-Prussian war; Napoleon III exiled; Germany takes Alsace-Lorraine
1871	Henry M. Stanley finds David Livingstone at Ujiji, East Africa
1872	Britain pays £3m damages for the Confederate raider *Alabama*
1875	Britain buys the Suez Canal
1876	Alexander Graham Bell invents the telephone
	Turkish atrocities in Bulgaria
	Congo Free State founded by Leopold II of Belgium
1877	Rutherford B. Hayes becomes president
	Russo-Turkish war
1878	Thomas Edison patents the phonograph
1879	Edison invents the electric lamp

	British legation massacred at Kabul, Afghanistan
1881	James A. Garfield becomes president
	Tsar Alexander II assassinated
	Garfield assassinated
	Chester A. Arthur becomes president
1882	Triple Alliance formed by Germany, Austria-Hungary and Italy
1884	US secures rights for naval base at Pearl Harbor, Hawaii
	Mark Twain publishes *Huckleberry Finn*
1885	Grover Cleveland becomes president
	Mahdi's forces kill General Gordon at Khartoum
1888	Wilhelm II becomes German emperor
1889	Benjamin Harrison becomes president
1891	Dual Alliance between France and Russia
1893	Grover Cleveland becomes president again
1894	Turkish massacres in Armenia
1895	Japan takes Korea and Formosa from China
	Cleveland denounces Britain over Venezuela boundary

---

for decisive action."

In 1860 it had become essential for the north to make its mind up on the greatest of questions. Now, when clear resolutions had to be taken, "we doubt if there is any public opinion in Europe surer than the American".

This was not at all an opinion that saw things the British way, nor was it rooted any longer in the original British stock. The two halves of the North Atlantic system had already drifted far apart. When, in 1874, W.E. Forster, one of Gladstone's ministers, spoke in New York of an "Anglo-Saxon alliance", the paper belittled him. It was "disposed to doubt the value of such bonds" and especially so between the Americans and the English. Immigration had radically altered the character of the American population and a common language had even become a source of irritation: "Every trivial and disparaging remark passed upon one nation by another in a language common to both rubs the sores of wounded vanity. This is particularly conspicuous in the case of the Americans, who feel keenly all that is said about them in England. If by a miracle the people of the United States could be transformed into a German-speaking population, it is probable that our relations with them would be improved, not impaired."

That was not how the Germans, among others, were to see things, but it said everything on what imperial Britain thought about prospective special relationships. More than that, the paper was highly suspicious of what Americans and British were liable to get up to if, by any chance, they did get together: "No race is fit to be trusted with irresponsible and uncontrolled power over other and weaker races; least of all a race like our own, which, in spite of all its splendid qualities, is in its relation to types of humanity which differ from it, coarse, domineering and often cruel."

If anything, it thought the Americans and Russians had more in common: "The two countries have one sentiment peculiar to them among nations, the rooted belief entertained by each that it is marked out for some exceptional fate and special position in the annals of mankind. This belief has for years influenced not only Russian peasants but Russian diplomacy, while it materially assisted the Americans in maintaining successfully the recent struggle against disunion."

This was high-flown but far-fetched. Like Lincoln,

Tsar Alexander II had freed the serfs and had been assassinated, but there was no sense of regret for an Alexander as there was even for a Garfield. South Russia was a grain exporter, like the American west, but unlike the west its corn was liable to be mouldy, its transport was unreliable and its costs were high. Still, at the back of the paper's mind, there was the extraordinary sale of Alaska for a mere £1m: "Russian finances are not, we believe, very flourishing, but still a million is far too small a sum to be a serious inducement."

So it seemed that the Russians recognised some United States right to acquire the whole North American continent. And that put Canada in question again: "The possession of Russian-America does not constitute a new inducement for the Union to conquer Canada, but it does offer a new inducement to Americans to tempt Canada into annexation."

In reality, the paper knew that Britain now had only two serious, permanent competitors: Germany and the United States. The Russians would draw British military expeditions all across Asia, as the French would do in Africa, but neither of them was a real threat because they were not commercial threats. The paper saw, and was highly conscious of, British supremacy slipping. It was regularly aware of German discipline and American machinery. It knew the habits of the skilled British working man and his unions. The misgivings would persist for generations to come.

It felt, however, that socialism might yet undermine the Germans: "a social struggle is evidently beginning which will disorganise the larger industries". The United States, it thought, had two problems. The first was that when protection finally went production deficiencies would be uncovered. The second was social disorder.

It suspected in 1878 that the big American plants, with their mechanisation, would produce unruliness on a large scale too: "Already the great manufacturers of America are few, all such work falling to companies which turn their men into machines, and produce among them the fierce irritation visible in the Pittsburgh riots of last year."

Against that was the inescapable fact that American ingenuity was working wonders: "In rifle manufacturing and sewing machines the Americans have driven us from many markets." Each of the three great rivals had their difficulties and their opportunities. The paper, sensible of Britain's remaining pre-eminence, its advantages and its reputation, looked both admiringly and uneasily at the American challenge. It spoke, therefore, in the only way it could bring itself to speak: as the candid friend.

STEALING AND CHEATING
President Grant's cabinet and the Republican Party managers all knew how to look after themselves

The paper had hopes of Ulysses S. Grant, the north's war hero, when he took the Republican nomination for 1868's election. There were no, or few, qualms: "It is scarcely possible to doubt that the great and sagacious General under whom the North gained its victory will be the national choice for the next Presidency." But he was an enigma: "General Grant would be an exceptionally silent man anywhere, and in a land where everybody talks he is regarded as a sort of phenomenon of silence."

He would restore order to the south, "if not contentment", but he was expected to pacify: "Generals who have seen great wars are not fond of wars."

The paper knew very little of Grant's cabinet either, a body of "unknown, and the most part, untried men". Yet the choices seemed fairly popular: "It may justly be said that the nation was never better pleased than it is with a Government in which a chief without experience is supported by Ministers without political reputation."

Before the year was out there were warning signs. The assistant treasurer at New York had had to resign and Grant "and the very highest officers in the State" were obliged to write disclaimers. The paper believed that because the government was its own banker, able to accumulate sizeable balances, "all its officials will be liable to foul suspicions". Grant's first message on the state of the union was itself disappointing: "General Grant has clearly talked fair sense, but he has done no more. He has set forth the views of moderate persons, but he has not given shape, and coherence, and a new vivacity to the views of those moderate persons. The nation has heard its most respectable thoughts respectably echoed back."

A Gladstone would have given precision and vividness to the country's understanding of its financial problems, and though "we are well aware that Mr Gladstone could not take Vicksburg or conquer General Lee" that was what the country needed. A distinguished soldier was simply the best that the system could, and usually did, produce.

When Grant disowned a Fenian incursion in Canada and arrested two generals in 1870, the paper thought him a "straightforward man" with sufficient popularity to adhere to international law, unlike "one of those unknown and therefore incalculable Presidents of whom America has unfortunately had so many". Of course Grant abused Britain from time to time. But the paper was sure that Britain was not America's permanent enemy and the British press was wrong to assume it was. It was even prepared to go along with corruption as a sheer inevitability: "In all countries where corruption is a great power—as it is, unfortunately, in the United States—the less change takes place the better. Hungry flies are always more greedy than gorged ones."

No one had any illusions about Grant, and certainly not the electorate: "There can be little doubt that General Grant has ceased to excite enthusiasm among them, that the imperfections of his character are very well known, and that his administration, as a whole, is not regarded with much pride." But when it came to the bit, "American common sense and conservative feeling" settled things.

After all, what had happened to the economy under Grant was, the paper felt, "exceedingly creditable on almost all points". Expenditure was under control, encouraged by Congress. Taxation was falling. Surpluses had emerged to start paying off the war debt. Grant was sound on getting rid of paper money for specie. This was, perhaps, almost as generous an endorsement of a president's financial acumen as the paper had ever made. Even in the bank panic of 1873 it noted, approvingly, of Grant that he was not actually contriving to make things worse: "If he is not doing absolutely nothing, he is doing as little as he can."

In the end graft was found in the cabinet. In March 1876, a bad time for a president thinking of a third term, the secretary for war, General William W. Belknap, was accused of taking bribes. He admitted that his wife had taken them. It was another scar on the Grant administration, but the paper thought too much ought not to be made of it: "Politicians in the United States rise high by the exercise, generally, of qualities which do not promise purity of character or refinement of feeling."

There were mitigating arguments even for the Belknaps. Governing the United States used to be a cheap business; it had become one of the most costly in the world. There was a revenue of $60m that had to be spent, "an immense power" put in the hands of subordinate officials. The salaries, even of cabinet ministers, were "fixed absurdly low". It would be an actual saving to the country if all official salaries were doubled, "from the President downwards".

The congressional elections of 1874 showed the more thoughtful Republicans that the writing was on the wall for Grant and his cronies, and even for the party unless it took a trick or two. The paper saw four causes for disillusionment: trade was depressed; the south was bitter about the war and its aftermath; the administration in Washington was openly corrupt; and there was a public dread of a third-term presidency. The wider world was disillusioned too: Gladstone's liberalism was losing its spell just as the anti-slavery cause had grown weary. Concessions in Ireland had done little to encourage loyalty to Britain; concessions to the negroes had done as little to restore order to the south. It was a time for new men, if they could be found.

Rutherford B. Hayes, the man the Republicans found at the Cincinnati convention, was an unremarkable but honest Ohio lawyer. He was, however, "allowed to be weak, and no change of policy can be expected from an Administration over which he presides". The Democrat, Samuel J. Tilden, had been nominated remarkably early, actually on the second ballot, at St Louis. He was a competent governor of New York and so a figurehead of the revived, post-bellum party. He was "a man made of stronger stuff than the average run of American candidates for high office". He would put a stop to corruption. His only obvious fault had been to ally himself with Thomas A. Hendricks, a soft-money man from Indiana, as his running-mate. The paper rather took to Tilden as the 1876 campaign progressed: "His policy would be a Free-trade policy on the tariff, a hard-money policy in regard to the currency, a policy strictly adhering to the practice of Republican Administrations in dealing with the National Debt."

Tilden, in short, had put together the formidable alliance of New York and the south. He seemed entirely likely to win. Indeed, when the results came in it seemed he had won. He took nothing in the populist

west except Hendricks's Indiana, but he was clearly ahead where it mattered. What had not occurred to many people, even to many Republicans, during the campaign was that they could still go ahead and, as the Democrats insisted, steal it. Three southern states, Florida, Louisiana and South Carolina, still under military rule, could give Hayes a majority of one in the electoral college if the Republican carpet-baggers declared their results for him. They did.

The paper was in a quandary: the result would turn on so many legal problems, besides plain corruption. It was a credit to the electorate that it settled down to wait for someone to find out how to work the constitutional machinery: "We can only wonder at the extraordinary patience and self-control with which the American people are awaiting the issue of this most unfortunate cast of the die."

When the device of an electoral commission was agreed on, effectively giving the casting vote on the disputed electoral returns to five Supreme Court judges, it seemed "no better course could have been taken in the emergency that has arisen". The paper was apparently not aware that the majority of the judges were Republican, but that decided it.

The country took it well enough, even most Democrats. It was a tribute to the businesslike moderation which made the Americans so political a people. The paper regretted, though, that the Republicans had not seen the merit of letting so reasonable and respectable a Democrat as Tilden into the White House for four years. It was 20 years since a Democrat had won. The Republicans should accept the principle that "open and cynical use of force or corruption" would be certain to defeat its own object.

THE SOCIALIST PERIL
*Labour troubles beset the factories and
railroads, and frightened the better-off*

Socialism was the new peril. In July 1877 strikes broke out on the Baltimore and Ohio railroad, and spread promptly to the Pennsylvania, Erie and New York Central. There was fighting with local militia in West Virginia. Pittsburgh was held for a time "by ten thousand armed roughs, who broke into shops, destroyed property, and spread terror until fatigue and drunkenness overpowered them". It was true, even "rather astonish-

The transcontinental railroad: Central Pacific locomotive near Salt Lake City, around 1869, the year the Central and Union Pacific lines met at Promontory Point, Utah. The coast-to-coast journey took over six days.

ing", that the price of railroad securities showed little change, but plainly something was up. The paper tried reassurance: "It must not be supposed that Communistic principles are gaining ground among the American people. In no country is individualism more sturdily rooted; in none is the institution of property more securely grounded upon popular respect."

The paper pointed out that the men had had their wages cut by the tycoons, and that agitators had fostered delusions. Even so, the vulnerability of the railroads, on which the country and its economy entirely depended, called for resolute action. The army had 30,000 men and fortunately no frontiers to defend. Indeed, politicians debated each year on whether or not they needed an army at all; administrations had a

regular problem protecting West Point. Now 30,000 miles of railway had been thrown into disorder because there were not enough troops to protect the junctions. Chicago had been lucky; it escaped because a brigade had been collected there.

Labour was trying to build itself up politically: "The organisation of a working men's party in the United States has made the regular politicians exceedingly uncomfortable."

The paper was uncomfortable, too, about the new party's programme. Some parts of it were "of a distinctly Socialist character". It wanted the repeal of all indirect taxation, the railroads and telegraphs to be controlled by the government, and all industrial enterprises to be run by free co-operative unions. This was not characteristic of the individualistic, property-respecting American working man. The trouble plainly was among the European immigrants, especially the Germans and the Bohemians: "Nearly all of the electors belonging to these nationalities are strongly Socialistic."

There was a worry that socialist ideas would spread among such roots: "We do see some danger of the uprising in every great American city of a formidable sect, penetrated with a creed which makes its members hostile to existing society, and willing to appeal to insurrection whenever insurrection seems to afford a chance of success." It would be particularly serious if the agitation were to spread into the south, with its large numbers of the uneducated, both black and white.

Where it was spreading quickly was among the small farmers, the freeholders, of the west. They were irritated with the system. The farmer paid no rent and very few taxes. He had enough to eat. He was warmly clothed and sheltered from the weather. But, despite this unique independence, "He is a very poor man; a man who labours very hard, and whose gains in cash are very small.... The capitalist who apparently does nothing becomes gradually an object of dislike, and if he can give him a little lesson he will."

The paper, however, had not much regard for the farmer's acquaintance with economics: "The American farmer is not better educated than most English middle-class women, and English middle-class women, if they ever try to consider questions of currency or trade, get lost instantly in an impenetrable fog."

Still, if the movement could keep clear of violence "and from advocating open plunder—not quite a settled point yet as to railway shares" they might get a sizeable vote. Most such causes actually did very little, though capitalists would feel the draught.

The paper put its confidence in the average American male, honest, paying his debts, proud of his government. And socialism would divide the Irish in the Democratic Party, anyway. By November 1878 this confidence had not been misplaced. The south had gone solidly for the Democrats, but elsewhere distress had been easing, business was slowly recovering, the harvest had been excellent, and the hard-money platform had won decisively in the north: "This is most satisfactory, and the more so because the decision is likely to be permanent."

PANIC AT THE BANKS
Hazards on the road to becoming the wealthiest country

The bank panic of 1873 enabled the paper to preach loud and long about the iniquities of an inconvertible paper currency. The war had caused it and railway speculation had depended on it: "In a rapidly progressive country even a fixed amount of such currency works an amount of harm which never could have been imagined beforehand."

The speculation had not been all bad. It had even been beneficial to the country: "It has covered its surface with railways, which eventually will probably pay, and which are sure to be very beneficial to the districts in which they lie, whether they pay or not."

The thing to do was not to discourage sound banking by helping unsound banking. "If you always help bad banks out of the difficulties, you will hardly ever have banks which are not in difficulties." It was unfortunate that the American government had no skilled intermediary like the Bank of England or the Bank of France because politicians could not resist popular demands to save bad banks.

Still, this time the authorities had a responsibility to make good their own mistake which had prompted the panic. They had taken $44m in notes out of the currency prematurely, too much for a rapidly expanding trade. The banks, especially in New York, had fallen collectively below their reserve limits and had stopped publishing their weekly reserve statements. Panic was not a surprise. What was needed was to put the money back in supply. When that was done the crisis was over.

The battle between gold and paper appeared to be going the eastern bankers' way, but the discovery of the Comstock Lode doubled American silver production in 1876 and by the end of the decade silver was in the ring. The west, which mined it, was determined to have its way. By February 1878 a resolution was passed by two-thirds in the Congress making it legal and honest to pay silver dollars, not gold, to holders of American government bonds. The paper was appalled: "An act of bad faith ... a proposal which identifies American credit with that of an openly repudiating State like Turkey."

It believed many Americans had simply caught a craze, a fever in which they were excited by tales of silver mountains, bonanzas which would remove all fears of debt. The very thought of bimetallism, or a "see-saw standard" for both gold and silver, gave the paper the horrors. The arguments for the double standard "remind one of the crude problems of the sixteenth than of the ripe experience of the nineteenth century". But silver was now established as the major political obstacle to free trade.

By October 1879 a trade revival was apparent, directly linked to the successful development of the new lands in the west. The investment had begun to work out: Europe was taking an ever bigger share of the crops. In turn the new and resuscitated railroad lines had brought a recovery in the British iron trade because Pennsylvania could not keep up with demand. The paper saw all this as a free-trade success.

Of America's total annual exports of $141m, $90m were still agricultural produce, chiefly to Britain. In return, British exports to America were no more than $23.5m. Britain's balance depended heavily on its investments and its return on financing America's trade with Europe and the Far East. The system worked, though in difficult years the talk of markets was how much bullion London would need to ship to New York. The paper was comfortable about it all: "We shall surely see her exports again largely exceeding her imports, which is the normal condition of American trade, for the United States having borrowed an enormous amount of foreign capital, they have of necessity to provide a surplus of exports with which to make their annual interest payments."

What was good for New York was even better for London: "It means that during the next twelve months we shall have abundant food supplies at low prices and that the most important of our foreign customers is likely to enjoy a prosperity that may be expected to react beneficially upon our industries."

America's success and wealth now seemed to know few bounds. Its population had topped 50m, leaving behind united Germany's 45m and Britain's 35m. It had put its investment into big plant and extensive machinery. By 1883 the Pennsylvania Railroad earned $21.5m a year; Britain's best, the London and North-Western, made only $10.7m. Of the Pennsylvania, "we may safely say there is not any joint stock company in the world which has ever controlled so large an income".

Perhaps it was the response to Bell's telephone that showed how far America was ahead and likely to stay

ahead. In 1882, because "private enterprise has been left free to work as it liked", the United States had 100,000 subscribers to its various companies (4,060 subscribers in New York alone). Britain had 4,946 subscribers in all (1,561 in London), France 3,640 (2,422 in Paris), and Germany 2,322 (only 581 in Berlin).

The panic of 1884 was little more than a footnote to 1873; a renewed railroad mania had broken out in 1880–82. In three years 28,000 miles of new line were opened and the railroad share capital and indebtedness were said to have increased by over $400m. (Later estimates even put the total higher.) This over-construction and over-financing were more than the market could bear, plus the gambling instinct inherent in the American appetite for grand coups based on the banks' money. In the end panic brought exposure. The paper was content that, taking its cue, British shareholders had had the chance to pull out.

PAYING FOR THE *ALABAMA*
Britain had a bad conscience and stumped up,
but not too much

The career of the Confederate commerce raider, the *Alabama*, built at Liverpool and allowed to escape to the high seas, still rankled with the United States authorities. It lay like a mine beneath the waters of the Anglo-American relationship. *The Economist* soon decided it was better to settle, and it had hopes of the Conservatives when they took office in 1866: "The Conservatives have for over thirty years had this great advantage with America that, being seldom in office, there were very few sore memories with which they were associated."

The paper wanted arbitration; it even foresaw a regular court of conciliation one day. An arrangement was reached, but the Senate jibbed: it wanted damages of over $2 billion. In the mind of Charles Sumner, chairman of the Senate foreign relations committee, and others there was even the idea that Britain could only atone by ceding Canada. The paper was worried that the issue might degenerate into permanent enmity. The first naval power had enough on its hands already: "Doubtless we must remain in that terrible uncertainty, on the awful nature of which the United States seem to plume themselves, whether when we next get into a war we may not have *Alabamas* swarming out of the American ports, or worse still, an American foe to meet in Canada in addition to the European foe."

It doubted if Britain were in the right anyway: "We are not by any means proud of the part the English middle-classes played during the American civil war. It was no doubt something of an ignorant and a jealous and an ungenerous part."

The paper believed that a great war with the United States must be "the most inconceivably mischievous, hopeless and murderous of all wars". It began to seem as if President Grant were thinking much the same way. When he put down the Fenian efforts to invade Canada the paper, in June 1870, had found its man: "General Grant … has acted with a good faith and a simplicity in the matter, which ought to inspire the English Cabinet with the sincerest desire to settle the disputed question of the *Alabama* claims with a spirit not only of justice but of cordial consideration."

This was discerning and timely. Although the paper initially approved of the humiliation of France ("a country which has always hated us") by Prussia that summer, Britain was shown to be powerless on the continent and could not afford any American distraction. Grant, it declared, might abuse Britain to get votes, but he did not always believe what he said. American feeling was misrepresented by the British press: there was "a deep root of respect and almost yearning towards England". An apology for the *Alabama* "would change the whole attitude of feeling towards England, and render it as cordial as it is at present sore".

Then in January 1871, with Paris besieged, it spelled out the facts: "Whether you may think that England's true position is that of a neutral state, standing aloof from the internal disputes of Europe … or whether, on the contrary, you hold that England ought to give her support to the cause of self-government and freedom, wherever it is endangered on the continent—in either case it cannot be denied that England gains immeasurably by being relieved from a chronic danger and menace in America."

The conclusion was one that it was "scarcely feasible to exaggerate": "If we can by any legitimate concession restore a cordial understanding between England and America there is no sort of end to be gained in our foreign policy so important and beneficial."

Much the same thoughts were being privately entertained by Gladstone (regretting his opinion in 1862) and his new foreign secretary, Earl Granville, and by Grant and his secretary of state, Hamilton Fish. Grant, indeed, had just told Fish that he wanted the English business settled before the 1872 election, and he did not expect the negotiations to produce Canada. Granville, who in October 1870 had asked Walter Bagehot, still the editor, not to write "anything which will give thoughtful Germans reason to believe that they have just cause of complaint against us", was a backer of arbitration with America.

By February Gladstone had accepted a commission which would try to settle all the outstanding disputes, which the paper thought was "judicious" of him. It was now openly committed to advocating the American connection politically, as it always had economically, although Grant would never touch free trade and dumped his interior secretary, Jacob D. Cox, and the special commissioner of revenue, David A. Wells (an *Economist* idol), because of it.

The paper's instinct for America was good. This initiative was the most important one it had taken since its publication began, although none of the leading articles which marked it has been attributed to Bagehot himself. The commitment which began then has been the most influential one in *The Economist*'s history, and it has never reneged on it. The ending of the estrangement between the United States and Britain was, in fact, to be the one great and lasting achievement of the Grant administration. It did not come about by chance.

The moment that arbitration was arranged by the Treaty of Washington in May 1871, Congress promptly floated the proposition that "England should be requested, as the first condition of a permanent peace, to retire from the American continent". This had been foreseen: "The American Government will lose a great deal more by exaggerating its grievances than by stating them moderately and in a practical fashion." The paper was not especially concerned about Canada. It thought it a burden but as long as it wished to be British its wish must be upheld: "The British people are not anxious to retain Canada; but they will defend it as long as it chooses to remain a colony, and will neither cede nor sell it."

It was agreed to submit to arbitration all border disputes, fisheries disputes and the *Alabama* claims. The arbiters were to be named by the president, the queen, the king of Italy, the president of the Swiss Confederation and the emperor of Brazil, so it "will be as fair a tribunal as we could wish for". The definition of neutrality under which the arbiters would work had still to be decided, but Britain expressed regret for the *Alabama* anyway.

The initial American stance was that the *Alabama* and the other cruisers had so prolonged the war that Britain was responsible for all the subsequent damage, although this even included Confederate claims that English loans had been raised on cotton which the Federal forces had then either destroyed or sold. This was "simply monstrous": "The exploits of the Southern cruisers added to the length of Southern resistance about as much as a hearty cheer from the shore might add to the length of a drowning man's struggle for existence—so much and no more."

The Canadians, too, were causing trouble. They wanted the United States to be liable to arbitration over the Fenian raids. They were bought off by the guarantee of a loan of £2.5m to be "used in the construction of a railway from Canada to the Pacific". Such were the beginnings of the Canadian Pacific a decade and a half later. The paper disapproved: "Scarcely anything is so objectionable as paying a price to some of your own subjects to do as you wish."

What was working London's way was the American dearth of capital and the rising cost required by the City so long as the *Alabama* action remained unsettled. By midsummer it was the Americans who blinked. They gave "a clear statement" that they meant by the terms of the treaty what Britain thought they meant. They also cut some tariffs by 10%, including a few on British manufactures. Nothing could have been more propitious.

Then to complete Britain's satisfaction the arbiters themselves threw out the $2 billion demand and decided on $15m (£3m). It seemed little enough when the chancellor, Robert Lowe, indicated his budget surplus would be £4.5m; no new tax, not even a penny on income tax, would be needed. The paper was highly pleased: "probably in the history of the world no tribunal ever was more fair".

It meant, it said, that all suspicious vessels would now be seized immediately. Britain had not seized the *Alabama* on suspicion because it had been relying on the existing law; now the law had been changed. In future, nations and their lawyers would need to take into account international damages to an aggrieved

state as well as domestic damages to an aggrieved owner.

Just a month after the decision Britain was content to lose again. Arbitration by the German emperor gave the San Juan islands south of Vancouver island to the United States. The paper was indulgent: "We see nothing whatever in this decision to call for any hostile comment."

One by one the greater and lesser obstructions to Anglo-American coexistence were being removed. It was what Britain wanted and, bit by bit, was prepared to pay for. It was what the paper wanted and would go on advising. Grant was re-elected, "a President who gave up nothing, but still did remove the principal causes of national ill-feeling".

The world had changed beyond recall in 1870–71. The French had been devastated and were adamant that Prussia would build a fleet and wait for an Anglo-American disagreement to declare war. (The paper had printed the first warning by the economist, Michel Chevalier, an instigator with Cobden of the 1860 Anglo-French commercial treaty, in January 1871.) *The Economist* believed Bismarck was too sensible to do that, but "a united Germany … is already stronger than Russia, and has more sway and influence". It was time the English-speaking countries contrived to settle down together: "If we can but keep temper, hot-headedness, panic out of the diplomacy between the two countries, we shall get along fairly well, just as an average family does, with no particular affection among its branches, and frequent disputes about money, but still with an underlying sense that somehow it has a common interest."

THE RAILROAD RUFFIANS
Greed and the good life on the Erie system, and elsewhere

Corruption was the great excitement: in the administration, in the judiciary, in the party machines and, above all, in the railroads. In the age of Grant, the railroads gave America its great successes and its abiding scandals. The paper thrived on both. By March 1869 the first transcontinental railway was nearing completion, "a great triumph of Yankee energy". Distance was being annihilated all right, and with it perhaps a frontier or two: "The first great step will have been taken to make the North American continent one country, all occupied parts of which will be in closer communication with each other than the counties of England a hundred years ago, or (say) the various provinces of Spain at the present day."

That was the hyperbole. When the last spike had been driven in the reality was a little more humdrum. The Atlantic and Pacific Railway stretched 3,305 miles; the time of the continuous journey on it was 6 days, 17 hours, 30 minutes, "which is probably a longer strain than the human constitution can stand". The ticket for the journey cost $23; too much, the paper thought, for impecunious immigrants.

On less pioneering lines the problem was rapacious owners and impecunious shareholders, usually British. The railroad companies regularly raised capital by advertising to coupon clippers in the paper, but

investors were advised to do without the business of the Erie railroad and the likes of Messrs Jim Fisk and Jay Gould: "Already the opinion of Americans is being strongly excited by the palpable mischief which the corruption of justice and the growth of irresponsible corporations practically above the law are producing."

They were all in it. The more respectable in American society had begun to dread, it seemed, what the Erie directors were going to extract from the United States government, the states and the governor of New York. Those who wished to hold on to their money should be warned off by the company report, which "proved to be remarkable for the fullness of its information regarding the improvements of the line and the absence of information regarding the financial position". Their methods were "brazen ruffianism" directed only to the benefit of the directors' lifestyles:

The western railroads brought settlers, cattle, the telegraph, towns and industry. It was done by enterprise, land grants, European capital and rascality. Wealth doubled in ten years, despite the civil war.

*Jim Fisk: speculator, capitalist, despoiler of the Erie railroad
finances. He tried and failed to corner the gold market.
Shot by a rival for his mistress in 1872.*

"They are absolute dictators—neither rendering accounts, permitting discussion, nor regarding any interest but their own. They openly maintain an Opera House, with Ballet and Orchestra, out of the revenues of the Railroad. By means of local judges as much in their pay as any lamp-cleaner on the Line, they have so far successfully defied every foreign bond and shareholder and every native dissentient from their proceedings."

Nothing less could be expected in a New York where "burglary, theft, and even murder, are incessant". The judges and the state legislature encouraged the game, and the press winked at it. These were the Tammany Ring's high days, spending "millions on millions of dollars" furnishing armouries and offices and carpeting court-houses. One tradesman had secured a contract for 70 miles of carpet at $5 a yard. This Democratic racket enraged Republicans and upstate Democrats

who did not share in it; the Germans also threw their vote against the Irish, who did. In the elections of November 1871 reform triumphed, not for the last time, and only Boss Tweed actually kept his seat as a state senator.

The Economist had learned, too, that the American minister in London, General Robert C. Schenck, who had been helpful over the *Alabama* claim, was the director of a dubious mining company, running the Emma silver mine in Utah, and had openly put his name to its London prospectus: "We should recommend him to withdraw his name at once, and we hope in any case that what he has done will not become a precedent." Schenck was reproved by Fish, but the mine's failure forced his resignation in 1876.

If the likes of Schenck were doing that it was not surprising what lowly judges would do, being so badly paid that "no lawyer of the first rank would dream of taking a Judgeship". For corporations like railroads which had to secure the support of judges in every state that the line passed through this was quite an expense.

Still, there were compensations. When Jim Fisk was shot in New York in January 1872, it might be something for "the long-suffering English owners of the railway" but the paper's obituary harped enviously on the deceased's marble palace, his jewels few Asian princes could match, his banquets and, of course, his opera house. It gave him an almost admiring send-off: "Robust and overflowing with animal spirits, energetic yet self-indulgent, full of a coarse humour and famous for a reckless generosity, Mr Fisk was a man who took the pleasant part of life as it came to him, and enjoyed it after his fashion, without a thought of the price he might have to pay."

It was naturally a surprise when Gould adeptly promised restitution of $16m (translated to English shareholders as £3m) because it seemed that he had "come down too easily for the result not to be distrusted". As more and more American stocks came on to the British market, it was something that it was chiefly American money that had built the 3,000 miles of new railroad that had suddenly come into being in the seven months to March 1880. The British who had gone into the "mania" of 1869–71 were, for once, well out of it.

CONTEMPLATING CUSTER
Not the time to criticise American methods

The Economist had minimum views to voice on relations with the Indians. But when the news of the annihilation of George Armstrong Custer and his immediate force of 240 men arrived and was digested in July 1876, it found it had something to say. What was startling about the Little Big Horn was that what the paper called "civilised warfare" had developed an elaborate code of customs among the powers over centuries, but savagery was still unusual and, therefore, exciting. The paper had little enough respect for the Plains Indian except for his fighting capability: "He has no dignity, no chivalry in his nature. He is a good fighting man, uses modern weapons with skill, has an unqualified contempt for work of any sort except war and rapine."

The Indian did not carry all the blame. He had shown his "unmitigated ferocity", but the white intruders into the Black Hills could not be kept out. They had heard talk of rich mines. Grant himself had taken an interest in planning a series of blows against the Sioux. The lesson to be learned now was that the borders needed to be watched by larger military forces.

There was no point in attributing blame for what had happened: "We do not know how far we have a right to be severe upon the Americans for their impatient rejection of humanitarian pleas on behalf of the Indian." It was not the time for that. The paper could also have said (but did not) that in a country having great enough difficulties with the Afghans, and shortly to have even greater ones with the Zulus, a considered silence was appropriate.

AT THE TURN OF THE CENTURY
The rural republic had grown up in awkward ways

The social changes in turn-of-the-century America were followed by *The Economist*, though its instinct for financial orthodoxy did not always let it encourage or approve of them. The United States had far outrun the thinking, the wealth and the morals of the rural republic it had been. To many British, as to many American, eyes the problems were specific and were surmountable if it were not for the insurmountable difficulties of the constitution and the system. The paper had never been happy with what the Americans had devised for themselves, but it was certain that political institutions, like the economic ones which had inflicted protectionism and deep crises on the country, had to be changed.

The presidency itself had not been designed to be strong. A Jackson and a Lincoln had made it that way, but most post-bellum presidents had neither been successful nor even tried conspicuously to impose themselves. The effective power normally stayed with the Congress. The Senate was still not elected directly, and was often perverse on foreign policy, the paper thought, especially when Britain was involved. The House was slow to reflect the shift of population and power westwards; and, as the paper regularly complained, a year could elapse between its election and its influence on legislation. All this was apparent, but no remedies were.

The paper had had initial hopes of President Grover Cleveland; at least it had hopes of his potential. It felt that Europe, at least, had not understood the advance of the president's power and influence: "There is no State so powerful, no people so numerous, as to be wholly beyond the range of the orders issued by the American President."

That was still before American imperialism set in. The paper's instinct was not wholly to trust such power: "Scarcely any man not an autocrat has such direct personal power over his fellow-citizens' fortunes, or can use it with so little responsibility except to his own conscience."

If few men on the planet enjoyed such a position, however, everything depended on the man who occupied it. The idea of a president as a great judge, who could weigh all the evidence and rise above personal temptations, did not work. The constitution and the system precluded it. It was not because the paragon did not exist. It was because the people could never know of him: "No one, except a soldier or a sailor, can hope to be recognised by the whole country."

Even the diversity and the regularity of American elections, the bloodstream of the democracy that the paper normally praised, gave it some bad moments. The normally coherent House of Commons procedure of effective party majorities contrasted favourably with one which could produce a Republican president and a Democratic Congress simultaneously. This meant more than deadlock, it meant constant uncertainty and speculation: "The Constitution, among its varied elements, good, bad, or indifferent, brings about the two great evils of constant political excitement, with its pernicious increase of power to politicians, and a singular barrenness of definite result which the multiplication of elections and the overlapping of electoral areas renders inevitable."

Then there was money. The paper was intrigued by the difference between the American and the British attitudes, what they meant and what they foreshadowed. Towards wealth Americans were straightforward, even simple: "The American who has made a great fortune in business finds nothing else so interesting, and goes on accumulating.... If the late Mr Vanderbilt had stopped dealing in railways, he would not have known what to do with himself, or have felt any excitement in his life."

In Britain, by contrast, things were much more complicated and, for some of the successful, actually disappointing: "The English millionaire, when his fortune has become large and solid, turns away to other things—takes to collecting, buys estates, founds a family, or interests himself in the much larger game of politics."

In the British economy this was patently true. For the aspiring British millionaire the reality was that he could not win a social position until his "days of speculation" were over: "While he is still in the market any squire of broad acres, or any poor Peer is his social superior."

To the paper, this was one reason for the progress and multiplication of the trusts and syndicates in the United States, where able entrepreneurs were never encouraged to give up. The paper and its correspondents were fascinated, intrigued by the American penchant for speculation. In 1866 it reported: "Every third or fourth merchant, manufacturer, cashier, manager, or other individual who has a bank account has bought 100 shares, perhaps 1,000 shares, of something."

When fever gripped them it was a phenomenon from which Europeans preferred to avert their eyes: "The transactions in options have exceeded all precedent. The wheat pit, long comparatively empty, has become a frantic, struggling mass of human arms, heads and legs, while the noise made shames pandemonium."

The very rich were addictive, with their own illuminating anecdotes, among them the impish Andrew Carnegie. In January 1885 the New York correspondent reported: "Mr Carnegie has publicly announced himself as a Socialist, and a keen sympathiser with wage earners in one breath, and, to the amazement of his men, ordered a reduction of from 10 to 33 per cent in wages throughout his works. An inquisitive reporter asked him if he were ready to divide up his wealth in conformity with his profession, and the iron and steel millionaire said 'No'."

The paper recounted regularly how widespread British investment had become. There were the massive railroad holdings; out west there were the "British holdings of vast cattle ranches and farming lands"; many of the profitable brewing plants, even in German Milwaukee, were in British hands; so were the big Minneapolis flour mills, and many iron works, gas companies and tramway properties. The paper saw this British ownership, like the spread of the trusts, a sign of the rapid change in the North Atlantic industrial world. It aroused controversy and comment in both countries. American protectionists declared stoutly that British investors understood at last what a success protection had become.

Besides British capital there were British hands, still arriving off the boats in company with the new millions from southern and eastern Europe. The Republicans wanted to bring in the aspiring states in the west, so incomers were welcome and, despite rising hostility towards immigrants among the indigenous workforce, the first restrictions, chiefly requiring a certificate of fitness for citizenship from an American consul, were not especially onerous for British applicants. The farmers and the railway constructors still said they needed hands from anywhere. Received opinion in Britain had long regarded emigration as the best answer to overpopulation and poverty, but by 1889 the paper had become uneasy at the loss of the skilled: "They are the adventurous and the brave among their fellows, and to pick them out of the less efficient must be a grave loss to any community, however industrious, as grave a loss as if the owner of a factory dismissed all his hands qualified to become overseers or foremen."

By the 1890s the pastoral republic of Thomas Jefferson's ideal had long disappeared. In the west farmers had got inured to debt, struggling from harvest to disappointing harvest. A special correspondent reported: "Our Western farmers are overburdened with debt, their farms have depreciated in value, profits have almost disappeared, and new sources of supply are increasing. It is only too plain, therefore, that they cannot long support families, pay taxes, interest etc, under present adverse conditions."

After the 1894 crash, Jacob Coxey, whom the paper called "hitherto an obscure member of the House of Representatives, sent up from some district in Ohio", had formulated liberal plans for public works, a country road system throughout the nation, guaranteed employment and an eight-hour day. The paper did not approve; nor did the Congress when Coxey's army marched to Washington. The ragged bands in the countryside were a threat to order: "The States, in fact, have as much trouble with the unemployed as we have, have as little work to give them, and lack, as completely as we do, the means of compelling them to perform any disagreeable task whatever. The existence of plenty of unoccupied land does not solve the social question,

nor does the fact that the nation is without a Sovereign, an aristocracy, or an Established Church."

There seemed to be no shortage of Americans who doubted if democracy had the answers. The smaller and more frightened the local authority, the faster the resort to force: "The smallest sheriff, once in motion, with armed villagers behind him, whether in pursuit of brigands or of Coxeyites who are threatening a town, orders his men to fire without the smallest hesitation. If the militia are called out, they pour in volleys on a hostile crowd just as if they were soldiers in an enemy's country."

Violence seemed endemic, especially in the south. The paper was appalled by the lynching of negroes, over 1,000 of them, it estimated, in ten years: "No European will ever believe that a State in which any mob can execute any man suspected of crime, unheard and untried, and escape punishment, is a fully civilised State."

This was not prompted by an unrealistic faith in equality: "Be it understood that we do not write as friends of the negro. The equality of races does not exist, and the whites, in granting to the negro the suffrage, have probably been guilty of a grave offence against Republicanism, as a system which assumes, and must always assume, the moral and intellectual competence of the citizen."

But it had no doubt that the system that had developed was corrupt and inhuman: "The whites should govern; but then, if their right is exclusive, they are all the more bound to govern justly, and they are not doing it. They refuse him arrangements for comfort which are granted even to horses—no horse would be excluded from shelter as negroes from inns; and when he offends, they put him to a death which is illegal, on insufficient evidence, by the verdict of a hostile mob."

In the industrial towns strikes were becoming frequent, chiefly for higher wages and shorter hours. The lifting of the fog of black smoke on a Monday morning signalled to a place like Pittsburgh that a strike or a lock-out was a reality. Chicago was another militant centre, deplored from the safe distance of New York: "The action of the mob at Chicago, where a good deal of incendiary talk has been indulged in, where a dynamite bomb has been used with fatal effect on the police, where several shops have been sacked, and where the effects of the negative and truckling policy of the Illinois governor is seen in six deaths and nearly one hundred wounded."

Miners' strikes were especially bitter. In the LeHigh Valley in Pennsylvania there was an evident desperation, which pointed either to their early success or to "widespread idleness, misery and wretchedness throughout the anthracite coal mining regions". The men earned $1 a day and were idle for up to a third of each year: "The wages received by this class of the labouring population are very small, the smallest relatively that are received by almost any 'trade' in this country."

The Pullman strikes in 1894 paralysed rail transport throughout the north. The Pullman workers said they wanted a living wage; neither the company nor the authorities were ready to listen, although Cleveland showed sympathy until militants derailed a mail train and took over strategic centres. The paper approved of the president's brisk response: "Mr Cleveland having no third term to expect, with characteristic decision ordered the Commander-in-Chief, General Scholefield, to place the whole Army of the Union, including the artillery, at the disposal of the Judges. The central railway points are, in fact, to be held by regulars, and all resistance to arrests is to be put down by firing."

It was the new immigrants from eastern Europe who invariably got the blame for violence: "These men, bred at home almost in slavery, are intoxicated with American liberty, and when opposed or oppressed—for of course their complaints are not all without foundation—they resort to violence at once, and display a

ferocity often noticed in Russia, Serbia and Hungary."

If anyone thought the administration's reaction excessive (Cleveland had said he would use every soldier in the army if necessary to deliver a single postcard in Chicago), there was legal reassurance: "In England a Ministry might be overthrown for using Gatling guns against the people, but in America, so long as the Government is within the law, as explained by the Supreme Court, it has nothing to fear."

This was the Cleveland, and the American executive, that the paper respected. But he remained an enigma to it right to the end of his second term. It believed he had not made enough of the presidency and the opportunity it gave any man. He was respectable, sound on gold, and tried to stop the interests that were exploiting public land. But Cleveland had faltered over the tariff; even his Democratic majority in the House had quailed before the habitual conservatism of the Senate.

The Treasury had had to struggle on with grossly inadequate resources once the Supreme Court had declared an income tax unconstitutional. All that was left to him was foreign policy, where the president probably had too much power, throwing the United States's weight about protecting the wrong people in South America. The paper's assessment of him was scathing: "William II of Germany ... could have done no more harm to prosperity than Mr Cleveland has done, and would probably, having his dynasty to think of, have felt a deeper sense of responsibility."

The flying machine: Wilbur Wright (above) and his brother Orville made the first, brief, power-driven flights at Kitty Hawk, North Carolina, 1906. They offered their knowledge to the world for $100,000, but were turned down.

4

WORLD HALF-POWER

1897–1913

TRYING TO BE FRIENDS

How British patience wore down American carping and complaining

The emergence of the United States as a world power, or at least as a world half-power, became increasingly evident in the early 1890s. For the century and more before that, from the very achievement of independence, the United States had had an effective foreign policy towards only one country: Britain. America brushed, officially, against no other power. It had bought territory from France and Russia; it had even insisted on France's withdrawal from Mexico; but neither its politicians nor its newspapers thought of the outside world except in the continuation of the strange, uneasy and exasperating relationship with Britain. Britain was supposed to be the country's only likely antagonist; Britain was responsible for more than half the country's trade; and Britain was the power that answered, in the end, for every little local issue along the frontier with Canada.

By the 1890s America had come to accept that Canada was not going to join the Union voluntarily, and that, congressional oratory apart, the thought of a United States stretching to the Arctic was no longer tenable. The 5m or more Canadians were going to be too much to swallow, even if many of them emigrated southwards as rapidly as they could. *The Economist* shared the British government's exasperation that the Canadians kept on finding issues to dispute with the United States, and the Americans issues to dispute with them.

There were too many fretful neighbours. In July 1886 the row was not only over how to apply the three-mile

---

CHRONOLOGY

1897	William McKinley becomes president
1898	US battleship *Maine* blown up at Havana, Cuba
	Spanish-American war
1899	US acquires American Samoa
	Second Boer war in South Africa begins
1900	Australian federation
	Boxer rising in China
1901	Queen Victoria dies
	First transatlantic wireless signal
	Andrew Carnegie sells to US Steel
	McKinley assassinated
	Theodore Roosevelt becomes president
1902	Anglo-Japanese alliance
1903	Panama cedes zone to US to build a canal
	Orville and Wilbur Wright fly at Kitty Hawk, North Carolina

1904	Russo-Japanese war begins
	Anglo-French entente
1906	San Francisco earthquake
1907	Anglo-Russian convention on spheres of interest in Persia, Afghanistan and Tibet
1908	Austria-Hungary annexes Bosnia and Herzegovina
1909	William H. Taft becomes president
	Admiral Robert E. Peary discovers North Pole
1910	Henry Ford's plant opens at Highland Park, Detroit, for the Model T
1911	Italy seizes Tripoli and Rhodes from Turkey
1912	First Balkan war begins
1913	Woodrow Wilson becomes president; free trade measures introduced
	Sixteenth constitutional amendment allows US income tax

limit in the perpetual quarrel over catches between the Maritime Provinces' fishermen and the New England fishermen, but even over the Americans presuming the right to buy bait in Canadian ports. It was all painfully inconsiderable and highly complicated: "The fair and reasonable interpretation of the old three-mile rule is that the line shall follow the winding of the coast, and on this head we suspect our American kinsmen have the best of the argument. But as regards bait buying, it is a valuable right which the Georgian convention of 1818 enables Canada to give or refuse. If the Canadians think they can get something for the concession, why should they be railed at as 'inhospitable' because they decline to part with it for nothing?"

One row was even more remote from British interests: it was over the Canadians who went catching, or poaching, seals in the Bering Sea. But as the secretary of state was James G. Blaine it became a crisis, even one of the earliest conservationist, environmental crises. The paper was not wholly worried about conservation: "We not only have no ground of quarrel, but we have no ground for suspicion, and would, if the United States would only permit us, be the most easygoing allies that one nation can possibly be to another."

When the prime minister, Lord Salisbury, accepted arbitration the paper, like him, was happy to wash its hands: "He probably would hear that all seals had retreated to the Polar Sea with immovable equanimity."

That, however, was little league stuff. The American sense of power and growing self-confidence took diplomacy into another dimension. With painful reluctance among the Democrats, American opinion was engaged in pushing itself into accepting wider responsibilities for its own defence. America was no longer Mars. The country would have to look to its own fleet, to its own bases and coaling stations in two oceans, and to the building of an American canal between the oceans somewhere in Central America. There were many Americans who wanted just that. There were others who did not.

Cleveland was sceptical about the privilege of annexing the Hawaiian islands, and, as the paper said, "paying the bills of the Kingdom and making its laws". But the paper's New York correspondent understood the strategy and "the necessity for a naval station in the Pacific Ocean, which shall command the entire range of our coast on that ocean, and the manifest improba-

bility of our being able to hold such a station without incorporating it and raising our own flag there". Such was the beginning of Pearl Harbor. The final annexation of Hawaii was announced by President McKinley in 1897, although the secretary of state, John Sherman, had just denied any such thing to the Japanese.

The paper was worried about the American propensity to protect all smaller Central and South American republics against all Europeans, not least when it was sure they were in the wrong and especially when they were defaulting on money matters. It remonstrated in March 1895: "Whether it is France which demands reparation from San Domingo, or Great Britain which requests justice from Nicaragua, or all Europe which is affronted by Venezuela, or the world which is astonished by the revolutionary authorities in Hawaii, the result is ultimately the same."

For Cleveland the British boundary dispute with Venezuela in 1895 was an issue requiring United States intervention. It had come out of a clear blue sky, and was unwanted by Britain; though Cleveland's time as president was now running out and elections were approaching. Even the possibility of war was widely canvassed.

The paper did not believe that the United States thought of war at all. If there were the possibility then "the only result must be an injury to civilisation". But the press on both sides was convinced that since Cleveland had made it an issue it must mean war unless Britain publicly backed down. It was Salisbury who had to answer Cleveland's remonstrance: "We presume he will deal with it in the only sensible way, by repudiating the charge of seeking any extension of British dominion, and then doing nothing, thus leaving to Venezuela or the United States the responsibility of aggression."

When Cleveland turned his intervention into a diplomatic note that could not be elegantly brushed aside—a 20-inch gun note, he said—the paper still saw no reason for panic: "We prefer to believe that the Government of the United States ... with its usual disregard of diplomatic forms, has said a little more than it means, that it is vexed by the refusal of its proposal of arbitration, and that its governing idea is rather to compel us to arbitrate than to make itself sole and uncontrolled arbiter of America."

It was disappointed that things had been made so difficult. But difficulty was the keynote of dealing with the Americans when the administration was in that mood, and the clue was to understand how the Americans thought, and how the English still refused to be provoked: "They watch all their kinsfolk do with permanent interest, sometimes appreciative, sometimes scornful, but always keen and active. They are always conscious, like members of the same family, of a certain rivalry, and always doubtful when surpassed in anything whether to be annoyed or full of hearty congratulations."

Whatever America felt, the paper, at least, was not going to rise to anything. It was the very mildness of the British that mattered: "'What an unfortunate mistake for President Cleveland to have made' nearly summed up their thoughts, and they waited, fully anticipating some late explanation."

There were doubts about Cleveland in Boston and on Wall Street, but what helped and what the paper grasped was that much of the United States was as unhappy as anyone at Kaiser Wilhelm II's commendatory telegram to the Boer president, Paul Kruger, in January 1896: "Our cousins have not shown the slightest disposition to take advantage of the German Emperor's conduct—are, indeed, half inclined to regard it as an impertinent interference with their own exclusive right of quarrelling with their relations."

The paper refused to believe that Cleveland meant an ultimatum. Common sense had gone beyond that: "We feel that war with America would be civil war, and desire to avoid it as much as we would an appeal to arms within the Empire itself."

It was reassuring that Salisbury, choosing the words for the Queen's Speech to Parliament in February, decided to put a favourable interpretation on everything coming out of Washington, that the United States merely wished "to co-operate in terminating differences" or had a "desire to come to an equitable arrangement". The paper thought this was entirely creditable: "As it is the wish of the country to avoid a war which they think almost fratricidal, those sentences are admirably chosen, for they in effect condone the interference of the United States, and assign to it an amiable reason."

When a year later the Senate turned difficult about passing an arbitration treaty with Britain, the paper was regretful. It thought of the United States as "a separate but not a foreign nation". Britain was beginning to be worried about its own isolation, so a friend might

be worth having: "We may rightly bind ourselves in the case of America in a way which might not be expedient in the case of other Powers."

It complimented Salisbury in not letting the senators ruffle him, showing instead "his anxiety to act towards our American kinsmen with the maximum of our courtesy, friendliness, and good feeling".

ROUTING THE SPANIARDS
The quick, successful war against lowly Spain
made the United States imperialist, and
annoyed all Europe except Britain

It was not Britain that would make trouble, or opportunity, but the expiring remnant of the Spanish empire. The Spaniards could not suppress the revolt in Cuba, but they would not give the island up. They distrusted American ambition and thought they had good reason to, from the plots of the Confederacy onwards. Hence, "their invincible reluctance to admit the interference of the United States in any shape whatever, be it mediation, amicable representations, or advice". The new president, William McKinley, was a moderate man, but he believed he could not ignore American opinion, now strenuously worked up against the Spanish military government. The paper warned against underestimating Spanish pride and stubbornness: "The Spanish are the last people in the world to submit to dictation unaccompanied by force, or to sell a dependency in order to avoid a war, and they do not believe that their defeat would be such an easy matter."

It was hard to believe that "bankrupt, worn-out and harassed Spain" could pull itself together to fight America, but the sinking of the battleship *Maine* off Havana in February 1898 left no alternative. The paper was suspicious of some American war aims: "Some leaders of the Republican party think that a war would offer the readiest means of escape from all their internal difficulties; others believe that the country really needs war to stimulate patriotic feeling; while others again, who have much influence, especially with the Senate, are devoted to the interests of great Trusts like the Sugar and Tobacco Trusts, which think the acquisition of Cuba, as of Hawaii, absolutely essential to their 'systems'."

The American regular army was only 27,000 strong and the Spaniards had 200,000 in Cuba, but the paper

The sunken Maine. *The explosion that sank the USS* Maine *in Havana harbour, 1898, was never properly explained, but it set off the Spanish-American war, which made the United States an imperial power, giving it the Philippines.*

had no doubt that the United States would win. It was fighting close to home, its people had "astonishing ability as mechanicians", and success in a maritime war invariably went to a maritime people. The paper was confident of British opinion, which was "always inclined to sympathise with Americans", but it still had a pang of regret for the luckless Spaniards: "It is difficult at the same time not to feel an emotion of pity for the ancient and proud people who find it so impossible to construct a government which shall fulfil any of their aspirations."

The Spaniards, however, had friends. The European ambassadors in Washington tried to mediate as a group to prevent the war. The British ambassador went to the group's first meeting, but not to the second. That stopped all idea of intervention to save Spain: "The whole of Europe will not intervene because Great Britain would abstain, and the Continent, always suspicious, would take no action while Great Britain was looking on, nor run the risk of changing the friendly feeling between England and America into an active alliance."

The connection was working. The American squadron in the Far East sailed for the Philippines after refuelling in the British colony, Hong Kong. A British squadron shadowed the German squadron operating there.

The war was fought and quickly won. The paper was not entirely impressed. The Spanish forts, it thought, should have blown Commodore (instantly Admiral) Dewey's squadron out of the water on entering Manila Bay. Enthusiasm was admirable, but all could see "the utter unpreparedness of the American volunteer forces, as complete in its way as the lack of preparation of the Spanish Navy". As for the Cuban rebels, they were "about as fit for a democratic Republic as the natives of Sierra Leone".

Now, at a stroke, the United States had an empire, which not all Americans thought they should have. The *New York Times* even suggested, briefly, the Philippines should be handed over to Britain. *The Economist* understood the American doubts. In the conquered 175,000 square miles were "some 12,000,000 of people, nearly the whole of whom are alien to her blood, language and institutions". If these colonies were taken on, it would mean a very different United States: "Isolation and freedom from armaments went together, but the new world-role will mean a very powerful navy and a considerable army.... The maintenance of great military and naval forces will also modify the character of the American Government, and necessitate the permanent adoption of a new system of taxation.... The attitude of the people towards the Federal Government will thus change."

There was no doubt the Americans could do it, if they wanted to: "If they can govern dark races well, the extension of their authority will be beneficial to the world, and certainly of no danger to Great Britain, but we wish they should act with their eyes open."

The Filipinos were "distant one-fourth the circumference of the globe" and most Americans were not happy with the idea of a helot class: that was why they had enfranchised their own slaves: "They would not have liked eight or nine millions of Seminoles in Florida, and the Seminoles were not so formidable as the natives of the Philippines would be if they took it into their heads to hate the new invaders."

The election victory of Theodore Roosevelt in New York in November 1898 after "making his fight for the Governorship of the State on annexationist, not to say on advanced Jingo, lines" was a sign of the way minds were being made up: "That the American people will declare themselves incompetent to perform a task which, as compared with the conquest of India, is a very small one, seems to us a delusion implying complete ignorance alike of their character and their history."

If it suited the Foreign Office to have a friendly fel-

Rough Riders. The charge up San Juan Hill, Cuba, led by Theodore Roosevelt, was hailed by the press and helped Roosevelt towards the presidency. It redeemed other American military failures.

low imperialist on the map, it suited *The Economist* to draw the most optimistic of conclusions for the future of Anglo-American relationships. It had declared in May 1898: "The two countries have recently drawn together in a remarkable way, understand one another better than they have done at any time in the last half of the century, and may, if the understanding continues, pursue certain objects together in a way which would lead to agreement for mutual protection."

The Americans, who, it said, had been "happy-go-lucky" about foreign policy, had discovered that they were not popular in Europe, where their industrial power was increasingly envied and resented. They had found, too, that war was not easy: they had "practically to make an army before they can as much as attempt to use one".

They had been warned: "They see clearly, in fact, that a great Power might for a time have beaten them, that they could not have faced a coalition of all Europe, and that they owe something to any Power which, by refusing to join such a coalition, has preserved them from such a danger.... Their only sincere well-wisher, in fact, was the Government of Great Britain, which they had thought secretly hostile—or, at any rate, unfriendly." Now the Americans themselves were being "very friendly, unexpectedly friendly".

So the paper dared to think that the "kindliest of races is rather ashamed of previous fits of ill-temper and acerbity". America should understand that friendship with Britain was an effective external defence. And now both America and Britain, with their interests in the Pacific, saw the very future of China with different eyes than those of the Germans, the Russians and the French: "Great Britain and America want very nearly the same things in the Far East, namely, peace, order, and freedom to trade anywhere at will, subject only to Customs House duties enforced against all nations alike. These things can be secured if the two nations are allied, and they have a strong interest in securing them."

The alliance idea, however, needed to be closely defined as the colonial secretary, Joseph Chamberlain, who wanted one, promptly found out. Chamberlain declared that war itself would be cheaply purchased if in a great and noble cause "the Stars and Stripes and the Union Jack should wave together over an Anglo-Saxon alliance". The paper's caution returned: "With this we entirely coincide, subject to the reserve that we want to know beforehand what the war is to be about." It thought the Americans would say the same.

When the Germans made life difficult for the Americans and British in Samoa in 1899, the paper was prepared to walk away: "Germany is welcome to the group or America, or any other Power, who is willing to relieve us of a condominium which, like every other condominium, is a source of endless vexation and of recurrent causes of serious dispute."

It was the Americans who mattered: "We cannot negotiate an exchange without being sure that the United States will be contented with the arrangement. The friendship of America is worth much more to us than that of Germany."

The Americans did not walk away. They had just found another reason to distrust Germany: "Washington can no more isolate herself than Berlin can, and by and by she will not wish to."

But just how far was the United States ready to go to implement its policies? The paper recognised the aspiration behind the policy of the secretary of state, John Hay, towards China. It was "in complete accord with the so-called 'open door' policy". But it could not see what precisely it meant or how it was going to be enforced. Elihu Root, the war minister, declared that America must one day either give up the Monroe doctrine or fight for it. The paper agreed. European states were seeking out new possessions. Germans were colonising in Brazil: there was room for 50m of them. That was pushing the anti-German cause, but America had no option. It was down from its separate planet. Its policy was no longer exclusively American; so a doctrine that suggested it should be was simply illogical.

Britain itself was now in an imperial crisis: the second Boer war, the last war it was to fight in the specific cause of expansion. It did not have an especially poor press in the United States; it was no longer the only player on the field. But politics were never dormant. In May 1900 a Boer delegation arrived in New York. The paper forecast it would be feted widely, especially in the mid-west, where there was the major constituency of German voters. The Germans did not like McKinley because he was felt to stand for American imperialism and for friendship with Britain. The Democrats had hopes of stirring things up. The paper felt it meant nothing more. That November McKinley beat the Democrat, William Jennings Bryan, for the second time.

The United States had come to the front in a world system which pressed it to conform with that system and British policy was intended to ensure that it did. World trade pointed inexorably one way. According to the paper's figures Britain still took 18.3% of it; Germany took 10.8%; the United States was now up and running with 9.7%. It had put Britain, on *The Economist's* reckoning, into second place in exports (many of them agricultural), but then 55.8% of all United States exports were to Britain and British territories. These seemed compelling figures to put beside the old claims of ancestry, language and history.

The paper was even impatient because the Americans were not yet ready to comply more closely with British interests in their new role. Europe had understood that they were prepared to act in bringing China, which had "gone mad with the old Asiatic fury", back to reason. But although all the powers had been, for once, on the same side against the Boxer rebellion, they had been far from united, and they had insisted on keeping the Japanese, who had real troops on the spot, on the sidelines: "It soon turned out, however, that America, with all her gigantic resources in men, money, and ability was not quite ready to encounter her new responsibilities.... She wishes to be great throughout the world, yet to avoid conquest, and as the two wishes are not always compatible, her ultimate policy can never be so far foreseen as to make dealings with her easy or even possible to other States."

Military rule persisted in Cuba three years after Spain's defeat. What was the United States really aiming at? "We should suppose that it would be advisable to avoid entanglements in China, but in that case there must be no pretence of leading European diplomacy. There can be peace in the Philippines, but it must involve the recognition of Filipino liberty. There need be no great difficulty as regards the status of Cuba, but it means that Congress shall keep its solemn pledge. The real question is whether American political morality will surmount supposed American material interests."

The Economist was convinced that in the world of the twentieth century commerce was going to be a big player in political decisions. The American industrial machine had been sufficiently successful, despite protection, to impose new policies. For the Republican Party the priority now was to persuade labour that overproduction in the United States must lead directly to more international trade and, with it, empire: "Production is far ahead of consumption; this serious disparity tends to bring about economic crises; to avoid such crises it is necessary to acquire or create outside markets for surplus products. Such is the syllogism which governs American politics under Republican guidance."

To Britain, which relied on American farm exports, there was no great fear of dumped American manufactures. Continental Europe thought differently. The Austro-Hungarian foreign minister, Count Goluchowski, proposed a European common commercial union to keep the Americans out. The Germans sometimes spoke the same way. (The Kaiser had first talked of an anti-American alliance in 1895.) The paper was scathing: the union "appears to us peculiarly absurd and impossible". The United States had nothing to fear: "For what is Europe, economically speaking? It is what Metternich called Italy—'a geographical expression'—nothing more." That was the received wisdom of December 1900.

Where the paper was certain United States power would expand next was Panama. The canal was an imperative: "They would occupy the Isthmus instantly if it were threatened by any European power, and we feel by no means certain that they would not consider its transfer to any power not as weak as the Panama State a direct menace to the future of their country."

When the secretary of state, John Hay, said the canal would be "for the use of all well-disposed peoples, but under exclusive American ownership and American control", the paper agreed. It saw no advantage in joint ownership: "A canal which shall be for the use of all well-disposed peoples is the only canal that we care to have."

Now the United States knew the reality of power. The figures of the older generation, the Clevelands and the McKinleys, were hesitant about it, needing to be pushed by the big interests, by the newspaper proprietors, and by what they interpreted as public opinion. In September 1901 McKinley's assassination brought the least hesitant of presidents to the White House. The new world half-power had found its man, its mission and its voice.

British diplomats trusted Roosevelt, argued and corresponded with him, and indulged him. (Sir Edward Grey even shared his interest in birds.) They knew who they were dealing with.

GOLD AND THE BANKERS

How not to run a successful capitalist economy

The Economist's unreserved preference was for gold and the honouring of debt, views which it shared with Cleveland. The silver interests and the pro-inflation lobby (especially western and southern poor farmers) had succeeded in passing a mild silver coinage act in 1878. The paper reckoned by 1885 that the Treasury had coined $37m but $28.6m was still in the vaults, because the public preferred the silver certificate bank notes and only $8.4m in coins had gone into circulation. It warned then that world production of silver was rising, the price was falling, and the coins in the Treasury were already worth less than 85% of the gold dollars, still the official unit of value. The farmers and miners had their own prognostications, but the paper was trenchant: "The more the American people learn of the silver situation, the less they will tolerate any plan of the silver mine men and silver fanatics to afford a market for silver speculation with the help of the Government."

The more silver depreciated, the more the customers insisted on being paid in gold: "It is clear, as President Cleveland states, that the United States cannot go on coining silver and striving by indirect means to force it upon the people, unless they are content to see gold driven wholly out of circulation."

The paper acknowledged that the United States was certainly not poor; it just had an unworkable system. The administration that was worried about gold draining away was running a huge revenue surplus, which the law still did not allow it to use constructively: "The law expressly forbids the Government to deposit in the banks any of the Customs revenue. The idea inspiring it seems to have been that by keeping the money in its own hands the Government escapes the risk of loss through bank failures."

When Cleveland was elected in 1888 he had time to think of another approach to reform—however inadequate—but the paper felt that the Harrison Republicans had merely been intent on making things worse. They reinforced the silver lobby by giving statehood to six western states, and bought their congressmen's support by passing the Silver Purchase Act in 1890. This required the Treasury to purchase 4.5m oz of silver each month at the market price in exchange for Treasury notes. The

paper thought this absurd. As the notes could then be exchanged for either gold or silver, the gold reserve was increasingly put at risk.

By July 1892 the paper reported gold had reached its "apprehension point" where people "will be disposed to make a rush to convert their notes, lest, if they delay, conversion will be impossible". Again, the law did not help a beleaguered Treasury. It required there to be a gold reserve of at least $100m (£20m), as security for the note circulation. That was a trapdoor just waiting to open.

There were many others. Increasingly, the west had grown indebted to the east, which held the farm mortgages. The farmers themselves had been short of funds since 1887. Even without a depression, funds had to leave the eastern banks and go westwards each summer to buy the crops and get them to the ports. This left the New York banks distinctly vulnerable, particularly when speculation, encouraged by the activities of the trusts, had become a widespread sport.

The over-ambitious Reading railroad "collapsed completely" in March 1893, having tried to get a monopoly of the anthracite coal traffic. The paper was vehement about American folly. The gold reserve in the Treasury fell below $100m by May, the announcement that payment in gold would continue only when gold was "lawfully available" causing "almost consternation". Of course, as always there was a reassuring voice, which the paper duly quoted: "Mr Henry W. Cannon, president of the Chase National Bank, and one of the delegates from the United States to the Brussels Monetary Conference, said to your correspondent that there will be no financial crisis at this time."

The Economist was not impressed. By the end of May the New York correspondent was reporting a "sudden and extreme liquidation" in industrial shares and the growing failure of banks in the mid-west: "a financial house of cards, built up of a lot of little country banks scattered throughout Northern Indiana, Michigan, and Illinois".

By June "bankers South, North-West and West" were "scrutinising commercial paper as they have not done since 1884". Failures were widespread. There was no source of reassurance left: "1893, even if we are fortunate enough to escape anything like the financial flurries of 1873 and 1884, will very likely go into history as a year of relatively extreme depression in trade, greatly restricted credits and discounts, and slight, if any, profits in staple lines, together with a much-needed, but somewhat exhausting, shrinkage in value of securities."

The paper, of course, blamed the silver lobby unreservedly. The 1890 Silver Purchase Act must be repealed: "One cause of the present breakdown has, undoubtedly, been over-speculation and to that nothing contributed more than the constant inflation of the currency through the issue of Treasury notes in payment of the compulsory purchases of silver under the Act."

Though the west strenuously disagreed, and went on disagreeing for a generation, the paper insisted that the currency expansion had been ahead of the growth in population: "Banks became lavish and not over-scrupulous lenders, and booming being easy, speculation of all kinds grew rampant."

The Erie railroad failed. So did the Northern Pacific (under its "corrupt as well as inefficient" management), the Union Pacific and the Santa Fé ("practically nothing that has been said by the officials in regard to the company position is deserving of belief"). The negligence of railroad management was nothing new, as shareholders found out. The paper's regular censure even prompted Collis P. Huntington, the boss of California and controller of the Southern and Central Pacific lines, to protest that the Central was not British-owned. He had, he said, expected better of "a paper of the importance of *The Economist*". He was told that American railroad managers generally were "deficient in morality".

But now the panic was on. Gold was draining out of the Treasury and out of the country, as predicted: "The doubt that had always been felt as to whether the Treasury would be able to maintain gold payments, if it went on adding to note issues while the gold reserve was rapidly depleted, had become acute, and gold began to be hoarded.... Banks, feeling the pressure, began to contract their loans and call in money; this led to forced realisations; some of the less prudently conducted banks had to close their doors, and a banking panic and general financial collapse was precipitated."

The Economist revelled in the morass. The president could do nothing to help the system because the Senate refused to do anything: "A few Senators, from motives of pure self-interest, are suffered not only to flout and defy public opinion upon the silver question, but also to bar these other necessary reforms."

The high tariff had reduced trade, and so reduced the essential customs revenue. The government was sinking into deficit. It considered an income tax on corporations and companies, but blenched at taxing individual incomes. When it did try, the Supreme Court promptly slapped it down. It repeatedly sold bonds for gold, which simply encouraged the purchasers to draw the gold to pay for them from the Treasury, which thus lost as much gold as it gained. It took four bond issues and the help of a Morgan-Rothschild syndicate to save the day. This did not improve the reputation of a Democratic administration with the Democratic voters.

The paper was aghast at the system which had brought the country to this pass. It was not that America was unable to pay its way, simply that the legislature had neglected its duty: "If necessary, the States could, without any strain upon the tax-payers, raise a revenue twice as large as that which now goes into the Treasury. But partly because the Legislature could not agree as to what taxes ought to be imposed, and partly because the income-tax it did sanction was declared unconstitutional, the provision made for the expenses of administration is inadequate."

The hapless Cleveland tried to force some measure of tariff reform out of his own party, but the eastern Democrats themselves had become increasingly protectionist as the industrial interests had got to work on them, and the president's authority had largely gone. The act which was finally produced was so weak he refused to sign it.

Disappointed in Cleveland, the paper was not greatly taken by the Democrats' new candidate in 1896, William Jennings Bryan. His oratory was lost on it. His advocacy of the extreme silver cause was anathema. It thought the Democratic platform on the issue amounted to a plain repudiation of debt: "They in effect demand that the debtor shall be allowed to pay his creditor ten shillings in the pound and demand a discharge in full."

The paper considered the silver issue a total irrelevance, without fully appreciating that the gold reserve was an insufficient basis on which to run a credit superstructure in what was a rapidly developing and prosperous economy. Bryan, however inadequately, was trying to find an answer. That aside it admitted that the Democratic platform was not, as other critics had suggested, "communistic and revolutionary". It thought, naturally, that the idea of a tariff raised for revenue and not for protection had "the sympathy of all reasonable men". It supported Bryan on trusts too: "That the Trusts have a most evil effect upon trade, and injure the interests of the poorer citizens, there is no possibility of doubting."

The paper's New York man was more scathing

been the "sound money candidate", but was not living up to it: "The whole question of currency reform, which was unquestionably the chief issue at the election, is pushed aside in favour of a drastic measure of tariff reform."

He would do nothing about the trusts either: his

*J.P. Morgan: banker, industrial organiser, the symbol
of Wall Street's financial power.
Saved President Cleveland in the 1895 gold crisis; formed US Steel.*

about the silver agitation in the campaign: "The result must prove an avalanche in favour of the defenders of sound money, or the misinformed, the unfortunate, and in many instances the malicious, will be encouraged to continue the fight for another four years. The snake must be killed, not scotched."

When the Republican, McKinley, duly won, the paper's relief was brief. It shared "the satisfaction so generally expressed at the triumph of Mr McKinley", but it forecast the price would be paid on the tariff. The bill turned out to be "a thoroughgoing measure of protection". That was uppermost again. McKinley had

pronouncements were the "embodiment of political anaemia". The trusts, concentrating businesses under a giant holding company or companies administered by trustees, developed remorselessly in the 1880s and 1890s. They meant enormous industrial power, usually organised by bankers like the House of Morgan. They crushed competition. They exercised decisive political power and influence. By 1899 the paper admitted it had been predictable: "Mr McKinley, as everyone knows, was mainly elected by the Trusts; his friend and political mentor, Senator Hanna, is the great leading representative of the Trusts, and during the Presidency of Mr

McKinley the power and wealth of the Trusts have grown to such gigantic proportions that it is now said that they control about 90 per cent of the industrial capital of the United States."

The tariff, it insisted, played directly into the trusts' hands, removing any prospect of proper competition: "It seems that, while special protection has been accorded to steel products by the legislation of Congress on the ground that it is an 'infant industry', the earnings of the big Carnegie syndicate have yielded a profit of 85 per cent.... We accept Mr Carnegie's figures as fairly accurate."

The same was true of oil. The paper never liked the Standard Oil set-up. It said: "The Standard Oil Trust, which combines many separate enterprises, is founded upon a most iniquitous series of preferential discriminating contracts; it has risen to its present position through so much that has been inferred to smack of bribery and corruption, and it has built up so many princely fortunes for its leading spirits, that trusts generally must at this time be associated with such methods."

Ten years afterwards it was still saying it: "The huge dividend just declared by the Standard Oil monopoly—coincident, be it observed, with a rise in prices—could not have arisen without special legal aid and comfort; so that, on the one side, the monopoly is almost created by money taken from the public pocket, while on the other side, when once consolidated, the monopoly proceeds to bleed every person who presents a demand for oil."

When McKinley won again in 1900 the American economy was booming again: "There can be no doubt as to the real cause of Mr McKinley's triumph: it is, in one word, prosperity."

The trusts seemed to be carrying all before them. Protection was again delivering the goods. But there were appreciable doubts. The paper noticed: "The fear coming over the American people that free institutions may be so manipulated by the union of rich men with their political tools that we may come to a Government controlled by rich men who will direct legislation to their own advantage. With militarism more and more supreme in Europe this would indeed open up a black prospect for mankind, as it would be a complete negation of the social hopes of a century ago."

In September 1901 McKinley was shot. While he still hung on to life, the paper, though it thought little of his policies, recognised an enviable political gift in an unassuming man: "He is not engaged in any enterprise which excites furious animosities. He is not the representative of any detested caste. He is a plain man of good character and kindly disposition, with a gift for acquiring popularity among the average kind of people, and for interpreting in his policy the average opinion." It was ironic that such ordinariness fell to an anarchist's bullet.

THE HIGH HOPES OF TEDDY ROOSEVELT
*The young Republican president who yearned
to be, and convinced himself he was, a
reformer*

Theodore Roosevelt was a puzzle to *The Economist*, as he was to many American voters. When the assassin Leon Czolgosz put him in the White House in 1901, he was the quintessential young man of the new generation and the new century. He was only 42, the youngest president ever, with the energy and optimism of a career that had taken him from Harvard to North Dakota, the New York police to the Navy Department, and the Rough Riders in Cuba to the governor's mansion in Albany.

The paper forgave his ebullience and recognised in him a man who took a world view, who understood the full potential of the presidency, and who was, at heart, a committed reformer. It was gratified by his overwhelming re-election in 1904. But most of his interests and, indeed, his chief successes, were not shared by the paper. Much of what it valued he could not deliver.

In his foreign policy, as in his own temperament, he saw things much as British diplomats, with whom he was invariably friendly, saw them. He talked of using the big stick abroad as at home, but seldom did: he helped to organise the end of the Russo-Japanese war and believed in the virtues of arbitration, but, like the American presence at the Algeciras conference (on the future of Morocco) in 1906, he was tempted by mere show. The issues that *The Economist* put first—the tariff, the currency, banking—he quickly tired of and left to his unfortunate successor, William Howard Taft. He annoyed the trusts but shrank from outright hostility to them and Republican interests. The long-sighted changes he brought about, the conservation of natural

Teddy Roosevelt: governor of New York, president, Nobel prizewinner, the epitome of reformist hopes. Failed in 1912 presidential bid.

resources, the forests, water power, irrigation, government supervision over food and drug standards, national parks, and even 50 wild bird refuges, were not among the paper's priorities.

Roosevelt's first great stroke was his intervention in the five-month anthracite coal strike of 1902 when, with winter about to set in, he summoned the mine operators and the miners to arbitrate. The owners refused and Roosevelt threatened to take the mines over and operate them with the militia. This was the making of the "square deal". The outcome was a victory for him and for the United Mineworkers' young president, John Mitchell, although it added to the mutterings among the Republican bosses, like Mark Hanna, who had only put him on the ticket in the first place to disarm him.

It was a debt that labour repaid, however, and while the paper, from the beginning, thought him hesitant over a precise policy towards the trusts, it credited him with slowing down Democratic gains in the mid-term elections. He had done it himself: "Precisely by hold-

ing out to the American people the prospect of obtaining deliverance from the grip of those colossal combinations of capital at whose will they are always liable to be, and very often are, fleeced in the same consciousless fashion as were our and their forebears by Tudor monopolists."

What pleased the paper just as much was the need to lift the tariff on coal to make up for the lost production of the strike. It was almost like the potato failure in the 1840s that had forced Peel's abolition of the corn laws: "Congress, at the earnest wish of the President, has passed, almost unanimously, a Bill, repealing entirely the duties on anthracite coal, and allowing a rebate of the duties on other coal for one year. An excellent step, no doubt, but if the duties had not existed, neither would the scarcity."

The paper's New York correspondent duly warned the Republican bigwigs not to drop such a man, whatever the likes of J.P. Morgan and his companies thought: "His friends could perform no better service for him than to permit it to be known that many of the possessors of millions, the great trust builders and their friends, were proposing to defeat a man in his candidacy for the Presidency who took sides with the wage-earner in his disputes with his employers."

Roosevelt, however, needed no coaching in election-winning. He pronounced that all remaining civil war veterans aged over 62 were entitled to a pension, doing it by executive act, not legislation. The paper was mildly sarcastic: "No one not blinded by prejudice can seriously suppose that he sanctioned the issue of the new pension order with a view to influencing the approaching election."

There was more good news. The Democrats for once dumped Bryan and picked the grey Alton B. Parker, who had been head of the New York Court of Appeals for 15 years. The paper was unhappy constitutionally about that choice: "We cannot but doubt whether, in the long run, American institutions will not lose more than they could possibly gain by the inclusion of the higher Judges among possible Presidential candidates."

It did not matter. Roosevelt was in his element. His platform, the paper said, was imperialism abroad and a check on abuses of the power of capital at home. The previous summer he had travelled 15,000 miles, making 300 speeches, through the mid-west and west. Modern campaigning had begun. His magnetism was infectious: "To tens, probably to hundreds, of thousands of his countrymen he became a clearly realisable individuality, representing large and high views of the destiny of the United States, and of the corresponding duties of its rulers and its citizens, and giving to those who saw and heard him the impression of a man exceptionally capable, if the opportunity were rendered to him, of carrying such views into practice."

A strike in the Chicago cattle market and packing houses was convenient. The New York correspondent reported: "His insistence that the Administration shall interfere in the Chicago strike ...; the President's action in ending the coal strike in 1902; and his more recent ruling in favour of an 'open shop' among Administration or Government employees at Washington, are all exciting a good deal of interest."

The paper's endorsement was enthusiastic: "President Roosevelt has been sobered by power: he embodies admirably some aspects of the typical American character, and expresses, so to speak, the manifest destiny of the United States. His strenuousness, his picturesqueness, his 'record' in sport and war appeal (we

are told) to the younger electors. He appreciates the fact that America has become a World-Power, and that, whether in the Pacific or in South America, it can play the part better, in the interest of humanity, than Germany or Russia."

When he won in 1904 by a landslide, the paper declared he would "enjoy the specially hearty sympathy of the British nation". It drew one particular lesson: "Democracies always like a man, and in President Roosevelt the great American democracy realise that they have got a man."

Just the same, the victor, talking of his plans for a big navy, world responsibility, and even an international police, did seem excessively high-flying: "It remains, of course, to be seen whether the American people will be ready to accept the role of magnificent knight-errantry thus indicated."

It was conceivable, if unlikely. After all, even "shopkeeping England herself" had once set out to suppress the slave trade. But moral causes were clearly uppermost in his mind: "The first important utterance of a President who has been reseated in the chair by the greatest popular vote ever cast for a single individual."

That was 7,626,593 votes in all, and the share, 56.41%, was the biggest since popular returns were collected. It meant that he found himself a popular, indeed a populist, president, and it appeared to give him the opportunity to put through the reforms he wanted. He said, and wrote, the right words. His message to Congress in December 1905 ("every line and every sentence contain evidence that it was written by Theodore Roosevelt") faced some of the more intractable problems. The paper knew them all too well. There were the trusts, about which he had talked and threatened so much: "In the United States, thanks, in great measure, to a high protective tariff, the operations of industrial combinations have been attended by grave abuses and gross oppression, and so long as that tariff is maintained on its present basis, it is difficult to see how internal legislation can eradicate the evil, though some mitigation of it might be obtained by more effective Federal supervision."

It was already apparent that the tariff was not going to be reformed by Roosevelt, even though, the paper thought, it would be more sensible of the trusts to let change happen under a friend than face, one day, the retribution of an opponent. On the trusts themselves it advised two things: to use only the existing law, but to make sure that the big offenders were brought to book under it: "While smaller criminals are relentlessly pursued by the law, these wealthy capitalists are allowed to escape with mere verbal censure."

That was only too true, and it stayed that way. Then there were the railroads and their discriminating freight rates. The paper recognised the immensity of the task: "The problem of regulating rates on so vast a system of railways as that of the United States is so difficult and so complex that it would be almost impossible to leave it in the hands of any tribunal, however able and competent that tribunal might be."

It recommended concentration on the two most unpopular devices: preferential rates and rebates. Roosevelt did get Congress to pass an act in 1906 which included regulation of storage, refrigeration and terminal facilities and sleeping car, express and pipeline companies. It eventually forced the railroads to give up their steamship lines and coal mines which they had bought to throttle competition. But the railroads had valuation tricks up their sleeves, which allowed for continued abuse in rate-fixing. Things did improve, but there was no elegant solution.

As Roosevelt's second term progressed he found himself increasingly unable to cut through the tangles of administration and the law, and as he became bored he called for more reforms and more powers. In 1906 he presented his programme to Congress as the thwarted champion of change: "It has one salient feature: it is, throughout, an appeal to Congress and the people to give much greater powers to the Federal Government. It reveals a strong man and an ardent reformer struggling against the limitations of a Constitution which it is almost impossible to amend; and it marks a further stage in the efforts at unification which have been visible since the foundation of the Union."

From the New York correspondent came the full, improbable list of what Roosevelt wished to set his hand to in his final two years. Many of them were sensible and were to become law eventually, but not as a package. He proposed an income tax and an inheritance tax, national marriage and divorce laws, meat inspection to include the dates of tinning on the label, the prohibition of corporate political campaign contributions, currency reform, an eight-hour day and arbitration between capital and labour.

He saw himself throughout his presidency as a moral leader and as a champion of the small man. But there was a limit to unfulfilled promises. By December 1907 he had ducked out of the banking crisis, and out of the trusts, the tariff and the currency. The paper, finally disabused, merely thought him hollow: "No American President has given so much excellent advice to his fellow-countrymen than Mr Roosevelt. His Messages if collected together would form a complete manual of citizenship. All the evils, political, moral and social, which the United States are heir to have been denounced in turn.... To some men eloquence is its own reward."

For him it had to be. So, having had his loyal lieutenant and successor elected, he went off to shoot big game, for the moment. The last act had still to be staged.

FINDING A ROLE
Britain was determined to appease the United States, and did so repeatedly, to the paper's satisfaction

Roosevelt went into the world of diplomacy on the spring tide of the Anglo-American reconciliation. This suited him, or, at least, the anglophile streak in him. His best man at his second wedding in London in 1886 had been the British diplomat, Cecil Spring-Rice, who was to be ambassador in Washington in Woodrow Wilson's presidency. He thrived on such friendships.

He inherited as secretary of state Lincoln's secretary, John Hay, who had been ambassador at the Court of St James and favoured the understanding. And just to ensure that there were no mistakes or misunderstandings, the Foreign Office sent James Bryce, the author of *The American Commonwealth*, to Washington as ambassador in 1907. It looked as the British meant it to look: a special relationship.

The difficulties with Britain were, therefore, few and far between. Their interests coincided in almost all parts of the world. In particular, Britain had no reservations about United States construction, ownership and control of a Panama canal. The Hay-Pauncefote Treaty of 1901 arranged that, and although Britain was miffed because Congress insisted on allowing American vessels to go through toll-free it kept reasonably quiet about it. Nor did the Foreign Office much like Roosevelt's virtual seizure of the strip of the isthmus where the canal was to be built, after a staged rebellion by a pro-American Panamanian junta against the local Colombian authorities, but it still kept mum.

The Economist had some quiet doubts too. It told Roosevelt directly: "The policeman of the Western hemisphere is apparently to be guided only by his own judgment as to when and where a case has arisen for his interference." When the Colombian senate rejected the Panama Canal treaty in August 1903, it observed that South Americans "are willing to accept American protection against Europe, but they distrust the Americans close at hand". The Panama coup in November settled that, and the paper welcomed the pragmatism: "We do not know that anyone, except the Colombian Government and the Pan-German colonial enthusiasts, need complain of this result. The Panama Canal will be open to all nations; it will be neutralised, and it will be a benefit to mankind."

When Britain, in an aberrant moment, sided with Germany and Italy in trying to force Venezuela to pay its debts in 1903, the paper was wholly opposed. The Europeans had even declared their readiness to go to war, and had claimed that countries using armed force would deserve priority in any repayments. The United States was disturbed. The paper was too: "We have not only acquiesced in an objectionable policy, we have actively participated in it, and have helped to create a precedent of a most mischievous character."

America still stood by the Monroe doctrine, and Captain Alfred Mahan, the great naval strategist, had been employed to justify it. The paper thought the issue was minor: "The United States is not quite the Colossus she seems to imagine, but her policy is not likely to be seriously challenged, for the simple but sufficient reason that no other great Power has anything adequate to gain by fighting her. Germany has most, because Germany might like a South American colony of her own. But she is not likely to make any great sacrifice to obtain one."

It also saw how British public opinion was beginning to side automatically with the Americans: "The building of new war ships for the United States is accepted as almost a compensation for similar action on the part of Germany. Unfortunately, the appearance of a new sea power is, at best, a doubtful joy. If it reveals a possible ally, it may also reveal a possible adversary."

It was thinking more of the Japanese than the Americans. The paper considered it absurd, and grossly expensive, to include the United States in the two-power standard that the Royal Navy was presumed to be able to defeat.

In South America the paper was determined that Britain should not be caught on the German side again, and when, under German inspiration, another plan for a "Central European customs boycott" of the United States was floated in 1903 it thought there was nothing more to this "strange propaganda" than "the impulsive irritability of an able, but fitful, Sovereign". It read the Kaiser a lesson in economics: "The United States could get on, with inconvenience indeed, but with no approach to disaster, if the whole of Germany's custom for their goods were cut off; but who will say that Germany could get on without inconvenience, and even distress, of a very serious kind, if she were to shut her ports to the products of the country which in 1900 provided her with considerably more than one-sixth of her total imports, and from which her imports have more than doubled within five years?"

The paper was worried about Japan. As early as 1895 it had thought it "a new power, not very friendly to European political influence ... which in a few years will possess a very good navy indeed, one equal to that of a European Power, and an army of 150,000 men, well drilled, well armed, and well disciplined". It doubted in 1902 if Britain were right to have taken Japan, a "yellow power", as an ally and its soldier against Russian imperialism in the Far East. The Americans might accept the alliance because it was committed to the open door in China, but the Japanese, "a nation of quick-witted artisans, very hungry for profit", might turn out to want to monopolise the trade.

In 1904–05 American opinion, like British, sided with Japan in the war against Russia, which was a relief: "There was a time, and that very recent, when Russia could rely on American sympathy, whatever might be British prejudice." Now, the paper thought, scales should have dropped from eyes: "For American feeling in past years has generally registered the high-water mark of what may be called natural and disinterested friendliness to Russia.... Even if the latest assurances of the Tsar's intention to respect the treaty rights of other countries in Manchuria are given bona fide ... they are absolutely futile because America at last has joined the rest of the world in recognising that Russia's word is never her bond."

It was gratified that the United States and Britain

joined forces to tell Russia about their joint definition of contraband. So much was proper in regulating a maritime war. It thought little of Roosevelt's idealism in announcing he would summon a second Hague peace conference while the war was on: "We cannot but think that the summoning of any Hague Conference during the course of the present war would be a proceeding of doubtful wisdom."

He did it, of course, only a little over a month before his 1904 election. The paper recognised how Roosevelt eventually "exerted himself with strenuous, almost passionate, zeal" to bring the Russians and Japanese to sign the peace treaty of Portsmouth, New Hampshire, although it ignored his winning the Nobel prize for his mediation.

The Japanese victory had stirred British pride, but the Americans and Japanese were natural rivals. In 1905 Roosevelt had to buy Japan's temporary acquiescence over the Philippines by accepting the suzerainty of Japanese troops in Korea. Japanese feelings were riled by increasing American hostility to immigration in California, an issue that ran counter to American moral claims: "All suggestions about international rights or the comity of nations are met by the question, How would you like your little girl to be seated next to a Japanese young man all her school hours?"

When the time came to renew the Anglo-Japanese treaty in 1911 the paper brightened at the new clause which removed the obligation of war against a third power which accepted the arbitration of disputes: "The mere contemplation of what might have happened, of the awful and ruinous consequences, not only to England and the United States, but also to Canada, of a mishap under the old treaty, will enable our readers to measure the value of the revised version."

The local difficulties between the State Department and the Foreign Office were, as usual, over Canada. There were four issues: the Alaskan boundary, naval building on the Great Lakes, the century-long disagreement over New England fishermen in Canadian waters, and the sensible regulation of American-Canadian trade in the age of high tariffs. The Foreign Office was bored with the whole business. The interests to be protected were Canadian not British; the real negotiators were Canadian; and Britain was blamed by both sides whenever anything went against them. Such was the continuing imperial burden. As befitted the new, correct diplomatic practice, everything had to be sub-

mitted to arbitration, about which the Canadians, watching the open courtship of Washington, were distinctly sceptical.

The Alaska boundary commission, faced with the complex problems of disentangling the terrestrial claims along a highly serrated and mountainous coast where Canada hoped to get harbours, had no chance of pleasing everyone. It did not please the Canadians at all. Since the 1860s they, too, had been building their own country, and they were not at all enamoured of the United States or its society, which the most nationalist of Canadian prime ministers, Sir John Macdonald, had publicly called "a mass of foreign ignorance and vice". It was never London that confronted the United States but Ottawa.

When the Alaska boundaries went largely the United States's way in 1903 the paper quoted a dominion official: "Just as a rabbit is vivisected for the benefit of science, so Canada is sacrificed for the good of the Empire."

THE CRASH OF 1907
The rich country with the worst currency system in the world

The Roosevelt administration was chary of financial experiment. It knew of the problems that beset the system, but had no comprehensive remedy. Another bout of monetary stringency began in 1902, in the president's first year in office, and the paper used it to recapitulate the self-inflicted wounds within the world's most powerful economy.

Each autumn as the crops were harvested the currency shortage returned. Cash was needed to pay for the crops and their transport from the west. The law, however, required that the banks could not add to their note circulation except on a par with the value of the government bonds deposited by them in the Treasury. The United States was still rapidly paying off its debts, so these bonds were by now too highly priced for the banks to want to buy them. The law further required that the banks must retain a cash reserve equal to 25% of their aggregate deposits; if the reserve fell below that, they had to stop lending at once until the statutory quarter was restored: "The banks, in other words, are compelled to keep large reserves, but are prohibited from using them in times of pressure—an obviously absurd arrangement."

The banks, of course, had not helped themselves by tying up too much of their funds in advances to the financial syndicates that organised the industrial combines and railway deals.

The country was comfortably off, revenue greatly exceeded government spending and the surpluses accumulated in the Treasury. The system did now allow the treasury secretary to deposit the receipts from internal taxes in banks that were prepared to give security for such deposits, but this was still forbidden with customs receipts, and customs were much the bigger part of the revenue. This total inflexibility meant that the banks were regularly living on a margin of deposits that was entirely unnecessary. When things got even mildly difficult they had to clamp down, both increasing and exaggerating the progression from company failures to forced sales to market collapses. This was puzzling, to say the least, to gentlemen in Lombard Street, but it seemed to be the way the Americans preferred.

There was a nasty little crash in August 1903, just as forecast: "The ceaseless pounding of stocks there, while due, in part, to bear attacks, has been largely caused by the merciless unloading by the banks of heavy loans they have been carrying, the collateral of which has so far depreciated in value as to render such action necessary."

Next was the resounding crash of 1907. This, the paper felt, was one of sheer, speculative overconfidence, allied to the system. The paper blamed the speculation induced by prolonged prosperity: the excessive inflation of values; over-expansion of credit; the exhaustion of the restricted supply of capital; the excessive use of new securities; abnormal interest rates; and, for good measure, the "aggressive attitude" of state and federal authorities towards the speculators' favourite investment, the railroads. It was a complex crisis, but the paper felt it could be succinct on such familiar territory.

By the end of the year it had identified the underlying causes of what was much more than a local, American crisis. There had been the destruction of capital by two great wars, the Boer war and the Russo-Japanese war. These had caused the unprecedented issue of debt around the world to pay for unparalleled extra armaments. At the same time unexpectedly good harvests in the decade had encouraged the expansion of trade and inflation of credit. There had been further

inflation as a result of the doubling of the world's gold output in ten years. Extravagant land speculation set in. American railway shares were manipulated to the limit and beyond. New companies were floated with reckless optimism. The inevitable happened: banks began calling in the loans, pricking the bubble companies around the world, trade steadily declined and serious failures began.

The paper's New York correspondent gave his reasons: "The disclosures that have taken place of the looting of corporations by high financiers as the result of Government investigations, the consequent undermining of confidence, and the action of certain unscrupulous capitalists in securing control of chains of banks and trust companies for the sole purpose of using the funds committed to their charge to promote and bolster up doubtful enterprises of their own formation".

The 1907 crash went all the way down. Gold attracted a premium in everyday life: "The ignorant man who hoards his money in his own house is a familiar anomaly in the United States, with its vast hordes of untutored immigrants, but when its smart businessmen deliberately choose the safe deposit in preference to the bank there is obviously a breakdown of credit."

The paper declared that the United States must at last determine to give itself a central bank, and to remedy the perpetual want of connection between supply and demand in the currency. But the collapse went on: "What we have seen is a dissipation of credit, a famine of cash, almost unparalleled withdrawals of gold from other countries to provide circulating medium and to catch up foreign exchanges."

The New York man confirmed that protectionism had simply added to speculation. Manufacturers had thought it safe to increase their capacity behind high tariffs, paying excessive prices for labour and material, and so over-capitalising their plant. Pig iron was imported "into this country, where we mine ore with steam shovels". Building prices in the cities went up by one-third, as did the price of farms, ore properties, timber and timber land. And all the time the currency system did not work: "As Bagehot says, nothing can more surely aggravate a panic than for the Bank of England to refuse to lend out the money that pours into it."

The chairman of the House Banking and Currency Committee, Charles N. Fowler, put it briefly. The United States currency system was "the worst in the world". His estimate was damning: "It dealt with bank resources aggregating 19 billions of dollars, and the products of the country which must be marketed by the aid of proper bank currency amount to 25 billions of dollars."

TACKLING THE TRUSTS
How Roosevelt took them on, with an unexpected ally

What Roosevelt brought to the administration's efforts to contain the trusts was what he brought to everything: publicity. He promised that it would be pitiless, that in its light the law would be enforced, and there would be no compromises except on the basis that the government won. This was the heart of the square deal for the consumer, for the plain man in the age of great corporations. But although Roosevelt had the populists and the muckrakers mostly on his side, so that United States Steel, Standard Oil, the Sugar Trust and the Whisky Trust had become objects of public mistrust—and only a few, like International Harvester, were admired—the corporations had managed to get the workings of the law very much on theirs.

So Roosevelt had to go on the offensive if he were to make good his promises. The paper could see the difficulties. It doubted if the courts were the right way. It was the competitive impact of free trade that alone could offer Roosevelt any sort of a panacea: "To convince him and his fellow-countrymen that in the reduction of the tariff rather than in special legislation lies the best remedy for most of the abuses which they feel or apprehend".

Roosevelt, of course, had no such intention. His reticence spoke for itself. Still, the trusts had to be brought to book: "The sinister influence of the Trust financiers is everywhere felt in the United States. Their power over the New York banks enabled them to compel those institutions to over-lend their resources with results little short of disastrous. Their attempts to dominate the industry of the country have been productive of grievous injury to the people, and the control which they exercise over the railway systems of the United States has given them the power to mulct the shareholders in a fashion that would never be tolerated here."

The Economist and Wall Street were surprised at the

answer that came to hand: the Supreme Court. To the trusts' derision Roosevelt had instructed his attorney-general in 1902 to start an action against the Northern Securities Company, a consolidation of the Harriman and Hill-Morgan railroads in the north-west: the Great Northern, Northern Pacific and Chicago, Burlington and Quincy. Two years later the court found by 5–4 for the president. Amazement and wonder swept the corporate world. Who would be next?

"It is notorious that the Sugar Trust, the Standard Oil Company, the Tobacco Trust ... would have quite as hard work proving themselves unable to restrict trade or prohibit competition if they so desired, as the Northern Securities Company has had."

Within a month the court struck again. The railroads controlling the anthracite coal country—the Philadelphia and Reading, LeHigh Valley, Delaware and Lackawanna, Central Railroad of New Jersey—were told they were discriminating illegally in their rates, faced prosecution and must produce contracts of their rates and prices.

In March 1906 it was another railroad's turn. The Chesapeake and Ohio had a neat trick under which it gave itself a rebate on the coal it carried and sold. The Supreme Court found against it. It was strict and specific: "The decision does not say that a railroad company may not be the owner of a commodity which it transports, but it does say that the price at which that commodity is sold must include its full published tariff rate, such as would have been charged to anyone else.... Common carriers cannot be dealers in the commodities which they transport in competition with other dealers if that results in discriminating in favour of themselves and their customers."

Roosevelt had scored significant victories, a continuing source of his popularity, but his campaign, which amounted to 45 prosecutions, was incomplete. He reached an unofficial armistice with J.P. Morgan, which reassured his party. The trust lawyers came back and got the court to accept that only "unreasonable" acts by monopolies justified prosecution. The paper acknowledged it was to Roosevelt's credit that he recognised many of the abuses, saw it was the administration's responsibility to act, and both in the courts and by the creation of the Bureau of Corporations as a policing agent, he earned the trusts' respect. They then devised new ways of outsmarting the law.

UNHAPPY TAFT

The chosen successor who managed to fail at almost everything

The presidency of William Howard Taft (1909–13) was the epilogue of the Roosevelt years, an unexpected failure though not an unmitigated one, the outcome of a mortal division inside the Republican Party and between Roosevelt and his own, hand-picked successor. Taft had his achievements: he managed to get constitutional amendments allowing an income tax and even the popular election of senators. Nevertheless he was a disappointment to the party's liberals, to Roosevelt himself and to *The Economist*. The paper had rather approved of his attributes in the election: "Probably Mr Taft is what we should call an Imperialist, but not of the noisy and flamboyant type, and he would doubtless prove a sober and fairly economical administrator. Great Britain, we believe, could count upon his friendship."

The paper's editor, F.W. Hirst, was in New York on election day, November 5th 1908, and sent his own impressions by cable. (His staff in London noted carefully: "The message will be found, we think, to be quite in accord with what we had written before its arrival.")

Hirst even managed to persuade himself that Taft might entertain ideas of lowering the tariff: "His interventions will be less histrionic than President Roosevelt's, but they will be powerful. He believes, for various reasons, that substantial reductions of the tariff would be beneficial. He is not at present in any sense of the word a scientific economist or financier. But neither was Sir Robert Peel in 1841."

The Economist still believed that reason, argument based on established fact, could determine policy, could even persuade politicians to change their minds and emancipate parties from their inherited dogma. Whatever politician in the United States was going to do that, it was not Taft. He wanted to build on Roosevelt's progressivism, but his political commitment to it was limited. Even if he had been committed, his actual political skills were few. Inaction was his preference and he dithered over the tariff.

Hirst sent regular reports back to London demonstrating where the tariff had failed. He understood about international exchanges, where protectionism, by definition, did not work. The tariff naturally denied to New York the very successes of London: "It prohibits exports of manufactured goods by making the cost of manufacture prohibitive, and it prohibits imports of manufactured goods by a heavy fine at the ports of entry. No wonder that the ocean shipping of the United States has steadily declined, until from the position of second in the world it has become almost insignificant."

To a British free-trader it was inconceivable that sensible Americans, aware of all the local benefits they got in their own continent, should not wish to extend them worldwide: "New York is the banking metropolis of the largest and richest Free-trade area in the world. She takes toll from 45 States. But their dealings and hers with the outside world are so hampered and embarrassed by the tariff, which is almost as fatal to banking as to shipping, that for these outside operations she has to depend mainly upon London."

Within three months of Taft's inauguration the writing was already on the wall. In the Congress the interests were organised; the public was not. "The pressure of protected producers affects the representatives more than the general and unorganised outcry of the consumers."

Now the tariff was going still higher. The detailed measures themselves the paper merely thought absurd: "What harm is there in dandelion root, prepared, that it should be taxed; while dandelion root, dried, goes free? Lava and leeches, manna and manuscripts, pulu and cudbear, salep, solep, and spunk; a paternal government has seen to it that though food and clothing may be taxed to the hilt, these at least shall be free to the American citizen."

The paper was free with its blame: "President Taft's policy of a scientific revision of the Tariff, schedule by schedule, deceives no one and appeals to no one. It is at best a plea for scientific protection."

In diplomacy, Taft persevered to the end with his principles and his policies. He meant well. He had bad luck. He took up America's mission to save China from disintegration. He said the United States took a "friendly and pacific interest" in China. The United States loan in 1910 had no strings; it would be used simply to reform the Chinese currency. The paper was not impressed: "An unfriendly critic might inquire whether a Chinese expert will be summoned to assist in the reform of the American currency."

Taft took more than a neighbourly interest in Canada. He wanted to expunge the quarrels of the past and he wanted a common market with the Canada of the present. Arbitration was the official keynote of American policy. Taft welcomed The Hague tribunal's findings on the Newfoundland fisheries dispute, a cause of friction for nearly 90 years. He wanted arbitration treaties with everyone. That was harder; it brought politicians with less high-sounding principles into play.

The idea of a trade reciprocity agreement between Canada and the United States also brought the British Foreign Office into the game. The Foreign Office had learned its lesson. It had to be helpful to the Americans if they really wanted a treaty. It could not stand in the Canadians' way if they wanted one. It had to provide its good offices while keeping a wary eye open and taking no part in the talks. This discretion was exemplified by the ambassador in Washington, James Bryce. The paper reported: "Mr Bryce introduced the Canadian delegates to Mr Taft, and kept closely in touch with them during the negotiations. He took no further part in them, beyond reminding the delegates continually of the regard that should be paid to Imperial interests."

Since London opinion, especially in the Conservative Party, was totally split over imperial preference, that was a properly ambassadorial view to take. Canada, too, was increasingly of a mind to make its own mark in the world, especially about its own business. Many suspicious Canadians "were demanding a permanent representative of their own at the American capital". It needed a sound touch: "It is only through the ability of Mr Bryce that this agitation has not come to a head.... Separate diplomatic representation ought to be far more trying to Imperialistic nerves than separate trade agreements."

Taft wanted a treaty badly. He thought the time was right for it. Both the United States and Canada had a common cause in maintaining wheat prices and not driving them down in competition. He thought Canadian manufacturers could be squared. He believed in Canada's future, taking the stump to remind Americans that, cotton and copper apart, Canada took more United States exports than Germany. It was a profitable market that should not be walled off. Its 7m population would, he said, rise to 30m. The paper was offhand, seeing another significance: "The Dominions have now claimed for themselves the right to exemption from the operation of commercial treaties concluded by the home Government."

In Washington it was the Senate that claimed for itself the right to annul treaties negotiated by the president. Europe had not thought much of Taft's arbitration policy, but the British and French, looking to the future, had signed up. The Senate stood on its rights in foreign policy. Taft took his argument to the limits: "This feeling will undoubtedly lead to the prosecution of the struggle for the ratification of the treaties with intense bitterness."

The bitterness was evident in Canada. When the prime minister, Wilfred Laurier, required his electorate's endorsement of the trade treaty he was summarily ejected from office. The treaty fell. The paper was sure that Laurier's popularity had been eroded anyway by time and minor scandals, but there were other prime causes: "The unpopularity of things American and the alarm of the Canadian manufacturing trusts have prevailed."

The farming vote was for the treaty, but not the protected industrial vote. America's experience was being turned back in its face. The Canadian Tories campaigned insistently on one argument: "That this Reciprocity Bill will lead inevitably to a political union with the United States, that the interlocking of tariffs will cause the interlocking of Governments. All the foolish speeches made on the subject in the United States have been quoted."

The paper affected no surprise, but it admitted, "perhaps", to some sympathy for Taft himself: "He is now left to face the electorate without a single achievement to his credit."

IN THE TWENTIETH CENTURY
*Why workers were better off; how San
Francisco rose again; and why the paper liked
planes, hated cars and opposed the* Titanic

The Economist studied workers' living standards in the United States and Britain. It found that American wages (excluding negroes) were 2.3 times those in Britain, and hours worked were shorter, except in engineering where they were three hours longer a week. American housing, outside New York, was bigger and more convenient, but at double the rent. Working men in America were buying their own homes out of their higher wages, and trusting to the higher value of land, which was relatively cheap to start with and steadily more valuable under pressure from the rising population. An American working-class garden was rare. Food was surprisingly similar in price, except, also surprisingly, bread. Clothing, fuel and luxuries were all dearer in the United States.

The editor, F.W. Hirst, was optimistic about the blacks he had met himself on his first visit, 1908–09, looking for a nascent middle class: "There are many thousands of coloured men who own their own farms, and form a contented class of peasant proprietors. The best cooks are often negro women. Most of the servants on the railroad cars are coloured men."

He did see something of the other side too: "Outbursts of crime and brutality are still terribly frequent in the South. But just as the old appeal to the revolver is slowly dying out in the West, so are the lynchings of the South becoming less frequent. Progress is painfully slow, but still there is progress."

He found almost a good word for the new European immigrants in the big cities: "The children usually speak English moderately well, and generally aim at some better occupation than the manual labour which satisfied their parents. They are also, it is hoped, less addicted to the personal use of knives and revolvers."

San Francisco rises again The paper said that the San Francisco earthquake in April 1906 was an economic as well as a human and seismological event. It saw in the destruction a commercial opportunity, as did many Americans. There was no question of appealing for state aid or interference. Capitalism could be depended on to do the job; and it did. The New York correspondent reported first in a despatch dated April 24th: "It is still too early to estimate the loss from earthquake and fire in San Francisco. With order maintained and relief supplies pouring in, much has been accomplished in a very short space of time. There is no doubt that the city will be rebuilt, a bigger and handsomer San Francisco than ever."

The enterprising businessman knew what to look for: "Another feature of the situation attracting widespread attention is the announcement that San Francisco buildings which had steel frames, as most large buildings at Chicago, New York and other large Eastern cities are constructed, successfully withstood the shock of earthquake in many instances. This will create a heavy demand for structural steel to meet the

wants of the city which is to be built, in the face of which fact, it will be recalled that leading domestic structural steel mills have orders from six to eight months ahead."

The optimism was justified. The system did its stuff. By October the following year, San Francisco was rising again, chiefly by its own efforts, from the ruins: "The city has recovered with remarkable rapidity from the effects of earthquake and fire, and the figures of its bank clearings actually show an increase over those of the year preceding the disaster. 6,500 new permanent buildings have been erected and occupied, and 3,700 are now in course of construction; the total number destroyed was 22,000."

This was just what the enterprise economy wanted to hear. One significant figure was that customs receipts "were far the largest in the history of the port". Imported steel and building materials were playing their part in the revival, even during the market crash of 1907.

Admired plane and despised car Two ambitious American developments caught the paper's eye: the aeroplane and the motor car. It was more enthusiastic about the first; or, at least, it had a more enthusiastic correspondent. Wilbur Wright demonstrated his machine in December 1908: "The Wright aeroplane (given, of course, freedom from gusty and variable winds) can be depended upon to fly when required, to keep flying as long as the supply of petrol for the engine holds out, or until the aviator becomes fatigued, and then to descend at any given point, a safe landing being assured even in case of accident to the motor."

This reliability must have been distinctly encouraging, especially as the reporter had a picturesque pen: "The machine, with its almost invisible whirring propellers, looked uncommonly like a huge dragonfly as it sped the mile-long length of the sandy plain where the experiments were being carried out."

It appeared that 60 miles was a reasonable journey, and £1,000 was a reasonable price for a plane. Still, the aviator had to be prepared to rough it a bit: "Aeroplanes are not yet equipped with comfortable seats and rugs, so it is cold work travelling in them, while the roar of the unsilenced motor, like that of a racing car, is not at all a pleasant accompaniment to an otherwise enjoyable experience."

The Economist did not think much of the car, or its

Conquering the west. The arrival of the cheap, sturdy automobile was a godsend to the farmers and all other American families. It broke down isolation and changed society. The industry soon became central to American prosperity.

prospects. The contraption was even a menace to the thrifty, economic American labour force that it believed in, a labour force imbued with the precepts of Adam Smith and hard money. By the end of 1910 the paper regretfully discovered a more spendthrift America, given to quite unnecessarily conspicuous consumption. It was "another wasteful drain upon the healthy purchasing power of the people which has been responsible for much evil. Many small merchants and farmers whose incomes do not really warrant the luxury, have had their savings swallowed up by the motor-car mania".

It is true that this was only two years after Henry Ford had first placed on the market a car designed for plain and even quite poor people, with evident success.

But the paper's blind spot was extensive: it had only just measured the performance of the motor car on English roads and had pronounced sentence under the reckless heading: "The Triumph of the Horse".

The Titanic moral   The paper's views on the sinking of the White Star liner *Titanic* in April 1912, with the loss of 1,635 people, many of them rich and famous, among them J.J. Astor, Guggenheim and Robelin, the builder of Brooklyn Bridge, were delivered with asperity. It was no advocate of giant ships, either mercantile or naval, and although it recognised that no modern disaster had so struck the public imagination or aroused such sympathy, it put the blame firmly on the big shipping lines themselves: "They have decided that, in bidding for public favour, it is necessary to build vessels of over 30,000 or 40,000 tons; that their lines must be advertised by constant additions to the splendour and rapidity of ocean travelling; that if their rivals launch a boat of 35,000 tons with a lift or a new type of café, they must respond with a vessel of 40,000 tons, and some fresh irrelevance of modern luxury—a fish pond, a billiard room, or perhaps a tennis court."

The *Titanic* had been hastening through fog when it hit the iceberg because it was aiming at a new transatlantic record. The paper was scornful: "The advantage of the additional speed is at least doubtful; in comfort there is certainly no gain; and, on the other hand, the big vessels are handicapped by disadvantages in diminished safety, in difficulties of control, in want of docks, and in over-concentration of human life and material wealth."

It was appalled at the insufficiency of lifeboats that the law required. There had been a statutory requirement of a minimum of 16 boats for ships of 10,000 tons and over since 1902. The *Titanic* was meant to be unsinkable, but it had too few boats on board for the number of its passengers: "There was neither rhyme nor reason even ten years ago in stopping at 10,000 tons. But as the register of the '*Titanic*' was 46,000 tons, it is still more amazing that a first-class shipping company should have been content with the minimum of boats required for a ship less than a quarter the size.... Whatever may be said, the shortage of boats is in hideous and glaring contrast with the pleasure equipment of all kinds which abounded in that vast palace of luxury."

The very concept of the *Titanic* was, it thought, the outcome of commercial rivalry, as the modern battleship developed from naval ambition: "The *Dreadnought* mania, after provoking a rivalry, very profitable to the great armament interests all over the world, was speedily reproduced in the merchant service, with the help of big shipbuilders, who wanted to 'lick creation'."

The shipbuilders had gone beyond the right formula: proper size, reasonable speed, safety, comfort and economy. Even if the ships were slower and less profitable, it would be better to run two ships "than to concentrate the risk of four thousand lives and several millions of material wealth in one gigantic liner".

This was the Wilson of the new age in American politics, the new spirit: a leader apparently remote from the machine bosses and vested interests, a leader who did not compromise, who kept his promises.

5

WILSON: NEUTRALITY AND WAR

1913–1919

THE NEW SPIRIT

He was the paper's ideal president, when he began

Woodrow Wilson could do no wrong in *The Economist*'s eyes at his inaugural in 1913. He was already the hope for a better ordered world. He was, simply, the apotheosis of what the paper expected America to achieve: "He sees the magnificent energy of his country, its limitless enterprise, its moral force, its desire to rectify wrong and alleviate suffering."

In his own self-possessed, self-reliant way that was what Wilson sought to do, and did. The paper was pleased, for a start, that he set about his speech at the inaugural by putting quality before quantity, breaking with the orotund style that had accompanied Republican disquisitions: "The Presidents of the United States had got into the habit of emptying a load of words into the public street, and calling it the inaugural address."

The essential beginning was on tariff reform. From the start the paper had been reassured that Wilson meant business. Just after the election it sensed that the Democrats planned a tariff for raising revenue only,

but when they put the needs of the poor on the free list, it saw they would meet what Peel had faced in the 1840s; and his solution was the right one: "He met it by imposing an income tax. And a similar way out may be found by the Democrats in the shape of a federal income tax."

The Supreme Court's obstruction to any such thing had required a constitutional amendment approved by three-quarters of the states. That was now practicable; opinion had changed even under the Republicans: "Already 32 States have notified Secretary Knox that they have ratified the proposed amendment and only four more are required."

The free-trade tariff bill confirmed expectations. The cost of its reductions was put at $80m, to be covered by $100m raised in the new federal income tax. Food would be duty-free; so would many raw materials and manufactures in agriculture, transportation and printing. There was to be a general reduction in many of the common necessaries of life, among them blankets, underwear, women's dresses, soap, rubber, knives and scissors. In announcing it Wilson broke with tradition again: "Mr Woodrow Wilson's brief and telling address,

---

CHRONOLOGY

1913	Second Balkan war		Russia leaves the war
1914	US navy takes Vera Cruz, Mexico		US declares war on Germany
	Archduke Franz Ferdinand shot at Sarajevo	1918	Woodrow Wilson's Fourteen Points outlined to Congress
	Great War begins in Europe		German offensive in France fails
	Panama Canal opened		Armistice signed in Europe
1915	German submarine sinks the liner *Lusitania*	1919	Treaty of Versailles, setting up new nationalities and the League of Nations
1916	Easter rebellion in Dublin		
	Naval battle off Jutland		Wilson suffers physical collapse; US Senate rejects the league
	Battle of the Somme		
1917	Bolsheviks seize power in Russia		

---

personally read to Congress, conveys an impression of victory, and his whole attitude is that of a great man who feels that he is endowed with popular authority to execute a large measure of commercial and economic emancipation."

It was impossible to predict how far prices would fall with the fall in duties. But the paper expected them to correspond closely enough in sectors like textiles where the trusts and manufacturers' agreements had held sway. The new income tax on the well-off would be little more than 9d in the £1 (Peel had kept his to 7d). The Washington correspondent gave Wilson all the credit: "There is considerable internal evidence that up to about March 4th the Bill was being drawn up on decidedly conservative lines, and that President Wilson's personal influence during the first month of his administration was seen in a marked readjustment of the duties.... President Wilson must meet the very extreme hostility of the communities which have been corrupted by over-protection for many years past, and whose only test of statesmanship at Washington is the dollar."

Wilson's very technique, his political daring, set his stamp upon Congress and the country. It bred resentment but in the beginning it seemed unchallengeable: "The political skill, and the amazing hold upon the country which the President has exhibited in all of these negotiations, as well as the disregard of the conventionalities which has permitted him to visit the Capitol in person and to summon Senators into the Executive Chamber, rating them like schoolboys and then sending them back to their work with an injunction to do better in the future, constitute a combination of qualities and capacities rare in an American Chief Executive."

The new tariff was, in fact, the lowest the United States had had for nearly 50 years. Wilson sought to put in place beside it and the income tax what was to become the Federal Reserve banking system. This was Representative Carter Glass's bill on currency and banking, and the administration wasted neither effort nor time in putting on the pressure: "Already Secretary of State Bryan and his followers have swung into line behind the measure, Mr Bryan giving it his 'unqualified approval'. This speaks badly for the soundness of the Bill as now framed, but greatly enhances its prospects of becoming law."

The paper was never reconciled to Bryan and his

radicalism, but it believed the bill gave the banks the chance to build a system that would at last allow a regulated expansion of credit across the continent: "Under the Bill an entire transformation of the banking system of the United States will be brought about if the banks themselves can, as seems feasible, be led or driven into more or less hearty co-operation."

The final stages of the tariff debate brought another novelty: the Senate, the home of conservatism, cut the rates proposed by the House by another 5%. The Senate was now the more radical in attacking special privilege. The reason was plain—democracy had broken out: "A situation of almost unprecedented character in American politics, and one which shows the great change that has come over the Senate since the introduction of the plan of popular election of Senators and the elimination of the old 'grand-ducal' ring of Bourbons".

It was possible for The Economist to be unusually unstinting in its approval: "President Wilson is to be congratulated on having, by his tact and firmness, enabled the Democratic Party to redeem its pledges to the consumer in the most honourable and substantial manner."

This was the Wilson of the new age in American politics, the new spirit: a leader apparently remote from the machine bosses and vested interests, a leader who did not compromise, who kept his promises. He was to face unrivalled challenge.

MORAL FORCE DIPLOMACY
It all depended on whom you were dealing with

Wilson was insistent that the new approach was applied in foreign policy. His first worry was in Latin America, where, under Roosevelt and Taft, the United States had spoken much of friendship but had not given up the dominant power's right to intervene. The country that used the Monroe doctrine to exclude European ambitions was resented in the Caribbean, both over its interventions in Mexico and over its virtual seizure of the Panama isthmus. United States trade was also directed and financed from Washington too often to be other than begrudged. This was not Wilson's idea of neighbourliness: "There is an undoubted and strong feeling of regret among the bankers that the Wilson

Administration will evidently refuse in the future to assist concerns which have heretofore relied upon aid from Washington in getting orders abroad, and in assuring themselves that they would be paid when the time came."

That was easier said than done: "Just what can be done to overcome the remarkably widespread and urgent prejudice against the United States produced in South American minds by the Panama episode is not yet certain; but something will be attempted.... The next twelve months is likely to be a period of almost continuous rebuke to the Roosevelt and Taft Administrations."

The first beneficiary of the American mood turned out to be the old enemy, Britain. The British had readily accepted the American presence in Panama: the Americans could do whatever they liked without rebuke from the Foreign Office. But there remained the refusal to cut the British in on the cheap, coastal rates to be allowed to American merchant shipping, which seemed to transgress the Hay-Pauncefote treaty of 1901. Wilson thought so, but the Democratic Party's policy in the election had been determined by a plank written at the urging of a Senator O'Gorman, "a bitter Irish Catholic and foe of Great Britain", and intended as a blow to British trade. O'Gorman, however, had only had his way because the convention had been exhausted by three days and nights of deliberations over the candidacy: "The insertion of the section in the platform was thus a recognition of the need for sleep, rather than an admission of the wisdom of the proposed plan."

When Wilson made it plain that he meant to stand by the treaty he was assailed by the shipbuilding and ship-owning interests as well as by the Irish, but he stuck to his belief: he thought it necessary to stay on good terms with London.

Mexico was more difficult. Wilson condemned imperialism and he also liked the concept of pan-Americanism, but he had no time for the Mexican revolution of Victoriano Huerta and his military clique, whom he privately described as butchers, and refused to recognise the regime, even if that increased the influence of Britain and Germany. The paper sympathised: "He cannot let General Huerta make himself Dictator, when there is a rival party representing the Constitutional Government overthrown by violence and by murder."

It believed that "Wilson clearly has the American people behind him": and the other Latin American states acknowledged the new moral attitude. Wilson was still determined to exert great influence, but to do it openly: "There is some feeling of satisfaction at the abandonment of the shifty and oppressive policy characteristic of President Roosevelt's term of office."

Wilson held off military intervention in Mexico, chary of any commitment which would be costly and lengthy. But in March 1914 United States sailors going ashore for kerosene at Tampico were arrested and marched through the streets, though they were later released. The United States demanded that a salute to the Stars and Stripes should be fired by the Mexicans, in part to assuage the bellicose press. The paper felt itself above such shenanigans: "If war is to be made on points of punctilio raised by admirals and generals, and if the Government of the United States is to set the example for this return to medieval conditions, it will be a bad day for civilisation."

Huerta refused any salute unless the Americans replied in kind. Wilson sent the fleet to Vera Cruz, and the town and custom house were seized after some fighting. The paper was scathing: "All because an irresponsible admiral has demanded a salute from a dictator whose existence he is not allowed to recognise!"

Wilson forced the British to withdraw their recognition of Huerta and Sir Edward Grey agreed: the Royal Navy did not wish to risk its supply of Mexican oil, but Grey held that American friendship came before oil. Wilson held off from military intervention "because of his reluctance to plunge the country into a lengthy struggle whose outcome could not be predicted and whose duration and cost would be very great".

Huerta gave up in July 1914 and it seemed that order had been restored. By August Europe was at war and Wilson had more on his mind than the next revolt by Pancho Villa. So had *The Economist*, though its commercial and editorial instinct committed it to a special supplement on the opening of the Panama Canal in December. It saw the event in strictly Wilsonian terms: "Of all the Great Powers the United States alone stands aloof from the contest of arms, and invites all the combatants to participate in celebrating one of the most magnificent achievements of engineering—a work often attempted, and now triumphantly concluded— the joining of two oceans."

Wilson found it hard to stand aloof.

TO THE NEUTRAL THE SPOILS

*The paper agreed with American neutrality
and American industry*

The Economist, like most Europeans, fixed its gaze on the war fronts and far from the United States. It was so clamorous, so exigent a war, so ruinous to the world that liberal policies and intentions had grown up with, that the paper's thoughts were held by events and not by reasons or solutions. By September 1914 it reported, almost dazedly: "It is admittedly and prevailingly true that the sympathies of the United States are with Great Britain and her allies as against Germany."

By October it briefly took stock of Wilson's neutrality. It approved: "The attitude of the President of the United States is a model of correctness." There was no expectation that the United States would, or should, join the war. The war was bound to be short. There was no American army. There was, however, a growing belief that the United States and Britain could be shaping up for another confrontation over just what a blockade entailed for neutrals. And, initially at least, the American economy had not made itself felt. United States exports fell, because the arms output for allied orders had not yet got under way. Only foodstuffs rose. Steel and coal were in difficulties; construction was down 15% on the year. Already, though, since it was a horse-drawn war, harness and saddlery were up. The paper thought it all rather strange: "In days gone by, when great nations were at war a neutral country had some reason to expect an industrial boom. This was our experience in the Franco-German War of 1870. But today the shock to the whole fabric of international exchange has caused such world-wide dislocation that the United States has to bear her share of the suffering caused by the war in Europe."

By December it was evident to everyone that the war would not be short and that American industry was going to be important in its outcome. Wilson had said so, but he had also identified American limitations: "The United States must mobilise its resources and take over the great commercial position which Great Britain, France, and Germany are leaving to a neutral power. But he finds this difficulty that, while the productive power of the United States is enormous, it has neglected the means of distribution.... The President deplores the many mistakes by which American Protectionists have discouraged, and all but destroyed, the

merchant marine, and have, 'it seems almost deliberately, withdrawn our flag from the seas'."

That was to be an elemental factor, still only dimly perceived. In January 1915 the paper reported that the Americans and British openly disputed what should be recognised as contraband going to Germany. After five months of war the Americans complained that "neutral commerce was still being unreasonably interfered with by seizure and dilatory search". The British view was unrelenting: "If an innocent manifest were (as has not always been the case hitherto) equivalent to an innocent cargo, the problem would be largely solved." The paper was dejected: "The Law of the Seas is in rags, which cannot be mended until the war is over."

As the costly stalemate persisted on the western front through 1915 British opinion became increasingly censorious of American complaints about the blockade. If neutrality meant taking equally to task the Royal Navy for searching ships and the German U-boats for sinking them, the United States was, it was thought, hindering the democratic cause. The paper did not agree: "It is absurd to complain of President Wilson for standing up for neutral rights. For Sir Edward Grey would have to do the same if we were neutral and the United States were belligerent."

Naturally, it had no idea of mitigation for the U-boats: "If Germany really wants to impress the United States with the 'barbarity' of English policy she might prudently have given her naval commanders a hint not to sink neutral ships loaded with grain for England."

To America's critics the paper highlighted the work of the American Relief Committee in Belgium, almost wholly under German occupation and short of food: "Those who criticise the neutrality of the United States government, who accuse the Americans of moral indifference to and of profit making from the agony of Europe, would do well to study carefully the report of the Commission for Relief in Belgium." The American businessmen running it had become, it believed, "the sole channel through which the people of Belgium are being fed".

When in May the *Lusitania* was torpedoed off the Irish coast and 1,198 passengers were drowned, 128 of them American citizens, American opinion was inflamed. So was the paper's. It thought it "a deliberate act", "an act of calculated barbarity". But it had its reservations: "The outrage has been denounced in the United States and in most neutral countries as a cold-blooded murder—though this does not prevent surprise that adequate precautions were not being taken on this side to prevent it."

The culprit, it thought, was Winston Churchill, First Lord of the Admiralty, who told the House of Commons that the priority was to protect the fleet, without which the war must be lost, and not the hundreds of merchantmen which sailed in British waters daily. This was not good enough for the Americans: "From the first wrath against Germany was accompanied by strong criticism of Mr Churchill for not protecting the most famous vessel in the British merchant service."

The paper thought this reaction was meaningful. It scorned anti-Americanism: "From the point of view of international interests, it is eminently desirable that there should be a strong neutral Power, above all a Power capable of assisting to bring about a just peace when opportunity arises. Such is the tone of American opinion; and we think it a service to present it to our countrymen."

The war had not disabused *The Economist* of its confidence and trust in America's place in the world, of its manifest destiny to uphold decency, honesty and fair-mindedness. If that meant being pro-American that was fitting. It was also politic. The "paper blockade", as it called it, was plainly not bringing the Kaiser to his knees; it was chiefly exacerbating American opinion: "It is clear, even from the most pro-Ally organs, that there is a growing irritation at the British Government's interference with the trade of neutral nations. The irritation is not sentimental, it is practical. American shippers and traders are losing money, failing to make the profits they, in their view, legitimately might expect."

German diplomacy, capitalising on this and anxious to bring the waverers in the Wilson administration and public opinion back from the brink, announced a remission in the submarine attack. It said passenger liners would not be sunk without warning and without ensuring the safety of non-combatants on board. By November the United States despatched a note to London setting out its grievances about the blockade. Again the paper sought the common-sense approach: "While the best thing to be said for our actions is that they are being done by way of reprisals, it must be remembered that reprisals must not be visited upon neutrals."

The longer 1915 lasted the more Britain and France depended on the rapidly expanding American armaments industries getting their output through to them, on American financial institutions organising and raising the money, and on the Wilson administration allowing the overwhelming imbalance in arms exports to persist, in an unneutral way, to the allies' advantage. For the American economy was in the war in a big way. In April the paper had commented: "The orders from European Governments to American manufacturers are too lucrative to be refused, and the easiest way of financing them is by loans. Hence, for economic and financial reasons, the policy of refusing to finance the war in Europe by public loans in America is being abandoned."

By October a British loan of $500m had been raised in New York. The paper was not particularly enamoured of this financing: "The British nation does not enjoy paying over 6 per cent for its accommodation, and nothing but the state of the exchange could justify the conditions under which we borrow.... We are not raising money on New York's terms because they are the best we can get, but because credit in New York is at the present time essential to the financing of our American trade."

The biggest single shift in economic power across the Atlantic was under way. By November the American motor companies were celebrating the "phenomenal prosperity" brought by the foreign demand for trucks and cars: "The four important concerns whose stocks have been making stock market history since the great war began are the General Motors Company, the Maxwell Motor Company, the Studebaker Corporation and the Willys-Overland Company."

Not quoted on the exchange but foremost among others sharing "generously" in the business was the Ford Motor Company of Detroit, Michigan. Almost everyone could share: "The enormous and constant demand for materials of all kinds that could be utilised on the battlefields or in domestic consumption in the warring countries has stimulated the formation of new companies to an unprecedented degree."

Neutrality more than paid its way: "Instead of being a debtor nation, the position of the United States is now that of a substantial creditor."

By April 1916, as the battle for Verdun was being fought and the battle of the Somme was about to start, the allies' needs from the American arms companies grew: "The most amazing exhibit which has emanated from any of these companies is that of E I du Pont de Nemours and Co. This report shows earnings equivalent to 94.3 per cent on the common stock, compared with only 13.6 per cent on this issue a year ago, which amounted then to a trifle more than half its present aggregate.... The aggregate of war orders booked by this company since hostilities began is stated to be $400,000,000."

Most British papers deplored such profiteering. *The Economist* would have none of that. It was gratified that Wilson and the United States still stood for upholding public international law and protecting small nationalities in the future. It also understood the turn the war had taken because it knew how to count: "To go on for years losing 1,000 men and five millions sterling a day ... they ought surely to be overflowing with politeness and courtesy to President Wilson and to the great people whom he represents. For without the friendly neutrality of America, where should we be in this war? How could the Chancellor of the Exchequer maintain the exchanges if the credit institutions of America did not co-operate, and how could we supply our Allies with food, munitions, and raw materials, but for the bankers and manufacturers of America?"

It never called for American entry; it seldom criticised Wilson or his words. It made a merit out of America's ability to intervene, even-handedly, at the point when Europe would be overtaken by war-weariness: "The war will still have to be ended by negotiation, by a series of bargains and compromises, which will satisfy none of the orators of war, but will, we hope, with President Wilson, serve as a chapter of liberty, law, and peace to all the nations of Europe for many generations."

For the present munitions industries thrived. The trade returns told the story: "Exports of commercial automobiles, which amounted in August 1914 to $124,000, were $3,388,000 in December 1914, $8,579,000 in June 1915, and $6,170,000 in February 1916. Aeroplanes, which amounted in August 1914 to $1,700, steadily increased month by month to $955,000 in July 1915, and went as high as $1,488,000 in December 1915."

One day Europe would have to foot the bill: "*The Economist* has been practically alone in pointing out ever since the war commenced how fast Europe is receding and the United States rising in commercial and financial power."

The paper was much more cautious in its prognostications for the 1916 election. Admiring though it was of Wilson, it saw that the German-Americans, centred in the mid-west, were far from enamoured of him now: "They think he has contributed powerfully to the success of the Allies by allowing the United States to be converted into a great munitions workshop for our armies and by permitting large loans to be contracted for us in New York. That is why they profess such enthusiasm for Mr Hughes."

However, it had no worries that a victory for the Republican, Charles Evans Hughes, who had resigned from the Supreme Court to campaign, would in any way upset American foreign policy: "There is no reason at present to suppose, in spite of the charges of the Democratic press, that the 'Americanism' of Mr Hughes is any more favourable to Germany or any less favourable to Great Britain and France than that of President Wilson."

This was more than tact. It turned out to be a close-run thing, and it was not until Wilson took California by just 3,000 votes that he was re-elected. The paper thought it was his progressive stance, his help for the farmers and his appeal to capital and labour to understand each other that had saved him in the west. It was not exactly sure what it meant: "For once the voice of the American people has spoken with an uncertain sound."

It certainly felt then that so divided a country would not allow any change in foreign policy, "at least until a later phase of the war". But that was what the Germans were contriving themselves. The resumption of unlimited u-boat attacks on shipping showed the United States that the military, General Hindenburg and General Ludendorff, had eclipsed the civilian chancellor, Theobald von Bethmann-Hollweg. Germany was prepared to risk the United States entering the war because it believed it could win before the Americans could offer anything but a token military force. This was what Wilson had supposed even before the Germans made their decision known. By the end of December 1916 the paper reported: "He sees that the United States may be driven into the war by that aggravation of the German submarine war against neutral commerce with the Allied countries.... This warfare, he fears, will constrain America, as the most powerful neutral, to range herself with the Entente Powers."

HOW THE WAR WAS WON

*Wilson's true merit was to see that the
economy came first*

When war happened, and Wilson, the man who had kept the United States out of it, had to ask Congress to vote for war, the paper complimented him on his sense of economic realism. It would ensure that the power of the United States would be brought decisively into play: "We could wish that the British people, too, would in all these matters take President Wilson as their guide and philosopher, as well as their friend. The President sees naval and military needs clearly enough, but he sees also what many of our rulers have been slow in seeing, that pressing indus-

trial, agricultural, and economic problems must first be solved if naval and military forces are to have the opportunity of victory."

It became a theme: "The American people, the world's champion hustlers, have now a rare opportunity to display their skill in improvising effective means of meeting a great emergency."

In its own way, the paper chose to evoke an old British image of the United States rather than the Uncle Sam of recruiting posters: "When Cousin Jonathan gets to work he works quickly. He has entered the war reluctantly, but, like ourselves, he has always proved as slow to leave off as he is to begin."

It saw two plain priorities: to get American industry to build the shipping that would negate the U-boat

*The decisive factor in stopping the German offensives on the western front in 1918 was the number of trained
American divisions that could be transported across the Atlantic in time. Shipbuilding won the land war.*

successes, and to transport an American army across the Atlantic to make up for the Russian withdrawal from the war and allied weakness on the western front.

The wartime paper itself was now a shadow of what it had been. Paper and staff shortages curtailed its space for comment, although it tried to maintain its statistical series. It supported Wilson's efforts, though intermittently, calling the United States "the Power which must now be recognised as speaking with the weightiest voice in the councils of the Allies", which suited it whenever that power spoke up for free trade. It was awed by America's ability to raise capital for itself and for the allies, although it noted: "America entered the war in a peculiarly powerful financial position. In the first two years of war, America's foreign trade showed an export balance of nearly 3.5 billion dollars."

It reported the success of each Liberty Loan as it was launched. It approved of Wilson's legislation to raise taxes on war profits, incomes and luxuries. It was less sure about the administration's aims in taking over the railroads to end the congestion of war supplies. But it was to shipping that it regularly returned. In May 1917, immediately after America's entry, it regretted that British yards, building and repairing for the Royal Navy and depleted of labour and materials, could no longer contribute as before: "Three years ago the United States were of little account in the lists of the world's shipbuilding; now they have sprung into a position of such great importance that the issue of the war will be decided in the American shipyards. The United States, and the United States alone, are able to redress the balance borne down against the Allies by the German u-boat attacks upon the world's commerce."

A year later it applauded their success, although with a touch of national apprehension: "Under the strain of war the United States have applied themselves to building on a scale never imagined by them in times of peace, and while we rejoice in the assistance they are now giving to the Allied cause we must not forget that their activity in war may have altered permanently our relative commercial positions."

This shipbuilding success meant that trained troops, capable of holding the line against the German offensives, could be brought over in 1918. By July it had been done. It was a stunning American success, even though half the shipping had been British: "To have

sent across the ocean, since the crisis at the end of March, nearly 640,000 men with supplies and equipment is an achievement unrivalled in the history of war." By October 1.75m American troops had arrived.

The u-boats had tried to starve Britain out, and had come close to doing so. Now the food crisis was over, too, and a future president was making a further reputation for himself: "Mr Hoover, the United States Food Controller, was able to assure us in a speech at the Mansion House on Tuesday that 'all anxieties as to the great essentials of food are now passed (sic)'."

The paper gave credit where it was due: "For this state of affairs we have in no small measure to thank Mr Hoover's masterly organisation, and the reduced scale of consumption which he has persuaded the people of the United States so ungrudgingly to adopt."

The last German offensive on the Marne carried its initial objectives, but then came up against what seemed inexhaustible American divisions: "No one who knows anything of America and the Americans can ever have doubted that the troops of the United States would be first-class fighting material. The only doubt was whether they, and all that they needed in food and equipment, could be brought across the sea. This has been done with a speed and success that is almost incredible, and has baffled Germany's hopes of this year's campaign in France."

As the allied counter-attacks grew the paper reflected on how the Atlantic campaign had been won. It had been a close-run thing. Success was due to three factors: "First, to the offensive and defensive submarine tactics of the Royal Navy, tactics increasing daily in effectiveness. Secondly, to the entry of America and the seizure of German and Austrian shipping at the moment when every ton was urgently needed; thirdly, to the expansion in American shipbuilding. The corner has been turned. Ships available for the use of the allies are now being built more rapidly than they are being destroyed, but we ran our luck very fine indeed. The war was nearly lost in the empty British shipyards during 1915 and 1916."

The armistice duly came and Wilson's programme headed the agenda for peace: "The world can start afresh with the fourteen points as its Magna Charta." Wilson sailed for Europe, again breaking precedent, but it was by no means going to be simple.

HOW THE PEACE WAS LOST

A president out of touch with his politicians

The Economist had repeatedly voiced its hopes in Wilson as the peacemaker. It thought his aims noble, a cut above those of European politicians. For itself, it seemed to expect a free-traders' nirvana, with the president conducting affairs benignly in the interests of all. While the fighting was still at its height it sketched a world that would not have disgraced the dreams of Richard Cobden and John Bright: "President Wilson's peace promises us a world in which mankind may be united into one great throbbing hive of industry, in which the best workers will win battles by turning out the best stuff, and the world's output and consumption of goods may be quickened to an extent undreamt of."

Other people had other war aims. The paper was suspicious of both those who wanted a protectionist world to emerge and those who planned to make Germany pay an extortionate price, a pariah shunned by the successful allies. In August 1918 it hoped for the best: "Under the preaching of President Wilson the League of Nations is now the credo of most English politicians. Many of them are lip-servers, but some, and we hope a majority, are true believers."

Even so, a continued economic boycott of Germany was more than a possibility: "If trade with Germany is to be prohibited, or severely rationed, Germans will be cut off from the Allies' sources of materials and food, while the European neutrals and Russia who border on

The three western statesmen who dictated unworkable peace terms at Versailles: left to right, Clemenceau, Wilson, Lloyd George. The US rejection of the League of Nations was fatal.

Germany will be in scarcely a better plight than Germany herself. Suffering from common troubles they would naturally tend to make common cause."

And two weeks later: "How can we expect security for the future if one of the strongest nations of Europe is convinced by a policy of boycott that it is an outcast among the nations until it has reasserted its position by force?"

When the outlines of the peace treaties emerged in May 1919 it was cautious: "The terms may result in success or fiasco according to the wisdom or the lack of wisdom in those who have to interpret them in action."

By June 1919 the paper's early hopes were fading fast: "A quartette of distracted politicians, doing their manful best, have produced a peace which leaves everyone dissatisfied and bitter.... Peace has been made by folk suffering from the after-effects of war hysteria."

It trusted to Wilson to save the league from his political opponents; if he failed not only would the treaties need rewriting but all sense of finality would be lost. It was relieved that Wilson's navy secretary, Josephus Daniels, had set his face against another arms race: "It was feared in this country that America's Big Navy programme, by forcing the resumption of intense armament competition, would kill the League at its birth. But now ... that programme has been abandoned.... This pronouncement by Mr Daniels is the happiest augury for the League."

However, as Wilson fell deeper into the toils of Republican opposition to the league, and suffered a paralytic stroke in September, the paper grew despondent, writing of rulers who had "been so busy in manufacturing a quite unworkable Peace Treaty", and admitting it needed "a robust optimism" to get an America preoccupied with domestic affairs to look abroad. Wilson's 1919 message to Congress, apparently "written by another hand from notes dictated by the President", did hit back, but to doubtful effect. Wilson said no policy of isolation could meet America's needs; the country must emerge from what he called the "provincial standards" of the past. The paper, naturally, spoke up: "'Provincial' is exactly the word which suits the attitude of the extremer Republican opponents of the Treaty of Peace, and its use will hardly conciliate them. But they have destroyed their only possible reply to the President by hampering the International Labour Conference at Washington, which, by

imposing better labour conditions on all industrial countries, would have helped to keep out the products of the low-paid labour of Europe, and still more of Japan." By then it was plainly too late. There had always been a majority for the league in the Senate, but never the required two-thirds.

DEBTORS' WORLD
Post-war America insisted its allies paid up.
They did not. Internationalism was dead

The post-war issue that concerned the paper almost as much was the repayment of the debt the allies had gladly run up in the United States when they were desperately pressed to hold Germany. In December 1918 it suggested terms: "Since our financing of the Allies was essential to the victory of the cause of humanity, it is surely reasonable that America, having gained great financial strength by the war, should give us time in meeting our debt to her by converting her claims on us into a loan, repayable in 25 or 30 years, or earlier, in so far as repayments from our Allies and payment of damages by Germany enable us to redeem it."

The paper was generosity itself towards Britain's own allies: "It would be a graceful act on our part, in view of their much greater sufferings from the war, to wipe their debts off the slate. That they should be our debtors for generations, owing to a war in which they fought on our side, is not a pleasant prospect."

Its estimate of what the war had cost the United States was substantial. It put the total cost at $22 billion, of which $15 billion was spent on the United States's own account, and $7 billion on the allies'. The numbers were beyond anything that an exhausted Britain could hope to raise, and far beyond the resources of France, Belgium and Italy and of a defeated and occupied Germany. As 1919 struggled on there were no volunteers among the allies, but the paper returned to its view, although realistically extending the time Britain needed to find the money: "We believe that this country can afford to write off the sums which we lent to them during the war, that this long ago should have been done, and that the sooner it is done the better.... All that we should ask from America, in our view, is ... that our American loans should be funded into a debt maturing in some 40 or 50 years' time, and that during the next four or five years we should be given an option of funding the interest if we wish to do so."

The youthful John Maynard Keynes, in his classic and quotable work *Economic Consequences of the Peace*, suggested that all the inter-ally indebtedness should be mutually forgiven. The paper, calling his chapters "a source of infinite rage or delight", stuck to its own view: "We still prefer this solution to Mr Keynes's for we believe that we can afford it if we work and reduce extravagance, and it is in accordance with our proud financial traditions."

But saying that was easier than actually finding the money, and the United States insisted that the money should be found. This importunity aroused new anti-Americanism, but the paper appreciated America's problems: "Critics of America's attitude must bear in mind that the United States has a debt charge on nearly $50,000,000,000, a very faulty tax system that not only hampers initiative but actually prevents the accumulation of any lendable surplus, as well as a railroad situation that will require for adequate rehabilitation nearly as much as the cash indemnity demanded from Germany."

No one, indeed, could see where any real money was coming from, so by the spring of 1920 fertile imaginations were unleashed: "The rumours that part of the British debt to the United States was to be cancelled by the transfer of certain of the West Indies Colonies has been denied by the Prime Minister, nor was this ever considered seriously in the United States, aside from irresponsible suggestions of the Press."

The paper itself was entirely dismissive: "Though in 1803 the United States purchased Louisiana from France, they are not likely—even if we were willing to sell—to offer so enormous a price for so small a territory, with which they have all the opportunity of trading they desire, and which could never prove a serious threat to them in case of war."

Even those who persisted in the belief that a prostrate Germany could be forced to pay up, a view strongly held in Paris, were plainly losing the argument and their own touch with reality. Retrenchment and frugality were the watchwords everywhere. The New York correspondent reported the change in the political atmosphere: "Like Great Britain, the people of the United States are tired of useless expenditures, and a storm of protest has arisen from all over the country against the issue of bonds for soldiers' bonuses, and the

remonstrances have come largely from the doughboys themselves. Every measure that comes before Congress bearing the earmarks of fresh inflation meets with the sternest resistance, and the incessant cry is to cut waste and extravagance and get back to sane living."

It seemed clear that the new mood was carrying the Republicans remorselessly back to power. The United States wanted out: it sought a return to old values and old ways, to times before the war and the draft, before foreign complications and wrangling. In this America Wilson represented only discord and uncertainty. He and his proxy, James Cox, governor of Ohio, faced overwhelming defeat.

When the end came it was a debacle. The Republican candidate, Warren Harding, took 60.3% of the vote, Cox only 34.17%. Harding won 16m of the votes, Cox only 9m. *The Economist* was impressed: "We must go back to the War of Secession and to the reconstruction period that followed it to find a more complete defeat of a Democratic candidate for the Presidency than that suffered by Governor Cox."

The real scapegoat, of course, was Wilson. He had declared that since the league had been defeated in the Senate the presidential election would be a great referendum on it. He had thought long and hopefully about running himself, despite his illness. His last secretary of state, Bainbridge Colby, even tried to get the party convention to nominate him by acclamation. It was no good. The league was far from being unpopular, especially in the south, although it was anathema to German-Americans (being a creation of the allies), the irreconcilable Irish and the isolationist progressives. What mattered was that the league was low in American popular priorities. When Harding declared that what the country wanted was normalcy not nostrums he was preaching to the converted.

Whatever the paper's admiration for Wilson in the past, it no longer showed: "The defeat is due mainly to the discomforts set up by the after-effects of the war and to resentment at President Wilson's policy and attitude. No President since Lincoln at the outset of his career, or Johnson just before his impeachment, has been so passionately hated or had such powerful opponents—at first because he maintained neutrality, then because he departed from Constitutional usage and seemed to claim autocratic power."

Not that the paper had any particular hopes of Harding: "The result is a President-Elect who has given no signs of rising above mediocrity, and whose political creed has shown itself elastic." This was very much what it did not want. It needed a president with some experience of the world, who understood Europe's economic weakness, who could grasp what the debt issue entailed, and who knew the limitations of protectionism as a policy. It recognised at once the new man's own limitations: "At present he stands for obedience to 'big business', for higher Protection, with discrimination against foreign shipping in United States ports and in the Panama Canal—even at the cost of a breach of Treaty obligations, as interpreted by the British Foreign Office; for something more than hegemony in Mexico and Central America, and for avoidance, as far as possible, of participation in the affairs of the struggling Old World."

Harding, the personification of small town America, was not likely to aim any higher than that. He was an American nationalist. His creed was clear: "to think of America first, to exalt America first". In the political language of the times he was written down as an isolationist. The paper was disdainful of the divisions, and so of the inertia, within the party that had brought him to the White House: "A few Republicans even support the League of Nations; many more, with many highly-educated mugwumps, chiefly women voters, have had to be conciliated by Mr Harding's declaration in favour of a combination of 'all that is good' in the League and in the Hague Tribunal; others, in the Far West chiefly, follow Senators Borah and Johnson in condemning in advance any participation at all in European complications."

Even so, it would not write United States internationalism off. The memories of the war were still too distinct, the unrivalled power of the United States was too self-evident, and the basic nature of American society too enlightened for that: "We may be confident that the American people, which, during the past six years, has kept a large part of the population of Europe alive and has rendered splendid service to the defenders of popular liberties, will not be found wanting at any great crisis in the future remaking of a distracted Old World."

When Wilson died in February 1924, six months after Harding, the paper still saw him as two men. This may have been reinforced, in part, by the arrival of Walter Layton as editor in 1922. Layton had been at Versailles; he had been a league man. The paper recognised Wilson's gifts; it did not try to conceal its disappointment in him: "Mr Wilson stirred to their depths the great elemental feelings of war-stressed human hearts; first, hope, faith, conscience, belief in the triumph of justice and the establishment of righteous peace—and then the bitterness of catastrophic disappointment."

It relived his glories: "It was he who with classic phrase, backed by the authority of recent re-election as the mouthpiece of America, lifted the struggle on to a higher plane, and defined in terms that appealed to the conscience of the world the peace for which America and the Allies were fighting."

But at Versailles the statesman had shrunk into himself, the theologian whom Keynes had called the "blind and deaf prophet": "As the conference wore on, he became more unapproachable, more autocratic, more unable to distinguish between his policy and his personal feelings—in short, more inhuman and therefore more incapable of dealing with his fellow-men."

AFTER THE FIGHTING: FIGHTING
Blacks, strikers, radicals, all felt the sting of peace

In the war's aftermath violence asserted itself in American life. Southern blacks who had moved north, and had seen army service, faced intimidation and even lynching. Radicals, reds and even inoffensive foreigners found the weight of the law and political judges against them. This was so, as often in the past, with the more aggressive unions in the labour movement. Strikes became endemic in 1919. Soldiers returned from the war to swell the labour market; there was the threat of cheap wages and cheap output abroad; wartime contracts that had fuelled the industrial boom were cancelled abruptly. By November a big steel strike had reached its seventh week; New York had a port workers' and a ferry strike; three-quarters of the bituminous coal miners were out in 15 states; a railroad strike was threatened in Chicago. Unions and employers met head-on over union recognition itself: "The Industrial Conference called by President Wilson, and representing employers, employed, and the general public, broke up a fortnight ago through the refusal of the employers, more especially Judge Gary, the head of the United States Steel Corporation, to recognise 'collective bargaining' participated in by the officials of the unions who are not the corporation's employees."

Judge Elbert Gary was not a man to be trifled with. When the workers, many of whom worked 12 hours a day, demanded an eight-hour day, he refused to talk to them, and branded them as communist agitators. The paper was surprised: "'Collective bargaining' is apparently repudiated by Judge Gary because the unions' leaders are extremists, and as being the first step to the 'closed shop' or exclusion of non-unionist labour, a thoroughly un-American institution."

It pointed out that the federal government had "weapons against strikers unknown in Europe". These included the constitutional obligation to secure interstate commerce, constitutional guarantees of individual liberty and property, and injunctions for contempt of court which were enforced by indefinite terms of imprisonment. Still, the unions were growing, helped by wartime prosperity. The American Federation of Labour had a paid-up membership of 2,725,000; the United Mineworkers had gained 367,000. Against these realities, it thought, "an attack on collective bargaining is an absurdity".

Tempers were high. The feeling that the law was on the capitalists' side embittered the workers. But the rest of the population, including business and the farmers, resented all labour movements and feared foreign workers. In iron and steel 58% of the labour force was foreign-born; in iron ore mining, 53%; in bituminous coal mining, 62%. Most of them spoke little or no English and were thought of as wild beasts who constantly threatened to break loose. It was a crisis in which the earlier Wilson would have used his interventionist

powers to get a settlement: "The situation demands conciliation as well as firmness.... President Wilson's ability to intervene is weakened by his illness." The strikes were broken.

Out west, more radical workers in the International Workers of the World—reds and American Soviets, as plain people talked of them—started spasmodic strikes on the Californian coast and at some mining camps. The paper reported that secret service agents deported 600 agitators and burned 20,000 tons of literature. The local citizenry "in at least three instances left swinging on the telegraph poles of public squares a ghastly warning to the alien element whose avowed effort it is to overthrow municipal and State government in these United States". Such was the New York correspondent's belief.

In London the editorial line demanded more of the hapless Wilson's efforts: "President Wilson, indeed, hardly goes deep enough; he does not demand recognition of the unions, and implicitly he endorses government by injunction, which is only justifiable in very acute emergencies, if at all."

The president was not altogether wrong: "He again urges the institution of a Budget—a reform long overdue. The fact that the United States has gone on hitherto without enabling Congress or the public to take a general view of its financial needs and their satisfaction is only explicable by local and historical reasons."

To European eyes there could be only one conclusion: "The controversy between capitalists and labourers is far less advanced in America." For a decade the influence and strength of the unions was to deteriorate markedly.

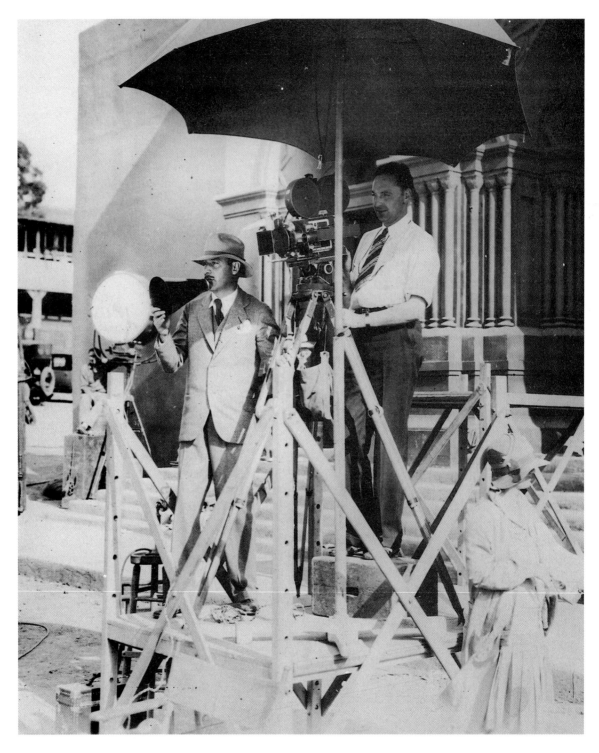

The age of the talkies. Warner Bros, frozen out of silent cinema circuits, produced synchronised sound on film to outwit their rivals. The Jazz Singer, starring Al Jolson, opened a new age.

6

THE TWENTIES: FALSE SECURITY

1921–1931

THE PROSPEROUS YEARS

When most Americans thought they had
poverty licked

The Republican 1920s, which Warren Harding summoned back to what he called normalcy, troubled *The Economist*. It was ready to applaud the country's productive capacity and the evident signs of prosperity, but it was apprehensive. It distrusted any system built on ever-increasing protection; it saw much of the wealth confined to a small class and not shared by farmers and most industrial workers; and it was apprehensive that the confidence on which the market depended was always vulnerable. Corporatist America had isolated itself from the world. It was impatient with the social ideas that permeated post-war Europe, ideas which, it thought, handicapped Europe's own industrial recovery.

At the height of normalcy's success, the Coolidge election triumph in 1924, the paper revealed its foreboding: "The returns mean that the average American elector has not yet begun to feel the pinch of the shoe, or at any rate not to realise which shoe it is that pinches. He still prefers the opportunities of his traditional system to the untried paths of social and constitutional change.... Still there seems enough prosperity to go round if the little fish are only left alone to browse quietly by the side of the great sharks and whales. Oil-wells still seem bottomless, the Pacific an impassable gulf, the American constitution sacred, American liberty impregnable."

There was envy in that. Europe, and Britain itself, had not had a successful return to peacetime and its irksome demands. The United States had turned its back on everyone, and flourished like the green bay tree. It was difficult to believe, but it worked: "Nowadays, so widely diffused is prosperity and comfort in the United States, and so conservative in their political

---

CHRONOLOGY

1921	Warren G. Harding becomes president
	Britain agrees to an Irish Free State
1922	US, Britain, Japan sign Washington treaty limiting naval armaments
	Benito Mussolini in power in Italy
	Turkey expels Greece from Asia Minor
1923	Calvin Coolidge becomes president
	Agreement on British war debt in Washington
	French army occupies the Ruhr
	Teapot Dome oil scandal
	Adolf Hitler attempts putsch in Bavaria
1924	Death of V.I. Lenin in Soviet Union
	John Logie Baird transmits first televised pictorial image
1925	John T. Scopes tried in Tennessee for teaching evolution
	Locarno non-aggression treaty signed by France and Germany
1926	General strike in Britain
1927	Charles Lindbergh flies the Atlantic
	First film with sound track
1928	Leon Trotsky and supporters exiled from Moscow
1929	Herbert Hoover becomes president
	Kellogg-Briand peace pact ratified by US
	Wall Street crash
1931	Collapse of Credit Anstalt, Vienna, starts German and European economic crisis
	Japan seizes Manchuria

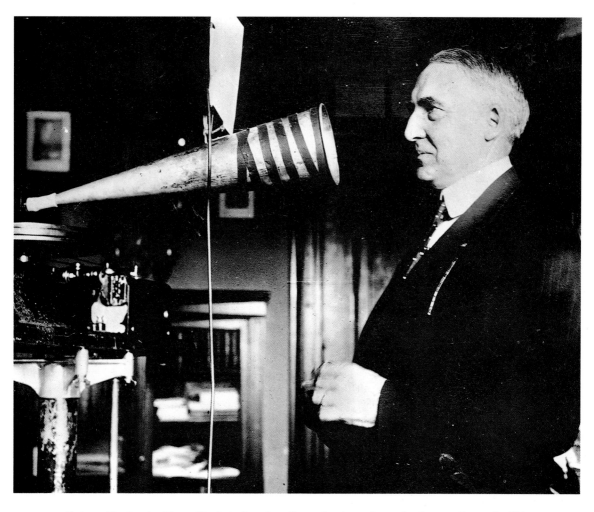

Their president's voice. Warren Harding, champion of normalcy, learned to make phonograph records of his speeches. His cabinet was tarnished by scandal, only revealed after his death.

opinions have even the working-classes become, that any kind of radical crusade directed against the plutocracy would meet with a chill response."

Even the losers, or enough of them, went along with this sort of philosophy. Farmers caught in a decade of falling income, miners and steelworkers, workers in the textile plants of New England, still believed that their turn would come, as individuals if not as a class: "Among all classes the idea is now firmly rooted that if the great corporations and their controllers are faring well, the rest of the country will somehow or other share in their prosperity, and that any legislation calculated to hamper their activities must in the long run be to the general detriment."

The national debt was diminishing, new capital was raised readily, taxes were being cut by the treasury secretary, Andrew Mellon, and even supertax had been halved from 40% to 20%. The boosters were winning: "From Cape Cod to San Diego the gospel is being daily preached in hundreds of chambers of commerce, Rotary, and Kiwanis clubs that the best interests of the nation will be served by frowning upon any legislation which will disturb the plans of the business world."

The achievements were considerable. Ownership, production systems and sales techniques in the automobile industry were drastically reorganised. When the

Du Pont-Morgan interests took over 51% of General Motors (Buick, Cadillac, Chevrolet, Oakland, Oldsmobile and Scripps-Booth models) in 1920, the paper's New York correspondent saw it "as a move to place the General Motors Corporation in the same position with respect to the automobile industry that the United States Steel Corporation occupies in the steel industry". Of a total world demand for petroleum of 700m barrels, 565m were for the United States. Annual car production rose to 3m in 1923: "It is predicted that the day is not far off when every American family will own a car."

In 1926 the United States had over three times as many motor vehicles on the roads as the rest of the world put together. The Ford Company personified American success: "In 1908-9 the world's largest producer, Mr Henry Ford, turned out 10,660 cars at an average price of $950; in 1924 his production ... was 1,993,419 at a price of $290."

Instalment buying had taken off. The paper reported that 75% of new cars were sold in this way in the United States (60% in Britain). But it did not believe that prosperity must be never-ending: "Trade does ebb and flow. From the beginning of time it has ebbed and flowed, and there seems to be no reason to believe that the Almighty has by dispensation set the United States free of the ordinary laws of action and reaction."

Still, as the years passed and car ownership rose to the dizzy height of one American in six (one in 100 in Britain), the paper's scepticism seemed foolish. The banking system had been reformed and the Federal Reserve kept a controlling hand; trade and credit would not be allowed to run away. The United States was an educated country, with booming colleges as well as movie houses. It was a new, exciting world in which habits, tastes and styles were changing. The story of wool textiles epitomised the trend in 1926: "The increasing use of central heating plants in offices and private residences tended to diminish the use of heavy woollen clothing as being too uncomfortable."

Only the very rich persisted with imported woollens. "American people began to spend less money on clothes and more on motors, radio sets and other luxuries. There was a time when the social status of an individual was rated by the quality of his clothes, but nowadays in the United States it is determined by the quality of his motor-car, and many men and women are content to wear old clothes as long as they will hold together, provided they can get an up-to-date motor-car every second year."

As the soon-to-be president, Herbert Hoover, began announcing, Americans were nearer to the final triumph over poverty than ever before in history.

DISARMERS' DREAMS
Sinking navies was worthy, but American and British admirals kept on quarrelling

Disarmament, and the many hopes, promises and schemes to secure it, was much in politicians' minds and on their tongues in the inter-war years, from Versailles onwards. The victorious powers were committed to it, and their electorates expected it; the defeated Germans had it enforced on them for a decade. But it was an uneasy world. The ambitions of Bolshevik Russia were feared. So were those of the even more expansionist Japanese. The newly established nationalisms of eastern Europe lived uncomfortably with their treaties and alliances. Most fearful of all were the French, conscious of their insecurity even when parading their military prowess. The one sphere where progress was possible was with the navies; there the Americans and the British, while their admirals still distrusted each other, were sufficiently dominant against everyone but the Japanese to draw up the agenda and to propose terms.

The Economist supported these worthy efforts, both for their own sake and as a means, like the Hague Court, of maintaining America's interest in substantive diplomacy without being a member of the League of Nations. To their credit Harding and his secretary of state, Charles Evans Hughes, saw it fitted their ends, and they invited the naval powers to a conference in Washington. To the paper it promised a relief from the innumerable conflicts of the Europeans, and did not seem too great a task for reasonable diplomacy to achieve: "Upon the sea there are now three Powers, and three Powers only, which are of any serious account: Great Britain, the United States and Japan. If these three Powers can bring their several interests to the test of calm discussion, and decide jointly upon a policy which will maintain peaceful relations among themselves, they can dictate sea peace to the world."

It believed two concessions were needed from Britain. First to go should be its pretension to rule the waves: "We in Great Britain must reconcile ourselves to the abandonment of the Two-Power standard. If the United States—now the richest and potentially the strongest country in the world—are determined to possess a navy at least as strong as ours, nothing that we can do will prevent them. If we are so foolish as to enter into naval rivalry with America, we shall most certainly be outbuilt."

Second should be the termination of the Anglo-Japanese alliance. This had suited Britain in blocking Russia in the Far East before the war, but it was now deeply disliked by the Americans: "The ambitions of Japan in the Far East have aroused the strong opposition of America.… If it be made plain that Great Britain will not support Japan against America, then it will be to the obvious interest of Japan to come to terms with America."

The paper sketched, with foresight, a Pacific scenario. Japan was intent on building an island network of cable and refuelling bases which could lead to "a very big war": "It could not for long maintain a war of blockade and attrition against America. The United States, whatever might be their early reverses, would and could build three ships to one against all the efforts of Japan." In addition, Britain was under pressure from the Canadians: "Most intelligent Canadians are keenly aware of the susceptibilities of their neighbours in respect to Japan, and are afraid that the renewal of the alliance may be looked at in a critical light by the people of the United States."

By July 1921 the American connection mattered most to London, and "the re-entrance of the United States into the arena of world politics provides the brightest hope that reason is once more dawning in international affairs". When in November the Americans came up with modest first proposals (Britain to have 22 capital ships, the United States 18 and Japan 10), the paper welcomed them "with profound relief and thankfulness". The moral it drew was its accustomed one: "There is no reason why we ever should fight America, and in making up our minds to that attitude, sentiment and common sense should be decisively reinforced by contemplation of America's undoubted ability to outstrip us if necessary in the ruinous race of armament construction."

Britain was on the way to accepting parity. It did not have the resources to do anything else. It accepted a final battleship ratio of 5:5:3; the Japanese were dis-

appointed.

The four Pacific powers, the United States, Britain, France and Japan, signed their pact in Washington in December, agreeing to respect each other's "insular possessions". On its ratification the Anglo-Japanese alliance was to cease. The paper was apprehensive about what it called the Japanese "militarist prophets of expansion", and it trusted to the pact to contain them: "The best proof that she repudiates their policy is her acceptance of the substitution of three Powers for one in a pact blocking a policy of expansion." It had few regrets about the alliance's end: "The alliance has been beneficial in some respects, but of late it has been a cause of friction, owing to the interpretation placed upon it in America and elsewhere."

The Australians had become increasingly worried. The paper reported the conviction that the Japanese were bent on controlling China, using the Philippines and other islands as stepping stones, and eventually flooding America and Australia with immigrants. The inclination of the age was to rely on diplomacy to defuse such nightmares. In the early 1920s it was not yet a delusion. But the paper was concerned that deep-seated issues remained, and the proposed treatment was superficial: "We venture to doubt … whether the great prestige of the Washington Conference will be enhanced by a paper agreement to abolish poison gas and to forbid the sinking of merchantmen by submarine. Indeed, a solemn declaration by America, Great Britain, and France of these principles without the assent of Germany invites the derision of the scoffer, who recollects the pious resolutions laid down before the war by the Hague Conferences."

The American absence from the league was a serious worry by 1924. The permanent French sense of insecurity prompted increasing demands on Britain. All league members were asked to sever commercial and financial relations with, and put an economic blockade on, any member state resorting to war. This, the paper insisted, could mean the Royal Navy going to war against the United States: "In the case of a war between two members of the League, one of whom has been named as the aggressor, we and the other members would be bound to do our best to prevent America from trading with the aggressor nation." If the navy dealt with neutral shipping as it did in 1914–18 "the United States would resist such interference with her commerce by every means in her power".

Silent Cal. Calvin Coolidge, renowned for his sparse conversation, throws out the first ball in a World Series baseball game. His presidency favoured thrift and a big navy.

Equally, there was the prospect of the United States in conflict with Japan in the Pacific, possibly over immigration pressure on what were still called the "white men's countries": "If America declared war, let us say, on Japan, having refused to submit the dispute to the League, we should be bound to co-operate at least in the institution of an economic boycott of America."

British public opinion, the paper said, would not agree to anything of that kind. It was relieved in 1925 when a returning Conservative government dropped what Ramsay MacDonald had been considering. But Anglo-American relations reached their nadir in the 1920s. Psychologically, it was the last decade when, the

paper thought, the two powers might have fallen into war. Britain was still powerful enough to defend itself at sea, and the United States navy ambitious and confident enough to take it on.

Despite the Washington treaty the Americans and British still disagreed vehemently over cruisers. The British wanted more 6-inch-gun light cruisers for commerce protection; the Americans wanted 8-inch-gun heavy cruisers of 10,000 tons to watch the Japanese who, in public, were intent on being reasonable. Anglo-American rivalry broke up the Geneva conference in 1927: "America openly misunderstands and disapproves our demand for more ships than we have today. We fail to understand and completely disapprove America's zeal for 10,000-ton cruisers and 8-in guns."

The paper did not mind what the United States did: "We have no reason to deny her. A co-equal navy will only in the long run thrust upon her joint trusteeship for commercial freedom—and, indeed, for civilisation—in many parts of the world." It was chiefly worried that the Japanese would follow the Americans. Nevertheless it was dismayed that the American and British admirals and naval staffs persisted in preparing for hostilities against each other. War was still possible: "It has certainly not been outlawed in the minds of the admirals of the two countries; and we say, frankly, that the time has come when statesmen should step in."

They did not. Instead, the British and French reached a private agreement. This was known as the Anglo-French compromise, which slowly unravelled, in which the British agreed to exclude French trained military reserves from land disarmament and the French allowed the British to build as many cruisers as they wanted while still wishing to restrict American heavy cruisers. The paper was aghast: "It should have been clear to the dullest mind that the United States would have nothing to do with the proposed pact."

In Washington, and especially in Calvin Coolidge's White House, this looked like a challenge. "Big Navy" legislation was promised. The paper thought it high time to put a stop to these dangerous misunderstandings. It might be done "if that personal intercourse which exists at Geneva between European statesmen could be established between those who guide the destinies of Britain and America". It was an idea just ahead of its time.

By the end of 1928 the paper feared that the American admirals, their political backers and the shipbuilding lobbyists would get the naval race they wanted. It was "the principal task of British statesmanship" to save the friendship between the British Empire and the United States: "That friendship cannot be taken for granted. It is not rooted in tradition. It is a recent and still precarious growth."

The American people, unused to foreign policy, would treat the British reaction as the acid test of their reception in a strange world into which they were being drawn out of their cherished isolation. If history repeated itself there would be a reversal of alliances: "The Powers which were jointly victorious in the war

of 1914–18 would proceed in due course to range themselves into two camps in order to become the protagonists in the war which the year 1945 or the year 1950 was to bring forth."

Should the United States and Britain fall out, Britain "in an age of aeroplanes" would become just another continental power grouped with France to offset "an Italo-German group". The job of arbiter would pass to the Americans, who might "drift through another world war into temporary 'world dominion' ". For an isolationist America this fate "would be as ironical as ours would be tragic". What had to be faced was the possibility that the United States could wish to wrest sea power from Britain by force: "That is what we did, in our day, to our predecessors, and that is what the United States will seek inevitably to do to us if, when her day arrives, the prize still exists to be fought for."

The paper accepted the inevitability of American economic power. The United States was bound to play in this century the part in the world economy that Britain had played in the last: "She will do it on a scale which will put our economic achievements into the shade. We have to adjust ourselves to this, and that is not easy; but it is certainly not impossible; while on the other hand, a refusal on our part to make the possible and necessary adjustment would court political and economic disaster." It was not hopeful: "This is the America with which His Majesty's present Government in Great Britain are confronted. They have not yet shown that they understand it."

There was even a plausible issue. In March 1929 the Americans were insisting on Britain recognising their full neutral rights under the law of the sea, while Britain was still asserting a belligerent's right to blockade an enemy. The isolationist Senator William E. Borah, who had helped to keep America out of the league, declared that unless the United States was promised the "freedom of the seas" competitive building against Britain was inevitable. It seemed a threat to end Britannia's rule in the clamour of the shipyards.

The public policy of the United States was artlessly pacific. Coolidge and his secretary of state, Frank B. Kellogg, had grown enamoured of the idea of a multilateral treaty among all the powers renouncing the very idea of war. Eventually 62 countries repudiated war as an instrument of national policy, Britain going along with it chiefly to placate the Americans. The paper was

Herbert Hoover delivers his inaugural address, 1929. He claimed Americans were closer than ever to the defeat of poverty, but his term ended in the disillusionment of the Wall Street crash.

dubious about the historic moment: "We cannot yet tell which kind of landmark it will be: a monument of a great and difficult objective achieved or a monument of one of those good resolutions which proverbially pave the road to hell."

Three things in the end stopped the Anglo-American naval competition. The first was public feeling. In America it forced the House committee for naval affairs to cut the Coolidge naval bill from 71 new ships to 16: "Since the failure of the Naval Conference of 1927, the American people has shown its determination that the failure shall be retrieved by rejecting the original 'Big Navy' Bill.... Meanwhile, the British people have shown the same determination by rejecting the so-called Anglo-French naval compromise."

The second factor was the improbable alliance of the new president, Herbert Hoover, and the British

prime minister, Ramsay MacDonald, who took their experts in hand and met, in the first Anglo-American summit, at Hoover's fishing camp on the headwaters of the Rapidan in Virginia in October 1929. The paper was pleased but decried the thought of an Anglo-Saxon "conspiracy", a "domination in international affairs" at Europe's expense: "There are two shores to the Atlantic, and one of these is the Continent of Europe.... A conception of international relations which sought to sever this country from the body of Europe would do violence to the national structure of the whole group of peoples on this side of the Atlantic."

Third there was the slump. In the same month that Hoover and MacDonald met the Wall Street crash started. The Anglo-Saxons soon had no money for naval construction; others did. When Hoover and MacDonald summoned a naval conference to London the following January the Americans and British settled their differences over cruisers, but the final terms included an escalator clause which allowed powers to break any naval limits if they felt threatened. The Japanese promptly did so when their militarists overthrew Baron Shidehara and the moderates who had signed the treaty and began a building race that made Japan the dominant eastern Pacific power. And in Europe a new name was in the headlines: "A witness at the treason trial at Leipzig, Herr Hitler, was announcing that his party, the National Socialists, who have just gained a sensational success in the German general election, would not recognise existing treaties and would evade or violate them by every means in their power. Many millions of people in Germany today are giving ear to Herr Hitler's threats."

The paper predicted the worst in the next decade of depression, fascism and rearmament: "Europe will again be divided into two rival armed camps, as she was during the twenty years that ended in 1914. We know the sequel."

It would be 11 years before the United States experienced it.

CONFRONTATION WITH JAPAN
But no one was ready to stop aggression across the Pacific

The Economist was regularly scathing about American efforts to supervise the American empire and spheres of interest. It saw that the horror of foreign political entanglements which stopped the United States joining the League of Nations was limited only to Europe. There were no qualms about behaving like a great power in the Far East: "She has annexed the Philippines; she has interested herself in China much as nineteenth century England used to interest herself in Turkey; and her attitude to Japan may be likened to the attitude of nineteenth century England to Russia."

The paper called this the "neo-imperialism of Washington" and it felt Washington had an advantage in that, although the newspapers played up trouble in Mexico and Nicaragua, the American public refused to take Central America seriously. It was a serious game: "The Americans intend to have peace in Central America for the sake of the canal. They also intend to develop the region without restriction. Both intentions

are served by the mysterious chessboard diplomacy which Washington has perfected, whose pieces are marines, elections, constitutions, the sale of arms, and treaties."

Coolidge had a masterful way with him. When the Philippine legislature passed an act for a plebiscite on independence he vetoed it. The paper was not impressed: "'All men are created free and equal', wrote the framers of the American Declaration of Independence. But if you happen to be born in the Pacific islands Mr Coolidge and the might of the wealthiest nation in the world will be graciously pleased to rescue you from so deplorable a condition.... In vetoing the Act the President points out that they have grown prosperous in the enjoyment of the great market of the United States from which independence would shut them out.... Clearly the American Government has no intention of shirking its disagreeable responsibilities in the Orient."

It was the arrival of Henry L. Stimson at the State Department in 1929 that perked up the paper's interest in, and respect for, American diplomacy. Stimson resolved to pull the marines out of Nicaragua by June 1931 after a peaceful election under American auspices: "In the half sordid, half pathetic annals of the relations between the weak and the strong, this is a welcome chapter."

Renewed banditry in Nicaragua and a revolution in Honduras did not dissuade Stimson from ending armed protection for American citizens in any or every emergency. Those who felt endangered were advised to get out: "In Nicaragua, within these last few days, several United States citizens are reported to have lost their lives. Mr Stimson's attitude in the face of difficulty is likely to make a deep impression, favourable to the United States, upon Latin-American public opinion."

As the year advanced Japanese aggression in China was the inescapable test for Stimson, and his opportunity. He promised support for the council of the league in trying to get a Manchurian settlement. The paper was enthusiastic; the United States was back on the world stage: "This is an event of first-class importance, for it has removed, at a stroke, in this Manchurian crisis, one complication—the uncertainty about American intentions—which has always been reckoned among the League's major unsolved problems hitherto. In taking this line, the Administration at Washington can count upon carrying American public opinion with them; for the traditional American horror of foreign entanglements is limited, like the similar British feeling, to the European continent."

Even though Stimson took the view that no territorial conquests should be recognised, the league proved powerless. By February 1932 the Japanese were at Shanghai. The paper declared that further inaction must send international relations to the abyss: "It means the death-knell of disarmament, and that means that all the nations will re-arm to the teeth and run to cover in military and naval alliances."

In particular, it foresaw the Commonwealth countries in the Pacific seeking cover "with their big brother, the United States". Stimson told the Japanese they must observe the treaties they had set their hands to, but the British hesitated; they said they saw no ground for action. The paper was annoyed: "This comes perilously near to British collusion with Japanese policy in Manchuria."

It repeated that the league assembly should back Stimson whatever the British government did. He went to Geneva to see the prime ministers of Britain, France and Germany, but Europe had its own worries. Stimson's efforts fell on deaf ears: "If Mr Stimson's speech means anything, it means that America is prepared to insist on the League's verdict on the Manchurian question being carried out, cost what it may. If we are not prepared to stand side by side with the United States in the leadership of world opinion and the mobilisation of world pressure in this test issue, we had better say so now."

No one was prepared to take the lead. The Japanese had picked their time; America was in the grip of the depression. Hoover and Stimson were soon to be out of office. The Pacific war was postponed for a decade.

WON'T PAY, CAN'T PAY

How American protection encouraged impoverished Europeans to forget their American debts

Europe's war debts were the bane of post-war diplomacy. Nothing aroused greater animosity among Americans than the Europeans' refusal to pay what they owed, or among Europeans than the Americans' refusal to lower their tariffs so that the Europeans could pay from their exports to the United States.

The Economist believed Britain could and should pay, although it doubted if Belgium, France and Italy, over whose territory the war had actually been fought, could afford to. It felt that the United States, after five years of war-induced prosperity, should recognise the difficulties: "For this enviable state of affairs our American cousins have in great measure to thank the quarrels and follies of this mouldy old hemisphere. They have lent it billions of dollars, but they will never get them back unless they help it on its legs again and take its goods and services in payment."

Its estimate was that Britain owed the United States government $4 billion. Britain, in turn, was owed $1.6 billion by the other allies, although as $568m was owed by Russia no one needed to have any expectation that it would be repaid. British opinion felt increasingly that it should only return to the Americans a sum net of what Britain was owed, but the paper did not agree: "This is not the way in which 'the word of an Englishman' has been made proverbial throughout the world as an expression of scrupulous honesty, and is the best asset that we own. America lent money to us, and we have to pay it.... Weakened as we are by the war, we are not weakened to that point or anywhere near it."

The United States would have nothing to do with the idea anyway, and the paper spelled out why: "The difference between the value of the promises to pay of our impoverished European Allies and those of Great Britain is very great, as any stockbroker's office boy could have told the Chancellor of the Exchequer. It was because of this difference that America insisted that, instead of her lending direct to them, we should borrow from her and lend it to the Allies."

Germany would not have been beaten in any other way. It had been the sensible thing to do: "We took this heavy burden upon us because we wanted to win the war, just as we have often enough in our history spent our money in inducing Europe to save its liberties and ours."

So it supported, even if the British cabinet had doubts, Stanley Baldwin's acceptance of the American terms in 1923: "It may seem a paradox that a decision binding Great Britain for 62 years to pay something over £32 millions a year should be so received, but the fact is that the American offer is an appreciable reduction in what the United States Government is entitled to ask us to pay."

The paper reckoned that the war had cost Britain more than any other country; it put the ratio of the cost to pre-war wealth (at 1913 prices) to be: France 21.5%, Italy 15.7%, Russia 13.2%, the United States 7.5%. Britain came out at 28.4%; defeated Germany at just 23.9%. But it counted on the debt settlement to remove the last obstacle to Anglo-American co-operation. America had washed its hands of Europe, and Britain envied it its isolation. This was the natural alignment: to keep the Americans interested, even if the interest rate Britain paid was higher than the American ambassador had led it to believe: "The task is within our power to perform; the promise to do so is a much-needed example to the world of the restoration of the sanctity of contract; and most of all, the removal of this source of misunderstanding and bickering from the realms of controversy has smoothed the path to an Anglo-American friendship and co-operation which becomes the more precious and the more vital the darker the European sky appears."

Whatever the European efforts and intentions, by 1931 the depression had made of them what the sceptics had suspected. What the paper called "the stately comedy of the War Debts" was drawing to a close with acrimony. Europe knew it had no chance of paying, of making good the commitments it had entered on in more hopeful times. The Americans, hard-pressed themselves, would not give up their title.

In June 1934 payment was suspended. Rancour remained. It was one of the lowest points in the relationship. It was hard even to be philosophical: "If the unhappy history of the War Debts has convinced the world that financial transfers are not possible without commercial intercourse, that an insane world cannot be expected to pay the debts it contracted in more rational times, the ink and the labour that have been expended on it will not have been entirely wasted."

THE CRASH THEY COULD NOT HANDLE
Why Wall Street kept falling and falling

When the crash began on Wall Street in October 1929 *The Economist*, like other analysts, initially underrated it. It saw the seriousness of the selling frenzy on October 24th, but thought it at first no more than a correction, which it welcomed, of the market's ebullience since Hoover's election. This was in keeping with the disbelief in the administration and among market apologists that the world could be so crudely turned upside down. In its issue of November 2nd the paper supposed that the chilliness of the coming Christmas would chiefly be felt among the investing class. Only the lucky ones had cashed in: "Now that losses, even if they may be only 'paper' losses, have to be met, there is many a family in the United States this autumn who will have to curtail expenditure, defer the construction of a projected new house, postpone the purchase of a car, a radio set or gramophone, give up the projected European holiday trip, and generally forgo some part of wonted consumption."

That was not quite the sacrifice that faced the industrial workers or the farmers, but the philosophy of the time still excluded the concept of a crash like those of 1873 or 1893 or even a minor one like 1921. The paper was worried about the consequences of purchasing on the instalment system: "If Wall Street losses cause many families to fail to meet their instalments, it remains to be seen how far the big commercial and credit system instituted to finance instalments will be able to meet the shock."

That was in keeping with its long-held doubts. There was another immediate worry even closer to home. Although the American economy had distanced itself from much of the rest of the world, British and Empire interests still depended on trade connections with the United States: "If the slump forces American cotton or grain to be thrown on the market, the Lancashire cotton spinner and the British farmer will be among the first to suffer. And though it is still too early to forecast confidently the course of events, there is reason to fear that a slackening of consumption in the United States may have repercussions on the demand for and the price of many important commodities, such as rubber, copper, tin and steel, whose effects on the world's markets may be far-reaching."

Still, with those qualifications, it preferred to look on the brighter side: "There is warrant for hoping that the deflation of the exaggerated balloon of American stock values will ultimately be for the good of the world. The material prosperity of the United States is too firmly based, in our opinion, for a revival in industrial activity—even if we have to face an immediate recession of some magnitude—to be long delayed."

The paper's New York correspondent, reflecting the

majority view in the market, tried to put the late October delirium into context: "What we have had up to now is a six weeks' recession, during which the Dow-Jones average of industrial share prices declined 15 per cent, and the corresponding average for rails declined 9 per cent. The decline has been orderly, with heavy selling rarely lasting for more than an hour or two."

He admitted that the selling had become heavier than hitherto, but it fell short of falls in previous years. He still thought it an orderly market. For much of the previous year he had not succumbed to the concept of an all-conquering optimism that would dispel doubt and hesitation. He thought the confidence was getting untrustworthy and the regulators at the Federal Reserve had failed to act. He had warned in February: "It is apparent that the Federal Reserve Board has once more failed to stem the flow of money into the stock market with half-way measures. Bullish sentiment has gained momentum ... and the bull party is talking enthusiastically of its 'victory' over the banking authorities."

He warned again in April. The Federal Reserve was making noises, but the business community resented it, partly because too much of the market was becoming over-extended and lived in fear that the easy money might dry up: "Businessmen are becoming genuinely alarmed lest money for their purposes become scarce, and lest a stock market crash, which would wipe out private savings, affect public purchasing of commodities and shatter confidence, crown the efforts of the Federal Reserve Board."

Without being alarmist he had advised prudence. Now, as November advanced, the dam was breaking: "The slow and orderly decline turned into a break that surpassed all precedent for swiftness and disorder."

In London the paper was still trying to be cool and dispassionate, though danger did lurk: "The one influence that could throw back the full brunt of the speculative collapse upon industry and produce a real depression throughout the country would be banking trouble." Although the banks might be presumed to have taken precautions some would be caught: "Many banks ... will have made very large bad debts, while others will have to finance customers for a long or short period. Some bank failures, no doubt, are also to be expected."

From New York came word of how the affluent were already suffering: "Luxury trades have already been hit hard. Furs are being offered at sharp reductions, and the large shops are having returns of all kinds of expensive articles. Jewellery, high-priced motor-cars, yachts and country houses will be much less in demand. The radio business is also seriously affected, the break having come just at the start of the heavy selling season."

Now the search was on for explanations: "There is growing recognition of the fact that the background for the decline was set by the excessive capital flotations of the summer and autumn, particularly in the field of 'investment trusts', by the summer boom in utilities and by the recession in industry that began about July."

It was a fair assessment of the preceding months. But the fundamental troubles and weaknesses had been hidden from all but the most shrewd. Industry was over-capitalised. Wage-earners and farmers could not afford to consume enough. Protection had cut off foreign trade. Public and private debt was crushing. And once confidence went there was no remission. Nevertheless, in December 1929 men and women still hoped and the machinery of government still ran, even concealing the extent of the predicament. Hoover's message to Congress and his budget statement would, the paper said, "be read in Europe with feelings akin to envy". Hoover felt comfortable with a surplus (of $225m) and although he greatly increased public works and crop-support spending in the face of depression, he balanced his books by cutting other expenditure.

The belief, stubbornly held, was that things would come right, that gloom was exaggerated, that every hopeful sign deserved encouragement. The New York correspondent took to this line at the end of that November: "During the past week the share market has supplied further evidence that distress selling has passed, and that a period of quiet, rest and recuperation has been entered upon."

He did not resist trying to correct some of what Wall Street frowned upon as sensationalist reporting: "Wall Street has been interested and amused at the descriptions of the recent break that have appeared in certain sections of your 'stunt' Press. Stories of streets clogged with the bodies of suicides and of savings banks stripped of funds reveal modern journalism at its worst."

There were no reliable unemployment figures so political calculations varied. In an era of large families, not least those engaged in subsistence farming, it was soon not inconceivable that the unemployed and their dependents came to 40m, one-third of the total population. Wall Street rallied, only to fall again. No one knew whom to believe: "Sober-minded observers feel that what has taken place is nothing more serious than the washing away of the price advances built up last winter and spring on hopes of an early trade recovery which failed to materialise. Others, who credit the share market with great barometric value, are fearful lest the current decline forecasts a considerable deepening of the trade recession later in the year."

It deepened. By January 1931 the signs of distress were widespread: "The crisis really finds the country without a national remedial policy or adequate relief machinery. And for too many the 'bread line' and the 'flop house' symbolise the only barriers between starvation and death from exposure in the merciless American winter."

The banks were running out of credit. They faced closure: "Failures of small banks in the South, Middle West and here and there in the East continues. It is probable that failures for the year will mount to 1,000, a new high record; but these failures are the inevitable result of unwarranted expansion of banking."

The pinch was universal. The depression reached Europe, initiating more American bank failures. Credit tightened again. Those with work to go to did not argue over wages: "Wage-cutting throughout the country continues, but with very little publicity, and, in many instances, with such devices as work days without pay, designed to conceal the real reductions. The major industries, which work on a more or less fixed scale, such as the railroads and the steel and building trades, have not cut wages; but undoubtedly they feel that it will be necessary to do so, whatever may be said for publication."

By September 1931 there were few or no optimists left: "The whole country has undergone a change in its frame of mind toward the business position. There is no longer a tendency to blink the fact of a depression, and less thought is spent on the probable duration than on ways and means of carrying on."

Hoover was active, even inventive. He set up the Reconstruction Finance Corporation to lend money to the banks and railroads, but it was lethargic. So were the Federal Home Loan Banks, set up to help with mortgages. His Federal Farm Board, which was meant to keep up prices, was swamped by surpluses of grain and cotton, so that the farmers were "thoroughly disillusioned and discouraged". Banks that had been

"staving off the inevitable for months have had to give up". Hoover's programme, built on the idea of self-help and an ingrained reluctance to spend federal funds, was not achieving what he, far less the country, desired. By May 1932 the weekly report from New York epitomised the end of expectations: "Industrial activity is as slack as ever. Some increase in steel activity is reported for the first week of May, but the daily rate of pig-iron output in April was nearly 9 per cent below the March average. Steel output is hovering around 24 per cent of capacity." It covered all industries: "First quarter output of 355,721 vehicles was 48 per cent below that of a year ago. Railroad traffic fails to improve, and net earnings for March ran about 28 per cent below a year ago."

That was how distant victory over poverty had become. Democracy in America, as elsewhere in the world, knew the ends it wanted; it was at a loss, whether its party was Democratic or Republican, about how it was going to get there.

ALL AMERICANS WERE NOT DRY
Prohibition was a disaster, but some managed to drink right through it

The anti-drink movement had agitated for almost as long as the United States had existed. The Methodists approved of it, as did other churchgoers, and by the 1890s and 1900s abstinence was a way of life, in some parts of New England especially, although it certainly was not in the big cities and the Prohibition party never got anywhere. The strenuous private campaigners, many of them women, with the redoubtable Frances Willard as their exemplar, did make headway among a generation which had reason to be impressed by the evils of booze, especially among the immigrant working class. Seven rural states succumbed easily to the drys, and by the time of the Great War the majority of the population was officially teetotal. The war itself, and its demands for civilian economy and efficiency, then gave the cause its chance to get legislation banning the manufacture and sale of intoxicating drink, and its adoption as part of the constitution by 1919. *The Economist* cast an eye on the grave of one of its mentors, Richard Cobden, and assumed that he would be stirred by the news: "That the richest nation on the earth should voluntarily have banished intoxicating liquor from their State would have seemed to him a miracle past belief. Nevertheless, miracle or no miracle, Prohibition has obviously come to stay in the United States."

That was precisely when the trouble began, especially for the owners, captains and pursers of British ships making a landfall in the United States where the authorities insisted on taking stern measures to curb the drinking habits of self-indulgent Europeans. Every liner had to be as dry as the ships of the United States navy. The law was there to be enforced: "The strict legality of the American action of seizing liquor on British ships entering New York harbour was admitted by Lord Curzon, and not disputed by Lord Birkenhead."

It was not popular with humbler transatlantic passengers, however, even though the paper pointed out that the main American motive, "apparently insufficiently realised", was to evolve a policy "that will effectually check the very considerable contraband trade which has sprung up, almost inevitably". It was the sort of dispute beside which the solution of the war debt issue seemed minor in the public's eye. It all depended on the proper observance of the three-mile limit: "The faintest suggestion that the British Government should agree by treaty to permit an officer commanding an American control boat even to smell the cork of a Scotch whisky bottle outside a limit of three miles from the American shores has been denounced as a betrayal of vital British interests, and an abandonment of principles as old and as eternal as the right to the Writ of Habeas Corpus."

The paper thought it essential that Britain should get the United States to reaffirm the three-mile limit, but it believed a mutual exercise of common sense was the best solution: "It would be an act of prudence and mutual comity for the United States to acquiesce in the carriage of prohibited liquor under seal in British ships through her territorial waters in exchange for British acquiescence in the search within, say, twelve miles of American shores, of suspected smugglers."

By February 1924 the diplomats got round to something of the kind: "The United States reaffirms in principle its adhesion to the 'Three Mile Limit', and consents to the import of alcoholic liquors into American waters by foreign vessels in transit and under seal, in exchange for British consent to the pursuit of detected or suspected contrabanders beyond territorial waters for a distance of 'one hour's steam'."

The paper was duly thankful. It had already decided in September 1923 that the prohibition experiment, however laudable its aims and objectives, had failed. It had done so on many counts: "It has admittedly failed to stop drinking. It has decreased the regard in which the American constitution and American law are held abroad. It has led within the United States to open and widespread contempt for and breach of law, which some critics have even described as the 'beginning of Bolshevism'."

American ingenuity produced its own, unexpected, winners too. Prohibition had brought despair to Californian grape growers. Vineyards were sold off and ploughed under; other crops were planted. Then the new Americans, the immigrant wine-drinkers from Europe, were heard from: "Each family undertook to provide its own supply of wine, and the demand for grapes quickly produced a market famine. Meantime the price of grapes and of vineyards skyrocketed, and thousands of acres of new vines were planted."

The paper had the details. In 1921 California had 362,000 acres of grapes under cultivation; 520,000 tons were produced, at an average price of $78 per ton. By 1926, under the rigours of the law, California had 662,104 acres of grapes under cultivation; 1,026,000 tons were produced, at an average price of $32 per ton. It seemed a fundamental point had been raised: "A vivid light is thrown by the official figures of five years later on the question of whether prohibition prohibits."

Investigation brought out the existence, almost the romance, of a popular and profitable new industry: "The long trans-continental haul is made in fast refrigerator trains, many of which cross the country loaded with nothing but grapes. In the harvest season the market streets of New York and other large cities are filled with innumerable boxes of grapes, while a little later the streets in the tenement districts are stained with the purplish residue after the 'joy juice', as it is called in America, has been extracted." It was all legal. Against the railroads' strenuous opposition, the Interstate Commerce Commission granted the growers' appeal for lower freight rates.

However, as the Hoover presidency disintegrated in the depression, unemployment and governmental incoherence, the evidence was overwhelming that the chief beneficiaries were not nice, urbanised Italian peasants but professional gangsters who, such was prohibition's failure, had almost got public opinion on their side.

By June 1930 the paper was crisp in its condemnation of the teetotal failure: "What prohibition has done in the great urban areas is to give an economic basis to those denizens of the underworld who have always been a troublesome element in the United States. They now derive enormous resources from their bootlegging operations, and in places like Chicago are able to reduce civic government to chaos. But an equally important development in the 'wet' States has been the growth of a widespread sense of resentment against the Federal Government as a hostile power which is attempting to impose a control completely antagonistic to the prevailing conscience of the people."

Prohibition's time was more than up. When Franklin D. Roosevelt ended it in November 1933 the paper gave it a brief burial: "Repeal marks the end of a chapter in the history of temperance which has had results calculated to horrify its original advocates."

SACCO AND VANZETTI ARE DEAD
And something called world opinion made itself heard

American and world opinion was strongly aroused and divided by the sentencing and electrocution of Nicola Sacco and Bartolomeo Vanzetti, described as philosophical anarchists, in a murder case that lasted from 1920 to 1927. The two had been found guilty of

The anarchists Nicola Sacco and Bartolomeo Vanzetti during their trial. They were found guilty of murder in 1920, but a prolonged communist and humanitarian campaign delayed their electrocution until 1927.

murdering a paymaster at South Braintree, Massachusetts, but their defenders were convinced that they were innocent victims of popular hostility to radicals, especially when they were foreigners and draft-dodgers. That xenophobia and antipathy to bolsheviks and reds were endemic in much of American society needed no demonstration, but the paper found serious defects in their conviction: "The crime for which they are to suffer the supreme penalty in 1927 was committed in 1920; the only judge who has heard the various appeals is the judge who tried the case and condemned the men in the first instance; there are grave doubts—to put it no higher—as to the evidence of identification; while a fellow-prisoner who confesses he was with the gang by whom the murder was committed has absolved Sacco and Vanzetti."

The two had tireless sympathisers in the United States, but there was also resentment in Europe. The paper had reservations about the origin of the agitation: "To begin with, no doubt, it was not unmixed with political partisanship. In the earlier protests, the most prominent part was played by the political organisations of the condemned men's fellow-Communists; and no doubt the Communist leaders, beyond their genuine and spontaneous feeling for their comrades, saw in this agitation a favourable opportunity for spreading the atmosphere of the class war."

It was more concerned about America's growing unpopularity, which it thought unjustified, but which American behaviour and predilections stirred up. The United States that turned its back on the world was inviting nothing but retaliation: "Another political current, again, has been derived from the gradually accumulated irritation against the United States which undoubtedly exists both in Europe and in Latin America, and which has found vent, in those continents, in a campaign on behalf of Sacco and Vanzetti, in which the 'bourgeoisie' has participated almost as heartily as the 'proletariat'."

Americans who saw their country and themselves as honest and even innocent bystanders in a devious and ungrateful world would be dismayed at this incipient anti-Americanism. It came from economic and social resentment, but just as much from the dissemination of America's own sense of idealism when injustice seemed self-evident. A new factor had entered world politics: "This characteristic is what one would expect of a public opinion in its infancy—as international public opinion (the child of such recent inventions as the Press, the telegraph and wireless) is obviously still in its infancy today. In this rudimentary stage, opinion is only aroused by the simplest and most forcible stimuli. We may take hope, however, from the fact that the rudiments are there."

In 1927 the news was conducive to the emergence of such an international and liberal opinion. The postwar world still believed that its political differences were capable of resolution. The depression had not yet struck. Instead of politics, the newspapers and the wireless were concerned with human worries with which individuals could relate in a compassionate way. Russia was not a threat; it faced a famine. Tokyo had been ravaged by an earthquake. The Mississippi valley had been submerged by floods; there were many drownings. Two men whom many thought innocent were about to be electrocuted. If this was what moved international opinion, it would now be moved again when it was not preoccupied with the perennial problems of political economy. As for Sacco and Vanzetti, the opinion grew after their deaths that Sacco might have been guilty but Vanzetti, the idealist, not.

Roosevelt calls on Congress to repeal the Neutrality Act on the outbreak of war in 1939 to allow the sale of arms to Britain and France. The US remained isolationist until Pearl Harbor in 1941.

7

THE NEW DEALERS

1933–1939

FDR'S WINNING WAYS

The public hero whose policy was hope

The Economist liked Franklin D. Roosevelt the politician. It looked for great things from him as president because only great things would do in March 1933 in the emergency which only he could confront. For it saw, however preoccupied American opinion might be, that the challenge had already been issued in Germany: "Whereas Herr Hitler, having promised the millennium, will presumably be accorded a little time to make his promise good, the task which confronts Mr Roosevelt of reviving the now wholly suspended economic activity of America is immediate and brooks not a week's delay."

It liked Roosevelt's sense of urgency: five immediate messages to Congress and its agreement to legislate on the banking crisis which had effectively closed half the banks, on reductions in expenditure and on ending prohibition. Farm relief and public works to reduce unemployment were also in the programme. But the paper was never as enthusiastic as the president himself about what he was doing or planned to do. It was Roosevelt's style that caught its eye, as it caught America's: "There is a sense, both at Washington and throughout the country, of confidence, almost amounting to elation, that action will be taken.... This is chiefly due to the immense personal prestige of the President."

It did not conceal its doubts: "Opinion in at least half of the world is moving rapidly towards the acceptance of deliberate inflation. It is consequently incumbent upon those who have for so long been preaching a policy of moderate expansion, to attempt to determine whether, in actual fact, President Roosevelt has found the cure for the depression."

If generating confidence would do the trick, FDR would do it. The paper admired the enthusiasm of Washington, in particular, and the overriding commitment and fervour of the New Dealers: "Washington is a new city, and with its vast mushroom growths of new

---

CHRONOLOGY

1933	Franklin D. Roosevelt becomes president		General Franco
	Adolf Hitler becomes German chancellor; Reichstag set on fire		Popular Front government in France
			John Maynard Keynes publishes *General Theory of*
	Roosevelt's first New Deal measures enacted in 100 days		*Employment, Interest and Money*
		1937	Japan attacks Shanghai and Nanking
	Prohibition repealed	1938	German troops occupy Austria
1934	Nazi coup fails in Austria		Munich agreement dismembers Czechoslovakia
	Britain begins rearming: Royal Air Force to be increased	1939	Germany occupies Czechoslovakia
			Italy invades Albania
1935	US passes Neutrality Act		German-Soviet pact
	Italy invades Abyssinia		Germany invades Poland; second world war begins
1936	Hitler reoccupies the Rhineland		in Europe
	Spanish civil war: Germany and Italy side with		Soviet Union attacks Finland

---

administrative staffs, its recruitment of the best brains in the country, its disregard of expense, consistency, and political convention, and its indifference to the ultimate effects of its measures, provided only they serve their immediate purpose of 'winning victory', is strangely reminiscent of Whitehall in war-time."

This ambivalence would persist. The paper recorded the initial failures of the New Deal with a sense of regret and self-justification. But it did hope; its hopes were in Roosevelt: "The next few years will clearly be a period of as great change in American politics as in the structure of the American economy, and it may well be that the accession to office of Mr Roosevelt will prove to have been as decisive a turning point in the political history of the Republic as that of Jackson or of Lincoln."

The paper accepted the need for his economic experimentation, because it accepted that it did not have all the answers. It relied on his own grasp of reality. The communist system would never be his, but he was ready to recognise the Soviet Union: "Recognition of the Soviet Government has long been overdue, and it is strongly reinforced by a description of the absurdities and anomalies, as well as the practical disadvantages which have arisen out of previous attempts to ignore the existence of a Government which has been firmly established for about fifteen years."

When the first New Deal did not deliver the goods, and business confidence waned while production fell and unemployment rose inexorably, Roosevelt's popularity with those who had voted for him remained undiminished; there were times when he took on even god-like qualities: "Even in the drought regions he was received as a public hero, and a population which was superstitious enough to believe that the drought was Divine retribution for the restriction of crops has not failed to draw its own conclusions from the fact that wherever he went he brought rain."

In the mid-term elections of 1934 his victory was "crushing and complete". "The vote was a Roosevelt vote rather than a Democratic vote or even a New Deal vote. No one man has ever, in the face of free opposition, won such unconditional support from so many millions."

The paper was pleased. It had discovered a new Roosevelt, not a revolutionary but "a sincere and powerful Liberal", from whom there had been little monetary experimentation and no currency manipulation for nine months. He was "less Radical but at the same time less frightening" than he had been in 1933. So he deserved a vote of confidence: "The President's policies, as they appear at the moment, consist of relief of the destitute, social reform and controlled expansion of individual business—a platform on which any Liberal in any country would be proud to stand."

It took little interest in the issues in 1936 for it was doubtful of the Republican, Governor Alfred M. Landon, thought Roosevelt unstoppable, and distrusted the opinion polls. The findings of the American Institute of Public Opinion surprised it: "The poll, one of a series, shows that Mr Roosevelt has suffered a substantial setback since the Republican convention, and now would win only 51.8 per cent of the popular vote; and that Governor Landon, if the election were held today, and the poll were a true indication, would have a majority in the electoral college and become President."

Sensibly, it ignored the finding: "Its rivals argue, with considerable apparent justification, that this election is the first in which the poor will vote differently from the rich, and that a ballot taken from the owners of telephones and motor-cars is therefore not sufficiently representative."

When Roosevelt won with every state but Maine and Vermont the paper gave credit where it knew it was due: "He is all that a successful politician should be. His campaign smile, his radio technique, his phrase-making gift, his surpassing abilities as a charmer, his rarely-failing instinct for what will appeal to the plain man, even his choice of enemies—all have helped him." His was the essential ability to represent democracy in the disasters and disappointments of the 1930s: "Mr Roosevelt has caught a little of the spirit which in other countries has been distorted and debased into Fascism."

The paper allowed itself one social comment. The Washington man, out in a fashionable New York hotel on election night, observed where the opposition in FDR's second term would be coming from. A party of New Dealers had gone out to celebrate: "After the election had been conceded by Mr Landon, the woman arose, lifted her glass and proposed for the entire room a toast to the President of the United States. The companions at her table promptly stood and lifted their glasses. But though a painful silence fell over the assemblage not another glass was raised. And the New Dealers, with one accord, gathered up their things and stole away."

THE OPPORTUNIST PLAYED ON

The New Deal had many tunes but too few hits for the paper

By *The Economist*'s reckoning, the New Deal failed to do what Roosevelt hoped for, and promoted, four times between 1933 and 1939. He and his advisers confidently tried expedient upon expedient, altered course and tactics, and adhered to no policy for long, or for only long enough to see it fail. Where others foolishly promised certainties, Roosevelt offered only pragmatism; the paper identified just relentless, searching, expectant pragmatism. It was seldom censorious. Its own ideas were more conventional than his, but it was modest in its expectations.

In July 1939, before rearmament, primed by British and French purchasing, began to rescue American industry, it remarked that the lagging recovery of that year, what it called the "re-recovery", had faltered and fallen below the attainments of 1937, let alone those of 1929 before the depression began. It ran through, politely, every solution that had been tried in six years of New Dealing endeavour: "We have had the depreciation of the dollar and the deliberate enhancement of the price of silver, the fostering of monopolies through the NRA and their prosecution by the Department of Justice, fiscal economy and deficit financing, pump priming and yardstick building, public works and work relief. The only remedy that has not been tried is a sustained attempt to lower the costs and encourage the expansion of the capital goods industries whose coma is, by common consent, the root cause of the laggardliness of recovery. It might be worth trying."

The paper respected the premises of Roosevelt's opportunism, as Wall Street never did, but it did not trust it. It respected the cause of reform that prompted what was being done in unemployment relief, social security, public works and conservation, and financial regulation, but it looked for economic results. It did not believe that more than a strictly limited use of inflation would be other than counter-productive. It distrusted the National Recovery Administration (NRA) from the outset in 1933. The NRA's codes, with a minimum wage of $15 and working hours cut to 42 hours a week for office workers, 52 hours in retail shops and 35 hours for factory workers, were part of the attempt to increase purchasing power and so tackle the depression and unemployment. By July, one month after the legislation, the paper voiced its scepticism: "An overweening spirit of optimism and confidence may suffice to counteract influences which would otherwise lead to a restriction of production and a deepening of the depression, but even with the strongest psychological impetus towards expansion the immediate future of American business will be watched with grave forebodings."

Roosevelt's first attempt "to drive the American economic machine up to the peak of the trade cycle in six months" soon petered out; by early September that was obvious, "as *The Economist* predicted from the beginning was likely to happen". The paper stuck to its own line: "The business stagnation that began in July still continues, and there is no reason why it should stop until a method is found of injecting fresh purchasing power into the system without increasing costs."

The NRA might be reorganising industry: "it may well be a political success". But its net effect had been to increase costs, not purchasing power. It needed to do "more than a mere substitution of the instabilities of inflation for the disequilibrium of deflation". By October the paper identified few voices raised for Roosevelt's policy; it found the spirit of hopeful unity had given way to "sectional, class and group antagonism".

"The inflation plan is recognised as injurious to the wage earner; the National Recovery Act is recognised as helping the wage earner at the cost of the farmer. Uncertainty as to the further application of the inflation programme and of the NRA is operating to restrain business enterprise. Behind these special interests is the growing resentment of the average urban consumer, whose income has not been increased and whose cost of living has been perceptibly raised."

The paper called the budget of January 1934 a "stupendous Budget". But it doubted if sheer spending were the answer: "America is thus launched upon a gigantic gamble. Heavy Government expenditures should undoubtedly assist in raising prices. But in his hurry to restore the National Income to its previous level, the President runs the risk of setting up a momentum of inflation which he will be unable to stop."

It disagreed with Keynes, whom it accused of advocating public spending "apparently irrespective of the methods or objects of the expenditure". What it did agree with was "government initiative in the trough of a depression to stimulate the capital industries", but it was worried about what some of Roosevelt's planners would thrust upon him.

It need not have worried unduly. The Roosevelt of 1934 was still pledged to budget balancing and still doubted all the claims made for public works. By August the paper reported that "the mainspring of the New Deal appears to be running down". The country was again looking to FDR to wind it up: "Inflation still has its attractions to the inflationists; they are talking of a further devaluation of the dollar.... On the other hand, those who have consistently called for the restoration of confidence and the freeing of private enterprise from the shackles of regulation have not changed their mind, and they have succeeded in driving the NRA into full retreat."

In September, as the New York correspondent reported steel production down to 18% of capacity, the head of the NRA, General Hugh Johnson, left the agency. For all his restless energy Johnson could not control the big corporations and he wasted effort and resources trying to regulate the small ones: "The very bluntness and dash which had served him well as a cavalry leader or a crusader became liabilities which in the end ensured his departure."

The farmers, beset by debt and over-production, were put under the Agriculture Adjustment Act (AAA) and their income steadily rose as they were subsidised, got compensation for limiting crops and were helped by the devaluation of the dollar; their mortgage worries were also lessened. The great drought and dust storms of the mid-1930s brought widespread distress in the mid-west, but the paper insisted on the reality; for all but the Okies the drought proved a blessing: "Broadly speaking, the farmer gained by it; for the increase in prices promises to prove more than compensatory for the decline in output. Second, surpluses have been largely eliminated. Third, cattle and sheep have been greatly reduced in number, and presumably several years will be required to build up flocks and herds." In October 1934 it concluded that the drought had given the farmer "the most prosperous autumn he has known for years".

The paper approved of the Tennessee Valley Authority (TVA) and cheap electricity. It was not persuaded by the private utilities' arguments and it commended Roo-

sevelt's general push for rural electrification. In March 1935 it commented: "In the past the utilities have been unduly timid in testing the effect of lower rates and they may discover that equally large profits can be made with a low-price policy."

Yet the depression persisted. Not even the paper's newly recognised liberal, Roosevelt, had found the answers. The paper, drawing up a balance sheet in May 1935, grew alarmed: "There are still about ten million unemployed and millions more on relief; the farming areas have not solved their financial problems, municipalities are in grave straits, and only heavy Federal expenditures keep the tide of discontent from expressing itself more forcefully. There is a strong, ultimate pressure for drastic reforms which might become revolutionary if conditions worsened."

Its advice to the administration was to do something to encourage the business community. There was credit there to be used, and business might be persuaded to use it, if only to forestall the demands for further inflation. But the biggest threat to the New Deal now came from the very heart of the constitutional system itself: the Supreme Court. In May the court struck down the NRA: "The Act, in giving the President power to promulgate and enforce industrial codes, was giving him legislative power, which belongs to Congress alone.... The power of the Federal Government to regulate inter-State commerce does not give it power to regulate matters such as wages and conditions of labour which affect inter-State commerce only indirectly. Accordingly, all Federal labour legislation is unconstitutional."

This cheered up Wall Street and the business community no end. Nor did the paper find any fault: "This decision obviously strikes at the roots of the New Deal. What is more, it is obviously good Constitutional law, as is, indeed, demonstrated by the Court's unanimity, and it is useless to blame the Court when it is the Constitution that is at fault."

The paper felt that, whether or not the NRA was resurrected under the same or different initials, management and unions were not likely to give up collective bargaining, minimum wages and maximum hours. The NRA had been too ambitious; it should have been restricted to the industries that clearly needed reorganisation, and it had encouraged labour costs to rise too drastically. It was not all bad: "Some of its achievements all will welcome—the prohibition of child

A ruined Texas family in the dustbowl drought that drove many farmers westwards to California in the mid-1930s. The drought deepened the depression in much of rural America.

labour, the virtual abolition of sweating, the introduction of reasonable labour standards into industries which were patently exploiting their workers." But it was suspect: "Some other of its results are undeniable, though their merits will be debated—the enunciation of the principle of collective bargaining and the great fillip given to the growth of trades unions, with an accompanying epidemic of strikes."

In January 1936 the Supreme Court declared the Agricultural Adjustment Act unconstitutional too. The paper thought this meant death to the New Deal. The act was one of its chief pillars, perhaps the most important enactment of the previous three years: "The majority judgment finds that any attempt by the Federal Government to regulate agricultural production is an infringement of the rights of the individual States, as guaranteed by the Constitution, and is therefore *ultra vires*."

It thought the Republicans were wrong to be jubilant; next time they were in office the court would make them impotent. But the court did uphold the Tennessee Valley Authority's existence: "The TVA is itself an experiment in regional rehabilitation of such great economic and sociological interest that it would be unfortunate if it went by legal default."

Through the summer and autumn of 1936 the paper found evidence of an economic upturn, in time for the presidential election. It thought it better than the indices suggested: "Non-residential building is depressed, and it figures heavily in the indices. On the other hand, every form of amusement is booming, and the amusement business, which is enormous in the aggregate, hardly finds even an indirect reflection in the indices."

Cars, too, were doing better, chiefly through consumer credit: "While the general level of incomes is by no means what it was in the boom years of the twenties, the demand for motor cars approximates to the heyday of the New Era, and all sorts of comparable items of household equipment find a similar demand –in instances, an unprecedented demand."

Just before the election the Supreme Court struck again, throwing out the minimum wage law for women in New York state, a decision which, the paper thought, invited political retaliation. Reverence for the court was dwindling: "Its finding against the NRA was widely popular. The nullification of the AAA was considered a hardship, but possibly a necessary price for the defence of local government against over-centralisation.... But the veto of the New York wage law has suddenly thrown doubt on the Court's ineffable inspiration."

That October the paper published a 24-page supplement analysing the New Deal to date: "Relief there has been, but little more than enough to keep the population fed, clothed and warmed. Recovery there has been, but only to a point still well below the pre-depression level. Reform there has also been, but it is slight compared with the reformers' blueprints. The great problems of the country are still hardly touched."

Roosevelt duly won, and a majority of the country enjoyed a more prosperous Christmas than any since the slump began. But the paper was still dubious: "Industrial production stands at little more than 90 per cent of the 1929 level, residential building is only about half the 1929 amount, the production of motor cars is not yet up to the figure attained in that year, and the loadings of freight on the railways are just over three-quarters of what they were seven years ago."

WRONG NOTES

Fighting the Supreme Court was hard enough,
but fighting business was ruinous

Roosevelt now began his attempt to reform the Supreme Court, seeking the retirement of justices aged over 70. The paper was surprised at the vituperation it brought down on him, providing "material for a psychological study of American political thought". FDR himself was caught unawares: "He expected opposition, bitter opposition, but he had not anticipated a neurotic outburst."

It had sympathy with his argument: "His case is that the United States is faced with a 'silent crisis', and that the elected Congress and the elected President cannot take steps to meet the crisis of poverty and economic instability because the Supreme Court insists on giving decisions based not upon the Constitution but upon the individual Justices' political opinions."

Although Roosevelt was beaten by the court and by what was called "articulate opinion", the court itself decided on a reluctant, but strategic, retreat. The older men stepped down and the others did not care to resist the verdict of the 1936 election returns. Collective bargaining on the railroads was upheld; so was a three-year moratorium on farm mortgage foreclosures; and so was the Wagner Labour Relations Act which gave exclusive bargaining rights to unions representing a majority of the workforce. Roosevelt had encouraged the unions, especially the Congress of Industrial Organisations under John L. Lewis, which fought its way into United States Steel and General Motors. The paper approved: "Industrial management, in agreeing to collective bargaining, has stepped with a single stride from the nineteenth to the twentieth century."

The unions went too far for Roosevelt and public opinion, however, encouraging sit-down strikes and combative picketing. Business grew jumpy, demanding that the unions adhere to the law. Roosevelt, misled by the relative prosperity of early 1937, wished to show business how sound he really was. He cut back government spending again and allowed the Federal Reserve to curtail credit. By October the financial world was in another bear market, not quite as bad as 1929 but close to those of 1920–21 and 1907: "About half of the shares listed on the New York Stock Exchange have fallen more than 50 per cent in price since early in the year."

The market was not out of touch. The paper was rightly disturbed at the floundering of capital goods industries: "More could be done to lower the cost of capital construction and to raise the margin of income of some industries, notably the railroads, which are at present unable to afford the re-equipment they require. Much could also be done by the adjustment of taxes which at present discriminate against capital expenditure."

Between autumn 1937 and the spring of 1938 industrial production fell by a third. Fear, according to the New York correspondent, did not reside with Wall Street speculators or industrial magnates alone; it was everywhere. So, in the administration, it was back to

exchanges between the president and business were themselves hindering any progress: "Mr Roosevelt is neither a Communist nor a dictator, nor has he aspirations to be either." But the paper held Roosevelt responsible too. Business had been led a perpetual

New Dealer: John L. Lewis (left), the combative president of the United Mineworkers, commiserates with the mine operators' Hubert H. Howard. Lewis's strikes forced both Roosevelt and Truman to take over the mines.

the drawing board: "The remedies of 1933 have been taken down from the shelf and re-examined, and the most effective of them has been re-adopted. The pump is once more to be primed with a Federal deficit.... And it is doubtful whether pump-priming of less than heroic dimensions will be of much avail, unless some truce is called in the present savagery of political conflict."

The immoderation, the sheer bad temper, of the

dance: "Some of his reform proposals have gone beyond the need for guarding against abuses and have become definitely penal in form; he has frequently seemed to be far less interested in exalting the humble and the meek than in putting down the mighty from their seats. There is something also in the charges of reckless experimentation; the course of monetary policy, of housing policy, the alternation between budget balancing and unbalancing, the attitude towards the attempts of industry to fix prices—all these have been unnecessarily and harmfully erratic."

So recovery struggled. When in July 1938 the first economic indicator of the demand that was eventually to push it into overdrive was revealed, it was hardly welcome: "Orders had been placed ... for 200 Lockheed reconnaissance machines and 200 North American trainers, at a total cost of over £7,000,000."

Before the rearmament tide became a flood the paper's exasperation was directed at the new Wages and Hours Act. Noting, dryly, that what had been called the doctrine of high wages had now become the purchasing power theory, it put most responsibility for the economic failure of the "re-recovery" on what it believed to be this fallacy: "In the present circumstances of the United States, when recovery has failed to progress beyond a very moderate point, when profits are well below the normal figure, and when the capital goods industries are languishing, any further increase in the cost of labour will have the effect of limiting the possibilities of recovery and depressing the total real income of labour."

The Economist was never among those who counted the New Deal a model for the future. It thought it should have been done differently, and better. However, it did recognise many of the New Deal's accomplishments and it did not regret the expansion of the scope and interests of the federal government. It cherished the truth that all was done for democracy by democratic methods. It regularly gave credit to Roosevelt that he asked the right questions of America. That was the abiding success of the 1930s against the dictators.

TOWARDS THE INEVITABLE
Roosevelt began with no foreign policy, but the Axis dictators left him no option

The Economist initially respected Roosevelt's reluctance to have an active international policy. It did not like it, but he was understandably preoccupied with the United States's own crisis, he was the inheritor of over a decade of isolationism, and, in an emergency, he was bound to give priority to the Far East before Britain's principal concern, the Nazi and Fascist dictatorships in Europe.

The paper had no doubt that Japan would have to

be restrained by compulsion or persuasion, but not yet. In January 1934 there was still time, it supposed, for words, and it found that the early Roosevelt had his own variety: "He diagnoses our present international malady as the work of a handful of criminals corresponding to the gangsters, machine politicians and fraudulent financiers who have been made the scapegoat for the present ills of the United States, and his international policy follows almost automatically from this. He proposes a rough-and-ready plan for isolating, exposing and pillorying these villains of the international piece until they are intimidated, by the enlightened and outraged public opinion of mankind, into abandoning their knavish tricks."

In other words, he had no policy. He left the routine business of diplomacy—disarmament, the war debts and reciprocal trade agreements—to his secretary of state, Cordell Hull. He sent observers to Europe who identified the steady drift to another war, to which isolationism remained the popular American answer. The paper spelled out the consequences in the Far East: "For Japan, Europe's prospective suicide opens up a prospect of wide expansion in Eastern Asia and the Western Pacific. For the United States, by the same token, the moral is that she had better quickly shake herself loose from the European mess in order to have her hands free to act when Japan gets to mischief."

The paper believed that the United States, with its Pacific seaboard, could not disinterest itself from Japan's attack on China in 1932. Japan, it said, was a victim of the shrinkage of international trade and the raising of national tariff walls. It needed to be restrained but it also deserved help. Neither was forthcoming. As the Japanese, "left free to run amok", pressed ahead, it was concerned there was no agreed Anglo-American policy: "The Japanese are doggedly pursuing their chosen path; but what is our line to be? Scavenging in the new lion's tracks? Or solidarity with the United States?"

In 1934 it felt there were "influential English minorities which are as unfriendly towards the United States as they are complacent towards Japan". The British Mediterranean fleet was supposed to be able to intervene in the Far East but, for an instrument of world power, it was markedly reluctant: "There seems to be a school which feels towards the Japanese Navy all the indulgence of a fond parent for an obstreperous child, while it cannot forgive the American admirals for having obtained, through 'parity', the privilege of having as big a toy to play with as our British admirals."

Again, some British business interests saw the Americans as "unwelcome competitors" and preferred trying for a timely deal with the Japanese. Oil companies were required to set up refineries and additional storage plant in Japan: "Are American, Dutch and British oil companies really to pay through the nose in order to provide facilities for the Japanese Navy to operate against the Philippines or Netherlands Indies or British Malaya in the event of war?" It was seven years to Pearl Harbor and the fall of Singapore.

The United States naval manoeuvres in the Pacific in May 1935 were to prove to be more to the point: "The main purpose of the present manoeuvres is evidently to discover whether the islands scattered over the North Central Pacific are capable of serving as stepping stones by which American air armadas might bestride the ocean from east to west until they come within effective striking distance of the Japanese Empire (or protecting distance of the Philippines, as an American strategist might prefer to say)."

American policy did not contemplate either demonstration or initiative in Europe, not least with the 1936 elections in sight. This did not stop Roosevelt abhorring Nazi behaviour, but the paper now believed strong words were no longer enough: "Whether we like it or not, we are our brothers' keepers; and the moral condemnation of the militant European dictatorships, which the President has pronounced and in which his countrymen certainly concur, is implicitly also a moral condemnation of this American determination to contract out of the common fortunes of humanity."

The Senate had killed an attempt to have the United States join the World Court. Congress had begun to pass neutrality laws which would impede arms sales to Britain and France. Italy had invaded Abyssinia. Germany was about to recover the Rhineland. The first test for collective security came with the proposal to impose an oil embargo on Italy. It came to nothing: "Owing to British and French timidity and equivocation, America has once more elected to 'contract out' of any understanding which might be interpreted as assisting the League, or Europe, indiscriminately."

The paper blamed the two foreign ministers, Sir Samuel Hoare and Pierre Laval, who proposed to hand half Abyssinia to Italy, for American antipathy to the Europeans. It was certainly the Americans who would

profit from a European embargo, but it did not believe American opinion would put up with it: "The imposition of the oil sanction will leave the oil companies of America free to do business with a war-maker, at the cost of Abyssinian, and of Italian, lives. No doubt they will seize the opportunity—at first. But we venture to think that the American Administration, Congress, and people will quickly withdraw from so invidious a situation."

A week later it reported regretfully: "American shipments of oil, copper, rolling stock and scrap metal to Italy and Italian possessions are now well above their normal levels."

When General Franco precipitated the Spanish civil war in July 1936, with help from Hitler and Benito Mussolini and their arms shipments, Roosevelt and Congress, with popular approval, insisted on a total embargo which cut off arms to the Spanish republican government. By December 1936 when Roosevelt flew to the Pan-American conference in Buenos Aires after his re-election, the paper's Washington correspondent reflected gloomily on the danger facing the United States if the dictators were to win the European war which seemed inevitable: "A Fascist republic in Latin America could be chosen partner in such an enterprise, and unless Pan-America adopts democracy with more courage and tenacity than at present there will be little mutual support of the Monroe doctrine."

The paper doubted if the United States could depend any longer on its insulation from the realities of the modern world: "Revolutionary political ideas are even harder to keep at bay than bombing planes; and Communism and Fascism may leap an Atlantic whose western waves are still physically ruled by the United States Navy."

This was the way Roosevelt's mind was beginning to move in 1937, although he had signed the Neutrality Act. He spoke of putting the dictators in quarantine, but with no specific system for doing so. When the Japanese bombed Shanghai and other open Chinese cities Roosevelt condemned them, but the paper doubted if it meant very much: "The American public has probably moved far enough from its erstwhile love of pure isolation to agree with the President that the avoidance of war cannot be secured by that route. Whether it has moved far enough to authorise him to join in 'concerted action' strong enough to achieve anything in the face of determined aggression is one of the

Japan drives into China: troops entering Shanghai, 1937. The United States and Britain disagreed on counter-measures. Japan's war party pressed ahead, eventually attacking Pearl Harbor and seizing Singapore.

questions to which only the passage of events can supply an answer."

In December 1937 the Japanese bombed and sank the gunboat USS *Panay* in the Yangtze, outraging the newspapers. *The Economist* had been there before. It underscored the differences between the Americans and British over the crises that really disturbed them: "The entanglements from which an American most shrinks are entanglements beyond the Atlantic, whereas entanglements beyond the Pacific do not

upset him nearly so deeply. For the United States the Pacific and the China seas are what the Mediterranean and the Indian Ocean are for the British Empire."

This time the Japanese apologised and indemnified the families of the victims, but the attack helped to justify Roosevelt's decision to increase naval tonnage by 20%. Even then the paper's Washington correspondent advised against any link with British rearmament: "If action has to be taken in the Far East it would be more palatable to American public opinion if it were taken alone, or at least begun alone. Certainly the emphasis is all on the lone hand, and it is worth noting that British friendship is, for the purposes of passing the Navy Bill, more of a liability, politically, than an asset."

In Europe the Nazi takeover in Austria in March 1938 and the Munich agreement in September which settled Czechoslovakia's fate were watched in the United States with resignation, and with relief that a European war had been avoided. Had war come there was no question of the United States joining it to save two small continental countries. It was the growing revelations of what Hitler's storm troops were doing to the Jews in Germany itself that were prominent in American headlines, and in American anxieties. The burning of synagogues, looting of Jewish shops and hounding of Jews out of their homes drew American eyes back at long last to what was happening in Europe. The paper was surprised at the significance: "The news of Munich gave American isolationism a powerful impetus; and it is one of Herr Hitler's most extraordinary feats to have thrown the movement of American public opinion into reverse by what he has been doing at home during these few intervening weeks.... The spontaneous expressions of feeling in the American Press have been answered by broadsides of Dr Goebbels' propaganda, in which the two great English-speaking countries are confounded in a common state of vituperation."

The United States kept up the complaints about the pogrom, ambassadors were withdrawn, and a formal German protest was turned down. The paper was not unhappy: "Relations between the two countries are now about as bad as they could be without a formal rupture. Whether or not this development is part of the Nazi plan, the attitude of the German press is doing everything possible to exacerbate matters still further."

In February 1939 Roosevelt began his campaign to remove the neutrality measures that would make it hard for the British and French to buy arms: "The higher pitched are Dr Goebbels' screams, the more is Mr Roosevelt likely to be pleased. He has, at the very least, openly stated a case in which increasing numbers of Americans are coming to believe. And at best he has changed the course of history."

He would do that, but not yet. The persistence of isolationism and pacifism in Congress had been underestimated, even as Europe was carried along towards the inevitable. *The Economist* tried to reckon what, exactly, America would do: "First, there is a very large goodwill for Britain and France as the (perhaps imperfect but residuary) representatives of democracy, a way of life in which the average American believes with emotion and conviction."

The paper thought that, in any war of self-defence, Britain and France could count on half the American people as their avowed partisans from the start. "Second, the more courageously Britain and France appear to be defending themselves, and the heavier the odds against them, the greater will be the degree of support. Third, if their opponents are Germany (especially), Italy and Japan, the sympathies of the American people would be powerfully reinforced by their antipathies (which are at present the stronger emotions). And fourth ... if the war involved heavy and unprovoked air raids on the cities of England and France the American reaction would be strong and violent."

In March Hitler seized all of Czechoslovakia, but the paper, adhering to its own advice, cautioned against high expectations of America's response: "British opinion is chronically at fault in exaggerating the willingness of America to take a hand."

In June King George VI and Queen Elizabeth went to Washington, the first state visit ever made by a British sovereign. The two got on well with the Roosevelts. It was a conscious diplomatic move, and much was made of it on the British side. The paper did not share such hopes: "The Royal visit to the United States is no more and no less an act of courtesy due to Canada's great neighbour; and it will not be misinterpreted by the American public." It had no illusions: "Not one iota will the King's visit deflect the course of American policy."

The Senate Foreign Relations Committee duly voted against repealing the Neutrality Act; it still believed there would not be a war. Roosevelt was powerless. Less than two months later German tanks crossed the Polish frontier.

Victory in Europe: US troops on the beaches of Normandy, 1944. Despite determined German resistance, France was liberated, the Rhine crossed, and Hitler's Reich forced to surrender.

8

FDR GOES TO WAR

1940–1945

RELYING ON AMERICA

As disaster spread in Europe British hopes
depended on Roosevelt's version of neutrality

The outbreak of war in Europe was seen by most Americans as ineluctable: many suspected that eventually the United States would be drawn in, but few showed a wish to hasten the day. The president called on Congress at once to revise the Neutrality Act, but under half of Americans polled were ready to send war materials to the Allies. The blitzkrieg was rapidly over in Poland, and though the u-boats' sinking of passenger ships like the *Athenia*, with 1,400 people on board, more than 300 of them American, incited anti-German feelings, American opinion was mystified by the quietness of the western front and the absence of air attacks on the big cities. It was soon called the "phoney war" by correspondents and induced scepticism in the plain man: "The consistently melodramatic bias of his press and radio in reporting foreign news has led him to suspect that there is some diplomatic dirty work behind the quiet on the Western front, and his suspicions emerge in the demand that the Allies should nail their colours to the idealistic mast by detailing their war aims."

Roosevelt's efforts to get neutrality reinterpreted in Congress still left the United States manifestly distant from any potential fighting: "It is very strictly, almost puritanically, a neutrality bill. Belligerents must take title for the arms or munitions they buy before the goods are shipped, and only non-renewable 90-day credits will be accorded. Belligerents must not sell securities in the United States. American vessels, by the bill, must carry no goods or passengers to belligerent countries, and no American vessels or citizens must enter 'combat areas'."

The paper commented on it austerely: "The guess may be hazarded that the dominant passion of American public opinion is to help in the overthrow of Hitlerism, provided the help can be given in a way that neither involves nor brings in its train the lending of

CHRONOLOGY

1940	Winston Churchill prime minister in Britain		Allied invasion of Italy
	France falls; Marshall Pétain sues for peace		Mussolini resigns
	Battle of Britain	1944	D-Day: allied invasion of France
	Italy invades Greece		Battle of Leyte Gulf, Philippines
1941	Lend-lease for Britain passed by Congress		Battle of the Bulge, Ardennes
	Germany invades Soviet Union	1945	Yalta conference (Churchill, Roosevelt, Stalin)
	Japan attacks Pearl Harbor, Guam and Philippines		decides eastern Europe's future
1942	Singapore falls to Japanese		Roosevelt dies
	Battle of Stalingrad		Harry S. Truman becomes president
	German Afrika Corps defeated at El Alamein		Germany surrenders
	US and British forces invade North Africa		Churchill voted out of office
	US naval victory at Guadalcanal		Atomic bombs on Hiroshima and Nagasaki; Japan
1943	Allied success in Battle of Atlantic		surrenders

money or the waging of war."

In this war the accepted opinion was that allied purchases had nothing to do with American industry's recovery. The paper's New York correspondent denied that the spurt in heavy industry had anything to do with a war boom. It was, he said, "a re-equipment or deferred maintenance boom, financed by undistributed corporate earnings". The real secret was psychological: "If there is little logic behind the new boom, there is plenty of sound and psychology. Wars notoriously breed sellers' markets and rising prices. It is a time to buy; it is imprudent not to buy while you can."

The paper was edgy about American attitudes and what seemed to underlie them. In January 1940 criticism of the phoney war rankled: "It is fear of war itself, not any question of the rights and wrongs of war, that dictates America's outlook. Their attitude is, in fact, pure Munich, and it is far too much to hope that they will draw the analogy and see behind Munich Prague, behind Prague Slovakia and Memel, behind Memel the dismemberment of the Polish State."

It recognised what Roosevelt was attempting to do to harden opinion. But the very monotony of the war served to encourage those Americans who concluded that if the allies thought they would win a war of attrition the United States was not needed. In February the under-secretary of state, Sumner Welles, was sent to take soundings in Rome, Berlin, Paris and London: "The United States does not want to be drawn into Europe. Neither does it want to be left out. The Welles mission exactly expresses this paradox."

For Roosevelt then the main import of 1940 was that it was another election year. The paper had expected for more than a year that he would run for a third term. Its reasoning was straightforward: "It is probable that, in a contest of nobodies, the Republican nobody would win. To save his party, and his policy within the party, Mr Roosevelt may feel constrained to fight again."

It was evident that the Americans disliked the allied blockade of Germany and their own government's restrictions, and saw no reason why they should not circumvent both. American shipping interests were getting impatient: "No American ship may now call at any European port between Bergen and Bilbao. This has been a shock to American shipping companies, which had confidently expected to be allowed to continue trading with Ireland, and possibly with Denmark, Holland and Belgium. Steps have been taken to transfer the register of American liners to Panama (and also, incidentally, to recruit non-American crews)."

The blockade was not difficult to outflank as long as Adolf Hitler and Joseph Stalin were still working together: "In January 2,000 tons of tin went to Vladivostok from the United States, the first shipment of its kind. Russian imports of rubber, copper, tungsten and molybdenum from across the Pacific have risen remarkably in recent months."

While the Royal Navy was stopping ships and, in American eyes, tampering with mail, the blockade was visibly faltering: "In the last four months of last year, American exports to Italy, Russia, the Balkan countries, Scandinavia, Holland, Belgium, Hungary and Switzerland—all countries accessible to Germany—are reported to have been valued at nearly 50 per cent more than the level of the same months of 1938."

In three months, April–June 1940, Denmark, Norway, Holland, Belgium and France fell to the blitzkrieg, Italy entered the war on the German side, and Britain was left to fend for itself. The widespread reversal of American opinion, the emergence of a popular will for intervention in Congress and not only in the editorial views of Atlantic coast newspapers, the readiness to vote aid for the allies and, above all, Roosevelt's ability to capitalise on the opportunity were decisive in Britain's survival. But the paper was concerned that what it regarded as the democracies' greatest asset, the American industrial machine, was not ready to give immediate support and would take years to make its critical impact felt. As France was falling, it analysed the limitations of the American wish to help. It indicated three priorities: "Perhaps the chief immediate assistance that the United States can render is in the delivery of machinery, and especially of machine tools. The American industry is already working to capacity, partly on Allied orders. Deliveries of these vital necessities to Europe could be speeded up if it were possible to give Allied orders any sort of effective priority over other exports, or even over certain classes of domestic demand."

Steel was the commodity in clamorous demand: "Steel, particularly semi-finished steel, is another material that will be urgently needed, together with scrap for steelmaking in this country, and priority rights, if America is willing to grant them, might also be of assistance here."

Only after these basics did it turn to what was

FDR at Madison Square Garden before his re-election, 1940.
He was seen in Britain, then fighting on its own, as the last great hope for survival
and his association with Churchill as a promise of the future.

uppermost in most people's minds: aircraft. It had reported absurdities under the neutrality laws which had required American planes to be towed along a border airstrip from the United States into Canada. That was over. But how effective was America's capacity going to be?

"Whether any immediate increase in the supply of aircraft could be secured by the same means is more doubtful, since the American aircraft industry is already working to capacity, and Allied orders already enjoy a substantial preference." No one had grasped yet the full potential and ingenuity of American industry; this was based on its capability in the summer of 1940. What the paper insisted on was realism. It was idle to expect too much, wiser to look to 1941 and onwards, though "its dimensions at that time are almost unlimited".

For the paper's correspondents the summer's events,

reversals and upheavals, and their significance, had made life difficult. The Washington man confessed in late July: "For the past six weeks, American opinion has been changing too fast for correspondence, even Clipper-carried, to have any pertinence by the time that it can get into print across the ocean."

For Roosevelt, and for those in the United States and Europe who had come to depend on him for a successful outcome of the war, with or without America's armed participation, one essential was his own re-election in November. In the first week of June, as the last of the British expeditionary force was brought back from the beaches of Dunkirk, the paper had a new personality to illuminate: "Mr Roosevelt is now certain of the Democratic nomination, and his chances of election are enhanced. But this very fact is driving the Republicans into angry non-acquiescence— the angrier because they realise that they cannot oppose the President's foreign policy. They may be driven to nominate an interventionist, and there is increasing talk of Mr Wendell Willkie, a progressive and independent-minded businessman."

When the Republican convention met at the end of June the paper was sorry for them. If they persisted in isolationism while London was being bombed they would alienate millions of their supporters; if they called for help for the allies Roosevelt was ahead of them. They chose Willkie, a surprising and imaginative candidate, and *The Economist*, among others, was grateful. It thought he would make "an able and distinguished President", but, more than that, his candidacy meant that America's alignment in the war had been taken out of the election: "The strong probability is that the next President of the United States will be Franklin Roosevelt; Mr Willkie's service to humanity— it is a very large one—will be to save the United States from its usual election-year predicament of having no foreign policy."

Even while the Battle of Britain was being fought over Kent and Sussex the paper had turned its thoughts to what the American reaction would be to another stalemate in the war. It was not at all complimentary: "American opinion will turn against us once more. Mr Henry Ford will think it is a 'phoney' war. Colonel Lindbergh will talk about the effrontery of Canada in fighting for democracy without American permission. And the team of Ambassadors to the occupied countries of Europe, longing to have their jobs back, will sing the praises of the Quislings."

Roosevelt, before the battle was decided, took a decision that Winston Churchill thought decidedly unneutral, agreeing to exchange 50 first world war destroyers for British bases in Newfoundland and Bermuda, outposts for the defence of the United States itself, and, in the West Indies, helpful in the defence of the Panama Canal. The paper saw no charity in this: Britain had also declared that, come what may, the Royal Navy would be neither surrendered nor scuttled. It showed how the two countries' interests were interdependent: "It means that in certain unlikely, but not impossible, circumstances the inhabitants of Great Britain would abandon themselves to occupation and starvation and would consent to be blockaded by their own fleet, rather than leave the way to the New World open to the Nazis."

It recommended that immediate steps be taken to counteract the growth of pro-Nazi feeling in Argentina, Brazil and Uruguay: the United States needed to guarantee a market for Argentine wheat and maize and Brazilian cotton. This would be wholly in American interests: "If Britain were to fall under Nazi occupation, nothing but distance would protect her from the menace of Hitlerism. If Germany could once secure an adequate air base in the Western Hemisphere, the splendid isolation of the United States would be a thing of the past."

In the election there could be only one British candidate: the man in office. Still, the paper was not going to compromise Roosevelt, however small and irregular its wartime circulation in America was. It was not until November 2nd 1940 that it actually cast its vote: "Perhaps it is permissible, in an issue of *The Economist* which will not reach the United States until after the election, to endorse, from the British angle, the comment that the known vices of Mr Roosevelt are to be preferred to the unknown virtues of Mr Willkie."

THE ARSENAL OF DEMOCRACY

It was agonisingly slow to deliver, until Pearl Harbor

The times were not easy: the London blitz was on. *The Economist's* offices were burnt out by incendiary bombs, and it appeared using unfamiliar type. American opinion was still overwhelmingly anxious to keep out of the fighting if it could. The paper put the best face it could on this: "Non-intervening America today is more committed to a policy compatible with its status in the world than was intervening America in 1918."

It was not true, but in January 1941 it would have read that way: "We want the tanks and the ships and the aircraft necessary to secure our victory, and we shall be only too glad if we can secure this help without plunging our great neighbour into the disaster and tragedy of war."

All it was tactful to say was that the United States was the arsenal of democracy, and that was what Britain had to be content with. The first idea of neutrality had gone, so had cash and carry, so had the policy of never opening fire. The resolution of the war would be determined, in the end, by American industrial production: "There can be no question that it is by far the most powerful economic unit in the world that is being thus mobilised. In national income, the most comprehensive measure of economic potential, the United States outweighs either Great Britain or Germany fourfold; its annual output is probably twice as great as that of the whole Continent of Europe, victors and vanquished alike." That was only potential armaments output: "By January, 1943, America will be a giant among nations; in January, 1941, she is the weakest of the remaining Powers."

Lend-lease, Roosevelt's solution to the rundown of British investment in the United States, meant the arms would still be delivered. Both governments, American and British, chose not to elaborate on who would pay in the end. The paper was not so diplomatic: "It is being very widely, and far too easily, assumed in this country that the problem will never arise in any seri-

The Flying Fortress: an early B-17 operating from eastern England, 1942. The build-up of US day-bombing strength, with the RAF at night, was airpower's contribution to victory.

ous form, that the apparatus of leasing and lending is merely a provisional substitute for an ultimate free gift.... But it is not the intention of Congress that the munitions and materials to be supplied are regarded as a gift. It is not the intention even of the majority who have passed the Bill."

It was obvious to the paper that the arsenal was even slower than predicted in producing the goods. In April 1941 it first put together an American section, hoping "that by the mere juxtaposition of so many different items, some idea will be conveyed of the breadth and colour of the canvas on which American democracy is painting current history". The reports were not encouraging. The New Dealers believed they could run war production better than business. Business was irked by the continuing New Deal controls. Walter Reuther of the Congress of Industrial Organisations (CIO) claimed the Detroit motor factories could turn out 500 planes a day; the experts demurred. The industry was aiming at up to 4,000 planes a month, but the March output was only 1,216 of all types. 100 tanks a day were needed; just three were being produced. It took time to get results, as it had in Britain: "Current expenditure on defence still represents little more than ten per cent of the growing national income. There has as yet been no reduction in the output of consumption goods, while the unemployed are still counted in millions."

At sea the war was "a race between losses and replacements" which the British yards were losing. Roosevelt himself admitted that the American and British yards together were putting into commission 1 ton of shipping for every 2 tons sunk by the U-boats. Then Hitler marched into the Soviet Union. It was "clear evidence that he believes he can end the conflict by a series of killing strokes before America's economic strength can be translated into military power."

There was no point at all in British appeals for a declaration of war: "They prove nothing—except that the British people would like to see America in the war, which everybody knows already."

American war production was disappointing, but no worse than the initial British efforts: "There have been unforgivable muddles, confusions, timidities, delays; but, if there had been no more muddle, confusion, timidity and delay than this in Great Britain in the days when it, too, was only a near-belligerent, it would be possible for an Englishman to be prouder of his country's achievements."

Things were beginning to happen. The symbol of visible rearming was the jeep. The paper's Washington correspondent welcomed the sight of it: "It is a new-type truck, known as a Jeep because it sounds like a Jeep. Ungainly and able, it rouses in the middle-aged American nostalgia for the model T Fords of his youth, the schematic, high-clearance moto-buggies that needed for their repairs only ingenuity, plus chewing gum or an occasional hair pin."

By August Japanese intentions in the Pacific appeared plain and ominous. The paper had no doubts of what was coming. It believed the United States and Britain must act together in the Far East and, in the face of Japanese ambitions, it was time to move from what had been "unmodified appeasement": "What they say together in the Far East now must be strong, forceful and without reserve. It is not a question of wilfully electing Japan as a new foe. Japan has nominated herself."

By the end of October it was looking at the American defences. It was not unhappy about them: "The Panama Canal is safe from attack so long as the United States holds Hawaii, the hub of their Pacific defence. Here, at Pearl Harbor, is the largest single defence area controlled by the United States military authorities. The Pacific fleet is stationed there, as well as an infantry division and a growing air force."

The gaps further west, the paper believed, were being sealed: "The islands are protected by Midway, Wake and Johnston islands, from which long-distance planes can patrol about 4,000 miles to the west of Hawaii. Midway is a fully equipped air and naval base, and Wake has only limited facilities; but both are being improved and expanded to the tune of a Congress grant of over $9 millions voted in March this year."

The final Japanese mission to Washington was, it thought, proposing no terms that could be acceptable. The Americans and British were being told, under threat of war, to give up their own and their allies' interests, in return only for a promise of immunity: "Mr Kurusu's mission is condemned to end in failure before he ever sets foot in the United States."

The paper viewed the Japanese attack on Pearl Harbor on December 7th as the ultimate in "this war of crisis upon crisis". It drew three particular conclusions. First, the Japanese had acted on a precise calculation of the consequences: "The Japanese have been persuaded in recent months that the realisation of their own ambitions in East Asia depends on who is master of the rest of the world. They have chosen their side and they are now implementing the Axis plan."

Second, it believed they had made a fundamental error: "The Japanese have, with forethought and intent, brought into the war against them a nation of 140 millions and the greatest industrial power in the history of mankind. They have performed the miracle of ending all American disputes overnight."

Third, it was helpful to Britain in more than the obvious accretion of military strength. The relationship with the United States had not, it thought, been entirely what was needed: "American generosity has been unbounded—but it has remained generosity, and gratitude has remained a commodity for import, not for exchange. All that is ended now—and a far more promising and satisfactory basis is laid for intimate co-operation on terms of real equality and trust."

The conduct of the war now came down to the conduct of the coalition.

THE UNCERTAIN ALLIANCE
Early failures brought on friendly fire
throughout the coalition

The Economist did not overindulge in grand strategy. It believed that American production would be decisive in winning the war; once that had attained its momentum, what was necessary was allied unity in aim, and, preferably, amity too. When differences became apparent it did not assume that Britain was necessarily right, but it believed that British policies and views deserved description and illustration. It could be annoyed by American criticism, especially in the mouths of old isolationists, but, like Churchill, it thought it knew enough to discriminate and, when required, to explain.

Occasionally it believed Churchill too forbearing. It was not greatly enamoured of high-minded charters and declarations; nor of summits. Before America entered the war the point it particularly fastened on in the Atlantic Charter was, true to its past, the restoration of equal trading opportunity and the repudiation of the theories of the 1930s which had elevated self-sufficiency into a principle of national policy.

The paper was not only concerned about the Anglo-American dialogue within the alliance; it believed it had the correspondents and the editorial experience to contribute to it in a way that other British papers were not equipped to do or mindful of doing. So in its issue of January 17th 1942 the editor, Geoffrey Crowther, started the American Survey section of the paper, a regular mainstay of its reputation to this day. He was fortunate to secure two outstanding editors, Nancy Balfour and Margaret Cruickshank, to guide its fortunes over its first 30 years. It was to be "a brief review of the major aspects of public affairs, political and economic, in the United States", although it showed a proper caution: "In the present state of communications across the Atlantic, it is not easy to secure an adequate flow of information. What is prompt is scanty; and what is detailed is delayed. In particular, correspondence arrives very irregularly." Just to prove the point, Roosevelt's budget message to Congress was hard to interpret: "Unfortunately, the cabled reports of this part of the Message are both cryptic and contradictory."

Britain's part in the war was soon under scathing American criticism, which persisted as long as the war itself, both of the British military performance and of Britain's apparent reluctance to forsake its imperial inheritance. After the fall of Singapore had come the unexpected collapse against Rommel's Afrika Corps at Tobruk. Churchill himself had heard the news of Tobruk in Washington: "Senator Ellender's outburst that he was 'sick and tired of British failures' was only one of many bitter comments which reflect American disillusionment with the British direction of the war. The Libyan collapse followed so quickly on the announcements of American victories in the Coral Sea and at Midway that an unfavourable comparison could hardly fail to be drawn; and the result is a growing feeling that the United States must assume more responsibility for the progress of the war."

The success of Montgomery's Eighth Army in the western desert silenced much criticism. So did the British part in the North African landings: "Rommel's defeat has put an end to the insinuations that British troops were unable to put American weapons to good use, or that Lend-Lease equipment was being hoarded in the British Isles."

The paper distrusted the isolationists in the Republican Party, among whom anglophobia remained latent. When in the mid-term elections in 1942 the

Republicans came close to controlling the house, its resentment quickly surfaced: "The real leaders of the Republican party have been at best tepid and at worst hostile to the idea of effective aid to Britain in the war against Hitler."

It put responsibility for America's own early reverses at their door, yet now the American voter was turning to them and putting Roosevelt's conduct of affairs in jeopardy: "It has not done any candidate any harm to have had a most vulnerable pre-Pearl Harbor record, to have voted against the fortification of Guam or for the disbandment of the army, to name issues which do not directly involve the question of aid to Britain or Russia…. President Roosevelt's position is weakened, not strengthened, by the repudiation of his friends and the election of his enemies."

The paper seldom took such a party-political line in its election analysis. What put it even more on its mettle was the deepening realisation that, under the rhetoric of Atlantic unity, a majority of American opinion had reservations about where exactly the British Empire was going to fit in. The failure of Sir Stafford Cripps's attempt to negotiate an agreement on India's future status with Gandhi and Nehru's Congress Party did not win American sympathy: "The people of the United States, for obvious historical reasons, are constitutionally inclined to regard all matters pertaining to the British Empire, and, in particular, to India, with the deepest suspicion."

Because of this "unfortunate" tradition and the propaganda of the Indian Congress Party over the years, American opinion did not want to hear the British side. The paper took issue with the magazine *Life*, which had been frank about British imperialism. Two concepts were, and had been, at issue within the relationship, going back to the idealism of Woodrow Wilson and his associates, self-confident enough to be intent on saving Europe from its failures and follies: "There is a sense in which, because of the size and strength and wealth of the United States, this must be the American Century. It was the firm belief, not only of President Wilson, but also of so staunch and clear-sighted a friend of Britain as Walter Hines Page, that the right result of the last war would have been American leadership. The chance was spurned."

It did not dwell on who had done the spurning. It was concerned that there should be no malignant or unavoidable difference now: "Now the door is open again, and it is the world's need that Britain and the United States should march through together, shouldering their responsibilities, with no narrow thoughts of prestige or precedence. To set the concept of the American Century, which has still to be understood, accepted and carried by the American people, in flat opposition to a concept of British Imperialism which is pure myth, is sabotage."

As the war progressed into 1943 American thoughts, especially among those who had the time, turned to the world after the war. Both Roosevelt's left-wing vice-president, Henry Wallace, and the Republican radical, Wendell Willkie, who still hoped to run for the White House again in 1944, were sceptical about what Britain might contribute: "Since the Battle of Britain, which brought a wave of enthusiasm for a time, a new picture has been growing in people's minds…. In the shadowy, indeterminate world of emotions and imagination, it would be untrue to suppose that Britain is making a good showing."

This fear, voiced by a staff correspondent in the United States, supposed that Britain's past could disqualify it, despite its efforts in the war and its natural place at the summits of Roosevelt, Stalin and Churchill, from an influential post-war role. It would be shouldered aside: "India, incredibly simplified as an issue between light and darkness, is universally discussed. Singapore, Malaya, Burma are still symbols of Imperial decadence. There is a real danger that the United Nations may come to suggest to people's minds an alliance of China, Russia and the United States for the purpose of liquidating—with the highest motives—the British Empire."

Nobody, the paper thought, was asking Britain to go socialist. It would even do harm if Britain did because the Americans were egalitarian, not collectivist. But Churchill had insisted that Britain meant to hold its own in the peace settlement, and Willkie, for one, had been shocked. With Hitler still far from finished and the allies still to land in France, these differences could prove dangerous: "The British Empire is in danger of becoming the object of a slanging match between British and American leaders. Nothing could be more unfortunate. Nothing could be more unnecessary. The Americans want to know what the British are going to do next."

If Britain made up its mind in a sensible, liberal way, and let it be known, the whole dispute would become irrelevant: "It should be perfectly possible to tell them in terms that might send them away whooping for joy over the British Commonwealth as the greatest, most creative experiment in the history of international relations."

Lend-lease continued to have its critics in the Congress. The administrator, Edward Stettinius, had to reassure them that Britain had provided two-thirds of the warships and transports in the original North African landing. Willkie's friends, who were not isolationist, continued to harp on Britain not even being allowed entrance to the United Nations unless it repented of its "imperialist sins". Five anti-British senators spoke of the British misusing the lend-lease supplies, and of "the efficient and single-minded way in which America's allies and clients", "notably Britain", were pursuing their own national interests. The paper was nettled. The criticism was "a surface and transitory phenomenon". It thought nothing of it: "That it should appear at all in the middle of a desperate war, fought in intimate alliance, can be explained only by an aspect of American life which Englishmen always find puzzling and for which they never make sufficient allowance—namely, its all-pervading irresponsibility."

The paper doubted if the repayment of lend-lease would turn out to be practicable, even if the Americans asked for it. While the war lasted the world was badly in need of American goods; when it finished, the world would need fewer, unless the Americans allowed it to sell goods to them. The only way Britain could pay would be in goods which normally (unlike whisky, textiles, oil reserves) it did not sell to the United States: "Whether America would be ready, when the time came, to accept free deliveries of British manufactures, presumably to be sold on the domestic market in competition with American products, is an interesting speculation."

ANSWERING BACK

Since Churchill never stood up to the
Americans, someone else had to try

The nadir of the wartime alliance actually arrived in the winter of 1944, when disappointment overtook the high hopes of the allied advance in the months after D-Day. The German counter-attack on a weakly held sector of the American front renewed criticism of other allied efforts. It was said that the British intervention to rescue the non-communist party in Greece was anti-Russian; at the same time the lack of British influence to help the Polish resistance holding out in Warsaw was too pro-Russian. That Britain was seen to be following both a balance of power and a spheres of interest policy, then anathema to the well-meaning, added to the familiar complaints: "Britain is stealing a march on the poor repressed American exporter. Britain has no intention of fighting the Japanese. Britain is not really fighting in Europe—it is even a subject of complaint that Rundstedt did not attack the British-held front for his break-through."

The accusations were cumulative: "Britain is imperialist, reactionary, selfish, exclusive, restrictive." Since this was not how the British saw themselves or wished others to see them, the paper judged it time to speak its mind, whatever it did to Anglo-American relations. It felt that a "journal whose general approach to the problems of the world is so obviously Americanophile" was the right one for plain speaking. It was plain enough: "To be told by anyone that the British people are slacking in their war effort would be insufferable enough to a people struggling through their sixth winter of black-out and blockade and bombs, of queues and rations and coldness—but when the criticism comes from a nation that was practising Cash-and-Carry during the Battle of Britain, whose consumption has risen through the war years, which is still without a national service act—then it is not to be borne."

It was the authentic voice of Crowther and his paper. So was his argument that followed. He ridiculed the suspicions which the American media had voiced. What were the British supposed to be hoping for: an Anglo-American alliance, exclusive and guaranteed, for the future or the worldwide protection of British territorial integrity? Or were they after a promise to put down aggression wherever it reappeared? It was all too improbable then: "There is no more possibility of any of these things than of an American petition to rejoin the British Empire."

That disclaimed, there followed the clearest exposition of the paper's attitude to, and outlook on, Anglo-American relations. It said it was precisely at times of crisis that nations saw their interests clearly: "If the ultimate extremity of 1940 should ever repeat itself, American action would be the same. No nation surely ever tried harder to keep out of war than the

United States between 1935 and 1940, but to no avail. No country surely ever blotted its American copybook more carefully than debt-defaulting, appeasing Britain, and yet we were given the aid we needed."

So it was in that confidence in the relationship, peculiar, undefined but confirmed by war and its demands, that the paper believed friends should speak to each other: "It is not reasonable to suppress legitimate British interests simply because they offend American susceptibilities. Let there by all means be a continuance of the policy of friendship and co-operation, and even of patience and forbearance under provocation. But let an end be put to the policy of appeasement which, at Mr Churchill's personal bidding, has been followed, with all the humiliations and abasements it has brought in its train, ever since Pearl Harbor removed the need for it." The candid friend spoke with proper Churchillian vehemence.

The recrimination continued once the Battle of the Bulge was over: why were the western allies short of reserves? Roosevelt and Churchill, the paper thought, had decided to put increased emphasis on the war with Japan as early as 1943, and waging the two wars with equal energy was accepted by Churchill in 1944: "Mr Churchill's government has conceived its role to be that of the honest broker. Its concern has been to see whether proposals and policies are acceptable to its Allies, rather than whether they are suitable and effective in themselves."

A distinctive British line would recover a freedom of movement which only Washington, Moscow and even Paris exerted in their own interests: "Mr Churchill would be relieved of the role of perpetual mediator, go-between and universal aunt."

The Yalta conference in February 1945 was the test for allied unity with victory in sight. The three powers decided on joint responsibility to set up democratic governments and arrange for elections. The paper was dubious: "This decision will, no doubt, be hailed in the American Press as a victory won by the President over British and Russian policies, with their desire for exclusive spheres. If to regard it in this way will make the policy of American intervention in Europe more popular and more enduring, it would be foolish to cavil."

If the arrangement were "properly interpreted and fully applied" it would be a genuine step forward. It was up to the Russians: "The British and the American Governments cannot shelve the issue.... The basis for negotiation must be the recognition of the major parties in Poland, the acceptance of their well-established leaders and the coming together of these men—all of them, or almost all of them—in a provisional Government."

The paper wanted terms that would put Stalin and his puppets to the test: "Secondary provisions are freedoms of the press, of speech, and of meeting within the limits set by military necessity—in short, a quick end to the suspicious unanimity of the Lublin regime.... Only under these conditions, formulated as precisely as possible, can the general provisions reached at Yalta be turned into concrete achievement."

It was only Stalin who got what he wanted. As the war ended, and with this evidence before its eyes, the paper was intent on the United States continuing to exert its influence in Europe. It feared a repetition of what had happened over the League of Nations. But other allies were not helping to ensure the Americans' interest: "Most agree that in the future Britain and the United States must swim or sink together. But Americans are much more reluctant to take commitments respecting France."

The Americans, it observed, would prefer international to French control in the Ruhr and Rhineland, but that was a French sticking-point. And when the Poles were still hesitating over assuming responsibility in Upper Silesia, their new lands, why should the Americans guarantee them? "The great dilemma of Americans, which Yalta sharpened rather than removed, is their unwillingness or inability to make their general commitments specific."

Their reluctance was annoying: so was Churchill's reluctance to press them firmly enough. The paper had been unhappy about a number of their projected schemes: for Germany's forcible dismemberment and its return to a purely agricultural economy. The next practical steps needed Roosevelt's authority behind them. But on April 12th 1945 at Warm Springs, Georgia, Roosevelt died of a cerebral haemorrhage.

AMERICA AT WAR

No bombs fell, but civilian America had to pull in its belt and get to its feet

War production was the key, and the war brought the production by the application of American industry's

The Big Three (left to right, Churchill, Roosevelt, Stalin) at Yalta, 1945. The paper disliked the plans for Soviet-dominated eastern Europe. Roosevelt's final illness was all too apparent.

resourcefulness and shrewdness. American plant had unequalled resources to call on: it was used to large-scale operation, there were reserves of manpower and womanpower, and there had been two years for planning and gearing-up. The civilian population, as a rule, co-operated with rationing, and the American effort ran potently, uninterrupted by bombing raids or blockade. It was the big firms that got the results. In September 1943, when war production was reaching its peak, the paper reported how industrial concentration was the winner.

Analysis showed that 70.1% of the war supply contracts worth more than $50,000 had gone to the top 100 firms in the period from June 1940 to November 1942. The leaders were, naturally, General Motors, Curtiss Wright, Bethlehem Steel, Douglas Aircraft and United Aircraft. The War Production Board was run by executives of big companies—Knudsen of General Motors, Nelson of Sears Roebuck, Wilson of General Electric—and, anyway, the armed forces preferred to work with

them because they knew them best. So, in a decade that had brought American industry from the pit of depression to the apogee of output, concentration seemed to be the secret.

Individual genius was there too, not least that of Henry J. Kaiser who cut the time for launching his ships from over 100 days to under a week. While the Battle of the Atlantic was going badly and the allies were on the defensive on almost every front, the paper grasped thankfully at the Kaiser record: "Today he has eight shipyards of his own, strung along the Pacific coast, with 73 ways to them; his boast is that he can build 10,000,000 deadweight tons of shipping on these ways next year." That had been Roosevelt's target for merchant shipping for the whole American shipbuilding industry in 1942. The paper believed Kaiser: "His boast has body to it."

By February 1944, three months before the D-Day landings in France, the paper reckoned the United States had been too successful with its war production:

"The existence of surpluses in a number of specialities, such as tanks and anti-aircraft guns, was recognised months ago. A number of ammunition plants have been closed recently. Several aluminium fabricating plants have been slowing down."

From Ohio came specific evidence: "Airplane engine parts have been accumulating to the point where one of the largest Cleveland works is laying off 1,000 men next week and reducing its working hours to 41.5 a week. Sunday work is being cut out in shipyards all over the country, and the Cleveland yard has had a cancellation of part of its order book." More followed in August from Gary, Indiana.

"The 36,000 steel workers ... are producing and partially or wholly processing more than 80 per cent as much steel as the whole of Japan."

Madison Avenue in uniform   The paper was struck by the highly successful war being fought by Madison Avenue. The North African landings and the Roosevelt–Churchill meeting at Casablanca afterwards produced advertising in the American papers to which British eyes were unaccustomed. Transcontinental and Western Air Inc addressed Roosevelt directly: "Thank you, Mr President. Your flight to Africa shows the great faith you have in aviation." American Airlines declared: "The human race now does possess the physical means of enforcing peace." And Alcoa Aluminium ("The metal that flies best") reinforced the strategy of air power: "Here is something bigger, more final, than

Women at war. Women shipyard welders not only showed what they could do in a man's job but promoted a new equality in industry which lasted into the peace.

our old earthborn belief in Freedom of the Seas."

The US navy had its own publicist on *The Economist*. Struck by the size of the Pacific fleet apparent in August 1944, the paper acknowledged the new dimension of the American way in war: "Larger than the entire British navy at the beginning of this war, commanding thousands of aircraft and landing craft, able to remain for months at sea supporting itself from its own supply train, this fleet is a veritable floating empire."

MacArthur's return to the Philippines was in sight. It had been a long haul from the early, panicky reports, such as of a Japanese submarine shelling the Bankline Oil Refinery at Santa Barbara, California, in February 1942, when the paper even sympathised with the apprehensive isolationists: it showed "that the fears along both coasts are not groundless or hysterical". In the east German u-boats were even more active: "Sinkings have occurred so close inshore that crowds on the beaches have been able to see them and have taken part in the rescue of the crews. The recent dim-out and black-out orders to coastal cities, including New York, are part of the attempt to reduce ship losses.... It is surprising that the United States has not instituted a convoy system along its coasts—unless the reason is that the escort vessels are not available." Convoys were brought in by July 1942, including in the Caribbean.

Enter rationing   The paper was intrigued about how Americans would respond to much of what had been accepted as part of everyday life in Britain. From the start, cars were in short supply: "As in Great Britain, the private car-owner will not be able to buy a new car. He will have growing difficulty in having his existing car repaired. There is the strictest rationing of tyres and, in some parts of the country, petrol rationing is a possibility."

The paper's Washington correspondent kept an earnest eye on the home front: "The housewife who went to the nearest schoolhouse last week and obtained Ration Book One (for sugar) obtained the first concrete evidence that something is being done on a national scale about the problem of price and supply. That was last week. This week ... car owners in the seventeen states of the eastern seaboard and the District of Columbia are being rationed again for gasoline."

The production of refrigerators for civilians was stopped by the summer of 1942; a year later many peo-

ple had no meat to put in them anyway. Shortages prevailed in both distribution and production: "It remains something of a shock to hear that Americans will be restricted to approximately a pound of meat a week, and realise that—if the ration is forthcoming—to many this will mean an improvement."

Los Angeles, swollen with war workers in the aircraft plants, was getting less than two-thirds of its 1941 supplies. New York City, too, complained that the war was hurting it. As late as the summer of 1942 it had 368,000 registered unemployed. It was still the world's biggest manufacturing city but it was making the wrong things: consumption goods, not war supplies. For some time the unions in the garment industry had been pricing themselves out of the market, especially in competition with the non-union south. It looked prosperous enough in the newsreels, but only in those parts of Manhattan which were catering for servicemen on leave. There the sky was the limit: "The crowds of sightseers on the streets are reminiscent of the days of the World's Fair in 1938–39, except that today most of them are in Service uniforms. Restaurants and night clubs are doing a land-office business. Seats are a premium for the better-known Broadway shows."

War earnings—and savings   Before the war the top tax rate had been 79% on those with incomes of over $5m; that had risen to 88% on those with incomes of $200,000. But war employment was making everyone better off: "The individual citizens of the United States have, in the aggregate, about $3,000 million more income, after taxation, every month than they had two years ago."

The paper did a quick calculation of what that meant for inflation: "Slightly more than $1,000 million a month is being mopped up in war savings bonds, leaving the enormous amount of about $2,000 million a month, or $24,000 million a year—considerably more than the whole pre-war British national income—as a net addition to potential purchasing power."

It did not think much of the solutions being proposed. There were wage formulas (which the miners' leader, John L. Lewis, was regularly "in the act of breaking"), price ceilings ("which are cracking") and the rights and wrongs of subsidy policy were being debated ("when, in fact, it is a problem of incomes").

The fight against prejudice   The war was rapidly

changing the lives of black Americans, often for the good but sometimes not. One of the first black heroes had distinguished himself on the first day at Pearl Harbor: "It is news—and good news—that the Navy Cross has been awarded by President Roosevelt to Dorie Miller, the negro mess attendant who, when the first bombs fell on Pearl Harbor, raced up from his galley and manned one of the machine guns that, by Navy regulations, no negro is allowed to touch."

Prejudice, the paper believed, was deep-seated: "The Navy still excludes all negroes from the service except as messmen; prejudice is rife in the army, despite the excellent record of negro soldiers in the last war; and discrimination against negroes in industry and Government service remains the rule, not the exception."

Necessity was to discourage intolerance, but far from everywhere. Industry drew a black migration northwards to the booming cities. In Chicago the number of commercial and industrial firms employing blacks had, by mid-1943, risen 400% in two years. The War Manpower Commission had been encouraging it: "Only 10 per cent of the firms that received defence contracts in this metropolitan area in 1940 had been employing negroes on the production line. In 1941, a broad sampling of industrial and commercial firms made by the Chicago Urban League (an organisation for inter-racial co-operation) indicated that 15 per cent employed negroes in skilled or semi-skilled capacities; now the percentage is 64."

In Detroit there was more trouble: "At least twenty-five negroes and three whites are dead, hundreds are in hospital, hundreds more are in jail, houses in Paradise Valley, the negro quarter, were fired; there was sniping, looting and at least one scene of open warfare.... It is alarming to find how quickly the violence usually associated only with race relations in the South has followed the migration of both negro and white workers."

Zoot suit battles   Even the distinctive male teenage fashion of the war years, the zoot suit, was a source of trouble: "The zoot suit, for all its eccentric specifications of coats below the knee, six-foot key chains, foot-wide shoulders and peg-top trousers, is not altogether a comic subject. About 500 men and boys are in jail and 150 in hospital in Los Angeles as a result of clashes between the uniform of the United States and that of the gandy-dancer, and Los Angeles has been put out of bounds for Service men."

Calling up the auto reserves   In April 1944 the paper reported that the worst was about to happen to American car owners. There had been a reserve of 2m cars unsold when the war began. It was now down to 50,000, all of which would be released to eligible buyers only by July 1st. It was a devastated and empty land: "Thousands of gasoline stations along the open roads of the country ceased business operations. Vacations by motor car became a memory. The retail tyre business all but disappeared. And that very special American institution, which over a generation had become very close to a religious rite, the annual showing of new automobile models, vanished with the rest."

There were even unimagined sights for the practised eye: "Old cars—very old ones—are coming out of hiding and rolling over streets and highways. One sees a surprising number of model 'A' Fords, and now and again even model 'T's. And names of machines whose companies long ago died or went into a different line of manufacture—Maxwells, Auburns, Reos—are mingled with the newest that remain after years of business competition."

For a moment it may even have seemed to some Americans that the allies were not winning the war yet.

THE LAST FIGHT
Peace seemed round the corner, but without Roosevelt

The Economist naturally favoured Roosevelt's decision to run for a fourth term in 1944. It was not worried about constitution or precedent. The war came first. Roosevelt then dropped his left-wing vice-president, Henry Wallace, for the almost unknown Senator Harry S Truman from Missouri; the Republican candidate, Thomas E. Dewey, chose the conservative Governor John Bricker from Ohio as his running-mate. Now the paper identified another rising star: "The scenes of mass enthusiasm daily staged in the heart of New York have nothing to do with either candidate or either party; neither with the war in Europe nor with the war in the Pacific. These public raptures are excited by the 'personal appearances' at stated hours each day of Mr Frank Sinatra, a singer of sentimental ballads."

It knew what the indices of approval and celebrity

showed: "Being a modest young man, Mr Sinatra would probably concede that Mr Roosevelt has greater charm, that Mr Dewey has a richer voice, that Governor Bricker cuts a finer figure of a man, and that Senator Truman is far more folksy. Yet every hour young women are swooning at the very sight of Mr Sinatra—and none of the national candidates has yet achieved that result."

It wasted little space on the actual campaigning, except to deplore whatever the Republicans did or attempted. The result did not seem in doubt. For the fourth time it welcomed a Roosevelt victory: "In a year when, for a variety of reasons, voting was surrounded by special difficulties, 50 million Americans would not have attended at the polls without a deep conviction of the importance of the issues at stake."

Though FDR had done his utmost to conceal his physical frailty during the election it did not need particular insight to recognise how infirm he was at Yalta; the photographs left no doubt. His death in April 1945 was still suddenly disconcerting. The paper advanced its own insight into his nature: "He had his defects; he was too good a politician to be a skilful administrator, and too good a fighter to conciliate the nation into complete unity behind his leadership. But when everything that can be said against him is said to the full, he remains a very great man and a very great President."

Now, on his death, it recalled what he had meant to Britain during its bleakest days: "No Englishman who lived through those twelve dreadful months from June 1940 to June 1941 is ever likely to forget how completely the nation's hope for ultimate victory rested on that buoyant figure in the White House, and how, stage by stage, the hopes found response in action."

Truman, now president, was a Democratic Party regular from the mid-west, slightly to the right, it was thought, of Roosevelt's views, and so a man of the dead centre. The man who was to authorise the dropping of the first atomic bomb in three months' time was freely patronised by those, including the paper, who simply did not know him: "It is no insult to Mr Truman to suppose that he is a good ordinary President."

Iwo Jima: US landing craft in the assault on Japan's outer defences, 1945. The Pacific war was dominated by the United States, but Japanese resistance kept up until the atom bombs on Hiroshima and Nagasaki.

At the Potsdam conference, 1945, the men of the cold war (left to right, Churchill, the newly-elevated Truman, and Stalin) failed to bridge the differences that Soviet ambitions revealed.

9

COLD WAR DUTY

1946–1951

FEELING THE CHILL

*The paper had early doubts about the
American willingness to stay in Europe, but
the Soviet Union helped*

There were few hopes of President Truman when he went to his first summit at Potsdam in July 1945. He was expected to follow Roosevelt's economic and social policies at home, but be out of his depth when it came to dealing with the Russians and the British. With the Conservative defeat in the British general election even Winston Churchill, who might have continued as the mediator, was removed from the conference table. But Truman had an incisive mind, he took decisions, and though he was a Roosevelt internationalist he did not wish to share the new world on Stalin's terms.

The Americans and Russians had been at odds at the United Nations conference at San Francisco. This was confirmed at Potsdam and *The Economist* thought its outcome was ominous: "At the end of a mighty war fought to defeat Hitlerism, the Allies are making a

Hitlerian peace."

Since what the Americans and Russians still had in common was the prostration and division of Germany that was agreed, although the paper doubted if it was either politic or feasible: "The system proposed is in the fullest sense unworkable. It offers no hope of ultimate German reconciliation. It offers little hope of the Allies maintaining its cumbrous controls beyond the first years of peace." Its consequences would not only push the new protagonists further apart, they would leave central Europe a wasteland to be fought over: "Its methods of reparation reinforce autarky in Russia and consummate the ruin not only of Germany, but of Europe. Above all it has in it not a single constructive idea, not a single hopeful perspective for the post-war world."

Churchill's speech on March 5th 1946 at Fulton, Missouri, in Truman's presence, in which he spoke of an iron curtain descending across Europe, was accurate and salutary; it was also unpopular. "Mr Churchill's expertly timed bombshell" the paper called it. He had

---

CHRONOLOGY

1946	Winston Churchill's iron curtain speech, Fulton, Missouri		West German republic established
			Chinese communists win civil war; Chiang Kai-shek flees to Formosa
1947	Truman doctrine: aid to Greece and Turkey	1950	US decides to make hydrogen bomb
	Taft-Hartley labour law		North Korean forces invade South
	US offers Europe Marshall aid		Chinese invade Tibet
	Britain gives India and Pakistan independence		Communist China enters Korean war
	Communist coup in Czechoslovakia	1951	European coal and steel treaty
1948	Britain ends its Palestine mandate		Iran nationalises oil industry
	Soviet troops blockade Berlin		UN forces recover 38th parallel
	West European treaty on defence		Truman dismisses General Douglas MacArthur
	Alger Hiss accused of being communist and spy		Churchill returns as prime minister
1949	North Atlantic Treaty signed		

"certainly stolen the show". But there were many on both sides of the Atlantic who could not believe ill of the Russians, or thought Churchill had been too acrimonious. Many Americans wished to limit the strength and the length of any commitment to the Europeans. Had there been a time when opinion could have turned back to the 1920s it would have been then.

However, modern weapons prohibited it. The paper agreed with those who saw the flying bombs that Hitler had sent against London as the precursors of those that would directly threaten the United States; twentieth-century science had "smashed up the eighteenth century doctrine of isolationism". Truman had used the atom bomb against the Japanese without hesitation or remorse. He and his advisers were prepared to organise a world system in which the bomb kept the peace. The paper advised strongly against nebulous controls or a spurious internationalism which might appease nuclear critics at the risk of great danger: "A system of atomic control which, however much it was dressed up as 'a promising first step' or 'an attempt to build up to a solution', in fact controlled the innocent while leaving the would-be-guilty free, would be a disaster without limit. It would make atomic war and the destruction of civilisation quite certain."

Before the Soviet Union, or Britain, had the bomb, it accepted the logic of the theory of mutual deterrence as the best prospect for safety: "It would be better to have atomic bombs in everybody's hands so that there would be at least the threat of retaliation to prevent, or postpone, the crash—a poor reliance, it is true, but better than the certainty of disaster." When the Soviet Union detonated its own atomic device in September 1949 the only alternative was one or other form of western pacifism, which had no appeal to the paper.

It was actually Britain that delivered, reluctantly, the decisive challenge to American ideas of how the postwar peace should be maintained. In February 1947 Britain admitted it could "no longer sustain the burden of financial aid to Greece". It had been backing the conservative monarchy in Athens against communist guerrillas and also backing Turkey against Soviet pressure in the Straits. Now the Attlee government had run out of money. (The paper's comment had to be delayed because a fuel crisis had also prompted the hapless government to stop the publication of periodicals for two weeks.)

Truman reacted vigorously, going to a joint emer-

gency session of Congress in person for a grant of, initially, $400m to bolster the Greek and Turkish economies. He also promulgated the Truman doctrine that the United States would support free peoples who were resisting attempted subjugation. It was to be seen later as a great turning point in American policy, but the paper (when it was allowed to print again) was dubious about the manner of its contriving: "If the President of the United States has to use such solemn tones and bold claims to persuade Congress to lend money and send advisers to the Greeks and Turks, then the American people have not begun to understand the international responsibilities claimed for them."

It was concerned about the popular reluctance to accept a permanent commitment to a continent that was still devastated, run by socialists and threatened, especially in France and Italy, by communists. Were the Americans determined enough? "If they have to be roused to half-measures of foreign policy by speeches claiming world leadership, how many speeches will have to be made, how many dangerous challenges thrown out, to maintain their support for an army of occupation in Germany?"

It had no doubt, though, that it was the end of Pax Britannica: "On February 20th, Mr Attlee gave notice that British troops would be out of India by June 1948. On February 25th, Mr Bevin proposed handling the Palestine problem through the United Nations. On February 28th, came news of the Greek withdrawal, with March 31st, one month off, as the financial deadline."

The paper's answer was greater European unity, which the Marshall Plan was shortly to encourage. It felt Europe had to show it was worth saving: "Those who remember the strenuous crises of the war will recall that President Roosevelt succeeded in launching Lend-Lease only after the Battle of Britain had been fought and won. The countries of Western Europe must similarly show, this time, that they have done all they can for themselves and that, if they are given the tools, there is a job they know how to finish."

It was to happen, eventually. As became usual, it was a Soviet threat that helped to strengthen allied resolve. When in the spring of 1948 Stalin decided that a democratically elected government in West Germany was against Soviet interests, he put a blockade round the three western sectors of Berlin. The legal position was unclear because the western powers had omitted to secure guaranteed access when they occupied their

The iron curtain falls. Churchill, ousted by the British electorate, went to Fulton, Missouri, to warn the West of Soviet intentions. Truman (centre) was there to introduce him. The speech was highly influential.

half of the city. The paper was sure about allied rights, uncertain about how to enforce them: "There can be no question of surrendering under pressure the rights in Berlin granted to the British and Americans at Potsdam; but there can likewise be no question of the Russian right to take reasonable measures for security checks on traffic along what, in present circumstances, can hardly be called the international highway between Helmstedt and the city."

The airlift by the United States and British air forces, which carried 2.5m tons of provisions into Berlin, solved both problems ingeniously and was a particular, and bloodless, success for the Truman administration. The Russians got the message, although the paper could not forget what it was costing: "They have undoubtedly impressed the Russians and they may have made them think again before embarking on any more offensives against the West. But the air lift can never be more than a temporary substitute for a constructive policy. For, though it may be cheaper than war, it is too expensive to be continued indefinitely in peace."

It turned out to be too expensive for the Russians politically. In May 1949 Stalin called it all off. Accompanied by the growing economic success of the Marshall Plan, it added to the momentum of the allied counter to Soviet pressure and the self-confidence of the European governments that Soviet ambitions could be stopped in their tracks. It underwrote Bonn's democratic constitution and democratic life in Germany. The Germans had been told that the balance of power lay with the West.

HARRY GAVE THEM HELL

Truman's troubles almost brought him down,
but some people still trusted his tenacity

From the outset the Truman presidency got a bumpy ride at home. Peace brought its intractable problems, but they were not the problems that had been expected. There was no post-war depression, earnings stayed high and a sense of prosperity pervaded the country. The problem was inflation. The public which had been denied its new homes, cars and refrigerators now demanded them, and it had the money to pay. Manufacturers and farmers saw they were in a sellers' market; they wanted to be rid of controls, especially price controls. But the reconversion of industry, even with American briskness, took time. Truman promptly found he was making enemies, including enemies in his own Democratic Party.

In April 1946 the paper tried to evaluate his first year and thought it promising, but that was principally overseas: "The past year has seen the final pledging of American strength and interest to the international organisations sketched by his predecessor; he has dealt courageously with the first major threat to the prestige of Uno; and he has kept a progressive domestic programme before the country."

By July it reckoned that the post-war boom was imminent: "The goods are now about ready to roll. The physical reconversion of plants is substantially complete; no more major strikes are likely before the November elections; most of the veterans are back in civilian status; and the shortages of basic materials and fabricated parts which have troubled the automobile, appliance and building industries are beginning to ease."

That was still optimistic. The labour unions were restless. John L. Lewis and the miners had challenged the administration, and although Truman had taken over the mines and the court had fined the union, it was Lewis who got most of what he wanted. Meat came off the market when the suppliers rebelled against price control. And all the time most prices were rising as the president's stock was falling; by October it had plummeted: "No Hollywood star has ever suffered a dizzier or more humiliating decline in popularity than that endured by Mr Truman during the past twelve months. Only a year ago he was, by the facile standards of the public opinion polls, a more popular President than Mr Roosevelt had ever been. Today that 87 per cent approval has shrunk to 32 per cent."

The immediate political price was paid in Congress. The Republicans took both the Senate and the House in the mid-term elections: "This is a reversal of political fortunes as sharp and as far-reaching as that which, in 1930, left Mr Hoover isolated in the White House."

The Washington correspondent was succinct: "The country is weary of controls, of strikes, of mismanagement, of Democrats." The youthful Senator J. William Fulbright of Arkansas had a suggestion that the paper found startling: that Truman himself should resign, "after having assured a successor who would have the support of Congress by appointing a Republican Secretary of State". That was not Harry Truman's way; Senator Fulbright later grew up. The paper was reassured that the reverse did not mean a reversal in foreign policy, though it feared it could end the low-tariff policy on which British exports depended.

The Washington man returned to the theme: "The two main reasons why people voted as they did were after all negative. People were fed up with the shortages, and they were tired of Truman's ineptitude. They put the Republican party into office as far as they could in an off year."

The paper also blamed the unions. They had become too demanding; they were resented; and the Democrats were the party identified with them. The country no longer saw them representing the underdogs: "The sympathy for labour's side which characterised the years between 1933 and 1945 and reached its climax in the Wagner Act has been strained since the war's end by strikes that have made labour look too big to be sorry for."

Lewis might win his strikes, Truman might have changed the New Deal into his own Fair Deal, but a prosperous America wanted something more: "In 1946 it is the public that feels small and unprotected. Public opinion polls show a hardening of the public temper and an increased criticism of union words and deeds. They reflect a growing impatience with free collective bargaining, and with labour's insistence on the right to strike when it chooses."

The Taft-Hartley Act of 1947 took the habit of fighting the unions further than the public expected or turned out to want. It outlawed the closed shop and secondary strikes and imposed a 60-day cooling-off period in disputes. But by subjecting the unions to a catalogue of obligations it promised to make them all but powerless. Organised labour had no option but to make its peace with Truman. When he vetoed Taft-Hartley Congress overrode him. It was an issue he knew how to turn into votes. The paper agreed with him: "The important thing is to get out the vote in the big cities, and most of America's 15 million union members and their families will go to the polls next year to register their protest."

Even so, Truman did not shirk fights with unions when he thought it necessary. By May 1948 he was using the army to run the railroads. He would not allow a strike because of the domestic chaos and because it would injure the European recovery plan. It happened that the railroads, which were subject to the Railway Labor Act of 1926, were exempted from Taft-Hartley, but Truman went back to an emergency law passed in 1916 and never repealed which authorised the seizure of the railroads in time of war: "Fortunately for this twilight zone of executive authority, a technical state of war exists."

The railroads themselves, once the masters of industry and the envy of all, were now sinking into default. Even the Pennsylvania and the New York Central reported deficits for the first months of the year. The companies had got by as long as road traffic had suffered from shortages of gasoline and rubber and air travel was on a priority basis. Now that was ending: "While the recent financial difficulties ... could be matched by those of their competitors, particularly the airlines and the inter-city bus services, the railroads have again been losing ground, particularly in passenger traffic. The difficulties of the airlines might be ascribed to 'growing pains'; the railroads are experiencing the infirmities of old age."

Truman, blamed for controls while they were on and for price rises when they were lifted, seemed beyond recovery. He pushed ahead, as no president had before, with civil rights and desegregation in federal employment and the armed forces, despite the outrage of southern whites who were the backbone of the Democratic Party. In June 1948 the paper commiserated with him: "He has tried to work with a hostile legislature and used the veto sparingly. But unspectacular achievement cannot compete with popular myth. The myth is that Mr Truman has failed."

The Democrats knew, and did not dissemble, that they were stuck with Truman. But the convention found a new Truman, a candidate with a new style, which he had been developing. The party had been all too aware that it had no dominant figure, no Cleveland, Wilson or Roosevelt, to turn to: "It was shown by Mr Truman's New Manner when he stepped up to take the nomination, and officially discarded the earnestness of the college valedictorian, which has characterised the reading of his major speeches in the past, in favour of the brisk, snappy, off-the-cuff technique of his press conferences, which was given a trial on his recent trip to the West."

It was to be a winner, but the experts disparaged it. The pollsters had made up their minds: "Mr Elmo Roper, the most reliable of the 'pollsters', has decided that the outcome of the Presidential election is so obvious that there is no longer any interest in reporting on the campaign." That was in September. There were few, if any, dissentients in October: "By virtually unanimous report, the American Presidential election is taking a course that will put Governor Dewey into the White House on January 20th next."

The paper had not given up hope for Truman. It watched his campaign and it admired his tenacity. On October 30th, in its last issue before the vote, it reported: "Both Mr Truman's energy and his optimism seem inexhaustible. On his trips he has made back-platform speeches from five in the morning until after midnight without appearing tired or losing his good temper. Contrary to prediction he has drawn larger crowds than Mr Dewey."

The paper basked in his victory: "Mr Truman, who was written off as a nonentity, has scored a personal triumph and deserves the world-wide tribute that has been paid to his cheerful, indomitable, never-say-die courage."

It felt confident the Democrats would not run amuck: they did not believe in the conscious management of the economy, but neither were they as committed against it as the Republicans. And they were traditionally the low-tariff party. People had relished Truman's success against the odds. It was a sporting instinct: "But there may ... be more solid grounds for satisfaction before Mr Truman's four years are over."

People liked "his homeliness, his friendliness, even his ability to lose his way in ... foreign policy", which were "in the American tradition". No one foresaw then that North Korea would invade South Korea.

CHANGING THE GUARD

Britain's economic decline made it essential
that America stepped in; delay increased
anxiety

What was happening in these years was the effective, and for the British the painful transfer of any authority in the western cause to the United States. The military and economic outcome of the war had left no other option for either power. It was concealed wherever it could be. The British government did not wish to admit it. Nor did the United States encourage the second power in the alliance on which it could invariably rely, socialist or not, to throw its hand in. History had no precedent of an unforced change among what were still conventionally called great powers. Even so, there were ructions along the way which *The Economist* felt it had a duty to explain and, where necessary, on which it ought to adjudicate. There was, first, the issue of the British electorate voting Churchill out and a Labour government in: "However mild and beneficial the Labour Government may intend to be, it is condemned before it starts in the minds of thousands of Americans to whom Socialism, Communism, Bolshevism, Collectivism and the Devil are all synonymous and all to be avoided. A possible resurgence of American isolationism could carry with it the nullification of American co-operation in both finance and politics."

That was the spectre, although British voters had ignored it. In a helpful coincidence, 11 days after the result of the British election was known, the first atomic bomb was dropped on Hiroshima. The paper felt it stifled the anti-British campaign in the United States: "Some might call it providential that the news of the atom-smashing bomb in the making of which Canada, Great Britain and the United States participated, was released just as the chorus of conservative complaint was climbing toward the danger point. For a day, at least, resurgent isolationists have been awed into silence."

Still, it also felt that too many American authorities were wilfully ignoring Britain and its interests. This was most apparent in the Far East where, although British forces had recovered Burma, Malaya, Singapore and the Dutch East Indies, and a British carrier force had helped at Okinawa, the United States had borne the heat and burden of the day: "American jealousy of any British presence in this area has been made obvious in a hundred ways—by the American attitude over Hong Kong and Siam, by the favours shown to American business in Shanghai, or by General MacArthur's unco-operative attitude towards British business in Japan."

It felt the second power had so circumscribed itself for unity's sake that it was losing out. The British were being overlooked: "Again and again, they have appeared in the role of Brilliant Second to American diplomacy. Over the question of the Balkan Governments, on the atomic bomb, on the Moscow Conference, America set the pace, forwards or backwards, and Britain followed."

In February 1946 the paper took it upon itself to assert British rights and involvement in matters that ought to concern "the two Great Powers who contest the possession of the English language". It was candid about American behaviour: "No nation is more firmly on the side of the angels in the long run; or more prone to wish its neighbours to the devil in the short run."

The United States had become accustomed to ignoring Britain because it had been allowed to. Churchill's great virtue in the alliance had been that he never allowed daily irritations to build up into a wall of hostility and resentment. But because he had had to rely so much on the United States, he had grown used to ignoring any difficulties: "He leaned over in the other direction; he tried, far too often, to hide the fact that there was any disagreement at all."

So the paper reiterated its policy when analysing American actions or intentions: "Let it be recited regularly, as a diplomatic litany, that agreement with the United States on the fundamental issues is a first commandment of British policy, with a superiority over all other objects. But let there also be no hesitation in stating the British point of view on specific issues with as much clarity and as little apology as possible."

It then set out to justify itself over the years: "No journal in Great Britain, it is safe to say, has given greater proofs of its passionate attachment to the cause of British-American community of purpose."

That it had published its weekly American Survey throughout years of paper shortage during the war and after was, it thought, evidence of its steady commitment to reporting and interpreting the United States to the British readership. It had the right to speak its mind: "No journal in Great Britain, it is also safe to say, has on occasion given greater offence in America by stating the British case with bluntness. Americans do not like being criticised any more than other people; but they should realise that, in the clamour that besets American public opinion, the only way the foreigner can be sure of being heard is by raising his voice."

Churchill's speech at Fulton showed the issues that the United States and Britain had to confront, each in its own way. They had to do it in association. There was no present prospect of anything as formal as an alliance: "The Americans, unimaginative about the difference in fortune between themselves and other peoples, are sometimes prone to act as if the real cleavage in the world today were between those who do and those who do not believe in private enterprise and thereby to obscure the fact that it really lies between those who do and those who do not believe in methods of freedom and consent."

That identified the Soviet opponent, if not yet the Soviet enemy. If it was to be faced efficaciously, by as strong a combination of free states as possible, there needed to be some new thinking: "It will be necessary for the British to realise that most of their natural allies are deeply suspicious of colonial imperialism, and for the Americans to appreciate not merely that Socialists can be democrats but also that the great majority of the world's democrats are now Socialists."

A week later it thought American opinion was beginning to crystallise, though still not decisively: "Americans do not want to be tied to a military alliance with Britain; they have no desire to defend the British Empire nor British colonial policy and they are not yet convinced—though their faith is badly shaken—that the last chance has gone of Big Three co-operation within the framework of Uno."

The British economic preoccupation with the United States in 1946 rested on the proposed loan of $3,750m (and another $1,250m from Canada) at 2%, to be repaid in 50 annual instalments from 1951. The paper, like John Maynard Keynes, thought it "a generous arrangement" although there were critics who thought the terms were actually too stiff. What worried it was the requirement that the pound should be made convertible in a year's time and Congress insisted on Britain accepting the obligations of a multilateral, non-discriminating system of trade and exchange. The British economy, beset by wartime debts, did not look

strong enough to survive the challenge. The credit would be used up by the end of 1948. Until then Britain needed a lot of luck: "If, at that time, there is reasonable internal stability in the United States, if dollars are not made scarce by a huge American export surplus, and if the British export drive has been so successful that British goods can hold, in the face of competition, the larger slice of the world's markets that they will have won, then all will be well."

It turned out to be not at all well. By August 1947 the paper could no longer hide its concern. The money was running out headlong. Given the choice between pounds and dollars the world chose dollars, but the paper thought too much was being made of this: "It is true that the date was far too early, and that it was its arrival which has apparently precipitated the crisis. But to restore some degree of convertibility to sterling is obviously a desirable objective if it is to survive as a currency of international commerce."

It blamed the allied stipulation of non-discrimination. America's trading strength was too great; the weaker countries and currencies needed to trade bilaterally; non-discrimination was actually throttling international trade. As it happened, convertibility only lasted five weeks. The act of generosity had been ineffectual. Now the Marshall Plan was indispensable.

However, Britain itself was not thought of by many Americans to be as deserving a cause as many others in Europe. It did not have its own distinctive voting strength or its own lobbyists: "Mr Marshall may have kindly feelings towards Britain. The average American Congressman has not. In the United States there is an Italian vote and a German vote, a Polish vote and an Irish vote.... Is Britain a commercial risk? Are its people capable of enterprise and initiative, and of standing up to the hardships that are part of pioneering a new future?"

By October 1947 there was a sense of desperation and even of despair in *The Economist*'s commentary, inspired by Britain's own crisis and the evident deterioration in continental Europe. It thought the United States was dilatory and the Europeans were indecisive. Could even necessity be relied on to bring them to their senses? Survival was at stake: "They are looking into a future in which all those decisions and acts will have been achieved not by the choice of free men but by the iron compulsion of necessity. Dictatorship of the Right or of the Left will have shattered European democracy and broken the strikes and the spirit of the European worker. Mass unemployment and a starvation ration will have brought up the coal from the mines in Britain and set the workers to work under the lash of hunger and the dole."

Nor would America escape if Europe were paralysed: "And in America, perhaps, at the end of the story, the most inexorable creator of availabilities, the most certain purveyor of rationing and control—war itself—will impose in their crudest and cruellest form the disciplines from which a leaderless America shrinks today."

It was the lowest point in the paper's disenchantment with America and Americans. It had not seen them taking up the full responsibility it had expected of them. It feared their withdrawal as they had withdrawn before. Now they did not have a Roosevelt. This was not an ordinary crisis. The paper knew it could deal with ordinary criticism of America. It saw through those critics: "They so clearly start from the conviction that the United States has acted in bad faith (because, of course, no capitalist can be sincere) and with the determination to prove that America is steering for a disaster (because, of course, no capitalist economy can be allowed to succeed), that they land in false evidence, pure fancy and bad economics."

Without America's clout, however, post-war Europe was going to go down in another defeat. The paper looked for a British lead. The Americans could not be expected to engage themselves in cases where Britain's own policy was still disengagement: "Geographically, Britain is now an extension of the European Continent, and it is isolationism, no less crass than that of which the Middle West is accused, to believe that a purely extra-European existence is open to Britain in the twentieth century. It is indeed a profound contradiction in British thinking to imagine that America can be drawn into a Europe from which the British wish to cash out."

MR MARSHALL MAKES AN OFFER

*How Europe was saved, and how the
American economy found the dollars, with
ease*

At Harvard in June 1947 the secretary of state, George C. Marshall, offered a vast transfusion of dollars for the world's anaemic economy, and invited proposals:

"Experience of American reactions in the past would suggest that on one condition only could that measure of approval be secured—if the policy were bold, sweeping, adventurous, and very big. In fact its chances of success would almost certainly increase in direct proportion to its size."

The Economist could be discerning in what enthused both Congress and self-interested European governments. The Soviet Union was not enthused, and it forbade its satellites to attend the conference organised by the French and British in Paris. The groundwork was laid by 16 nations, and the Truman administration's response was unequivocal. That November the paper could write of "the generosity and the grand sweep of the Marshall proposals". To those who doubted it was sharp: "It has to be made clear to the 245 million people of Western Europe affected by them that two-thirds of the aid for the first stage of the plan will be a straight gift—a gift of some $3.5 billion; and the execution of the plan will mean difficulties and sacrifices for the American producer and consumer, even controls and restrictions alien to their way of life."

The Marshall Plan was just what the paper had looked for, what it had expected of American liberality, and what it had believed modern America would have to accept to keep western Europe out of the Soviet sphere of influence. It was politics, but it was more than that: "All this may indeed be enlightened self-interest, but the degree of enlightenment is so infinitely in advance of any yet shown by a great nation in time of peace that it may well be questioned whether it comes into the category at all."

Congress was not so sure. It hesitated for two months. Then the Soviet Union, as so often, came to the rescue. It got the communists to seize power in Czechoslovakia. Congress approved the plan and in April 1948 Truman signed the Economic Co-operation Act which put $6 billion into the first year's effort. The paper was elated: "A year ago the project would have been inconceivable—Congress was then making desperately heavy weather over only $400m for aid to Greece and Turkey. Ten years ago such an initiative would have driven the nation en masse into the arms of the America Firsters. And search back as one may through the annals of the United States or of any other Power, there is no record of a comparable act of inspired and generous diplomacy."

What did worry the paper even then was the prospect of a world dollar shortage that, aid apart, would last for ever. It recognised there had been a fundamental change in international trade since the war. For a century before then free trade had depended on the dominant economic country, Britain, being compelled to buy its food and raw materials abroad, and having its chief investment opportunities abroad. That benevolent system had ended: "It is not a matter of relative skill or clumsiness in managing an international system, or of a relative willingness or unwillingness to 'act as a creditor should'. It is a simple matter of geography. The continental United States, unlike the tiny British Isles, can produce all the food and most of the raw materials it needs. There is no compelling natural reason embedded in its geography to make it purchase supplies in large quantities overseas."

As there was going to be no early way out, it needed careful handling: "America does not, as Britain did even in the days of its ascendancy, inevitably buy as much abroad as it sells there. Any economic equilibrium between America and the rest of the world is naturally precarious and if it is once upset is difficult to restore."

At the start of 1952 the paper summed up the Marshall Plan's obvious success; it had put western Europe back in business: "Europe has not squandered America's generous gift. It has increased output; it has re-equipped its industry, it has worked as a unit in certain fields and it has expanded both its total exports and its exports to the United States and Canada. Its major deficiency has been its failure to bring under control its internal inflation."

For the Americans themselves, it had been money well spent: "From the United States' point of view the disbursement of $12 billion of aid under the Marshall Plan has been a successful investment, and it is worth remembering that the sum is only half of what was originally considered necessary."

It had not been faultless: "By making the European countries beg for their dollars every year, it risks corrupting both them and Congress and turning an alliance of self-respect into a confederacy of clients. And by treating each country separately, on an assessment of 'need', it has put a premium upon failure to achieve solvency."

Furthermore, on its familiar theme, the paper repeated that so long as there was a dollar deficit, the non-dollar countries had no option but to restrict and discriminate against the dollar, whatever Congress said. Still, it was beginning to think that its own prognostication might be too gloomy. In mid-1952 the United States, like Victorian Britain, was in the course of becoming dependent on the resources of the outside world: "It is possible to foresee a time when the United States, not by choice or policy but by compulsion, will have to buy from the rest of the world enormous quantities of raw materials. This is a real hope."

The West's post-war recovery had depended not on hopes but on one great economic engine, whose continuing success had outrun all expectations and prophesies: the United States itself. In May 1950 the paper studied, admiringly, the unending boom: "Before the war ended in Europe five years ago this spring, a considerable number of people both in America and elsewhere were prophesying that the cessation of hostilities would soon be followed by, at best, a major recession and, at worst, a serious depression in America."

Almost every day since then someone, somewhere, had proclaimed the onset of the slump: "American business men, labour leaders, farmers, economists, publicists have all hailed it in turn, with a continuous accompaniment from Moscow and a sporadic one from other foreign sources."

It did not happen: "During the entire five years, production and trade, income and employment, while they have fluctuated, have remained at very high levels. There has been no depression, and there has been no serious recession."

The paper put it down to a series of agents. There was the deferred consumer demand from the war years. The administration was spending extensively among the defence industries. The United States was profiting from the economic and social reconstruction programmes abroad. Even the despised Republican eightieth Congress had cut income tax; the labour unions had forced up wages; the nascent welfare state had put in an appearance. Consumer confidence had encouraged a large and rapid rise in borrowing to buy cars and houses. This conglomeration of favourable impulses had not exactly been planned, but it had not been wholly unplanned either.

The record was good enough to suggest that American Keynesianism might have discovered, or had thrust upon it, the secret of persisting prosperity. The boom psychology had gripped individuals, businesses, the

The Berlin airlift. The Soviet attempt to cut off West Berlin was answered by an American and British airlift which kept the city's 2 million people alive and working until Stalin admitted defeat, May 1949.

stock exchange and the administration's own programmes. It was a fortunate moment, one of the apogees of American self-confidence in the world after 1945. Inflation lay in wait. So did the challenge of the cold war. It was in the assurance that it knew how to deal with its own difficulties that the United States assumed a world responsibility and its increasing costs and burdens.

LIVING WITH DANGER

The bomb and communist China made life difficult, and Britain was playing up too

The rivalry of the cold war and its enlarging dangers preoccupied *The Economist* in the early 1950s. The United States and its allies, constant and inconstant, faced the predicament of containing the Russians, detecting the aspirations of the Chinese and managing the deterrent effect of nuclear weapons. The end of the American nuclear monopoly had been expected, but

when it came in 1949 it was disconcerting, especially when announced by the Soviet representative at the United Nations, A.I. Vyshinsky, the former prosecutor of Stalin's enemies. The Soviet Union had the bomb, and there was no prospect of international agreement on its regulation: "Between, say, Britain, Canada and the United States, an international atomic system could doubtless be devised. The precondition of confidence exists. But Mr Vyshinsky has left the western world in no illusions about his Government's views."

When early in 1950 Truman declared that the United States would go ahead and manufacture the hydrogen bomb, the paper thoroughly approved. It opposed any idea of trying for a limited atomic agreement, however popular it might be. It believed the West should betray no sign of weakness: "Nothing can rob the United States of its incomparable lead in industrial techniques and scientific research. The added risk lies in the preference of the western world for an easy, non-belligerent life, for normalcy, for the pacific conduct of affairs. Even a limited agreement with Russia might be taken as the signal for a slackening of vigilance and a weakening of the defensive effort all along the line."

The bomb by itself was not the whole of the problem: it was the Soviet system and its ambitions. If there was to be talk it should be on all the major issues of policy: the elimination of hostile and inflammatory propaganda, the concept of spheres of interest, and general disarmament. These were the sources of distrust: "There is thus every chance that an accord with Russia covering no more than the atom bomb would increase the risk of war by leaving the major aspects of Russian hostility unchanged while lulling the west into a false and lazy security."

Communist China's intentions had still been largely unrevealed at the end of 1945 when the paper had welcomed General Marshall's appointment as ambassador. It did not accept that American foreign service officials had sympathised with the communists to the extent of encouraging their successes. The policy of full and uncritical support for Chiang Kai-shek in Chungking had, however, antagonised much of liberal America and deserved scrutiny. Now, by February 1950, the paper had made up its mind. Communist China was bent on aggrandisement: "It is only too clear on which side time is working in and around China. There may develop, in a matter of years and in ways not now predictable, important fissures and strains in the Sino-Soviet front. There certainly will develop, in a matter of months and in ways already predictable, a landslide in the border states of southern Asia towards co-operation with Communist China, unless they are told clearly and quickly where the stop-line of the western governments is to be drawn."

It was the line that the paper repeatedly called on the United States to draw for the next 25 years and more. It was to argue that the battle was worth it, even if only half-won, as in Korea, or lost, as in Vietnam, because it allowed the newly independent countries further south to establish themselves not only independently but as anti-communist states outside China's orbit. It gave unreserved support to the evaluation of the secretary of state, Dean Acheson: "The free world cannot afford a repetition of the Chinese debacle, in which a government committed fully to national independence lost the support of the people because its economic and social outlook was too conservative and static."

The allies that offered themselves were not, as Amer-

ican policy was to discover, always the allies it needed: "The greatest difficulty underlying Mr Acheson's admirable analysis of Asian nationalism lies in the fact that the new nationalist regimes are not necessarily committed to those economic and social changes which are as much a genuine Asian aspiration as independence itself. With Communism pressing down upon the frontiers of south-east Asia, nationalism is not enough."

The paper was appeased by the integration of Japan with the western community, in which it thought the Americans showed an adeptness that the British were not displaying in Europe: "In so far as the great majority of the Japanese people now have a genuine hope for the future within the non-Communist zone of the world, they may be counted as willing supporters of policies designed to preserve their country from Communist conquest."

It preferred General Douglas MacArthur to the Foreign Office in London: "General MacArthur has made his mistakes in dealing with the Japanese, but he is not afflicted by those moonbeams of the larger lunacy which inspire British policy towards Germany. He does not go out of his way to provoke Japanese enmity four years after the surrender."

The paper saw Britain at the opening of 1950 as the awkward member of the squad. It felt the Attlee government's views had become merely negative and restrictive, showing the withdrawal symptoms of a dwindling power: "No imperial power has ever been so fortunate in its successor and there is little excuse for the streak of sullen isolationism that has appeared in so much of British foreign policy."

It thought the government unwilling to surrender anything, especially sovereignty, even to friends. It was "the impression conveyed—for instance in most negotiations concerned with American investment in British colonies—that America is an intrusive outsider; the resentment, reinforced by ideological prejudice, of any suggestion touching Britain's internal economic policy even from those who are underpinning it to the tune of a billion dollars a year. If the Americans have yet to learn to treat Britain consistently as a respected partner, the British have yet to learn consistently to behave like one".

The Foreign Office was jibbing, in particular, about having anything to do with the plan by the French idealist, Robert Schuman, to begin the process of making a future Franco-German war impossible by tying the two countries' coal and steel industries into one community. It was the first step towards a European economic union, but the Attlee government thought little of it. The paper disagreed: "Solid reasons, both of general policy and of economic interest, exist that should lead the British Government to join wholeheartedly in the examination, drafting and establishment of the proposed council. Cautious hesitation has become too invariable a factor in the formulation of British policy."

It was the first issue on which the United States, with discretion, indicated to Britain that it thought its future was with, if not in, Europe, and not in trying to remain an independent world power. The paper's first impulse was to insist that this was going too far, too fast: "One can be deeply distrustful of the French and American leaning to the dangerous and difficult principle of federalism, and disappointed at the failure to realise how much sovereignty has already been pooled in defence matters by much less spectacular and more workmanlike methods, in which the British have been the reverse of backward."

That was to become a familiar Foreign Office reaction over the next 40 years and more, but the paper did not succumb to the instinct. It showed no doubt: "When all these things have been said, the fact remains that at the bar of world opinion the Schuman proposal has become a test. And the British Government have failed it. Those throughout the world who suspect that in this island, of all incredible places, an attempt is seriously to be made to live to ourselves alone have had their suspicions confirmed." The endless argument had begun.

To much liberal and all anti-American opinion in Britain and Europe the compelling issue was the bomb and whether and how it could be used. The paper had made its mind up firmly. The bomb might be "the unmentionable weapon", but in Europe's own state of defencelessness in July 1950 it was the essential one: "First, do members of Parliament realise that the only sure method now available of countering a Blitzkrieg aimed at Germany or the Middle East is the threat or the fact of atomic bombing?"

Scorn directed at politicians was a regular stratagem, and logic was the paper's best argument: "Second, when and how precisely do those who protested on Monday propose that the decision for or against its use shall be taken? In fact, the decision lies entirely with the President of the United States; and those who are content that the presence of small American forces in Germany should be accepted as the best deterrent to Soviet aggression are, in fact, relying on the power of atomic weapons without taking any responsibility for their use."

When in December the British Labour Party believed the Americans meant to bomb Chinese Manchuria and use Chiang Kai-shek's remaining forces in Formosa to bomb the mainland, and when it was put about that this could include using the atom bomb, Clement Attlee felt he had to go to Washington to find out what was up. He was cautious in his public remarks, both on arrival and after his talks. The paper, which had feared a demand for conciliation, as the Labour left wanted, was greatly relieved, and turned on the erring media: "Having succeeded in scaring London with their messages from Washington, the news agencies, associated and united in their irresponsibility if in nothing else, proceeded to scare Washington with reports from London of impending Munichs and a government bent on 'appeasement'."

There had been something approaching panic in both London and Paris that the United States was planning unilateral action. Attlee learned this was not so and was able to reassure the Commons. It was his own priority for the alliance that won him praise: "It was a relief to everybody when the door of the Cathay opened and the British party filed out with not an umbrella to its name."

Attlee, as prime minister, did not belong to the Chamberlain wing of his party. To the paper, it was only the innocent who misunderstood the benefit of the bomb. It reported each new sophistication of the weaponry with approval: "The atom bomb came of age last week, for the fourth of the atomic explosions now taking place in Nevada was the twenty-first in the series that began in July 1945. The atom has matured very satisfactorily, for the latest detonations were of bombs of different sizes and types, with ground troops participating for the first time."

The paper believed tenaciously in the tactical use of nuclear weapons, not least in central Europe, and accepted evidence of their feasibility from the start: "The Congressional observers were able to report that atomic bombs can now be used on the battlefield and followed up immediately by attacking forces without danger from radiation."

Then, and in the years that stretched forward, the paper's policy was to be counted among those who, convinced by the practicality of the policy of containment, were not to be lured away by deception, fear or laziness. But the anchor had to be sure: "The basic truth—which Europeans, as they play their domestic politics, are apt to take for granted and leave unexpressed—should be plainly stated. However much indifference to the Atlantic Alliance there may be in America, there is very little in Europe."

THE KOREA TEST

Defeating aggression and fighting a limited war were both major American successes

North Korea invaded South Korea in June 1950. Truman promptly replied by ordering American troops back into the South. This set the pattern for 40 years of the relationship between communism and western democracy until the collapse and disintegration of the Soviet Union. That aggression must be met by determined western resistance was in the forefront of *The Economist*'s beliefs, and it commended Truman and the American military commander in Japan, MacArthur, for their reaction. It declared at the outset that the communists had miscalculated, and in so doing had negated their own strategy of exploiting every western weakness: "For the reasons that might have been found for doing nothing in Korea would have cast their shadows into the future, would have become arguments for doing nothing in Persia, Jugoslavia, Indo-China and Hongkong. That, surely, is the lesson of the early thirties, and to have spent the early fifties relearning it would have been disastrous."

So the first, crucial engagement in the cold war, in containing communism, was begun in substantial allied unity and even, because of a Soviet oversight, with immediate United Nations approval. The anti-American instincts of left-wing socialists, especially in western Europe, set off agitations and fellow-travelling explanations, among which was the complaint that the communists had been misled. The secretary of state, Dean Acheson, had been a public critic of the South Korean regime under the highly conservative Syngman Rhee, and when Acheson had set out an inventory of countries essential to American security neither South Korea nor Formosa had been on it. The paper was

unimpressed. It was unimpressed, too, by the corresponding complaint from the Republican right that Acheson and the State Department had been intent on selling South Korea out.

It accepted that the State Department had threatened Syngman Rhee in April, telling him to put his house in order or American aid would cease: "This was not pro-Communism in the State Department—though it may seem so to Republicans of the McCarthy vintage—but a common-sense declaration that the American taxpayer's money was not going to be spent on training horses that will not run."

It should be a principle of resistance to communism that it must be aided and organised in countries that were at least aspiring to democratic standards: "Successful resistance can only be offered to the Communist menace in the Far East by a state which can avoid the disintegrating effects of uncontrolled currency inflation and can provide a constitutional outlet for popular discontent."

The paper was not a political admirer of MacArthur's, but it acknowledged that he had his usefulness in helping to keep unreconstructed isolationists in line with Truman. He had even become, by accident, a symbol of bipartisanship: "The incidence of left-wing generals in the United States Army is not high—their political views usually run parallel to those of French generals under the Third Republic—but only General MacArthur seems to radiate that particular brand of conservatism which reassures Middle Western Republicans."

MacArthur's spectacular landing at Inchon on the North Koreans' unprotected right flank meant the invasion ended in rout. It was patently a Soviet reverse. But the paper was already worried about China. North Korea was not a Chinese satellite, but its defeat would bring American troops up to the Chinese frontier on the Yalu: "The more speedily Peking can be admitted to the counsels of the United Nations, the better will be the chance of achieving some permanent settlement—as opposed to a precarious truce—in Korea. It is quite uncertain whether Communist China is prepared to play the good neighbour, but as long as it is excluded from the community of nations, so long will it be tempted to behave like any outlaw."

When, against MacArthur's forecasts, Chinese troops did intervene in imposing numbers, the paper was insistent that this could not justify a strategic extension of the war. It was not part of the United Nations' aim: "That purpose is not to win a complete victory in the Far East, except in so far as the winning of a victory helps to contain Russia all over the world. There is real doubt whether General MacArthur sees that point." What was all too evident was that the first military response to a communist invasion was in rapid retreat: "The spectacle ... is one that neither Asia nor Europe will forget."

China was not, to the paper, the principal enemy; a full-scale war would only be to the Soviet Union's benefit: "About twenty of the best American, British and French divisions are now tied down in the Far East, without a single Russian soldier being engaged. Nothing could please Stalin more than that the Western powers should still further reduce their defences against the Red Army."

Now western policy needed closer definition: "This is not a plea for the abandonment of the Far East.... The right strategy is not to abandon the continent altogether, but to exercise a strict economy of resources in continental adventures, to defend on the continent only the most vital areas and those where the air and the sea are at a maximum advantage."

The paper was to change its mind on tactics from time to time, especially over Formosa, but it did not desert its basic analysis. The ferocity of the Chinese attack in Korea did alter its belief that some appeasement, such as the seat at the United Nations, would now make much difference. It did not wish to be counted among the faint-hearts: "Those who cling, rather pathetically, to the belief that, with one or two small concessions, the Chinese Communists will be ready to settle down as good neighbours, are flying in the face of obvious facts. The evidence is that Mao's policy is as aggressive and as expansive as Stalin's and that, if he is prepared to treat at all, it will be for purely tactical reasons."

Although it was prepared to defend MacArthur, accepting that he had not disobeyed the UN's instructions by invading North Korea, it was wholly opposed to any wider war, and it blamed Truman for his aberration—"the real Munich of this war"—which led him to agree to MacArthur's demand for attacks on the far side of the Yalu. Truman certainly regretted it, and although he agreed to the neutralisation of Formosa he did not allow any invasion of the Chinese mainland. The stabilisation of the Korean front on, or just above,

the 38th parallel even encouraged hopes of negotiations. But in April 1951 MacArthur went behind his orders and appealed to the Congress to accept no substitute for victory. Truman dismissed him. The paper understood MacArthur's view: "It is not yet certain that he was wrong in believing that Korea is the test case for the free world's ability to deter aggression in future by defeating and punishing the aggressor now."

But it could not accept his wider war or his insubordination: "There is a natural and healthy distrust of generals who appear to be running ahead of Ministers and courting the gravest risks of spreading conflict."

The paper's Washington correspondent was confident that, whatever histrionics MacArthur got up to, Truman was the one who was going to survive: "It should be recorded ... that after conceding the stiff price that is being and will be exacted, some well-educated guessers in Washington now think that the often derided, often underestimated, but doggedly single-minded tenant of the White House will come out on top once again."

In the modernising of American policy which the paper relied on, the compulsory fading away of the old soldier was a necessary constituent. America had been converted to a new ideology. It was one demonstrably, and unusually, based on self-restraint: "To an extent quite insufficiently realised in this country, the policy of containing Communism while avoiding a world war has been stated in this campaign."

The paper thought it remarkable in a nation of such immense potential strength: "In this campaign, enemy aircraft leave and return to their Manchurian bases in perfect safety. Chinese anti-aircraft batteries on the north bank of the Yalu do not trouble even to use camouflage, so confident are they that the Americans will not dare to attack them. Such restraint has been based on the confidence of Americans in the Administration's claim that the United Nations purpose can be achieved without extending the war."

So the sense of limited war entered the calculations of military staffs and electorates. For all its drawbacks it proved more popular, and more enduring, than the all-out variety.

When Churchill returned to Washington in January 1952, on his first visit as a peacetime prime minister, he settled the issue of British policy towards Formosa. He praised the American decision to keep the communists out. The paper predicted he would hear about it in the

Commons when he got home: "He can, however, with full justification make the defence that if he has succeeded in convincing the Americans that he is a trustworthy ally in the Far East as elsewhere, he will have far more opportunity of influencing American policy towards moderation than ever Mr Attlee did."

The Americans were now committed, for better or for worse, to Chiang Kai-shek and were taking, the paper thought, the first steps towards other obligations. When Dwight Eisenhower, a month after his election, went to Korea to see for himself, he was cautious and came away pleasing the State Department. If the aim was to close down in Korea and let the peace talks drag on, as they did interminably, then the Americans needed to reconcile their aims there with the developing struggles elsewhere on China's borders: "In particular, the conviction is growing that the United States can no longer have a Korean policy, run jointly by the Pentagon and the American mother, separate and distinct from its Far Eastern policy in general. Containment of China may in fact require that greater attention be paid to Indo-China than Korea."

The Americans were to be tempted in due course, as the British were not, to intervene to save the crumbling French empire in North Vietnam. But Eisenhower the general was the man to resist such temptations, rightly or wrongly. One of his first decisions was to allow the Chinese Nationalists to operate against the mainland, as his Republican backers wished, but without the necessary American firepower in support they were not going to get anywhere on their own: "For those who applauded it in Congress on Monday almost certainly expect too much from it, and those who attacked it in the House of Commons on Thursday almost certainly fear too much from it."

The Eisenhower years began in the Far East as they were to end there, conservatively: "There is ... no reason for thinking that the American chiefs of staff have changed their view that to get involved in full-scale hostilities against China would be to wage the wrong war in the wrong place."

LIKING IKE
And accepting Nixon with him

The paper respected Eisenhower the general, the wartime commander who had organised the allied suc-

cesses in North Africa and Europe, and thought him, as an internationalist broadly following Truman's policies, the best possible Republican candidate in 1952.

Eisenhower had had to accept as his running-mate a right-wing senator from California, Richard Nixon, a figure execrated by liberal Democrats. But the paper thought: "Mr Nixon is a remarkable vote-getter in a politically critical state, and his selection will please the booming west coast; he has youth, and though once connected with the Un-American Activities Committee—he put the first finger on Alger Hiss—he has never been guilty of Senator McCarthy's excesses."

When the Democrats nominated another internationalist, Adlai E. Stevenson, the paper was satisfied with the choice before the voters: "General Eisenhower is a world figure of rare personal charm; Governor Stevenson is an orator and an intellect of Wilsonian force. May the best man win."

Then came the charge that Nixon and his family had profited unduly from campaign funds raised by a group of Nixon's admirers. Nixon replied theatrically and the paper sanctioned his argument: "Some $75,000 was spent this week to enable him to put his case to the country on television and radio, which he did so effectively that there is apparently no longer any question of his resignation.... Senator Nixon's case is certainly not unique, and the law on political contributions is so unrealistic and out-of-date that it is often difficult to draw the line between proper and improper conduct."

Eisenhower had distanced himself from the affair, but it was another reason why a commentator across the Atlantic should, almost by instinct, return to the habitual Democratic alignment now the virtually unknown Stevenson was making his mark: "The speeches he has made ... have made a great impression, not simply for their grace and eloquence (though these qualities count) but also for the evidence they have given of a man who has thought things through, who has built up his principles and will not allow himself to be pushed off them. On the other hand, General Eisenhower's friends are at a loss to understand what has happened to him."

Election night despatched these doubts. Stevenson had been overwhelmed everywhere except the illiberal south; for the first time since 1928 the Republicans had won a national campaign and also had made gains that showed they were a national party. But it was not

Madly for Adlai. The Democrats' liberal candidate, Adlai E. Stevenson, in 1952 and 1956 was admired in western Europe but failed to dent Eisenhower's popularity. America preferred a father-figure.

a party victory: "Americans from every part of the country and from every walk of life want General Eisenhower. It is a measure of his personal magnetism that he was able to overwhelm such an intelligent and inspiring opponent as Governor Stevenson."

However, in choosing the man they had not chosen the party: "The American voters have put General Eisenhower above his party. If he can pull that party up to his level by making it accept the basic continuity of American policy, he will earn both the gratitude of the world and a place in its political history."

ISRAEL HAS ITS WAY

It won its existence with America's help, and taught the Foreign Office a lesson

The Economist had no illusions about the predicament in which post-war Britain was caught between Arab and Jew in mandated Palestine, or about the determination, persistence and political influence of Zionism in America. In 1944, before the allies landed in Europe, it reckoned that most Americans were not primarily interested in the Middle East so that if Britain came forward with, and carried out, a reasonable compromise in Palestine, it would get American moral support. The British authorities recognised that they would have to go back on the policy they had followed before the war and, in early 1946, they published the report of an Anglo-American commission which proposed the admission of 100,000 Jewish victims of Nazism.

This alarmed the Arabs, but the paper was not despondent. The proposal was risky, but if official American support was assured there was a chance of success: "If the American Government accepts the Report and is ready to give unstinting political and economic support, if the British reform and strengthen the Palestinian Administration, if adequate compensation can be found for the Arab League in other areas, if the Jewish community make a generous and not a one-sided use of their new opportunity—if all these conditions are fulfilled, the Report can mark the opening of a more hopeful phase in Palestine."

It was entirely wishful thinking. By July the paper was casting around for something down-to-earth and better reasoned, like partition: "If the political disadvantages of every other solution slightly incline the balance of advantage towards a policy of partition this is not due to any inherent virtue in the policy itself."

The more it looked at it, the less it liked it: "It would be geographically complex, politically cumbersome and economically retrograde. Neither Arab nor Jew would accept it willingly.... There is no magic formula which can mollify the disappointed Zionist, the recalcitrant Arab and irresponsible American politician."

By January 1947 it was thinking again, always with the United States much in mind: "The alternative courses now are either to admit failure, abandon the thought of a British base in Palestine and lay the matter before the Uno with a recommendation that it partition the country and guarantee the frontiers so as to avoid a coup by either Jewish or Arab force, or else to dictate and uphold a partition of British manufacture. The Zionists of America are not the only element to be considered."

The paper, like British public opinion, bitterly resented the American Zionists' campaigning. The British ambassador in Washington protested, and the paper was appalled by Zionist advertising: "The latest of these is a letter from Mr Ben Hecht, the Hollywood scenarist, in which he writes: 'Every time you blow up a British arsenal or let go with your guns and bombs against the British betrayers, American Jews make a little holiday in their hearts.' "

By that August the British government had had enough. Jewish terrorists had blown up the King David Hotel in Jerusalem; British soldiers had been killed and their bodies found in a ring of booby traps; that was normal and could be borne. What could not be was the refusal of the Truman administration, under Zionist pressure, to share responsibility in seeking a settlement: "A change in policy there can and must be, one which relieves the British taxpayer and the British soldier of the impossible burden of internal policing and administration in Palestine. There is only one such solution—the partition of Palestine and the creation of

a small Jewish sovereign state, if necessary with certain transfers of population."

If the United States would do nothing on its own initiative, there was only one option: "The only reason why the Palestine situation today is for the first time a new situation is because Great Britain has decided in the last analysis to quit. This is the only instrument by which the Arabs and the Jews, the Americans and the whole United Nations can be forced to face their responsibilities."

The paper's correspondent in Jerusalem recounted the outcome: "Even those who appreciate the Arabs' lack of preparedness, organisation, equipment and knowledge of modern warfare are astonished at their complete and abject collapse and panic flight."

For the paper, it underlined one of its own guiding principles: little or nothing could be counted on from British influence or military muscle in the region if it went against the predilection of American policy.

IN A NEW WORLD
Changing America: forewarned was forearmed

The Economist took an ironic look, from time to time, at how American fashions and manners were changing in the post-war world. It was going to be a younger America and a better-off America, but whether it was going to be a more contented one was another matter.

The paper was not surprised by the baby boom. It had been calculable that the birth rate began to rise in 1940. The economic revival, the marriages generated by the thought, and the event, of war, these encouragements to child-bearing came after a decade of unemployment and suppressed parenthood. Then the return of men from the forces pushed the rate higher, where it stayed unexpectedly. There was a "revived and thriving Goddess of Fertility" in American life: "In spite of war casualties, the American population has increased by about 8,000,000 in the last five years as compared with an increase of less than 9,000,000 in the whole ten years between 1930 and 1940. The unusually large excess of births over deaths, in conjunction with a small increase through immigration, brought the population to almost 140,000,000 by July 1, 1945."

The large increases in the numbers of first and second children showed the fertility was in new families, not in already large ones. Things had hardly begun.

This population seemed intent on doubling itself before the century ended.

Fast food takes off   By August 1946 the paper expected a boom in fast food: "During the war at many factories hot meals were packaged ready to be taken home by factory workers coming off shift. Is there a commercial future for such services in a good many cities? (In New York such meals are obtainable both in a fairly high price range and at the Automat.) Pre-cooked package foods, frozen foods, prepared mixes from soup to cake, were doing well before the war and are now reappearing on the grocery shelves." For British readers the editor felt obliged to define the automat: "nickel in the slot cafeteria".

Space: scepticism on the frontier   In the same month it discovered space, and saw in it the prospect of a new frontier in American history, encouraging the rebirth of the pioneering spirit, taking over from the impulses generated by war: "A possible outlet for these thwarted race desires is suggested by the activity of that scientific section of the War Department which is said to be busy planning interplanetary rocket flights."

A young scientist had been heard declaring at the Pentagon in Washington: "I fully believe that I will stand on the moon in my life-time." The paper's innate scepticism was not going to let it swallow that precise prophecy whole: "Does it look as if Mr Truman could sweep the Moon in 1948? With its traditions, does it not appear probable that the lunar votes may be counted in the Isolationist column?" Twenty-three years later the Eagle had landed.

Broadway revisits the past   The paper's caution occasionally disconcerted even itself, such were the world's worries. "*The Economist*," it declared once, "lays no claim to be escapist literature." It gave few hostages to hungry fortune: "The peace, for all its faults, will be, on balance, more enjoyable than the war."

Prudence could not go further. So the paper was alert to post-war Broadway's retreat to the past: "Escape to 1860 with Bloomer Girl, to 1880 with Nellie Bly, to 1890 with Oklahoma! and Life with Father, to 1900 with I Remember Mama, even to 1920 with Billion Dollar Baby. Of the 18 plays and 14 musical comedies on the boards at the time of writing, seven are revivals and

seven more are re-creations of the American past before author and audience grew up and began to take life and war seriously."

Its psychological explanation was that Roosevelt was dead; the father figure, like him or not, had been removed, so the public was unconfident. People felt they had to be on the lookout to ensure that the new president made the right moves; they had to watch Congress: "They express opinions, they take sides, but they are uneasy and would like to forget. So they stand in line for tickets to Oklahoma, and dream themselves in a two-gun day when action was enough and no one insisted they think things out."

The Ford legacy   Early in 1947 Henry Ford died. He was a man who did more than anyone to make America mobile, and settled its modern lifestyle, its distribution system, and even its mating habits: "Ford made an age. He created modern industry. He found automobiles expensive because there were so few of them, and so few of them because they were so expensive. He made his hundreds of millions by one simple act of faith—that if he produced cars in sufficient numbers for them to be cheap, people would buy them."

Ford's very name was redolent of the heroic epoch of the American car and the road it ran on, his foibles and quirks those of a man who saw himself in a epic tradition. His generation was over, but not the precept he taught: "In economic terms, he discovered the elasticity of demand for the products of industry. In retrospect it sounds simple, just as simple as the original invention of the wheel, which exists nowhere in nature. But it was hardly less fundamental."

To a Britain that was not then well acquainted with the motorised age the paper shortly introduced the Ford legacy to it: "There are the 'motels' (individual cabins with place for a car to park alongside), and the tourist camps—some of which are now comparable in architecture, convenience and facilities to the good hotels of the cities—the 'drive-in' movies, where the picture is flashed on an enormous screen visible from the parked cars, the 'drive-in' banks (some 250 of them) where tellers' windows are ranged along a ramp, the roadside restaurants with 'car-hop' service, on trays attached to the open window."

Thus, valiantly, the paper carried out its interpretive responsibilities.

The America of the 1950s warmed to the reliable, conservative figure of Ike and accepted with him Richard Nixon as his vice-president and heir. Eisenhower's caution nullified the Franco-British invasion of Suez, 1956.

10

THE FRUSTRATED FIFTIES

1953–1960

THE ALLIANCE THAT DULLES RAN

There was agreement on big issues, but
personalities did not help

The Eisenhower presidency formalised and organised the western response in the cold war. It instituted no great initiative, not even on the death of Stalin in 1953. It did nothing, in keeping with the president's own nature, that was hasty or ill-considered. Much of its preoccupation was with military technology. Its biggest crisis was not with the communist powers but with its major allies over their Suez expedition.

This was, as it happened, largely in step with what the paper advocated for the 1950s. To the editor, Geoffrey Crowther, who formulated the paper's policy until he chose to resign just before Suez in 1956, and influenced it as chairman thereafter, what had been essential was that the United States should accept its historic responsibility and settle down to exercise it responsibly. The collective failure of the democratic powers between the wars, when they lacked both foresight and understanding, would not be allowed to be repeated.

Crowther himself, in his signed, final article, emphasised the difference: "The important change, to my mind ... is the emergence of the United States as a full-time great power and its willingness to form and lead a Grand Alliance."

The times might seem desperate, but they were far from hopeless: "It still seemed most unlikely, when the second war came to its end, that the United States would actually accept the obligations and commitments of a permanent formal Alliance. But the miracle happened (thanks to Stalin) and the transformation it has brought about in the diplomatic position is revolutionary.... The essential point is that, for the first time in modern history, the defending powers are virtually as strong, and as ready, as the potential aggressors."

Eisenhower the commander left most of the concepts and all of the details of diplomacy to his staff, as the State Department had expected him to do. This left regular responsibility, and most attendant blame, to his secretary of state, John Foster Dulles, by far the most experienced Republican expert. The paper was not wholly sure of him: "He is an extremely skilful nego-

---

CHRONOLOGY

1953	Dwight D. Eisenhower becomes president		Soviet Union invades Hungary
	Death of Joseph Stalin	1957	Treaty of Rome setting up the European Economic
	Armistice signed in Korea		Community
	Soviet hydrogen bomb	1958	Nikita Khrushchev in power in Soviet Union
1954	First atomic submarine, *Nautilus*, launched		General de Gaulle returns to power in France
	French defeat at Dien Bien Phu; loss of North		US troops in Lebanon, British in Jordan
	Vietnam	1959	Fidel Castro takes power in Cuba
1955	Eisenhower has heart attack		Archbishop Makarios returns to Cyprus
	West Germany in NATO	1960	U-2 spy plane shot down by Soviet Union
1956	France gives independence to Morocco and Tunisia		Paris summit collapses
	Anglo-French-Israeli attack on Suez Canal		Anarchy in former Belgian Congo

tiator whose religious convictions do not blind him to the beauties of a hard bargain. It is no use pretending that he is not a controversial figure or that his career does not reveal great inconsistencies of view."

Dulles had ambitions and ideas. In particular, he did not consider the communist structure to be immutable, least of all its advances in eastern Europe since 1945. It should be no part of western policy to sustain the system that wished to eradicate what the alliance stood for. But even announcing this, which Dulles liked to do with relish, was too advanced for most of the allies: "The Europeans, conscious of their weakness and exposed position, are afraid of such calculated taking of risks as led to triumph over the Berlin blockade and President Tito's defection from the Communist camp."

The paper expected nothing from Stalin's death, except the opportunity for the West to drop its guard. It insisted that no one knew how to predict what the Soviet Union would do: "The surest way to relax the vigilance of the West—which may now be more necessary than ever—is to suggest that the news from Moscow is good. It is not; it is deeply disturbing."

It did value the armistice in Korea; that, at least, was tangible. The war had achieved its primary aim: "In fighting it, the United States and its allies have kept alight the faith in collective security that was so often allowed to die in the days of the League of Nations. In the 1930s, Abyssinia, Austria, Czechoslovakia and China itself were left alone at the mercy of the aggressor; in 1950 South Korea was not. History may record this as a unique turning point."

Eisenhower had confirmed that he was no warmonger: "No better piece of work has been done by President Eisenhower since he assumed office than his repeated insistence, both publicly and privately, that a diplomatic solution is more desirable than a military solution for any international problem."

That had helped the cohesion of the alliance. So, in its way, did the explosion of the Soviet hydrogen bomb: "It will bring the Americans themselves closer to understanding what Europeans—even the bravest of them—feel when they think seriously about atomic warfare; for if the H-bomb race goes on the United States will feel threatened as never before."

The paper understood why American opinion differed from world opinion in not seeking clemency for the atomic spies, Julius and Ethel Rosenberg. Human

feeling was there: "Americans, too, have been made sick at heart by the Rosenbergs' protracted ordeal, and have been troubled by the fact that never before have American civilians been executed for treason in time of peace."

But there was more to it than that: "Since the case (unlike that of Sacco and Vanzetti) lacked, in the eyes of the overwhelming majority of Americans, the one basic ingredient of a judicial tragedy—any real doubt about the guilt of the accused—the campaign for clemency had little chance of success, despite the skilful Communist attempts to exploit the pathos of the case to its full."

In early 1954 the nuclear race was uppermost in the minds of western liberals. The paper had not changed its views. The bomb, and the willingness to use it, was essential to western defence: "There is clearly something in the doctrine of deterrence. There are some wars that it can prevent."

It recognised that nuclear weapons could not be expected to stop all wars. Nor would they necessarily be always in the possession of dependable men: "There is a risk that the decision for or against their use should be left entirely in the hands of one man. Free men may trust President Eisenhower to act with wisdom, courage and restraint. Can the same be said with certainty of all his possible successors?"

Still, it found some scientific consolation: "One of the hydrogen bomb's nicer characteristics is that it is very reluctant to explode. Extraordinarily high temperatures and intricately adjusted conditions are needed to set it off. In this respect it sets something of an example both to public opinion and to public men—an example that might be better heeded." The Bikini atoll tests were supposed to seem less fearful after that.

The crisis of April–May 1954 was, anyway, in a war that the bomb could not influence. For seven years the communist Vietminh guerrillas had been getting the upper hand over the discouraged French forces in the north of Vietnam in the old French Indochinese colony. The French had put their last hopes in a fortified position at Dien Bien Phu, which the Vietminh invested. The Americans, who were virtually paying for the war, were persuaded that Vietnam should not be lost to the communists. Eisenhower himself said that it was first in a row of dominoes which would fall, one after another, if it were knocked over. The American military proposed an air strike to save the French. The official British view was more moderate, but the paper regretted that Britain did not have an influential voice: "If the British could send even a token force to Indo-China now that the Korean commitment is being reduced, they would be in a much stronger position to use their influence with both sides."

When Dien Bien Phu fell most French opinion concluded the war had ended in defeat, and looked, as the paper did, to a conference at Geneva to reach some acceptable arrangement that would leave South Vietnam, at least, outside the communist sphere. But already the paper was intellectually committed to the domino theory because of the British interest in the countries further to the south. While the negotiations went on it considered Britain could be "faced with a brutal choice" between helping the French to win victory and sharing in the disastrous consequences of their defeat. It had made its own choice: "Then we shall have to choose victory, facing now and in company the risks we would cheerfully confront rather than surrender Malaya and the road to Australia."

That was why and where the paper was ready to advocate making a stand. It had no time for wilder accusations or proposals. It was contemptuous of certain senatorial fancies: "Not only does the squalid McCarthy circus go on and on, without any apparent prospect of cutting the Senator down to size. But even the majority leader of the Senate himself, Senator Knowland, is allowed to parade his irresponsibility daily, urging war with China and, when others hesitate to involve themselves in it, writing them off as unworthy allies."

The Geneva outcome allowed a South Vietnam to continue, but the paper observed how the Americans and British, although ostensibly making common cause, were becoming divided in their approach to the issues. Dulles and the British foreign secretary, Anthony Eden, agreed over Vietnam and over not going to war with China, but personalities were showing up: "Mr Eden is not an appeaser; but he is prone to believe that any problem can be solved by skilled and patient negotiation. Mr Dulles is not a warmonger; but he rather fancies himself as a Gordian knot-cutter. Both men have that form of vanity that is apt to take disagreement as an affront."

Equally, it believed, the need to make political responses had made the State Department and the Foreign Office behave as if they were further apart than

they really were: "The trouble has been that the State Department, plagued by Senator Knowland, has had to pretend to be more aggressive and anti-Chinese than it really is, while the Foreign Office, needled by Mr Attlee, has had to pretend to be almost as ready to appease Peking as he is."

In this artificial atmosphere, in the presence of growing ambitions and in the absence of clear understandings about aims and initiatives, even over allied status in those parts of the world where it had been left unclear, existed the origins of the divergence over Suez. Eden was not Churchill, although he had been trained by him; as prime minster he did not have Churchill's ability to conform to American wishes. Dulles's abilities did not extend to managing coalitions: that was Eisenhower's responsibility. As the paper had spotted, the alliance was on the verge of making itself highly vulnerable.

SUEZ: NO END OF A LESSON
The alliance's worst moments taught the West to face facts, and not just in the Middle East

The Anglo-French expedition to the Suez canal in 1956 was the most damaging break in the western alliance during the whole of the cold war. It was taken more seriously by Eisenhower, who thought it a personal affront, and by the British than it was by the French. It was the last initiative that the British took as a major power and its failure marked the end of Britain's ability to manipulate the Middle East in its own and the alliance's interests. It marked, too, the first signal success of an Arab country, Colonel Nasser's Egypt, in an international confrontation. Eisenhower himself had no doubt that Eden, acting without American approval or support, had made a fundamental error; the rebuke was driven home without remorse. But it was Eisenhower who then decided that United States policy was best served by the restoration of Britain as a primary ally. It was a role that Eden's successor, Harold Macmillan, was prepared, and equipped, to play.

The paper, which might have been faced with a test of loyalties, had no apparent doubts: it believed American policy was right, British wrong. It said so. It was not a crisis in which it was to put much trust in Dulles, the secretary of state. But it thought Eden's handling of it was bad in itself, as well as separating London irretrievably from Washington while it lasted.

In July both the United States and Britain cancelled their offers of aid to Egypt to build the Aswan dam, a favourite project of Nasser's to capitalise on the waters of the Nile. Nasser had tried to play the Americans and British off against the Russians, and the western cancellation was abrupt. The paper had its doubts: "They cannot congratulate themselves on a brilliant stroke of policy." But it thought the decision was right: "Western aid is far too precious to waste in obstructing the Russians, but should in general be applied on its own merits, where it is most needed and where it will be most effective. The fear that if the West does not help, the Russians may, is a bad counsellor and leads to false decisions."

When the western powers, as a group, tried to devise a strategy to stop Nasser nationalising the canal in retaliation, the options were few and barren: "The real shock to the West has been ... the appalling discovery of its own vulnerability."

In early August it was already clear that the western powers did not see eye to eye. The Americans distrusted Nasser but, in an election year, they were wholly unwilling to set off any detonations. Dulles wished to use ingenuity, not force: "He is thoroughly disillusioned with Colonel Nasser, whose flirtations with Moscow and rancour against the West led Mr Dulles to cancel the offer of aid for the High Dam and thereby to spark off the Canal crisis. But if the Americans disapprove of Colonel Nasser, they disapprove hardly less of the Anglo-French brandishing of force."

To Eisenhower there was no question of needing force; he insisted on negotiation, on "sober second thinking". That was the word from Washington: "There is no support here for an imposed solution, still less for a military adventure."

While Dulles and numerous volunteer statesmen tried to bring pressure on Nasser through the Suez canal users' association it became increasingly apparent that the Egyptians had the ability to run the canal themselves, with the approval of the Russians and much of the third world. Dulles then proposed that all transit dues should be paid to the users' association, not the Egyptians. It would, effectively, be a boycott because the Egyptians would stop all ships that did not pay them: "Such a boycott, with the United States in, promises to be many times more effective than if Britain and France had embarked on it alone. The most

surprising feature of the scheme is that it is an American scheme, originating with the American government."

It may have looked sound, particularly to those whose overriding motive was to avoid fighting, but it did not survive close study. By early October the paper could see that Dulles had left Eden isolated. American opinion, caught up in the election campaign, was against the coercion of Egypt: "Americans, mostly to their discomfort, had serious doubts about the merits and justice of the British and French case. They wished that case were stronger, but found it rather weak.... The Nasser-Hitler analogy never seriously caught hold in the United States."

It was still, however, central in Eden's thinking, and Eden was getting impatient: "When the users' association scheme for applying pressure broke down—in large part because of inherent weaknesses which Mr Dulles himself had failed to realise in advance—the pent-up ire of the British and French burst upon him."

With the West divided and Eisenhower preoccupied with re-election, two crises now became one. Stalin's successor, Nikita Khrushchev, faced with an anti-communist revolt in Hungary, took his chance to send the red army in to suppress it. The British and French, too, believed they had an opportunity to repossess the canal and, in collusion with Israel, moved without consulting the United States. The paper called it acting in "splenetic isolation": "Britain and France may have had cause to complain of Mr Dulles's vacillations over the Canal dispute and the Users' Association, but their action now puts his failings in the shade."

The Israeli army won a crushing victory in the desert; the British and French intervened, ostensibly to protect the canal, but were slow to get their forces ashore in strength; and Eisenhower was duly returned to the White House. The paper was appalled at the consequences of what Eden had set out to do, and of what, as sterling was imperilled, he had been stopped from completing. The price of Suez had been exorbitant: "The Anglo-American alliance is badly hurt; the Commonwealth is at odds; the uncommitted nations are alienated; the canal is blocked; there is the soaring question mark over Suez's effect upon Hungary."

The paper's sympathies were with Eisenhower: "No man was more shocked or more affronted both by what the British and French governments did in Egypt and by the way in which, without consultation or warning to their allies, they did it. Yet no man, after the first anger, was more intent upon rescuing the partnership."

Once again it was the Russians against whom Eisenhower and the administration reacted instinctively. The red army had been sent into Hungary before the Anglo-French landings: "The President is a man of simple faith. The re-entry of Russia bearing menaces confirms again his conviction that, at all costs, the western powers must stand together."

Hungary might have helped to restore a sense of reality to the bickering alliance; it also demonstrated their impotence: "The lessons that should be drawn from the Hungarian tragedy, especially by the under-developed countries of Asia and Africa, are bound to be at least partially obscured and distorted by the Anglo-French intervention in Egypt, and this is lamentable. But to the extent that they do strike at home, the sacrifices of the Hungarian patriots will not have been entirely wasted."

The lesson the American public drew widely was that its allies were as inept and old-fashioned as their critics had always said: "The Administration decided that this alliance must be preserved at almost any cost once the Russians had attacked Hungary, but most Americans, sick at heart, believe that this attack was encouraged by, if not the direct result of, the immoral and outmoded 'gunboat diplomacy' which the British and French were pursuing on the Suez Canal."

Although the paper had read the crisis better than the British government, it denied itself any elation; that was not its style, nor the style of the new editor, Donald Tyerman. What it saw two weeks after Suez was months, if not years, of opprobrium and a suitably humbler British part in western counsels. It rebuked those Tories who fantasised that Britain should have gone on alone, if necessary, until it had imposed its will on Egypt. That would merely have jeopardised the alliance and Britain's place in it still more fatally: "There is no substitute. We cannot, as we should now know, go it alone. It is no answer to say that, if the Americans will not act, we will act without them; we cannot. The facts of power remain: Russia cannot be resisted, whether the challenge is by direct attack or by indirect subversion, nor can the United Nations be activated, without the Americans."

To a paper with more than a century of eliciting the right arguments for a tenacious relationship, or even

liaison, with the United States, which had always written as if assuming parity of respect if not of economic and military power, it was the nadir of a long intellectual journey. It had ended at bedrock: "We must learn that we are not the Americans' equals now, and cannot be. We have a right to state our minimum national interests and expect the Americans to respect them. But, that done, we must look for their lead. And they, on their side, must accept, as they have not done, the obligation to protect our interests and provide, as they have not provided, clear leadership."

Cautiously the professionals began to put the connection together again. The paper noted the State Department's reluctance to do anything too obvious: "It appears to be that the lonely asset surviving the wreck of western influence in the Middle East is the moral advantage of America's speedy initiative in the United Nations. It is considered essential not to compromise this by any manifest collusion with the British and French, such as a 'big three' meeting or a guarantee of fuel supplies, so long as the invading troops are in possession at Port Said."

The paper did not dissent from this realism. It wanted, then and thenceforth, an end to artificiality. It had said it before, but it had not been listened to: "There has, to be blunt, been altogether too much use of the vocabulary of comradeship without the reality of genuine expression. The doubletalk of mutuality has induced a kind of deafness to plain words and a garbling of clear situations. For nearly a year Britain and America have been shouting at each other without hearing, Britain saying it would use force in the Middle East without waiting for the United Nations, and the United States saying it would countenance no such procedure."

It then knocked some obvious heads together: "The British and French grossly exaggerated the paralysing effect of an American election: the Americans did not grasp the intensity of Anglo-French despair at Mr Dulles's disappearing solutions. The British for a time gave Mr Dulles the impression that they were prepared to let the United Nations settle the matter. But Mr Dulles had equally failed to explain to the British his own, much-prized long-term plan for bringing Colonel Nasser to his downfall within a year by political and economic pressure."

There had been too many unmistakable and unsubtle faults on the transatlantic line. For week after week the paper kept up its analysis of painful actuality: "The British have assumed too easily that it must always be an American interest to preserve Britain as a power—without considering that the Americans might have views of their own about the kind of power that they wanted Britain to be, or might come to desire British influence to be strong in one place and weak in another."

If that were true, as the paper believed, so was the corollary: "The Americans, in the weeks when they blew hot and cold over Suez, at times appearing to support Britain and at others blandly putting on an air of detachment, took it for granted that Britain was too loyal to go off on a violent diversionary action of its own."

So the paper pronounced its verdicts. To the United States, replacing British influence in the Middle East with its own tripwire and $400m immediately to friendly countries, it gave the award for responding to the obvious: "The makers of American policy have at last resolved that the Middle East can no longer safely remain as a hiatus in the American system of alliances and power positions which stretches round most of the world. Spectators in London will feel that it is high time—as indeed it is."

To the British government and its diehard supporters it prescribed a dose of economic common sense: "If the ceasefire had not been sounded on November 6th, it is really extraordinarily difficult to see what Britain could have been doing now—in mid-December—to avert devaluation of the pound."

For the Hungarians and other east Europeans it drew a disdainfully anti-American moral: "Events have shown that the Western powers lack any means, short of atomic war, of restraining Russian conduct. President Eisenhower has reasserted that the east Europeans were never encouraged to start a hopeless struggle. His specialists in psychological warfare had not made this message clear in advance; disillusioned hopes now breed a bitterness in Hungary which gift parcels, however generous, will not allay."

Eden's illness and resignation, and the arrival of Macmillan as the British prime minister, put a better, calculated face on Anglo-American relations. Macmillan had served his apprenticeship in the wartime alliance in North Africa, where the Americans had brought him out of his intellectual shell; he had also devised for himself the conceit that the British were the Greeks in the American-run Roman empire. He set himself to restore the association in this guise. The paper did not see things in that way: "It is quite clear that there is not, and cannot be, anything exclusive now in the relationship.... The new Europe, as well as the Commonwealth, has to come in to redress and hold the world balance."

However, in the world of 1958 Macmillan knew that Europe and the Commonwealth were chiefly concepts; the residual capability and experience of Britain were facts, and would be there when the United States next needed them. In July the anti-western coup in Iraq and the threat of revolt in Lebanon and Jordan gave him the opportunity to return to joint, preventive action. He was entirely open on what he was about: "When Mr Macmillan said somewhat wryly on Tuesday that he would almost prefer to be wrong together than to be right separately he was only just misstating a fundamental truth of western policy."

For Macmillan the relationship was back in being. For the United States there was a new complication. It had gone into the Middle East to block Soviet influence. The paper did not think the Iraqi coup had been engineered by men under Moscow's influence but serving pan-Arab nationalism: "When the American marines splashed ashore among the sunbathers of Beirut ... they were intended to readjust the political balance of the Middle East; instead, in the long run they may prove to have readjusted American thinking about the Arab world."

Or, at least, the paper hoped so.

STUMBLING INTO SPACE
America's early embarrassment was a military one too

The United States' first, often stumbling steps in space were seen by *The Economist* with decided scepticism. Sub-orbital lobs and even planned flights to the moon were not its sort of priority. In August 1955 it was barely civil: "The dramatic announcement that the United States was planning to launch into outer space the first man-made satellite has excited the imagination of scientists, the art of science fiction writers, the ingenuity of international lawyers and the instincts of investors on the New York stock market.... And what if, by some mischance, the first satellite should fall before reaching its orbit and kill some chickens in Khazakstan or a cow in Jersey?"

When in October 1957 the first satellite turned out to be Soviet, it was fully prepared to congratulate the Russian scientists and to allow that it had not been done by espionage, but it had no truck with a Soviet claim that it showed the inherent superiority of the communist system: "This claim would be more convincing if some of Russia's older satellites were in better shape. A skyful of balls will not solve Mr Kadar's problems, or Mr Gomulka's."

Having chastised Hungary and Poland it turned on everyday efficiency in the Soviet Union: "The sight of the whizzing 'moon' punctually keeping to an announced timetable is superb; but down below, in the world hitherto known as the Soviet sphere ... timetables are rare and risky, transit is often slow and inefficient, and even five-year plans sometimes fail to run their predestined course."

The paper promptly decided that the success was unmistakably an authoritarian one: "A more decisive factor was surely the ability of a totalitarian regime to concentrate a vast amount of talent and resources on one group of projects. A free society has difficulty in achieving so much concentration—especially when the projects are essentially military and political, with little bearing on economic progress or welfare."

That was true, and it saved some faces, but when the Russians quickly did it again with Sputnik II and the dog Laika, neither the military nor the political consequences could be brushed aside. The West was lagging dangerously in strategic firepower: "If the Russians can self-confidently throw half a ton of equipment and a living creature into their proper orbit in the sky so soon after the first satellite was despatched, they must hold an even longer lead over the Americans than was first thought."

Just two months after excusing the difficulties of a free society in this competition, the paper admitted to doubts, if only propaganda ones: "To a simple man who says: 'If communism can put a dog in the sky above my head, surely it can raise my condition', it is going to be difficult to explain the perils of taking Moscow's way."

Russian cynics, though, did not fall for the full Soviet story: "Up there a dog's life is over. Down here it's still going on."

One month later the perils in the American pro-gramme were made all too apparent by an explosion at Cape Canaveral. It was a chastening blow and the paper did not trouble to alleviate it: "Few nations have seen so many of their basic assumptions shattered so swiftly as the Americans have in the weeks since Mr Khrushchev propelled his first sputnik into space."

It was the point in the cold war when, superficially at least, the West faced the prospect of its technological lead diminishing and even disappearing, not only in its military capacity but in the very society on which its superiority was based. American opinion took it hard: "They have been made to realise that their technicians are not in every possible respect the most efficient in the world, that their educational system has some dangerous flaws, and that soon they will no longer be able to protect their homeland against nuclear attack. Even their special pride, the efficiency of their economy, has been challenged by the Russians' demonstration that in one narrow field at least they can deliver the goods sooner and better."

The Economist had no doubts that America's natural instinct was to keep up in the race, but, so disconcerted had the paper become, that might be part of the Soviet machination. Khrushchev was a schemer: "In the next few years he may produce startling figures of Soviet coal production—or butter, or cement—with the implication that the United States will lose face unless it can match them ton for ton. He is inviting Americans to a series of races in which he marks out the course, names the conditions and plants the finishing post. This would set precisely the wrong criterion for the Americans' economy: not what is necessary, but what a self-appointed rival can perform in his chosen fields."

The most urgent decisions had to be taken on security. The apparently widening Soviet lead in intercontinental missiles meant that the West could no longer be confident that the power of nuclear retaliation could be relied on. The United States was, to that extent, now interdependent with its allies. Reliable allies had responsibilities to take up; to station shorter-range missiles near Russia: "In this situation Britain's responsibility ought to be plain. Whether or not the missile sites will enhance the beauties of the English landscape, this is the most sensible place for them to be deployed."

Critics in Britain thought the idea missile madness. Those who were not anti-American by conviction did not wish to take the risk. Nor, in the 1950s, did a policy of stationing nuclear weapons on West German soil, within the grasp of West German politicians, carry any expectation of popular support. There was only one option: "Placed here, they do not involve any addition to the list of nuclear-armed powers, which it ought to be the aim of western statesmen to keep as short as possible. Putting them in Britain does not do the political harm that will be done if they are put in Germany."

The paper saw no qualitative or quantitative difference between American bombers on British airfields and American missiles on British sites. The changing needs of the deterrent had to be satisfied. It was an argument it was prepared to sustain for as long as the cold war.

Meanwhile things were still going wrong at Cape Canaveral. In August 1958 it was a Thor missile that failed, the first stage in an attempt to put a rocket round the moon: "In surviving only the first ten of its 250,000 miles to the moon, the much-heralded rocket at least justified the deliberate official pessimism which surrounded its launching.... After a little more than a minute in flight, it disintegrated in the customary burst of flame and smoke and headed, in many pieces, for the ocean bed from whence divers are endeavouring to collect the fragments for the inevitable post-mortem."

Within two months the air of resignation was dispersed. It was not a complete success, but it did confirm that the Americans were in the race. They had not given up by any means: "The success of last week's 'lunar probe' in penetrating nearly 80,000 miles into outer space and in sending back a stream of information about conditions there is the American way of celebrating the first anniversary of the Russian sputnik and more than offsets the failure actually to circle the moon."

The Pioneer had gone incomparably farther than any previous space vehicle, and what it reported was found to be pertinent for the future: "Reports are arousing the most immediate interest since they suggest that the belt of radiation revealed by an earlier satellite is less deep than had been feared and will not prohibit the passage of human beings into outer space if they are in protected vehicles."

The hectic days of repeated American success in space were still distant.

COPING WITH KHRUSHCHEV
Eisenhower was too canny a man to believe in Khrushchev or be tempted to challenge him

The serious business of American policy was understanding and dealing with the new force in the Soviet Union, Nikita Khrushchev. He was a change; he was not Stalin. He was human; he was highly unpredictable. He was less than an ogre; but he enjoyed personal power and he relished the prospect of Soviet imperialism. When in February 1956 he told the twentieth party congress, in secret, of Stalin's crimes the Eisenhower administration saw him as an improvement, but an unstable one: "Despite their unaltered conviction that the congress did mark a step in a better direction, the Americans have since become very dubious about making progress with Mr Khrushchev. Above all, they do not want to throw away what they regard as the chance in a century to bury the German menace for ever, which is offered by the willingness of the present government in Bonn to tie Germany inextricably to European institutions, for the sake of a quick, superficial reconciliation with Russia."

This preference for dealing with the known rather than the unknown was characteristic of Eisenhower, and when Dulles went to hospital with cancer in February 1959 the sense of caution was reinforced. The United States, the invigorative power, was becoming the most conservative one: "The apostle of change may go down in this period of history, perforce, as a twentieth-century Metternich, the pillar of the established order."

When Dulles died in April the paper acknowledged his tenacity, conscientiousness and sheer hard work. He had been the man whose abilities and experience would have made the right negotiator of a momentous settlement, but fate had decided otherwise. Dulles had believed in the assumptions of the policies he had inherited in 1952: "They included the necessity to hang on without a major diplomatic settlement until the effective containment of Soviet expansion had produced some major changes in the Marxist reckoning of foreign relations. The tragic implication has been that he who was so well equipped to negotiate a settlement on behalf of the West has had to end his service without achieving even the opportunity to try."

Few epitaphs on Dulles were as charitable. Now the United States faced the Khrushchev peace offensive with curiosity and caution. The first visitor to Washington was the Cuban dictator, Fidel Castro, for whom the paper had scant sympathy: "Dr Fidel Castro, invited to Washington in the first flush of enthusiasm for his victory in Cuba, arrives this week with bloodstained hands held out for economic aid which his record so far shows little to justify."

Khrushchev came in September, to be shown America before talks with Eisenhower at Camp David. The paper thought it extraordinary: "The frenzied scurry with which the police hustled him through New York, and Hollywood's bizarre notion that he would be beguiled by actresses' posteriors, were a caricature of the United States."

Khrushchev's own behaviour varied between truculent claims for communism's superiority and exhibitions of folksiness to outdo anything done by his hosts. He was on his best form at Santa Barbara, just north of Los Angeles: "The security arrangements were relaxed, and the crowds who were thus able to see Mr Khrushchev in the flesh decided that they rather liked what they saw. From then on the mellowing was mutual; the uncanny silence which had greeted him earlier in the tour dissolved into the expected mixture of applause and boos, roughly in dry Martini proportions, five to one."

The talks suggested that progress could be made on both Berlin and nuclear weapons, and the visitor left amid growing hopes of a success at the summit: "It is possible, of course, that he was deliberately bullying at the start and deliberately cajoling at the end. An eyewitness can only report ... that he arrived genuinely worried about the Americans' sincerity and goodwill, and left relieved of his worries."

Eisenhower and his new secretary of state, Christian Herter, came to believe that Khrushchev wanted a settlement. The idea was urged too by Macmillan and, more circumspectly, by de Gaulle. Whether, indeed, the Russians had matters of substance in mind, they gave priority to a propaganda success. For years American reconnaissance planes had been photographing Russian installations from a height which the Soviet anti-aircraft defences could not reach. The Russians had been so unsettled by what they said was aerial espionage that when a missile did bring down a U-2 plane Khrushchev broke the news just 11 days before the summit was due to begin in Paris. The paper had certainly thought the conference worth attempting, but, unlike

much of the western media, it was undismayed by Khrushchev's revelations: "Mr Herter and Mr Eisenhower should have convinced even unsophisticated Americans, shocked to find the American government dabbling in the same dirty tricks as the Russians, that not only is this nothing to be ashamed of, but a necessity if a nuclear Pearl Harbor is to be avoided."

But the Russians had successfully caught the State Department out in a lie and Khrushchev kept up his abuse, even withdrawing an invitation to Eisenhower to return his visit. The summit was driven on to the rocks.

Eisenhower's presidency seemed to be ending the same way. Khrushchev was one thing, now the Japanese government had to ask him not to go there because riots threatened to disrupt his visit. That the Japanese, who had been reliable and even docile adherents to the western system should have had to make such a confession seemed to suggest deeper causes than the commotion of "neutralists, pacifists and screwball students": "The President of the United States who came into office saying 'I will go to Korea' is now going out of office being told 'You cannot come to Japan' and something more than humiliation is involved. The failure of the summit conference marked no more than the failure of a diplomatic move upon which most Americans had embarked hesitantly and reluctantly a mere nine months before. The cancellation of Mr Eisenhower's invitation to Japan shows that the foundation upon which the United States has constructed its whole policy for the past fifteen years is riddled with termites."

Eisenhower made the best he could of it, declaring that Japan's ratification of the treaty with the United States far outweighed the blocking of his visit. But now, just as the 1960 election campaign moved into top gear, the paper suspected a more dangerous Russian conspiracy against the United States, centred on Cuba. Castro had been given financial help and sympathy, which the Americans strongly resented. The paper thought it time for an avuncular warning; Castro was a difficult and intemperate young man, but he should not be built up into a bogeyman: "The shrill bellicosity with which some American newspapers and politicians have built him into a king-sized enemy has a whiff of the uncontrolled exaggeration that led the British not so long ago to make a Hitler out of President Nasser—with the important difference that the American administration, unlike the British Government of that day, has so far kept its head and its sense of proportion."

Khrushchev announced that he would go to Havana himself: "The apparent purpose of these Soviet tactics is to goad the United States into just the kind of angry stroke against Dr Castro that would promptly alienate the rest of Latin America." Eisenhower was not the man to succumb to the temptation; it would be left to his successor to do that.

When in September Castro descended on the United Nations "with beard, battledress, and a front seat in the hall (on its extreme left wing)" the paper was pleased to observe him "squirming in the unfamiliar torment of having to listen to other people's oratory". Khrushchev's own arrival must, the paper thought, be part of a considered policy, but the Washington correspondent was still left wondering what did make "that complicated man" tick: "Mr Khrushchev, a true choleric if ever there was one, is showing precisely the same extremes of temper as he showed last year. His outbursts in the General Assembly reveal the same violent dislike of being argued with as he demonstrated when meeting American trade union leaders last autumn; he has once more displayed in his kerbside interviews that earthy, human and rather attractive gusto for life which makes such a startling contrast with Mr Eisenhower's thin-blooded manner."

The comparison was pointless by then; Eisenhower had only three months left in office. The new generation now had its chance with the complicated man.

A VOTE FOR YOUTH

America had become bored with old faces and old ways; John Kennedy was the answer

The politics of the Eisenhower years were predominantly conservative in both parties. That, in its way, was reassuring to *The Economist*, as to many people in Britain, because it meant they knew what to expect. When the Democrats won the mid-term elections in the House in 1954 it was, in British eyes, a return to normalcy. They were, after all, the natural majority party.

Nevertheless, the power in Congress was still kept securely out of liberal hands. Actual shifts in the political spectrum were rare: "The new committee chairmen will nearly all be conservatives, the majority coming from the South. Curiously enough the President's main difficulty with the new House of Representatives may well be that it is too conservative for him."

The man in the White House, being essentially conservative himself, was no Keynesian. He was committed to protecting and stimulating private capital investment, took no chances in relying on consumer buying power as the way to economic growth, and was reluctant to spend his way out of a mild recession which might jeopardise his own chances in the 1956 election. Eisenhower saw himself as the model chairman of a company staffed by model businessmen: "The modern conservative wants to preserve a free market and a free price system as a means of rationing goods among consumers. He wants to keep incentive and reward among the principal propulsive forces of a free economy. He advocates equal opportunity, not equal shares. He dedicates himself to a sound dollar, regarding it as indispensable to a sound economy."

So great was the sense of conventional politics that the paper had no hesitation in January 1955 to forecast a *déjà vu* election, Eisenhower against Stevenson again: "Unless things change radically in the coming eighteen months Mr Stevenson will be the next Democratic candidate and his chances of ever being President will probably depend on the personal decision of Mr Eisenhower. If Mr Eisenhower runs, he will, again unless things change in the meantime, defeat Mr Stevenson once more; it is doubtful if any other Republican can."

The surprise in October was Eisenhower's heart attack: "When President Eisenhower's heart faltered, American politics awoke from a trance." It was mild. Eisenhower was able to put thoughts of being a one-term president behind him and consented to an expansive budget. The economy could afford it: "The Budget which President Eisenhower has just sent to Congress is, perhaps more than anything else, the symbol and reflection of the country's enormous wealth. With many governments elsewhere retrenching—or feeling they ought to retrench—a Republican Administration in Washington has chosen to expand, and it is the amazing American economy which made that choice possible. The President has asked Congress to approve an enlarged role for the government in literally dozens of different parts of the national life; he has been able to do so without unbalancing the Budget because revenues are so ebullient."

The economy and Eisenhower's determination to keep out of Suez were more than enough to settle things.

Liberals strongly condemned what they saw as the wasted opportunities of the Eisenhower years, the failures in the slums, schools, hospitals and public transport. One popular economist, John Kenneth Galbraith, embodied this school of thought in his best-seller *The Affluent Society*, but the paper's opinion was not so enthusiastic: "*The Affluent Society* is penetrating, fresh, knowledgeable, humane and—though it gets off to a slow start—entertainingly written. It is also perverse, muddleheaded, provincial and dangerous."

It accepted the book might make salutary reading in its native land, but elsewhere it would only encourage delusion. However, the thinking was making an impact, especially among young people, and as 1960 approached it acquired an appropriately youthful spokesman. Senator John Kennedy, who had only just failed to get the vice-presidential nomination at the Democratic convention in 1956, was sparing no effort to go further next time: "He has the advantages of youth, a brilliant war record and a very wealthy father able to contribute to the party's empty coffers. But he is a Roman Catholic of Irish background and political pundits are trying to decide whether this would be a drawback or an advantage in a national campaign."

The paper believed it was worth taking the risk. There was an estimated Catholic vote of about 14m: "There are relatively few of them in the South and in the agricultural regions of the Middle West. The states with a high proportion of Catholics are the heavily-populated ones which cast a big electoral vote and are pivotal in determining who wins the Presidency. They include New York, Massachusetts, Pennsylvania, Ohio, Michigan, Illinois and Wisconsin."

The decisive test in the primaries came in the small, poor and Protestant state of West Virginia. It was a Kennedy prize: "The Democratic voters who, in a proportion of three to two, preferred him to Senator Humphrey—Mr Kennedy had expected, in public at least, to be beaten by this amount—proved that his Roman Catholicism does not count against him."

When the campaign proper began the paper was struck by what it saw as the similarity of the Republicans' Richard Nixon and the Democrats' John Kennedy, whatever their publicists claimed: "The two men are strikingly alike, except that Mr Kennedy is rich, Mr Nixon poor—an odd reversal of the usual distinction between their two parties. Both are ruled by their brains not their hearts and are efficient young executives making a career out of politics. Both are tough, articulate campaigners, determined to succeed, and masters of the compromises on which political triumphs are built."

For the first time both candidates agreed to a form of televised debate, Nixon apparently counting on his superior experience with the medium to offset the new promotion it gave Kennedy. The paper was cool about the opening encounter: "To the disappointment of those hoping for some of the real argument which has been missing from the campaign so far, neither candidate had anything new to say, nor did they strike any sparks off each other in the hard-hitting tradition of President Truman. Calm, moderate statement and gentlemanly discord characterised the hour-long discussion."

The paper missed entirely what everyone else had decided was the yardstick of success and failure: the deficient application of Nixon's make-up under the studio lights.

When by the end of October the Kennedy camp began to sense victory, the paper agreed that he had mobilised most of what it called "the country's permanent potential majority of Democrats". He had had three consecutive successes: "By explaining his views on church and state to the Protestant ministers in Houston last month he diminished the danger—at least for the time being—of a massive outpouring of anti-Catholic votes against him. By showing in his television encounters with Mr Nixon that he was as well-informed as his opponent ... he blunted the charge that he was immature. Above all, in his appearances all over the United States, he has created an impression of enthusiasm, sincerity and thoughtful concern for his country."

Its forecast of the result was close: "Senator Kennedy will win by a fairly modest majority of the popular vote transposed—by the peculiar mechanics of the American system—into a comfortable majority of the electoral college."

His popular majority was only 118,000 out of a total of 68m votes, although duly transformed into an electoral majority of 303 to 219. The paper's Washington correspondent thought the voters had returned "a divided, indeed an evasive, reply". It would mean difficulties for Kennedy: "The exquisite narrowness of his majority in the total number of votes cast makes it clear that the United States has not rallied whole-heartedly and convincingly to his appeal for new exertions in the nineteen-sixties. Half the country, to all intents and purposes, has accepted Mr Nixon's assurance that there is nothing wrong with America."

In the broad sweep of history, the paper felt, it was all for the best; it was time for another generation there and elsewhere in the alliance: "There is a rhythm in the affairs of a democracy, a sequence of pauses for consolidation and fresh bursts of energy. There is no need or cause to decry unduly what the Eisenhower regime has done, both in the world and in holding the line at home well to the liberal side of old-time Republican reaction. But the time has come in the United States, as indeed in Britain or in west Germany, for a new dose of adventure and imagination."

The post-war world had come to an end.

CIVIL RIGHTS: WAKING UP

The campaign against racial prejudice produced Martin Luther King, and troops in Little Rock's high schools

The slow erosion of racial segregation in the border and southern states was hastened in 1954 by the Supreme Court's decision reversing the long practice that school facilities were not illegal if they were separate provided they were equal. In the case of Brown v. Board of Education of Topeka the court ruled that separate meant unequal. The court had proceeded slowly, delaying a decision the previous year and preferring to rule on minor matters such as compelling restaurants to serve blacks in Washington, DC. But when the court made up its mind, unanimously, it opened the door to a new, though still hard, world for black people especially in the deep south. While United States governments spoke for the democratic way of life, what counted for news from some parts of the country had read differently. In January 1954 the paper reported: "In 1953, for the second successive year, there were no lynchings in the United States."

It was such good news that the Tuskegee Institute which collected the lynch statistics decided that it should start a new index emphasising economic and cultural progress. The paper was delighted by the court:

"It ... means, or should mean, that both races will take their first lessons in the responsibilities of good citizenship together. The effect on the superiority complexes of the white children should be as satisfactory as the Court expects it to be on the inferiority complexes of the coloured ones."

It gave great credit to Chief Justice Earl Warren: "His liberal humanity and his practical experience of young people certainly lie behind the Court's readiness to make modern psychological knowledge, unknown in the last century, a factor in its decision that today segregation retards the educational and mental growth of Negro children."

The segregationists turned their faces firmly against acceptance. They sent in their experts: "The Southern lawyers emphasised, as reasons why the Supreme Court should stand aside, the traditionally local character of school administration; the moral impropriety of overriding the parents' wishes on so basic a matter as the mixing of their children with those of other races; and the priority of the individual states' police powers, which embody the elementary right of any government to preserve good order and public morals."

The court disagreed. It ordered in May 1955 that the schools should desegregate with all deliberate speed: "These words, 'deliberate speed', can be widely interpreted and it appears as if the Supreme Court is trying to give the South as much opportunity as possible to comply in its own reluctant way."

What the court had insisted on was a "prompt and reasonable" start to the process. It allowed a wide range of responses. In September 1956 racial segregation was abolished at a stroke throughout the publicly financed school system of Louisville, Kentucky: "As was to be expected, a substantial city, with a strong liberal newspaper, a university which has already been integrated and two years of intensive preparation by social agencies, managed a major social reversal with more grace than small, backward communities with long traditions of rugged conservatism."

It was very much harder wherever racial feeling was ingrained in everyday life. In April that year the paper looked at the pastor of the Dexter Avenue Baptistry in Montgomery, Alabama; the youthful Dr Martin Luther King had been active in the bus boycott to stop the practice of blacks having to give up their seats to whites. The paper liked him: "The main innovation of the young, northern-educated intellectual has been his

Civil rights. Gaining strength and momentum, black America's insistence on its rights grew from the Supreme Court's decision ending segregation in schools. The young Martin Luther King was dedicated to peaceful progress.

passionate emphasis on non-violence and the creative power of unrequited love."

King's church, pushing up its steeple at the foot of the Capitol building in Montgomery where Jefferson Davis had taken the oath as the first and only Confederate president, was itself the symbol of the approaching, unending struggle. The paper sympathised. Like the authorities in Washington it grew impatient with the organised resistance put up in most parts of the south, among them some unexpected ones. The governor of Arkansas, Orval Faubus, called out the state's national guard to stop black children attending desegregated schools in Little Rock in September 1957. The paper was puzzled: "What inspired the Governor's theatrical challenge is the great unanswered question; until recently he had been a moderate on racial matters and it was his liberalism which first carried him into office. One suggestion is that he wants a third term, almost unprecedented in Arkansas, and thinks that his only chance lies in an extremism which will appeal to the poor white farmers among whom he himself was brought up."

Eisenhower, "who a few months ago was saying that he could not imagine ever using force in the South", now had to act. He put the national guard under federal orders and sent in paratroopers as well to enforce the court's orders. Faubus got the "sorry distinction" of being the man who took "the first irrevocable step away from peaceful acceptance". But there were no winners: "The despatch of paratroopers to Little Rock was a painful blow to Americans. In the South there are bitter tears and rage; in the rest of the country there is gloomy support for the President's show of resolution."

There had to be a lengthy process of adjustment. In the end the parents of Little Rock preferred some integration to no education at all for their children: "The four Negro pupils who for the past week have been attending classes in Little Rock's white high schools without being molested have wiped out the stain smeared on their city's name by Mr Faubus."

That was in the autumn of 1959, however, two full years later. Where there was southern compliance it was a token one. The paper spelled the failure out: "Of the eleven states which formed the Confederacy in the Civil War, five obeyed the Supreme Court to a modest extent during the school year which ended last June. If Texas, which has made some genuine progress, is excluded, this means that exactly 206 coloured children, out of a total of more than two and a quarter million, were admitted into previously all-white schools in ten states."

The paper had regularly recorded the violation of civil rights in both north and south, but normally with an underlying belief that federal exertion would succeed. In January 1960 it had to comment on a killing at Poplarville, Mississippi, which showed that lynch law continued, a warning to the civil rights demonstrators in the deep south in the ensuing decade: "The Negro, Charles Mack Parker, was charged with raping a pregnant white woman. Local residents were bitter at the prospect of his Negro lawyer cross-examining her in open court about the sexual attack. Some thirty-five men planned the lynching, then drew straws to see who would carry it out. Those chosen wore masks. The gaol was unguarded and the keys nicely available. The mob drove Parker to the Pearl River, shot him and threw the body in."

If anything, factual reporting from the south at the end of the Eisenhower presidency suggested that the Supreme Court's actions had set race relations back. It was, the paper said, "a sharp reminder" that the United States was a federated country. In Washington the attorney-general, William Rogers, naturally condemned a "travesty of justice" but he had to admit he had no power to intervene to bring the murderers to trial. Now resolute, and often bloody, campaigning by a young generation of activists was about to start.

THE NEW SOCIETY
Catching up with automation, frozen foods, aerosols, the Edsel and Hopalong Cassidy

In post-war Britain *The Economist* was particularly interested in everything new that came out of America, and which its British readers might expect to see, and even experience, ten years later. In industry the future was plainly in automation. In May 1953 the paper looked at a new car plant in Ohio. The progress was impressive for the day: "The Ford Motor Company has just opened in Cleveland what is described as the first automatic factory in the automotive industry where, it is claimed, electronic devices enable 250 men to turn out twice as many engines as 2,500 men could make in a factory of the older type. Remarkable as that record is, a factory which requires 250 men for its operation has not yet reached the fully automatic stage."

The paper's forecast was that proper automation would not happen for 5–10 years. But new processes were happening: "Large sections of the communications industry are already self-controlled. In metal working, in the production and distribution of electricity and gas, in machinery manufacturing and in the chemical, petroleum, ceramic, textile and food industries great strides have been made in the past two years in the use of instrument control. The unattended oilfield, the electricity generating station, the 'cat-cracking' plants which have revolutionised petroleum refining, have become familiar sights, working quietly along with only an occasional man to check the dials."

What was true in the factory was as true on the farm: "The tractor, the combine, the maize-picker, and a host of other machines have greatly reduced the amount of hired labour needed on grain and livestock farms. The combine long ago drove into folklore the hordes of men and boys who 'rode the rods' under railway goods wagons from Texas into Canada to bring in the wheat harvest. Some combine crews still make the great trek, but they are skilled workers and the owners of expensive machinery, not footloose hoboes."

Two-track railroads   On the railroads there was now a two-tier system. The airlines and the buses had made big inroads into the business, as had the family car. The consequences were all too visible: "The traveller who crosses America by train these days is struck by a contrast when he makes the inevitable change at Chicago. The train that brought him from the East is drab-looking, the equipment run down, the service indifferent. But the one that carries him westward is brightly painted, comfortably equipped and attractively decorated, and the service is efficient and courteous."

It was all down to money. The Pennsylvania and the New York Central, hemmed in by their competitors, were running huge deficits; they cut back on repair and maintenance, reduced their labour forces, abandoned services and pinched pennies. The western railroads still reported sizeable profits, especially the Southern Pacific and the Atchison, Topeka and Santa Fé. They carried relatively few passengers, which were usually unprofitable; they had no commuters; but they were still competing with the airlines for trade because they advertised scenic routes; and their long hauls helped to beat the trucks. They were the last, stylish railroad days, with vista-dome cars on the Santa Fé Super Chief and the Union Pacific's City of Los Angeles, on which passengers paid up at premium rates. The railroads ran their own trucking systems, they were into commercial property and real estate, and they had a growing stake in oil. It was not to last.

Flying into prosperity   There was a time in 1952 when the paper worried about the future of the airlines; they were losing, collectively, $1m a day. Overcapacity was ruining them: "The competition from

privately owned automobiles is growing rather than declining, with the construction of such direct super-highways as the 110-mile New Jersey Turnpike. As for taking more customers from the railways, the airlines have already won about half the first-class travel market, and have almost monopolised it in some areas; on the New York to Houston runs, for example, it is estimated that aircraft carry 80 per cent of all first-class through traffic."

The obvious source was building up coach traffic, which had just been extended to transatlantic flights "where the airlines offer a reduced fare in exchange for the elimination of such fripperies as free hot meals served aloft". But the paper was sceptical. It was wrong. Three years later the figures were just what the airlines wanted: "With airlines carrying three million passengers a month, with one out of every three persons who travel long distances by public transport going by air, and with air passenger traffic up by 20 per cent over last year, the boom is flying high."

A name to forget   Among those who were in trouble for once was the Ford Motor Company. In September 1957 the paper covered the launch of the new product, the Edsel car. It was impressed: "The centre of all this is another low, wide and handsome automobile in the prevailing super-powered American style, whose chief distinctions are a vertical oval-shaped grille in front which makes it look down its nose rather than grin through its teeth, and a proliferation of push-button controls and warning lights."

It seemed as if it had been designed to be the intellectuals' car: "Preparations for its birth involved ten years of planning, the expenditure of a quarter of a billion dollars, and a long correspondence with Miss Marianne Moore, the poetess, about its name. The ultimate choice, which is pure prose, was not hers; it commemorates the father of the company's present head, the son of the first Henry."

It appended the first sales reports on the forthcoming disaster: "Early orders 'greatly exceeded' the original estimates, whatever these were."

Novelties in the sound world   Everyday life had untold excitements in store. There was the novelty of long-playing records in 1951: "The introduction of these long-lasting records, needing a special needle and revolving at the new speed of 33⅓ r.p.m., was hailed with almost universal enthusiasm by gramophone enthusiasts, and with as universal forecasts of financial disaster by everyone, outside the Columbia company, who was connected with the business side of recorded music. As it has turned out, the industry's gloomy prophecies could hardly have proved more false."

And there was another novelty, the tape recorder: "In its present form, the tape recorder (of which excellent examples sell for less than $1,000) is by far the cheapest as well as by far the best method of making 'masters', or recordings of original performances for later transference to disc. Ironically, the tape recorder's reputation was finally made when it was used by Mr Bing Crosby to 'can' his radio programme for later broadcast."

The housewife's choice Quick frozen foods, started by Clarence Birdseye in 1923, were now making an impact on the market, by 1953 accounting for $875m of America's $64 billion spending on food: "The quick frozen food industry has been a godsend not only to the housewife, but also to the economies of food-producing states. The New England fisheries benefit because their catch goes straight to the freezing plants. Florida's frozen citrus industry has grown to fabulous proportions.... California is relying more and more on its fruit and vegetables. In 1944 it was responsible for 8 per cent of the national production of fruit and 17 per cent of that of vegetables; today the figures are 20 per cent and 26 per cent. The poultry raising states are also doing good business with their 'cut-up-and-ready-to-fry' packages."

Summer's status symbol Air conditioning was in great demand, moving the peak of electricity consumption to July, not January: "In the most comfortable country in the world, a new form of luxury is rapidly becoming a necessity. Air conditioning, which before the war supplied a $200 million market largely confined to factories and commercial buildings, had by 1953 become an industry with a total sales volume of $1.7 billion, nearly 25 per cent of which was for residential use. The ugly rump of a 'packaged' air cooler protruding from a window sill of a block of middle class flats has become a social symbol as significant as a television aerial."

The aerosol invasion By 1955 aerosols had arrived,

too: "Aerosols, a group of products packaged so that the contents spurt out vigorously at the push of a button, are invading almost every counter in America's drug stores. Low-pressure aerosol insecticides, the sophisticated development of the original high-pressure army 'bug bomb', are still the most commonly stocked product, but ... more than half of all customers would also prefer their room deodorants and hair lacquers pressure-packed."

TV's winners—and losers Television was having it all its own way by now. The paper was prepared to see the best in American television, and it ridiculed the restrictions that were imposed, and accepted by the BBC, in Britain: "In the United States, the notion that television should not begin at all until three o'clock and that when it has started, it should sign off, sign on, and finally retire for the night, like an elderly lady, at a little after ten, suggests an apathy verging on coma."

The programmes it praised ranged from *Meet the Press* and *I Remember Mama* to the latest Howdy-Doody and Hopalong Cassidy instalments. It also found dross: "Nevertheless, when all of this has been said, it remains true that, for anyone who is prepared to sift and select, there is a great talent, originality, charm and inventiveness to be discovered in American television programmes."

It was intrigued by the commercial saga that the Hopalong Cassidy production had become. A silent film actor, William Boyd, penniless and jobless, had jumped at the chance of a series of western, horse-opera films "even though he could stay on the back of a horse only with great difficulty". He had been the central character in 66 films in eight years, sartorial elegance and clean-living being his hallmark. He bought them all up after the war for $400,000 to use on television. In 1952 they were shown simultaneously in 62 of the 63 cities with television stations. From the royalties on sales of Hopalong Cassidy Enterprises he earned $1m a year. The paper carefully recorded what this entailed: "Hoppy ear muffs, rain sets (hat, coat and gun), bow ties, polo shirts, dressing gowns, bedside lamps, lunch pails, bathroom rugs, fountain pens, greeting cards, games of all varieties, colouring sets, television chairs (to sit in while viewing the Master), window shades, clothes hampers, linoleum, laundry bags and the Hopalong Cassidy Bath Roundup which contains a sculptured cake of Topper, Hoppy's famous horse, in pure castile soap, and two large cylinders of Hoppy's favourite bubble bath, pine scented ($1 retail)."

This was the future, and it was to be highly competitive: "Hoppy's six-shooter, bubble-bathed and pine-scented though it may be, seems to be giving way to the Space Cadet's Atomic Disintegration Ray Gun."

The paper's correspondents fell happily for quiz shows and engineered profound reasons for doing so. The *$64,000 Question* was a shining example: "The programme has no sex and no violence; it has no famous Hollywood film stars and no politicians or comedians. But it does have 'empathy'—the vicarious identification of the viewer with the anguished and dramatic decisions of the participants. The actors are warm and intriguing ordinary people with unexpected gifts.... The happy sponsor of the show, Revlon Incorporated, the maker of 'Living Lipstick', is reported to have doubled the sales of some of its products."

The unhappy uncovering of the reasons for the success of Charles Van Doren, a clever young competitor on the *Twenty-One* programme, in 1959 naturally caused disappointment and heart-searching: "Mr Van Doren, a university lecturer and an attractive member of a famous academic family, won in all $129,000 as a result of being given advance notice of the questions. He justified this deception to himself by the respect which his success and fame would bring to education and the intellectual life."

It went deeper than that, however. There was anger at the deception and a deepening suspicion that it was a "specifically American tragedy": "The ease with which Mr Van Doren and the others were corrupted is the seamy side of a society which puts too much emphasis on material success. Thus poor Mr Van Doren is already, for many of his countrymen, a figure in the cold war, a symbol of the weaknesses through which Mr Khrushchev hopes to bury them."

It was better to turn to the more conventional and trustworthy pleasures of *I Love Lucy*, which also happened to reward its performers well: "Lucy rapidly endeared herself to women as the housewife addicted to lying and other forms of minor deception to get her own way with her husband, and to men for the way in which she bungled her efforts. In addition, Miss Ball won high marks for her readiness to roll in the mud, fall in a swimming pool and—in one classic episode—engage in a grape-slinging contest while trampling grapes barefoot in an Italian wine vat; that was a time

when most actresses on television relied on glamour and grooming."

It was illustrative to learn that Miss Ball and her husband were now comfortably situated. CBS paid $4.3m to Desilu Productions for the rights of 153 episodes. Desilu itself owned the former RKO studios in Hollywood and Culver City. The Hollywood correspondent summed up: "There was no clowning about this."

Fans of jolting Joe   There was no clowning either about the commercialisation of sport. In 1951 the paper reckoned that baseball, still called America's national game, was bringing in $66m in admission fees each year, and such exponents as Joe Di Maggio of the New York Yankees was earning $125,000, second only to Ted Williams of the Boston Red Sox who got $150,000, "being the most powerful hitter in the game today". Still, Di Maggio had extensive sources of income. Among gifts received in the year: "$7,191 in nickels, dimes and quarters sent in by 3,000 devotees throughout the country (Mr Di Maggio lost no time turning over this sum to charity), a Cadillac motor car from New York fans and a Dodge motor car for his mother from his followers in Hoboken, a Chris-craft motor boat from New Haven, Connecticut, a cheese from a Wisconsin baseball team, a four-year college scholarship from Il Progresso, the Italian-language newspaper in New York City, for any boy Mr Di Maggio might choose, 300 free taxi rides from the Brown and White Cab Company, and 300 quarts of ice cream from the Joe Cardani Ice Cream Company."

But baseball was well down the earnings list. The paper's estimate was that sport (including fishing, motor boating, golf, bowling, softball and skiing) was already bringing in $4 billion a year.

For those concerned about more intellectual pursuits in the United States, the paper offered news of success and challenge. The United States had, if student and amateur groups were counted, over 1,100 symphony orchestras: "Some are world famous, notably the 'big three', the Boston Symphony, the New York Philharmonic and the Philadelphia Orchestra. Others are growing up with the newer centres of wealth; in Dallas, San Antonio, Houston, Tulsa and Oklahoma City orchestras are beginning to tap the oil men's millions.... Yet despite such prestige and support orchestras almost everywhere live on a thin margin of security."

Here, too, the answer was hard work: "Almost all are very busy. They must be; it is the price of their survival."

Bookworms: a threatened species Books, which ought to have been readily accessible in a literate society, were surprisingly hard to get in 1959: "There are in the United States only between 1,200 and 1,500 really well stocked book shops and book departments in large stores. The latter are among the least efficient and the least profitable of department store operations."

The book shops provided no more than a meagre livelihood for the book-lovers who owned and ran them with a minimum of commercial instinct. There were no big concerns: "There are two substantial chains of book-shops, Brentano's Incorporated and Doubleday Book Shops, which have introduced some modern marketing techniques, but between them they are responsible for only three to four per cent of sales."

But then, away from the east coast, *The Economist* itself was not easy to get.

Dallas: November 22nd 1963. John F. Kennedy is shot and liberal America mourns its hopes. But others, like the paper, questioned if his performance lived up to his promise. He was chiefly a portent.

11

IMPERIAL PRESIDENCY

1961–1968

THE KENNEDY STYLE

From the beginning, there were doubts about his caution and detachment

The Economist was attracted by President Kennedy, the representative of a new generation taking charge of America, but it was far from overwhelmed by him or his policies. It was the same when it saw his cabinet. Dean Rusk, from the Rockefeller Foundation, took the State Department, Robert McNamara of Ford took Defence and Douglas Dillon, a Republican, the Treasury. This might be a sensible response to the narrowness of the election but it might be symptomatic: "Most of Mr Kennedy's nominees are like him not only in the virtues they possess but also in the virtues they lack. They seem for the most part to be prosaic men whose strength lies in efficiency rather than in imagination, in cool application to the tasks of administration rather than in the service of any passionate belief."

This diluted the heady intoxication of Harvard speech writers and MIT brains trusters. The paper dismissed Kennedy's inaugural speech, widely admired for its eloquence and idealism, as an exhortation, not an analysis. It did respect the wish to organise the public mood and to take risks with the new technology that was to hand: "His decision to let the television cameras broadcast his press conference live—with all the dangers this involves of a slip on the icy ground of diplomacy—is based on the need to stimulate public interest with the prick of electronic immediacy."

It saw the enlistment of Edward R. Murrow, "the outstanding commentator in the world of television", to head the United States Information Agency as integral to this policy. The United States was to be presented more effectively: "To Mr Murrow this means with scrupulous truthfulness."

With the invasion of Cuba by anti-Castro forces coming up it was to be an unrequited task. However,

---

CHRONOLOGY

1961	John F. Kennedy becomes president
	First man in space: Yuri Gagarin orbits earth
	Bay of Pigs invasion fails in Cuba
	Berlin wall built by East Germany
1962	Algeria gains independence from France
	China invades India
	Cuban missile crisis
1963	De Gaulle vetoes British entry into Common Market
	Nuclear test ban treaty
	Kennedy assassinated in Dallas, Texas
	Lyndon Johnson becomes president
1964	Johnson declares war on poverty, the aim of his "great society"
	Nikita Khrushchev removed from power

	Labour government in Britain
1965	First US combat units land in Vietnam
	Voting Rights Act to encourage black voters
	Riots in Watts, Los Angeles
	Southern Rhodesia declares independence
1966	Indonesia calls off confrontation with Malaysia
1967	De Gaulle's second veto on Britain in Europe
	Military coup in Greece
	Israeli victory in Six-Day War
	UN resolution 242 on Arab-Israeli relations
1968	Johnson withdraws from the presidential election
	Soviet troops invade Czechoslovakia
	Martin Luther King shot
	Robert Kennedy shot

Cuba apart, the paper thought the Kennedy aim was to lower expectations. The missile gap was played down, and the recession began to look as if it might be what the Republicans had called it: a breathing space. The Washington correspondent passed on the anecdotes: "Visitors to President Kennedy who have ventured to contrast the moderation of his immediate intentions with the way he used to talk when he was a Senator report that they have got the pragmatic answer: 'That was when I was a Senator, but now I'm the President.'"

It was not at all like the early days of the New Deal: "There are those who would have him challenge cruel fate by a declaration of radical intentions, but his reactions have been to show extreme caution, patience and calculation."

The Kennedy wish to open negotiations on risky issues with the Soviet Union was part of a new international climate, but it ran counter to many Americans' predilections: "It is hard for a nation brought up on the code of the frontier to accept the idea that the sheriff must try to come to terms with the gunman so that they can both drink in peace in the saloon."

As the months went by the paper became progressively more puzzled by the coolness, the self-possession on the New Frontier: "A President all for growth, surrounded by Harvard teachers of economics, has opposed a steady orthodoxy to their heterodox proposals—to reduce short-term interest rates, for instance, or declare a tax holiday."

It was Kennedy's own doing: "Invited at his press conference to discuss the prospects for the economy, Mr Kennedy dodged the broad question and instead rubbed in the risks of renewed losses of gold. Is this the man who, the bankers said, would ruin the dollar?"

The paper found him engaging in his stonewalling, "elegant, drily witty, aloof yet urbane", but his detachment extended even to urgent social issues: "Mr Kennedy criticised his predecessor for failing to provide 'moral leadership' on Negro rights, but last week he himself kept almost silent during the racial violence evoked by the Freedom Riders' protest." As civil rights was predominantly the problem that demanded the awareness, the very conscience of the Kennedy generation, the paper concluded that his response was due to his own personality: "His liberalism is cerebral rather than the product of his own experience. It represents not his passionate faith but his reasoned judgment."

The first visit to Europe was a prodigious publicity success for "the personable young President" and his wife "an American Queen of Hearts", but the meetings with de Gaulle and, especially, Khrushchev were unproductive and Kennedy seemed to show it: "Mr Kennedy's attempts to deal with every issue personally will either threaten his health further or force him to leave some of his essential functions undone.... The spectacle of an obviously harassed President, unable quite to keep up with his job, would alarm American public opinion more than anything else."

Even the foundation of the Peace Corps, the quintessential Kennedy concept, putting together the energy of American youth and the needs of the third world, the paper met with scepticism. Naturally it saw the political opportunity: "To vote against the Peace Corps Bill will look like voting against American youth and American idealism and only very curmudgeonly southern Congressmen will dare to do that. Even Senator Goldwater, the leader of the right-wing Republicans, is claimed as a backer."

But it doubted the practicality of the scheme as a major contributor in helping poorer countries: "Teachers ... are in short supply in America. So are doctors, nurses, medical auxiliaries and veterinary surgeons, largely because of the restrictive practices of the professional bodies. America is an importer (though also a trainer) of such skills rather than a supplier of them to the needy."

The first year, the paper thought, proved its point: "About two-thirds of those now overseas are liberal arts graduates who have gone into teaching. The great disappointment has been the difficulty of recruiting people with specific skills." Not enough were black, either. Nevertheless 20,000 had offered to go, and Kennedy was asking Congress for $63.75m. He wanted much more help for education in America as well and directed Congress's attention to the consequences of past neglect: "A million children fail each year to finish secondary school. There is a grave shortage of teachers and one in five of the country's 1.6 million teachers in elementary and secondary schools is not fully qualified.... He wants more adult education, because there are still almost 3 million illiterate grown-ups."

Kennedy wanted to spend $22 billion on college building over ten years and $20 billion a year on educational expansion and improvement, a 75% increase. He tied it to the campaign to keep up with the Russians in engineering and science, but Congress did not see it that way: "At the same time as it gave him money for bombs and the moon, Congress frustrated Mr Kennedy's request for federal aid to education, so that children by the hundred thousand will continue to learn their lessons in double and triple shifts in hallways and basements, in the richest country in the world."

It was not turning out to be, in the paper's opinion, a distinguished or fortunate presidency, but then it was not captivated by the romance of Camelot. It was not above reporting the car bumper sticker sighted by a correspondent in Los Angeles: "I Miss Ike. Hell, I Even Miss Harry."

Nevertheless it gave him credit for trying, for having the right aims and instincts even if the performance had been disappointing: "Americans have been very loath to face the problems presented by their sluggish economy, their choked cities, their inadequate transport, their exploding population and consequently overcrowded schools, their polluted water, their neglected countryside, their increasingly adverse ratio of dependents to breadwinners and their growingly restive Negro semi-citizens. Now, spurred on by Mr Kennedy, they are debating some of those matters vehemently."

Kennedy was still plainly in this trough two months later when he was faced with the biggest test of his presidency, if not of the cold war itself: Khrushchev's despatch of missiles to Cuba, a momentous threat to American security. That Kennedy's success was complete made his reputation.

Even then, however, the paper suspected that Kennedy's style, greatly admired by his middle-class supporters, did not make him popular; it certainly did not exempt him from criticism: "His eye is too fresh and too penetrating by half. He sees the things that are basically wrong and the important things that have to be done; but because he takes a long view, his proposals go too deep below the surface of day-to-day problems and day-to-day living. He fails to rouse the people."

It was to rouse the people with the 1964 election in mind that Kennedy and his motorcade were in Dallas, Texas, on November 22nd 1963. The paper avoided too much emotion on his death. The president, it thought, had disappointed too many people, for different reasons: "The truth is that John Kennedy was a portent as well as a person. He did not, in fact, succeed in setting

the Potomac on fire."

The paper offered no revelations or speculations on why he had been shot or who was to blame. It was just perplexed: "What the revelations so far have proved is that, while Oswald's past was unusually well documented—from New York City school psychiatric reports to Soviet Union consular files—nothing could have predicted that he would kill a President."

It had no reason to dissent from the Warren Commission's report a year later: Oswald was a lone assassin. The Washington correspondent believed a defective personality was a sufficient explanation: "The report is almost sympathetic as it traces all the failure of his twenty-four years of life. He had no father and his childhood was miserable. He was a misfit in the Soviet Union when he tried to become a figure by going there. He could not hold a decent job in the United States. His wife complained about his sexual inadequacy. One understands why he was 'profoundly alienated from the world in which he lived', why he fancied himself as a great man in history."

Kennedy had approached, in many ways, The Economist's specifications for the United States' chief executive. He was young, intelligent, active, imbued with high aspirations and a sense of duty and history, and he had the sense and means to ensure he was well advised. It felt he erred, for all his polish and style, through innate caution.

VINDICATION ON CUBA

The manner of the Soviet reverse made Kennedy's international reputation, although The Economist *had been highly sceptical*

Cuba was almost the breaking, and then decisively the making, of the Kennedy presidency and of Kennedy's own reputation, especially in The Economist's eyes. Kennedy inherited the first Cuban crisis. Although Eisenhower would have nothing to do with an exiles' invasion, the idea was widespread among the agencies and the deficiencies of Castro's Cuba were increasingly widely propagated. The refugees had spread through Central America but they were concentrated in Florida and the Central Intelligence Agency (CIA), under Allen Dulles, took a purposeful interest in them. There was nothing official in this, but ambitions grew. Expectations of an invasion and an attempted coup flourished.

The Kennedy inaugural. The paper was scarcely impressed by the rhetoric and saw in him a naturally cautious young man who, despite his battery of Harvard advisers, would be circumspect in his policies.

The paper was worried in early April 1961 by reports of American involvement: "If such help is given, and the invasion still fails, it will be a major disaster for the reputation of the United States."

A week later it said it again: "Win or lose, the odium will fall on the Americans. If the invasion now fails, the United States will be laughed at for bungling as well as blamed for bullying. A win might have proved the Americans right about the Castro regime, if the invaders had been greeted as liberators; but it would have left the rift between north and south in America wider than ever."

When the fiasco was duly confirmed, the paper was more inclined to blame the Pentagon and the CIA than the Kennedy administration, inexperienced as it still was: "General Lemnitzer is reported to have endorsed a sketchy plan that would have frightened an infantry major. Overborne by the brass hats and the undercover boys, the Harvard contingent in the White House failed apparently to question the assumptions or the logic of the scheme. Caught in this web of circumstance, the President gave the green light."

The president plainly had to take the responsibility, but the paper was not unhappy about caution in foreign affairs: "The image of Mr Kennedy as a cautious and sure-footed young leader is inevitably tarnished; but at least he has stumbled early in his Presidency and is determined not to be misled again."

He was, or felt he was, when Khrushchev, disturbed by the swelling flood of East German refugees escaping through the western sectors of Berlin, ordered the building of the wall dividing the two halves of the city. The Russians were on the defensive, but the wall took the Americans by surprise: "Nobody had warned the President that the Russians might indeed seal off east Berlin and when they did he found nobody had made any plans for that contingency. The idea then went around that, as Mr Khrushchev had now staunched the haemorrhage of refugees from east Germany, however brutally, negotiations would become easier.... Whereupon the Russians made the first of their menacing gestures against the air routes into Berlin and heated up the atmosphere some more."

Kennedy sent a battle force into Berlin without incident; force had been shown to pay in dealing with Khrushchev. He did not exclude talks, but his expectations had been sharply reduced: "Like Mr Eisenhower, he seems at one time to have flirted with the idea that a process of intelligent negotiation might usher in a new period of tolerance, perhaps even of goodwill, between East and West. The President still believes in the value of negotiating, but he now regards it simply as a means of avoiding the worst dangers of what he clearly expects to be a long and intolerant tussle between America and Russia."

Kennedy's prudence put a clamp on adventures and risks in international relations, and he got Congress's approval to improve the nuclear deterrent by weapons such as Polaris and to build up specialised conventional forces as well. He got the resources, too, to develop America's challenge to Russia in space, the new war almost by proxy, with scientific and military consequences and prolonged propaganda campaigns. In May 1961 he declared the United States would land a man on the moon before the end of the decade, a claim that seemed imprudent when the Americans were still so far behind in the race. But he was counting on the worldwide benefit of doing everything as an open society should: "Together the massive publicity given to Commander Shepard's parabola in space and the modesty and intelligence of the astronaut himself made a propaganda triumph out of a short flight which came a poor second, in scientific achievement as well as in time, to the Russian Major Gagarin's orbit of the earth."

The gamble paid off again in John Glenn's flight in February 1962 when the paper emphasised the value of a working, human pilot against the claims of computer-driven research: "A rocket probing the radiation belts beyond the earth, measuring the solar flares or even exploring the moon is not really required to exercise judgment. But the military, toying with the ideas of space bombers in orbit, dare not entrust such weapons to a dim-wit computer with roughly the same intellectual capacity as an earthworm."

It was not war by proxy that came to a head in October 1962 but the cold war itself, and for once *The Economist* wavered, unwilling to see in the Soviet arms preparations the justification for hostilities that might end in nuclear war. The paper, it seemed, simply did not share the United States view that the presence of Soviet bases off the American shore and within immediate striking distance of American cities and defences was a legitimate cause for intervention. When American opinion began to get visibly worried about Khrushchev's intentions, the paper's reproof was stern. There were, it said, plenty of good reasons to be worried about Cuba, especially the American state of mind: "It must be admitted that Cuba has fallen under communist influence more quickly and completely than many people thought likely a couple of years ago (including this paper). But that has been past history for a good many months. The military aid Russia has been sending to Dr Castro since the middle of July brings no change in the situation inside Cuba itself—except in the roundabout sense that it makes it harder to change that situation by military force applied from outside."

To see the issue as primarily an internal Cuban affair was one divergence from the paper's usual approach in the Caribbean. It then foresaw a Soviet reaction with conventional forces in locations around the world: "If the Americans were by any chance to invade Cuba tomorrow, it would be no use asking for whom the bell tolled. It would almost certainly toll for the western access routes to Berlin, and for American servicemen in South Vietnamese outposts."

The blame for this was put firmly on a traditional American policy, with which Britain had disagreed at times in the previous century, but which the paper believed was now inapplicable: "Such is the mesmeric effect of the Monroe doctrine (or that part of the Monroe doctrine which it is fashionable to remember) that a unilateral declaration made 139 years ago is apparently thought sufficient to insulate what the United States does in the Americas from what can be done to the United States elsewhere."

This was a second divergence from the primacy that the paper gave to the alliance in an evident emergency. Kennedy, having seen the photographic evidence from a U-2 plane over Cuba, instituted an armed blockade to turn back Russian ships still approaching the island.

The Macmillan government, beset by doubts itself, thought this illegal, but the Russians slowed down. The paper appeared to be concerned that the United States might interpret this "in a dangerously wrong way": "They may be persuaded that by forcing a showdown over the shipment of Russian arms to Cuba the United States has publicly and triumphantly made Mr Khrushchev back down; in other words, that the United States has achieved that decisive victory in the 'contest of wills' which the extremists of both East and West have been pursuing, like a will o' the wisp, for years past."

The paper believed, as did many others, that great powers, once in active confrontation and seen to be so, were unlikely to back down and be seen to back down: "The possibility of the fatal spark being struck in the Caribbean has not yet vanished, or even seriously diminished. Mr Khrushchev's feeling that he cannot make a 'confession of weakness' (how it twists the heart to hear these identical phrases tripping from American and Russian tongues alike) may yet lead him to try to push a ship or two through the blockade to Cuba; just as the western powers would probably feel obliged to push a convoy or two up the Berlin autobahn if the Russians imposed a blockade there."

The paper was certain that the real question was how could the powers "back away from their perilous confrontation without having to eat dirt"? It proposed an international inspection system under the United Nations: "Might America conceivably accept a control that left Cuba with an armament sufficient to deter an American attack but not capable of devastating the United States?"

This was indisputably not what Kennedy had in mind. He had not accepted advice to attack Cuba but had imposed an arms embargo. He was not likely to accept the reliability of United Nations inspection in Cuba. But he had not given up the prospect of a peaceful settlement. In fact, when Khrushchev put forward two possible methods of proceeding he accepted the statesmanlike one. The Soviets withdrew their offensive weapons, and the United States agreed not to invade Cuba. When this solution emerged the paper was ungrudging in its praise of Kennedy: "He played his hand as a strong hand should be played: the bid called exactly, the moves unhesitating, the objective, once stated, adhered to."

The pace had been hot, but the judgment accurate:

"Perhaps only this can explain the astonishing speed and (within the limits of the matter at issue) the completeness of the Russian retreat. Mr Kennedy thereupon showed that he knew not only how far to go, but precisely where to stop. His acceptance of Mr Khrushchev's retreat was unreserved and handsome."

The paper's compliment placed the president in the top rank: "There was not a touch of the intoxication that confuses success with victory, not a sound, in this final moment, from the demon of generalisation who tempted Woodrow Wilson and Franklin Roosevelt."

It thought the commitment not to invade Cuba was entirely sensible: "It is for all of us to acknowledge that the promise can be, in the prevailing American political climate, an irksome one to have made, and to give unstinted credit for it."

The Washington correspondent quickly confirmed that the commitment was one meant to be kept, although some Americans hoped it could be forgotten: "In fact, however, and not for sentimental reasons, invasion is unattractive to the Administration. The tiger does not wish to eat the goat."

Kennedy had kept in due touch with Macmillan in Downing Street during the crisis. Macmillan had backed him firmly. Kennedy, in turn, was obliging about British priorities, among them the supply of Polaris missiles to continue the British deterrent agreed at Nassau in December 1962. He nourished the British wish to join the common market, partly, at least, as a counter to the more authoritarian and less accommodating stance of Konrad Adenauer and de Gaulle: "Mr Kennedy feels that the western thrust towards European unity and Atlantic interdependence is too strong for one or even two old men to stand for long in its way.... There is, in fact, plenty of evidence that President Kennedy was amazed and outraged by President de Gaulle, while among Americans there is growing distrust of Europe's postwar strong men, once so admired. Americans want Britain in Europe as an aqueduct for parliamentary democracy as well as a bridge between continents."

The Americans and British worked together to impress the Russians with the need for the test-ban treaty in the summer of 1963: "It is hard for the same Americans to believe that Mr Khrushchev, who smuggled missiles into Cuba last October, has suddenly become a lovable character. The test-ban treaty is welcomed—provided there is not some catch in it."

However, by then the paper had accepted, almost without reservation, Kennedy's ability to run a successful alliance. When by November the Americans were worrying about their balance of payments deficit and threatening economies in their defence spending in Europe, it gave its customary vindication: "The allied critics have to demonstrate that they, too, are putting in their sufficient contributions to perhaps the hardest of all human enterprises—a wartime alliance in peacetime."

It was clear-eyed about it. The American conversion to interdependence across the world had been "uncertain often, ham-handed sometimes, but always inescapable". The motives were as mixed: "It is in the national interest of the United States to be entangled in the world. That way lies American safety—and American prosperity as well."

Within two weeks Kennedy was dead.

ALL THE WAY WITH LBJ
A difficult, proud man met a battered end

Kennedy's successor, Lyndon Johnson, was a very different and underestimated man. Johnson resented this. He did not have Kennedy's style, but he believed he had a vision of America that was as valid as Kennedy's and of a range that equalled Franklin Roosevelt's. He

LBJ hastens his Great Society. With his vice-president, Hubert Humphrey, and his exemplar, Harry S Truman, to confirm the date, he signs the Medicare Bill in 1965. The Vietnam war overtook his plans.

also knew, from his 23 years in the Congress, that he could get it to pass the legislation that Kennedy had failed to get through. From the outset the paper saw him as a determined man: "Certainly there is an unmistakable streak in Mr Johnson which makes it unlikely that he will flinch from risks he judges to be unavoidable."

He had not been majority leader of the Senate for nothing. Johnson knew about the reality of power, he was a manipulator, and his roots were deep in the philosophy and the reasoning of the New Deal: "What is not so widely appreciated outside America is another, rather un-Texan element in his temperament, a pensive reluctance to push disagreements beyond the point of no return. To judge from what he has written and said, the new President's deepest felt sympathies are egalitarian and humanitarian, his turn of mind pragmatic."

The paper had hopes of him, which the Kennedy people would never admit to: "If President Johnson should manage to get passed by Congress legislation dealing with medical care for the aged and other improvements in social security, with federal aid for education and with civil rights and tax cuts, it will probably be by a stick-and-carrot technique that Mr Kennedy either did not choose, or did not know how, to use."

Using his experience and the sense of national urgency that followed Kennedy's death, Johnson did carry social legislation that had come to a standstill; he got tax cuts, and set out on his own programme declaring a war on poverty in America. The paper was enthusiastic. It felt it was back in the New Deal frame of mind: "The proposed Job Corps, intended to enlist at first 40,000 and later 100,000 youths between the ages of 16 and 21 for training and work on useful projects—in the national parks, for example—seems to resemble President Roosevelt's Civilian Conservation Corps. The Work Training Programme and the Work Study Programme recall the old National Youth Administration. The Work Study Programme is a roundabout way of getting young people without money through college, by enabling them to work their way in the American manner."

It liked the Community Action Programme too: " 'Community action' is intended to include improvements in health services, housing and education; in various ways it runs up against entrenched congressional prejudices—for instance, by channelling funds directly into local authorities, not necessarily through the states, and by enabling the children in religious schools to benefit from federally-financed efforts."

Johnson spoke emotively of the "great society" he had in mind. The United States was booming economically, most Americans were better off than ever before, but Johnson was trying to bring about an intellectual change in American society and how its problems should be tackled. To British liberals there was no contest in America; Johnson seemed to personify the caring, kindly social order that affluence should strive for. There was new thinking on the radical Republican side too, but of a kind abhorred by the British middle classes who were about to vote for Labour and Harold Wilson. The Republican Party had changed drastically in three years. Richard Nixon, the inheritor of the Eisenhower centre, had gone grudgingly to defeat trying for the governorship of California: "Though Mr Nixon strained every mental and facial muscle to appear as a broad-minded and even jovial anti-communist non-reactionary, apparently he left on the voters' retinas only the image of an inquisitorial scowl."

The way was open for the candidate of the new right, Senator Barry Goldwater of Arizona. The paper, judging his performance in the New Hampshire primary, did not believe in him: "He has implied that he advocates withdrawal of the United States from the United Nations, repeal of the old age pension scheme and military control over the use (or non-use) of thermonuclear weapons. No Republican can go that far to the right and expect to be nominated for President." When Goldwater did well enough to be nominated, the paper could conjure up the spectre of catastrophe: "This sets the stage for a disaster of monumental proportions for the Republicans."

When Johnson joined the campaign it was a triumphal procession, though he took care to switch his emphasis from legislating for minorities, useful as their votes would be, to the basic appeal to middle America: "The graceless phrase, 'the Great Society', has not caught on and the President no longer uses it much."

What he did insist on, and the boom allowed him to emphasise it, was that his was not a spendthrift government relying on higher taxes: "While he has loaded his money-saving campaign with essentially meaningless gimmicks, like the turning off of lights in the White House and a reduction in the number of chauffeur-driven government cars, nonetheless the drive for economy is clearly real and he has had some success. Mr Johnson's motive, however, has been to reduce, not the part played by the government, but only the amount spent by the government."

Johnson's professionalism and his ample lead in the polls encouraged the paper to put in the kindest word it could for the obvious loser. Goldwater had his points: "He is a warm and lovable man with many attractive qualities and in office he would very likely not have been so terrible as a large part of the world supposes. But he has completely failed to endow his campaign with any consistent intellectual concept, a thing that would seem to be necessary to a man purporting to attack root and branch the political status quo."

Johnson duly won with 61.1% of the vote. The evidence of American prosperity seemed so abundant that he believed the wealth-creating process itself would be expanded further by his welfare schemes. This was the spirit of his inauguration. The paper was not so sure: "In his presumptive two terms he can expect a growth of 23 million in the population of the United States, a need for 8 million new places in the schools and colleges, a demand for 10 million more new jobs and 8 million more houses and for the expanded and remodelled urban life and services that such a growth, superimposed on to the arrears from the past, makes urgent." Its conclusion was candid: "Matched with reality, the Great Society may sound like the empty promise of a golden age."

Golden it was. The budget for 1965 was appropriate for the richest country, and for Johnson's targets: "The mind begins to boggle at what the government of a rich country can do if the government is mildly Keynesian.... Spending is raised on health, on education at various levels, on poverty—rural, urban, among old people, among young people—on the unemployed, on the unskilled, on under-developed parts of the country— more than $6 billion in all. In addition, as a sort of bonus, taxes are cut (in this case excise taxes) by nearly $2 billion."

What LBJ and almost everyone else had not yet grasped was the size of the commitment he soon felt obliged to make in Vietnam. Nor were the consequences of inflation in the overstretched economy appreciated. Beside the grandiloquence of the re-election the paper inserted an unwelcome thought: "The involvement in Vietnam goes on yielding unhappy results."

But it made no more of it then. These were still early days, when everything continued to be done to conceal the extent of America's increasing involvement, however unwillingly the obligation was accepted. As he was steadily drawn in Johnson continued his pressure for reform in Congress, but within six months of his re-election the paper saw how his influence dwindled with his new preoccupation: "At a time when the President spends hours on end deciding the details of bombing in North Vietnam, responsibility for Congress has been delegated to White House aides."

Predictably, opposition grew. What LBJ could not take, for all his political experience, was criticism, especially criticism so soon after he had won one of the most conclusive of election results. His anguish was palpable: "Painful decisions have refused to be circumvented. They have tormented his emotions, taken up his time and drawn heavily on his strength. What is perfectly plain is that the President takes failure hard. Not only is he an emotional man, he is also a man always in need of reassurance, of concurrence (the more heartfelt the better), of affection and admiration. This causes him to take criticism badly."

As the problems beset him—Vietnam, desegregation, the growing alienation of those parts of American society where he craved approbation, especially the young—Johnson withdrew into himself and into the conduct of a war which he had persuaded himself it was his duty to win. When he had first gone to Congress for the wherewithal to keep an American presence active in South Vietnam in May 1964 the paper had warned that the risk would become cumulative: "This decision may, in the event, turn out to be mistaken; it may never produce 'victory', or it may lead to a more painful defeat than another policy might have produced."

When he went ahead and The Economist produced, over the years, a consistent and coherent backing for his endeavour, he was grateful for advocacy that he felt too often he missed in America; he was glad, he said, to have the paper's "understanding". When in April 1968 he confessed himself beaten, unable to run for the White House again, the paper understood: "President Johnson is a battered man. For the last two years he has been abused, in a manner that has sometimes recalled the McCarthyism of the 1950s except that this time the abuse has come from the left, for having drawn the logical conclusion of his predecessors' policies towards south-east Asia. It has been enough to bludgeon any man. And the Americans are a battered people."

VIETNAM: NOT THE RIGHT WAR

And not in the right country, nor for the right regime, but it did not have to be fought again

The Economist began with grave doubts about South Vietnam. It did not like the regime there; it doubted the optimism of Kennedy's military and security advisers; and it feared (as Eisenhower had apparently feared) that the United States might have to go in deeper than it wished. It noted in December 1961: "The President cannot feel happy to be told by General Taylor and Mr Rostow that South Vietnam may be saved without the dispatch of large American forces only if the South Vietnamese government accepts American advice, when South Vietnamese newspapers under government auspices are accusing the United States of interference for the sake of profiting from capitalist imperialist exploitation."

It was far from a major issue. In March 1962 Robert McNamara, the defence secretary, conceded that 4,000 Americans were training the Vietnamese to deal with the communist guerrillas who were helped by the north. They were doing so under combat conditions, and there had been a handful of casualties. The paper was surprised: "The most remarkable event ... however, has been the dogs which did not bark at the news of how deeply the United States is now involved in Vietnam."

Kennedy had been careful. He had consulted the leaders of both parties in Congress. Nixon had announced he strongly supported the policy. Nevertheless the American commitment was going to grow inexorably. There was a big step in February 1964 while Johnson was still campaigning on a peace platform: "The purpose of America's enormous and costly mission there (some 15,500 military men at present, with aid flowing at a rate of some $400 million a year) is a limited one: simply to get South Vietnam into a condition to keep down insurgency within its territory and to resist infiltration from the North. Something short of victory would do."

By midsummer the paper had made its mind up,

even if Johnson was concealing, perhaps even to himself, what he thought it right or ineluctable to do. In June it put together the enlarging American participation in Vietnam and the existing British commitment to Malaysia in Sarawak and Borneo, where British troops repulsed Indonesian insurgents, and said they were the same operation for the same end. To the paper it was inconceivable that the American presence in Vietnam was somehow felt to be different from the wars against communism in Malaysia and the Philippines, which could not have been conducted, far less fought to an acceptable standing, had not the United States taken the heat and burden of the day in Vietnam. The paper was positive that it was all the same South-East Asian war: "In the predominantly Buddhist northern part of the area, it involves an American attempt to keep a centre of non-communist power in existence between Saigon and Rangoon. In the predominantly Moslem southern half, it involves a British attempt to establish the equally non-communist (and by virtue of the British inheritance much more genuinely democratic) Malaysian government firmly on its own two feet."

The extent of the eventual commitment in Vietnam, with all its political consequences in the United States, served to diminish, in American eyes, the effort that was being made elsewhere around the South China Sea. The paper always thought of it as a demonstrable advantage from the Vietnam war.

In March 1965 two battalions of American combat troops were landed in Vietnam, and the demands of the war on American resources thereupon took off. In August Johnson contrived (as it later emerged) a collision between Vietnamese gunboats and the US Seventh Fleet, from which there could be only one victor. The paper was doubtful: "It is vastly odd, on the face of it, that the mosquito of the North Vietnamese navy should attack the tiger of the Seventh Fleet. But then it was vastly more odd that Mr Khrushchev should have risked slipping missiles into Cuba, and the purpose in both cases—to test the adversary's intentions—may have been identical."

The Washington correspondent saw it much the same way: "The accounts do not explain why, unless they have taken leave of their senses, the North Vietnamese should have acted as they did."

After a week the paper concluded that the engagement in the Gulf of Tonkin was an "attempt to frighten

Caught in the Vietnam jungle. As US conscripts were drafted in to contain the communist Vietcong, Johnson found both the war and political support at home slipping away from him. He did not seek re-election in 1968.

North Vietnam into disengagement". (It was not wholly confident: "This article is pure speculation.") It was hesitant about accepting the Johnson version: "The Cuba crisis was a textbook example of how to manage the infinitely careful diplomacy that these confrontations demand. Is this one being handed equally well?"

The South-East Asian correspondent thought the clash would be briefly influential: "On fleeting judgment the whiff of grapeshot in the Gulf of Tonkin has helped to clear the steaming Indochinese air for, say, the next three months."

On LBJ's re-election that November the paper noticed how he worried publicly about the growing calls to attack North Vietnam directly. It was, it thought, in "the character of a man who not only

prefers peace to war, but also looks very carefully at any proposal that is in the nature of a gamble and turns it down if it does not offer a return fully commensurate with the risk involved". But if he wished to persist then the alliance should side with him: "If President Johnson decides that the Vietnamese battle must be fought through to the finish, then the United States will be faced with a long and wearisome haul. The military situation in South Vietnam is bad, and to put it right it will almost certainly be necessary to mount air strikes against North Vietnamese targets. If this has to be done, Britain and other western countries should resolutely resist the temptation to make small noises of distress."

Despite its doubts about local tactics, the paper believed that the elemental justification of the policy of drawing the line was that it had succeeded up to then in the cold war in Europe and Asia, and that it had even come to give guidance to the communist powers which they respected when it was done effectively: "A succession of confrontations with the Soviet Union helped the rulers of that country to realise that very definite limits are set to their freedom of action on the international scene; this has been a major cause of the emergent understanding between Russia and the West."

It thought the same approach and the same determination applied in South-East Asia: "To inculcate the same realisation into the Chinese government and its hangers-on is the main justification for continuing to draw a line in south-east Asia. This policy was in the past called containment. It could also be called education."

That resolution, the paper believed, could and should be enforced. It was within the capability of the Americans to do so. But the South Vietnamese were another matter. They obeyed their own inclination; they sensed themselves to be in desperate circumstances and behaved in that way. The paper had no time for their atrocities: "Shooting prisoners (defectors or otherwise) is, quite simply, wrong. For months past there have been photographed instances of South Vietnamese brutality (the knife pressed against the prisoner's throat, the head held under the water). But it is harder to maintain a distinction between the degrees of violence—short of methodical torture—that happen during interrogations than it is to make and enforce the simple rule; one must not kill prisoners. That this should be done by the side supported by the West makes it worse."

In the monsoon season in June 1965 the Vietcong guerrillas attacked in strength and American troops were drawn in. The paper was unworried: "Nobody ever thought they went there just to garrison a few islands among the Vietcong's paddyfields."

The strategic objective should be plain: "The correct aim of the United States in Asia is to draw a defendable line somewhere between China and India, and hold it." As more and more American troops were shipped in it was obvious that Vietnam was not just any line, it was the line on which American policy depended. In July the paper noted: "American military strength in Vietnam has risen since 1963 from 15,500 to something over 72,000. This has not prevented the state

of the campaign from deteriorating."

By November 161,000 American troops were there: "The facts that the domestic condition of South Vietnam is still deteriorating, and that its political structure still looks hopelessly unsound, give a possible clue to the motives of the communists in refusing at this stage to accept the inevitability of defeat. At all events they do refuse. Their military effort has grown in scale and has become more aggressive than ever."

The Washington correspondent confessed to doubts about the wisdom of the American liability, which now seemed open-ended in numbers and cost: "The Administration may be half way through the Vietnamese forest, or it may not. There is no view of the further edge. President Johnson's own position in the matter is a puzzle. It does not appear to be in his character to take on a commitment of undefined extent. Yet this is what he seems to have done."

LBJ was going to see his policy through and he had American public opinion well on his side. Gallup showed 64% agreeing that United States forces should be involved, compared with 52% in May. The paper was intrigued at how the intellectuals were divided, in a way reminiscent of Britain in the nineteenth century: "The combination of intellectuals studying the interest of the state at one end of the scale while other intellectuals protest in the name of humanity at the other reminds one irresistibly of British political life during most of the past century. To this extent America, the new society in a new technological environment, working out new purposes, has suddenly come to look astonishingly like the old imperial and liberal Britain writ large."

It was not imperial in the sense of outright conquest, however; resolute Roman containment was always the paper's aim: "There can be no victory in the classic sense. The best that can be hoped for is a gradual improvement in which military successes generate a growing political stability, which in turn improves the military prospects. North Vietnam will not have been defeated—that is not the aim—but South Vietnam will have been saved."

That calm, dispassionate strategy looked good and read well, but South Vietnamese politics were nothing of the sort. In April 1966 Air Marshal Nguyen Cao Ky in Saigon had got into trouble with the Buddhists which showed him neither to be a strong man nor a practising politician. The paper found it irksome and tedious. There was nothing new in the discovery that "the junta is rickety and politically inept, and that the militant Buddhists are restive and expert at setting off demonstrations"; but this squabble had serious consequences: "What was new was the revelation that the military leader whom President Johnson had rashly embraced at Honolulu in February was himself so rash as to disrupt the junta's own unity, and to get into a position where he had to concede, in a humiliating manner, the militant Buddhists' demands for civilian government."

When within a month Ky had flown his marines into Da Nang, deceiving the Americans, meaning to arrest the Buddhist leaders and failing, the paper was contemptuous: "In a war like Vietnam's a man can play dirty tricks and still qualify as a leader. But the really important thing that has been destroyed in this week's mess is Marshal Ky's standing as a leader capable of pushing ahead with the fight to keep South Vietnam out of communist hands."

The paper had no solution to provide to Vietnamese politics. When the word went round Washington that summer that America's allies might try to be of military use, even if only as a gesture (the band of the Black Watch was in regular demand at the State Department), the paper was rather cagey: "Covetous eyes are being cast on the jungle-trained British troops who by late July may no longer be needed in Borneo to hold off the Indonesians. The Americans realise that there is no hope of getting even a token British force to Vietnam itself. But it is thought that such a force might be sent to support the 20,000 Americans in Thailand, a Seato ally which has two insurgencies on its hands."

Nothing came of that. Where the paper felt on surer ground was rebuking the British Labour Party for its occasional rebellions against the official policy of support for American aims in South-East Asia. They were, it thought, jeopardising general British influence in Washington. Its reasoning was true to type: "The rule is that Britain goes along with the main aims of American foreign policy in return for the right to nudge the Americans back on course when they seem to be deviating from those aims. It is a fair exchange."

It felt that Attlee had done this over confining the war to South Korea in 1950, Macmillan in urging the Americans towards the summit in 1959, and Wilson in sinking the concept of a NATO nuclear fleet in 1964. This was not going to be contrived with LBJ in 1966. He was preoccupied with Vietnam in his very emotions. The Washington correspondent reported: "When he lists America's allies in Vietnam, as he is given to doing, Britain is not among them, nor is any European country. Australia and New Zealand are and their stock has risen dizzily in Washington."

There was no doubt that the war was difficult and messy, and especially so for troops wholly unaccustomed to the country, the people and the tactics of such a campaign: "It is a land war, fought by relatively small formations of very brave men who are prepared to persist for years with the tactics of ambush and terrorism until the other side's nerve cracks. Those who believe that this technique of 'people's war' should be opposed, because its aim is to set up an unacceptable form of society, have little choice but to fight it on its own terms: that is, by a land war."

It was turning into more, much more, than the Americans had bargained for. The paper admitted the worry: "It is not the 'right war in the right place'. Defensive wars seldom are. It is not the sort of war that the Americans will be able to bring themselves to fight time and time again in other parts of the world. But if it comes out right in Vietnam, it will with luck not have to be fought all over again elsewhere."

By December 1966 it admitted that Johnson needed a settlement: "He has persuaded the Americans to accept the war, but it is not a popular one, and it could give him a lot of trouble if it is still going on when he runs for re-election in 1967."

The paper advised a compromise, provided the integrity of South Vietnam, the drawing of the line, was not prejudiced. This was realistic, or seemed so: "The military situation next year will still fall a good deal short of the clear-cut victory the purists want. This can be accepted—provided North Vietnam in return will accept the principle of South Vietnam's right to stay non-communist. That is the essential principle the Americans have been fighting for. If it is accepted, anything else is negotiable."

Three weeks later it spelled out what it thought ought to be reasonable: "South Vietnam need not be tied to the United States by a military treaty or the presence of an American army. It could be part of an internationally guaranteed neutral belt in south-east Asia. There could be a place in its political structure for most of the people in the National Liberation Front who come from the south, as distinct from those who have been imported from the north. It would not remain a generals' fief. There would be an amnesty."

As 1967 progressed Johnson still found the polls backing him, but support, as the paper recognised, was slipping. It identified two particular worries: television coverage was, intentionally or not, losing the war in American homes; and the intellectuals, or a sizeable proportion of them, were despairing and deserting. The imperial presidency, as its critics called it, had fallen foul of the new technology: "It was Kipling's Private Mulvaney who said there were many things done in war that never got into the papers.... Mulvaney and his kind were professional soldiers, and knowledge of the kind of death they might die ... did not greatly disturb Victorian England.... In Vietnam the theatre of operations is swarming with cameramen and reporters, and the war they are covering combines the unpleasantness of a regular campaign in difficult country, where there is always enough of death and terror, with the extra unpleasantness of a counter-insurgency operation. This is the material from which television conducts its documentaries on the horrors of war."

That was essentially the problem of conscript forces. The college graduates, the "huge numbers of bouncy, young intellectuals", who saw in LBJ "the defects of the frontier breed", were inclined towards the arguments of the doves and gave them political credibility even when they did not entirely accept them. The paper questioned if they were really alienated: "That is putting it a bit high; many of the country's most intelligent people think that Mr Johnson is doing the right thing and many of his angriest critics are far from being intellectuals. But the sense of unease is manifestly there. Quite a lot of Americans, of the sort who would describe themselves as believers in the American dream, are feeling lost. They recognise that something new is happening and they have not yet adjusted themselves to it."

It was, in its way, the disillusionment of the new internationalists: "Asia being Asia, they are sometimes going to find themselves supporting allies who are less than wholly desirable and fighting enemies who are no Hitlers. This is what happens when a big country deploys its power for a long-term end."

In May the paper hoped, as did some in the White House and the British prime minister, Harold Wilson, that the talks which the Russian leader, Alexei Kosygin, was to have with Johnson at Glassboro, New Jersey, and Wilson at Chequers would put a restraint on Ho Chi Minh and the North Vietnamese government: "Mr Johnson has a powerful interest in keeping moderate men like Mr Kosygin in power in Moscow, just as they have an interest in good relations with him. He also has little reason for believing that a purely military approach to the Vietnam war will crack the problem soon, or even surely."

It came to nothing. The war of attrition—even if that had not been the original American hope—had to be pressed on, but the South Vietnamese army, as the paper repeatedly complained, was not playing its part. American units were diverted from their main job of taking on the communists' big formations, and Vietcong-held territory was not being reclaimed: "In addition to corruption and inefficiency, there have been security leaks at the highest South Vietnamese military levels.... Local people have long since learned to live with the Vietcong and are not willing to jeopardise their lives by putting the finger on their neighbours and friends. As a recent confidential intelligence report showed, enemy forces are getting at least two hours' notice of most American military operations in South Vietnam."

Failure on the ground and mounting American casualties moved the opinion polls away from the war. The Louis Harris poll showed a precipitate fall between July and October: "The number of Americans willing to go on supporting a limited war fell from 51 per cent to 26 per cent. The number who wanted to 'get out as soon as possible' rose from 24 per cent to 44 per cent."

To compound this cheerless prospect for Johnson, the military and the advocates of the war, came the news on January 30th 1968, timed for the opening of the primary election season, of the Vietcong's Tet offensive. Part of Saigon was seized, Hué was overrun and 30 provincial capitals were attacked. It had a devastating impact in the United States. The paper argued against undue depression: "Its aim is political; if possible, to shake American public opinion into electing a peace-making president in November; failing that, to get negotiations going on relatively favourable terms before the Americans' firepower eats deeper and deeper into the communists' hold of the back country." The paper was anxious.

"This is it," it said, declaring, correctly, that if the Americans did not reassert their control over the towns they "will have to negotiate their way on to the troopships" but that, militarily, the shock would be withstood. The Vietcong, it thought, could not have been stopped from getting into the cities and that merely impressed the nervous. But, incorrectly, it underestimated the nervous: "The probability is that it will also end up as a propaganda defeat for the Vietcong."

The decisive blow fell on Johnson, and it fell in New Hampshire. Johnson's name was not even on the Democratic ballot in the primary there; he had relied on his position, on his record as a vote-puller four years before. The name on the ballot was that of Senator Eugene McCarthy, a liberal with a growing student following and a persuasive opponent of the war. Early in March the Washington correspondent, reporting from Manchester, New Hampshire, estimated how the support for Johnson was simply disappearing. It had nothing to do with him not being on the ballot paper: "Mr Johnson's Vietnam policy seemed to be well accepted in New Hampshire and the regular party organisation was solidly on the President's side.... But matters began slowly to disintegrate for Mr Johnson about a month ago. The Tet offensive by the Vietcong perceptibly diminished the enthusiasm for the war."

He essayed a guess at the outcome: "Mr McCarthy's total could conceivably reach as high as 40 per cent, a vote unthinkable not long ago."

McCarthy got 42%. He was actually beaten, but the extent of the disaster to Johnson surprised many Americans. The paper pronounced his political obituary on the morrow of the result: "He may not get nominated by his party in August, and if he is nominated he will very likely not get elected in November.... The New Hampshire voters have set the stopwatch; they have told him how long he has got."

He told the country on television on March 31st that he would not seek and would not accept his party's nomination. The paper was disappointed, not with him but at what had forced his decision: "The Americans now seem to believe that they cannot restore the situation to what it was before January 30th, at least in the near future, unless they send something like another 200,000 soldiers out to Vietnam. Mr Johnson has decided that neither his balance of payments nor the temper of American opinion will allow this."

But the war was not over; nor did the paper think it should be concluded. It should certainly not be concluded in defeat. There were four more years to go before the troop total, which reached 543,000 in 1968, dwindled eventually to 39,000. The United States was to have to take many more casualties, more demonstrations and disruption, and much more disillusionment before there was peace, or what passed for peace, in Indochina.

RIDING TO FREEDOM
On the laborious road to civil rights

The Economist followed the civil rights agitation, demonstrations and dismaying violence with sympathetic attention. It favoured Kennedy's aims but, unlike him, it was overconfident about the prospect of rapid success. It thought him slow to react to the attacks on the freedom riders, demonstrating for the desegregation of interstate buses, in Alabama in the summer of 1961. It needed the attorney-general, Robert Kennedy, putting in hundreds of federal marshals to save the day. This demonstration of what central authority could achieve encouraged the paper's optimism. Sooner or later, right would prosper: "It will be possible for Negroes in the South, as in the North, to use golf courses, libraries and swimming pools, schools and colleges, as well as all the restaurants and restrooms in bus and railway stations—and it will be a crime to prevent them from doing so."

It was pleased that the Department of Justice had been able to take a long stride forward "as the result of the blooded heads and arbitrary arrests". But the resistance was rooted in the prejudice of centuries. When a black air force veteran, James H. Meredith, tried to register at the University of Mississippi it needed federal troops to enforce his rights. In 1963, the centenary of Lincoln's proclamation of black emancipation, Martin Luther King encouraged widespread, non-violent demonstrations which were answered in Birmingham, Alabama, by police dogs, fire hoses and electric cattle prods organised by the local police chief, Eugene ("Bull") Connor. Again the president seemed powerless: "The moral considerations were clear; the photographs of a policeman kneeling on a Negro woman's throat and a police dog attacking an unarmed Negro boy did not leave room for doubt."

However, law enforcement was a local and state government responsibility: "There is no federal criminal law enforcing the rights which Negroes in Birmingham sought to obtain—the right to eat with white

Black Power at the 1968 Olympics. The two black US athletes in the men's 200 metres in Mexico City, Tommie Smith (centre) who came first and John Carlos (right) third, showed their solidarity with campaigners at home.

people at a lunch counter, to demonstrate peacefully, to be employed without racial discrimination."

The paper agreed with the attorney-general. Birmingham was only a preview of the future: "As the Negro becomes better educated and more politically conscious, his demand for equality is put with greater insistence. The Birmingham episode will encourage mass protests in other repressed communities."

The time for tokenism in civil rights was over: it was

no longer acceptable. The desegregation that had been won was incomplete and discouragingly slow: "At the rate at which this is being done—viewed by many southern whites as alarmingly fast—it is claimed that it will take another ninety-three years to end the colour bar in education."

It was a matter of economic necessity in the black community: "The issue in the schools has ceased to be one of abstract justice and has become a life and death matter for Negroes. Automation threatens to shut them out permanently from almost any job unless they can improve their standard of education. Fear and frustration regarding not their own but their children's futures are what chiefly embitter them."

The Kennedy administration, reluctant to rely on laws which might be blocked in the Congress, produced a civil rights bill in October 1963 which it thought was at least a three-quarters loaf. The paper thought it adequate: "It will enable Negroes to register to vote, schools to be desegregated and colour bars to be broken down in hotels, restaurants and places of recreation.... It is ironical that it is the Attorney General, whom so many have accused of being too fiery, who is now being upbraided for being over-cautious."

It was Johnson who brought the bill to reality, breaking the southern filibuster in the Senate on the way. Blacks voted overwhelmingly for him in November 1964. In the week he was inaugurated the paper reported dissidence in Selma, Alabama: "Clearly the city of Selma ... is not worried about public relations. The day after it reached international fame—as the place where the Negro leader, Dr Martin Luther King, was attacked while signing a book in a hitherto all-white hotel—Selma's sheriff arrested 63 Negroes who wanted to register as voters. The next day he arrested 200 more."

The black community in the south was anxious to register, but the white zealots' resistance in Alabama, Mississippi and South Carolina was unyielding. In March 1965 the paper reported on the numerous counties where intimidation and violence still held sway: "Dallas County, Alabama, can show only 1.6 per cent of its eligible Negroes registered to vote; this is the county where Selma, the chosen stage for this year's conflict on voting rights, is situated. In four southern states there are counties where not a single Negro is on the voting register."

King insisted on the voting rights issue being settled by legislation, and the march from Selma to the state capital, Montgomery, had federal encouragement. The act required federal examiners to go in wherever 50% of the population of voting age remained unregistered. Registration soared.

There was another side to the black rights debate, however. The paper took it up; it was "a subject which liberals prefer to skirt; the breakdown of the Negro family which is responsible for much of the poverty,

crime and aimlessness of young Negroes. Fewer than half of all Negro children reaching the age of 18 have lived all their lives with both parents".

When the chiefly black Los Angeles district of Watts erupted in rioting, incendiarism and looting the paper was careful not to emphasise the racial aspect. It saw Watts as one of a series of outbreaks in problem urban areas around the world: "This was an insurrection, but not against the economic order (which is the marxist fallacy) and not even chiefly against white men's domination (which is going to be the Afro-Asian fallacy). It was an insurrection of anarchy, an outburst against any kind of system by the people left at the bottom."

There were 34 dead in Watts, most of them black, more than 800 injured and treated in hospital, some 3,800 arrested and damage to property put at $175m. It brought the underclass to the surface: "Outbreaks like this are part of the price we are going to pay for a society in which more and more people live in cities and do deadly dull work and waste their leisure.... These are the people who do the dullest jobs of all, and are the worst paid, and live in the ugliest parts of crumbling old towns. They have a high rate of illegitimacy and broken marriages. Their religious and cultural roots have been cut."

It was an analysis which applied to the left-behind in all cultures, races and religions: "They know they are the natural bottom layer; they have been deprived of the social and religious consolations of the old rural life; there is no legal outlet for young male violence; and every now and then they go bang."

It was in Harlem that the reality of degradation could not be concealed. The failure of black urban society was alarming: "When a white American enters Harlem, it is helpful if he comes armed with detachment; otherwise the degradation and despair around him are likely to bring him quickly to his knees. There are rats in the tenement buildings and refuse in the streets. Families are often crowded into dark pest-holes. Violence, ugliness, disease—the impersonal charts and statistics only confirm what the cold eye picks out."

It would have been surprising had it not led to alienation from American society: "Of New York's 30,000 drug addicts, nearly two-thirds live in Harlem; juvenile delinquents commit twice as many crimes in Harlem as they do in the rest of the city. There are six times as many murders. Whatever the social sickness— prostitution, alcoholism, brutality, disease—Harlem is engulfed by it."

One outcome was the black power movement, in all its forms and varieties: "The exponents of 'black power' insist that the concept is not intentionally anti-white; nor is it, they say, a form of black nationalism. It is designed to counteract the Negroes' sense of inferiority and insufficiency, something which they can only get rid of by and for themselves.... While non-violence will still officially be the rule in civil rights demonstrations, it will no longer be interpreted to preclude self-defence. The great advocate of non-violence, Dr Martin Luther King, has openly denounced the new slogan."

King himself was drawn into the anti-war movement. In April 1967 he led a march of 125,000, organised by the Spring Mobilisation Committee to End the War in Vietnam, to the United Nations Plaza in New York. This was disliked by those who thought he should concentrate on black causes: "His Negro critics feel that he is down-grading their cause, 'making a serious tactical mistake', diverting attention from the basic work that is still badly needed for civil rights and repelling many sympathisers."

The next step was extremism, the world of Leroy Jones, Rap Brown and the black separatists, directed at the discrediting of liberal reform: "What they are saying, in effect, is that different races cannot coexist within the same society. They believe the sense of racial antagonism goes so deep that the majority will never agree to share its privileges with the minority, and that in any case the minority would not want to be assimilated into a society shaped by people of a different race."

Because of the war, the paper felt there could be serious ramifications: "They are counting on white vigilantes to force Negro soldiers and ex-servicemen to become black nationalists, contributing their expertise and, where possible, their weapons. There are at present 100,000 Negro soldiers in Vietnam, and perhaps as many serving elsewhere in the armed forces."

It was, in many ways, the lowest point of American self-confidence. The paper was not despondent; the society was strong enough to come through: "It is embarrassing for the United States to have its racial problem spattered about the world's headlines as if it were an American peculiarity.... But in the long run the United States is better able to cope with this crisis than most other countries are."

Even the shooting of Martin Luther King in April 1968. The paper recognised his virtues but seemed more concerned about public order: "Dr Martin Luther King is buried. Not all the white politicians who flocked to his funeral in Atlanta had fought as they might for Negro rights, but otherwise it was seemly and dignified. The Negro looting and fire-raising in America's cities flares up and simmers down by turns. But so far control has nowhere been lost. It is a mercy."

It thought, rather despairingly, that the looting and arson in black districts on King's death would have taken place, in some way, sometime that summer. The Washington correspondent gave a friendlier appreciation: "He remained the leader commanding the largest hearing, the respect of the widest spectrum of Negro groups and great reverence among the Negro poor, rural and urban. Never a man for accepting the established order if it was wrong, he maintained to the end of his life that there was a course of action, in between violence and acquiescence, by which changes could be forced."

The paper was unhappy about the manifestations of black power in 1968. It partly took the side of the Olympic athletes, Tommie Smith and John Carlos, "who stood with clenched, black-fisted gloves and downcast eyes" while the American national anthem was played; it did not think the whole track and field team should be disqualified as officials wanted. It did take exception to the strong-arm groups that attached themselves to otherwise inoffensive causes. One of them was the Poor People's Campaign, camped in Washington: "The black toughs stand at the gates of Resurrection City, USA. You have to be poor, black, convincing or devious to be allowed past. These are Dr Ralph Abernathy's marshals, chosen to control the poor people's campaign ... they consist largely of street gangs, out-of-work hoodlums and militantly black students from northern and mid-western colleges."

The paper was going to miss Martin Luther King's example and philosophy.

NIXON'S THE ONE

In an election shambles America decided—
just—for the man it thought it knew

Johnson's withdrawal after New Hampshire opened the presidential race in a way it had not been for 20 years. The radical Democrats were divided between the followers of McCarthy, who had done the upsetting, and the more professional machine put together by Robert Kennedy, who had long distanced himself from the Johnson administration. The centre and right of the party looked increasingly to Hubert Humphrey, who had had to live down his liberal past in his years as LBJ's vice-president. Johnson himself, retaining control of the Vietnam issue both in diplomacy and in the conduct of the war, held Humphrey to the official line.

The danger to both Republicans and Democrats was the reappearance of George Wallace of Alabama as the candidate of the American Independent Party. His reactionary policies, geared to the taste of blue-collar workers in both north and south, were disliked by the paper, but it retained a sneaking respect for his platform style, and his vote-getting: "He is an engaging rogue, who calls girl hecklers 'Honey' and male ones 'Fellow' and has a night club comedian's knack of turning a rude remark against his opponent. He has a stock speech and a set of reflex answers to the questions which he knows will arise." He was also too smart a demagogue to let himself be labelled a racist.

In an America beset by the agitation against the war, by black activists and by the unease, if not despair, of ordinary people, the election came to be dominated not by political argument but by the shadow of the gun and of rising violence in which sections of the police gladly took part. In April Martin Luther King was shot. Kennedy was beaten by McCarthy in the Oregon primary ("more than a setback," the paper said, "it was a disaster") and moved on to California in a last, desperate effort to regain the initiative. There he was shot. The paper was not of his way of thinking, but it recognised his quality: "Robert Kennedy's complex character led to his being misunderstood—and hated and loved—as few candidates for the Presidency have ever been. Rude he often was, but the damaging reputation for ruthlessness was greatly exaggerated. Some of his troubles stemmed instead from excessive loyalty and softness of heart—and maybe from a need to achieve something before the fate which he expected overtook him."

The paper was lukewarm about the Republicans' re-tread candidate, Richard Nixon: "He has been chosen as a representative of the Eisenhower centre of his party, but he lacks ex-President Eisenhower's greatest advantage. Whereas Mr Eisenhower was generally liked even by his political opponents, Mr Nixon is rather generally disliked by a disturbingly wide stratum of opinion."

It had more confidence in Humphrey as a person: "He is genuinely a warm, good man, he inspires trust and affection and, to people alarmed and repelled by all the criticism and bickering, he is a natural refuge."

Human qualities, though, were no guarantee of success in the party. The Democrats were divided, not just about the past or even ideas of the future but about every war communiqué and the gloss that Johnson was putting on them. Humphrey's people wanted signs that Johnson was winding the war down, otherwise they despaired of their man's chances. The more radical, especially the young, were intent on making their views and feelings known in the convention, or in the streets of Chicago. To this Chicago's mayor, Richard Daley, and the police, tired of the radicals' taunts, had their own reply: "At first the over-reaction of the police was laughable; it quickly became ugly.... Tear gas filled the air and spread into the hotels. The police made less and less distinction about whom they went after. Anyone who paused or who was simply unattractive to a policeman was likely to be attacked, usually with a club, sometimes with Mace, the irritating chemical spray. As dark fell the police took to charging in a body, sometimes helped by guardsmen. The frenzy of some of the beatings they administered almost passes description."

Humphrey's nomination that night was not helped by the accounts of police behaviour which filtered into the hall and flooded into the television news and the headlines. To the paper Humphrey was the party's only rational or winnable choice: "An active, sanguine, emotional, gregarious, talkative party by habit, the Democrats chose from among their presidential candidates the one who most closely resembles themselves, Vice President Humphrey. Their choice was more instinctive than calculated."

The paper agreed with many of Nixon's policies, not least on Vietnam, and was to support his refusal to accept outright defeat there, but its conclusion was against him: "Few people really trust him, fewer love him, although many admire him. Thus, when Americans go into the polling booths on Tuesday week, alone with their consciences, more of them than Dr Gallup allows for are probably going to vote for Mr Humphrey. In the final balance *The Economist* would like to be one of them."

It was not to be, although with five days to go Johnson did appease the anti-war protesters by calling off the bombing of North Vietnam. Nixon won with only 43.4% of the popular vote; Humphrey got 42.7% and Wallace 13.5%. The paper thought it a draw: "So America's year of trial and upset has ended in the most conventional choice of all for the Presidency: the electorate has played safe, and has played it even safer by giving Mr Nixon an almost unchanged House of Representatives." It was not a confident prospect.

LIFE IN THE SIXTIES

The new economics, two ways not to smoke,
and some very proper bunnies

In the changing intellectual disposition of the mid-1960s *The Economist* picked up the dare directed at the Keynesian establishment by Professor Milton Friedman of Chicago, one of the principal instigators of the new liberalism. But it was not instantly convinced. Friedman, the paper said, asserted that the money supply was the dominant factor, the senior partner, in determining the general level of business activity and prices. There were two cornerstones to the edifice: "The first is that when data on money and on industrial production are compared over a long period, there is a clear and stable relationship between the two. But this in itself proves nothing."

Having dismissed the years 1867–1960 to its own satisfaction, it continued: "The second and crucial hypothesis is that the turning points in the money series precede and determine the relevant turning points in the output series. This is extremely difficult to establish by statistical manipulations alone. And having attempted the exercise, Dr Friedman admits that at most his efforts merely establish a 'strong presumption' in favour of his thesis."

Friedman was to become a Nobel laureate. From the paper he got a pat on the head: "In the end Dr Friedman's work may serve simply to strengthen the case for an active monetary policy."

Norman Macrae, the paper's deputy editor, visiting the United States in 1969, gave Friedman proper recognition, acknowledging the influence he already exerted in the offices where it mattered: "The guts of the argument between Dr Friedman and at least some of the Fed used to be whether the level of money supply had

any direct importance at all. It is fair to comment that most reputable economists now accept at least part of Friedman's statistical proof that to some extent it does; changes in money supply do affect total demand after a varying time lag, which Friedman thinks averages around six months under present American conditions."

In the post-war years, Macrae pointed out, the chiefly Keynesian policies of Democratic presidents had encouraged phenomenal growth. During the Eisenhower years of the 1950s the average annual growth of real GNP had been under 2.5%; during the Kennedy–Johnson years it was over 5.25%. As a target for the new Nixon years he provided a Friedman-adjusted rate: "The fashionable figures to argue for now are a rate of expansion of some definition of currency plus bank deposits of between 5 and 7 per cent per annum; the favoured rate used to be lower before people realised how swiftly the American economy can grow."

The perils of Telstar   The paper was entertained, as before, by television's continuing growth, and especially by the arrival of satellite transmissions across the Atlantic. In the exchanges on Telstar it noted the self-abasement of many American critics: "The strange sense of inferiority which European culture often inspires in Americans was revived by the first formal exchange of television programmes through the Telstar communications satellite; some American critics berated as superficial and banal their country's offering of baseball, Cape Canaveral and a Red Indian in exchange for the Sistine Chapel, Tosca and the Winged Victory of Samothrace."

The paper preferred to look on the brighter side: "The morning-after assessment should have been cheered by the fact that the first live presentation to Europe of a presidential press conference brought the almost immediate granting of Mr Kennedy's wish to strengthen the dollar; following his insistence that there would be no devaluation, gold shares fell swiftly on the London Stock Exchange.... The exciting glimpse of the Chicago-Philadelphia baseball game, moreover, was as enlightening to Europeans as the display of medieval works of religious art in Communist-dominated Yugoslavia must have been to Americans."

Breaking the habit   One of the most influential

reports of the decade was the United States surgeon-general's condemnation of smoking, which eventually produced a widespread change in middle-class habits around the world: "Cigarettes, the scientists report, are a major cause of lung cancer in men and possibly in women as well (the statistics are not complete here). In addition, they are a significant factor in coronary heart attacks, are the most important cause of chronic bronchitis and make some contribution to cancer of the larynx, the oesophagus and the bladder."

There followed the necessary warning about political impossibility: "Any sentencing by the government looks extremely doubtful. The harsh facts are that this is an election year, that several key southern states depend on the $8 billion-a-year tobacco industry for their income and that some 3.5 million people are employed in making or selling the cigarettes which nearly 70 million Americans, most of them voters, smoke for one perverse reason or another."

Hippies do their thing The communities often, though not always, guilty of illegal smoking, the inhalation of drugs, were the hippies whom the paper found interesting if wayward dissenters from capitalism. In 1967 there was trouble in New York's East Village where the hippy population had fallen out with censorious Slavs and the Puerto Ricans: "To the police, most of the blame attaches to the hippies, the unwashed, passive, barefoot, nineteen-sixties' brand of alienated youth."

They had virtually taken much of the village over: "The small shops have given way to pubs and coffee houses and book shops that specialise in avant-garde literature; 'Mod' boutiques and baroque antique shops now nestle between Jewish restaurants and small, low-priced furniture stores. On all the streets and in the community's central mall, Tompkins Square Park, there are hippies; long-haired men, barefooted women, bizarre costumes. They are all quite harmless."

They were all, apparently, bourgeois too: "Like most other rebels against the middle class, competitive, urban American way of life, the hippies come from recognised families and schools. It is their greatest source of protection in New York; they may need it."

The hippies of Haight-Ashbury (or the Hashbury) in San Francisco were the most celebrated and publicised of the communities. The nerveless correspondent did not feel threatened by them or their habits, and television viewers in that week of July 1967 enjoyed the sight of the two most famous ballet dancers in the world, Margot Fonteyn and Rudolph Nureyev, hauled in by the San Francisco police who had raided a hippy drugs party. It was the done thing: "The police seem almost benevolent towards the movement, at least until a "be-in" in Golden Gate Park winds up denuding the place of flowers (the hippies pick them and wear them, contending they belong to God, not the City) or an impromptu street dance snarls traffic or a noisy party in a crowded communal hippie pad turns into a drug-for-all—as Dame Margot Fonteyn discovered this week. Shopkeepers in the district, those who have adjusted, are doing well, in spite of the fact that hippies are supposed to be unemployed and flat broke."

Young America's modest sex life The paper also ran its eye over what was publicised as a daring and even mildly salacious institution, the Playboy clubs, which it found entirely decorous: "The Playboy Clubs are in fact the soul of respectability, catering mostly to transient visitors—businessmen, airline stewardesses on a date, suburban couples having an evening in the town. The whisky is not watered, the owners are not associated with the underworld; the bunnies are neither bar girls nor prostitutes. Indeed, though they may be stuffed into tight, revealing costumes, their virtue is carefully protected by the management. The girls are forbidden to get in touch with any member or customer after working; to ensure that the letter of the rule is observed, a private detective agency keeps a continuous eye on things. Since the waitresses earn close to $300 a week in salary and tips, they are usually ready to accept the conditions of employment."

For those of more modest means who wanted technological assistance in developing their social experience the paper looked into the novelty of computer dating: "After posting his (or her) answers and the $3 fee, the applicant waits for fourteen breathless days. Then the envelope should arrive containing the names of five members of the opposite sex—within easy travelling distance—whom the computer has deemed most likely to please. The male does the telephoning. The female presumably accepts. Then they write back to Operation Match and tell them how things went."

It reported only one particular outcome: "One boy found a bride but refused to be grateful: 'It was just luck. The other four were dogs.' "

Skateboarders unite For young and even old skateboarding had become the rage: "The craze is said to have originated a few years ago among surf-riders in the Santa Monica Bay area of California.... Providing skateboards may be a business worth as much as $100 million this year; this represents retail sales of some 10 million at an average price of $10.... Boys and girls in the desert and even in middle western farm communities acquire skateboards eagerly as the entrée into the world of surfing which is a passion among the American young. On the strength of owning a board they adopt the hair styles, clothes and jargon of the surfing set. Now the craze seems certain to become international."

A wig's her best friend The arrival of the wig as a regular item of women's wear was properly recorded in September 1962. This fashion had been greatly encouraged after President Kennedy and his wife had visited the de Gaulles in Paris a year before, when Mrs Kennedy had shown herself a pace-setter. The industry had become a $40m proposition: "Wigs have emancipated women from the time they used to spend at the hair dressers. Now they begin their daily shopping routine by dropping off the wig at a beauty salon, where it is dressed; they pick it up again at the end of the day.

They can swim and engage in other active sports without having to worry about the state of their hair. Some women, in fact, have been able to say goodbye to their psychiatrists because their inner turmoils have been erased by the possession of a wig."

Every luxury in the modern world could be lavished, the paper reported, on pets and their owners. The products and services at their disposal were startling: "Should an American dog suffer from halitosis—and one company in the veterinary field claims that 40 per cent of American dogs do, in fact, have bad breath—the owner can obtain a product designed to combat this complaint. If he wishes to take the dog on a trip with him, he can consult a 48-page directory listing 6,000 hotels and motels throughout the country which accept guests accompanied by pets. 'Reproduction control' products which are now on the market enable him to regulate the number of litters his pet produces and he can eliminate fleas by giving the dog a tablet which is absorbed into its blood stream and poisons the hungry insect. False eyelashes are among the novelty items for pets which are gaining favour."

A strange sense of inferiority was known to overtake British and European readers when they compared their unassisted, uneventful lives to those customarily lived throughout the United States.

The eagle has landed: July 20th 1969. The American Apollo 11 astronauts beat the Soviets to the moon. Buzz Aldrin was photographed by Neil Armstrong, the first to set foot on the surface.

12

THE TWO NIXONS

1969–1975

WINDING DOWN TO NEW HORIZONS

Nixon's rearguard action in Vietnam was not allowed to block his main objective

Nixon had two options on the Vietnam war when he entered the White House. He could break with the past entirely and sue for peace on terms that he thought most Americans would find degrading. Or he could transfer the burden of the fighting on to the South Vietnamese, reassuring the peace party by staging successive withdrawals of American troops. He chose the second and thereby decided the fate of his first four years. He ended by pleasing nobody, but he got the men out.

The Economist was not unsympathetic. It reckoned that Nixon was trying to find a way out of the war by walking backwards through it: "Mr Nixon is talking as if he had reversed the policies that took the United States into Vietnam, while in fact doing things which show that he remains essentially loyal to them.... He has settled for, at best, the uneasy acquiescence of the muddled middle of the American electorate."

The sleight of hand depended on good timing and keeping a substantial majority of Americans behind the programme. At the end of the first year the paper was dubious: "It has to be assumed that he will probably have to go on providing the doubters with a fairly regular diet of troop withdrawals. He will want to keep the casualty lists down below the figure they were running at earlier this year; and that may mean pushing too many half-ready South Vietnamese into the fighting too soon, with results like the beating they took in the Mekong delta on Thursday."

As more months passed and the negotiated peace Nixon wanted stayed elusive, his impatience grew. In May 1970 he sent American troops into Cambodia to intercept the Vietcong's lines of supply and reinforcement. Student protests erupted on university campuses, and four young people were shot at Kent State University in Ohio. The paper was deeply unhappy that Nixon had shattered the consensus he had slowly built up on a gamble that it did not think was wholly necessary anyway: "For the fact is that, until last weekend, Mr Nixon's plans for Vietnam had never seemed

---

CHRONOLOGY

1969	Richard Nixon becomes president	1972	Nixon flies to Peking
	De Gaulle loses referendum and resigns		Nixon's first visit to Moscow
	Mary Jo Kopechne drowned at Chappaquiddick, Massachusetts		Watergate break-in
		1973	Britain joins European Community
	US astronauts, Neil Armstrong and Buzz Aldrin, land on the moon		Israel wins October war; Arabs invoke oil price weapon
1970	US troops invade Cambodia	1974	Vice-president Spiro Agnew resigns
	Four students shot by National Guard, Kent State University, Ohio		Nixon resigns
			Gerald Ford becomes president; Nelson Rockefeller appointed vice-president
1971	Dollar devalued		
	India defeats Pakistan; Bangladesh independent	1975	South Vietnamese army routed; Saigon falls

---

to depend on getting the North Vietnamese and the Vietcong out of Cambodia."

It even seemed that the president himself was falling apart. He had much on his mind: "He slept for only an hour or so in the small hours, and then at 4.55am, in the dark, he left the White House alone with his valet and at the Lincoln Memorial had a long chat with some student demonstrators who happened to be there, not about the subjects that had brought them to Washington but about the world in general. No doubt bewildered at finding themselves suddenly talking to the President of the United States in the dark in the Lincoln Memorial, the young people were more bewildered when he had finished: 'He just kept rambling,' said one, 'and he didn't make any sense.'"

If Nixon had miscalculated over Cambodia, however, he could still read the American voter correctly. There was still support for the war, for the belief that the strongest power in the world should not be humiliated, and there were other issues in people's minds, too. The typical American voter was said to be the machinist's wife in Dayton, Ohio, who was worried about drugs and whose brother-in-law was a policeman. In the mid-term elections in November it emerged that Nixon had managed to deflate the Vietnam issue: "The election has made it abundantly clear that the machinist's wife is very worried indeed about drug-taking and law and order. Her worry is a real issue, not an artificial one in any way. But she is also worried no less by the presence, or the threat, of unemployment in her family. That was a real issue too. But Vietnam, seemingly, was not."

In February 1971 Nixon risked inciting the demonstrators again, allowing the South Vietnamese, with American support, to go into Laos: "The South Vietnamese have identified the enemy's present Achilles heel. The doubt is whether they have the teeth to bite into it."

The paper's conclusion was that they had done better than might have been expected: "This has not been the stroll across the Ho Chi Minh trails that some of South Vietnam's generals seem to have thought it would be. But neither has it been the flop that so many hand-wringers expected."

What Nixon had up his sleeve was the idea of a rapprochement with communist China. He plainly intended it to be an asset in bringing pressure on the North Vietnamese, in playing off China and the Soviet Union against each other, and in persuading the anti-war party that he meant business. The paper reported the possibility that he would take the road to Peking in March 1971: "President Nixon, as a Republican, an ancient hounder of communists, an old champion of the now declining China lobby, is better placed than any Democratic politician to lead the way back to a non-dogmatic approach to China based on cold national interest."

Nixon and his national security adviser, Henry Kissinger, were at one in developing this policy, and the paper agreed that there was merit in winning Chinese smiles: "To many querulous and puzzled people in the United States, prepared to believe the worst of what their intervention in South Vietnam has done, and encouraged to believe by their news media that they are even more divorced than ever from President Nixon, the Chinese action is guaranteed to be as welcome as the Chinese intended it to be."

However, recalling its own lengthy train of thought that the American intervention in Vietnam was part of the necessary containment of Chinese aggression and expansion, the paper recognised what a reconciliation with Peking would do to the thesis. If North Vietnam had a protector and adviser it was still the Soviet Union. Making up with China would merely leave new questions: "For if it is not the China of maoist frenzy that confronts America and its friends but the bland, cultivated China of Chou, the real China that must have been there all along if the Americans had only been smart enough to spot it, then what (it will be said time and again) can possibly remain of United States policy in south-east Asia?"

That was a minor issue that Nixon was prepared to ride out. He was demonstrating that he had his own peace policy and that he could deliver it. Two lesser issues inside the United States, both integral to the beliefs of the war and anti-war parties, then intervened. One was the trial of Lieutenant William Calley for war crimes committed by his platoon at the village of Soon My or My Lai 4, when no fewer than 22 Vietnamese had been killed. The second was the attempt to stop publication of the so-called Pentagon Papers in which Dr Daniel Ellsberg used confidential papers to attack Lyndon Johnson's decision to intervene in Vietnam. The paper was strict about Calley, but saw it as no more than a normal concomitant to ground war: "Whenever one commits an army to war it is statistically almost inevitable that some of its men will do something atrocious. An unforgivable act was committed by certain Americans at Song My. Its authors must be punished. But it does not change the issues that lie behind the war."

When Calley came to trial three years after the event

motives but it believed that he and his supporters were naive intruders in the real world. It mounted a considered assault on the intelligentsia: "It consists of that part of the middle class which with a reasonably good education behind it, keeps up its interest in public affairs afterwards on the basis of what it calls left-of-

Nixon's coup in Peking, 1972. The president surprised the Soviets and his liberal critics by patching up relations with Mao Tse-tung (left) and the communist leadership in China.

he was sentenced to life imprisonment. The paper did not dissent from Nixon's decision to remit the sentence: 79% of people asked by Gallup thought the punishment too hard anyway.

The Ellsberg case was, in its way, more important to many middle-class liberals because it concerned the freedom of the press. The paper understood Ellsberg's

centre politics. It is arguably the most influential body of opinion in the western world today. It is civilised, rational and concerned for others. As President Johnson and now President Nixon have discovered, no policy can be sustained for long without its consent."

It then put the knife in: "It has one over-riding characteristic when it applies itself to the problems of international politics. Its emotions understand the misery of war, but it does not possess a matching intellectual grasp of the way cause and effect continuously operate among the powers of the world. Its feelings are international, but its reasoning remains parochial. Because it is so nice itself, it is unwilling to look too closely into the minds of adversaries its country has to deal with."

Ellsberg's argument was that Johnson had deceived the public during the 1964 election by professing peaceful intentions while plans were being made to intervene in strength in Vietnam. The Washington correspondent gave the answer: "It is necessary to remember that American governments in those days feared not the pacific instincts of the public but its bellicose instincts. Mr Johnson feared the war party more than he feared the pacifists and he wanted to keep the freedom to launch in Congress the first sustained Democratic programme of social reform since the 1930s. Thus he let the public be told that the war was not such a deadly serious thing as it turned out to be and he probably told himself the same. His misfortune was that, though the legislation was passed, its execution was largely frustrated by the cost of the war."

That was not enough for the Supreme Court, which upheld the right to publish. But later that month the Chinese came through with their invitation to Peking. The paper had no doubt that Nixon should go; his decision, whatever the right wing thought, "deserves acclaim": "Mr Nixon has been invited to Peking, not to Canossa. Concessions on both sides are involved, and they consist mainly of the sensible type of concession that amounts to an acknowledgment of realities. Neither Mr Nixon's obvious hopes of improving his chances of a second presidential term, nor his past record of warnings about the need to use a long spoon when supping with those devilish Chinese detract at all from the essential sanity of his initiative; rather, they enhance it."

The paper duly recorded that the definitive unpopularity of the war, growing month by month, could not be concealed. Equally, American army morale was falling like a stone: "What is quite clear is the anger and resentment of the professional soldier against ... the society that sent him to war and then refused to support him; second, the government that never gave him—in his terms—plausible war aims; and third, the army itself, which increasingly comes to resemble one of those sleek American conglomerates, all purposeful

conglomerate image on the outside and chaos within."

Courting China meant some old allies had to be disposed of. Taiwan was expelled from the United Nations, naturally against official American opposition: "Of the 76 member states who had voted against America on this issue, more than 40 were recipients of American aid—a point that was thoughtfully drawn to the Senate's attention by Senator Fulbright."

Nixon had his reward in February 1972 when the Chinese let him fly to Peking. It was a major diplomatic step, which the paper acknowledged, but it worried about what it would realise in hard, diplomatic terms: "A reading of the tea leaves of last week's meetings tells virtually nothing about how far all the bridge-building, long-marching and wall-destroying actually went. The communiqué put it prosaically but probably rightly in terms of hopes for the future: that the visit would open up 'new prospects for the relations between the two countries'. The qualified concession on Taiwan was the price Mr Nixon had to pay if he wants to persuade China to agree that the non-communist countries of eastern and south-east Asia should stay that way."

When Nixon had won the 1972 election the end of the war in Vietnam, however it happened, became of less importance to him than his wider diplomacy among the powers. He was soon preoccupied with Watergate and its consequences, but his diplomacy continued. In a Vietnam from which almost all Americans had been removed the battle might be allowed to decide. It was certainly not American policy to see the South Vietnamese lose; the commitment to support them was unchanged. But terms could be made more flexible: Kissinger had said, as Americans voted, that peace was at hand, but it still entailed the bombing of Hanoi to force the North Vietnamese to accept it.

Kissinger went back to Peking to underline American wishes: "The Chinese know as well as anybody just how tough and dynamic a people the Vietnamese are; a united Vietnam could easily become the dominant power in mainland south-east Asia. So the Chinese are probably as anxious as the Americans to keep Laos and Cambodia out of North Vietnamese hands."

For the paper the truth was that the United States had failed. American public opinion had given up: "It never seriously tried to come to grips with the idea that a war can be fought on behalf of the rather better against the rather worse, or that it can be fought for the sake of the next couple of generations as much as for the present one. It never got down to the calculations that lie behind a balance of power war. It wanted a simple war, and when it found that it had not got one it either gave up, or swung right over to the opposite simplicity of supposing the other side were the heroes."

RE-ELECTING THE PRESIDENT
*Watergate turned out to be much more than
just a human failure*

The paper found the first news of the Watergate break-in mildly amusing; it thought it of little importance. Employees of the Committee to Re-elect the President were found by a night watchman in the headquarters of the Democratic National Committee in Washington on the night of June 17th 1972: "It is a scandal to warm the heart of any Democrat."

They seemed to be amateurs: "According to those who know about wire-tapping, it is not uncommon for candidates who are up for election to bug the offices of their rivals. The experts also say that, if the Republicans wanted to discover the Democrats' secrets, there were more effective ways of doing so. The five were caught with equipment which went out of use in the 1950s."

The culprits were tried and convicted, Nixon went on to his overwhelming victory in November, and most people had found it easy to forget the affair; but neither the *Washington Post* nor Judge John Sirica of the district court forgot. By March 1973 enough had come out about the work of the dirty tricks operation that the new administration found itself in the mire. The paper's Washington man looked closely at Nixon's diminishing options: "Mr Nixon has powers and opportunities of action available to nobody else. He can change course, introduce innovations and steal the opposition's clothes, as he has done before. He can even clean house in an ostentatious manner, if he chooses. The alternative, to sit tight, defying Congress and where necessary ignoring the courts, is practicable for him as a second-term president, but it would have unfortunate effects which he, no doubt, can see as clearly as anyone."

Nixon chose, in his own words, to tough it out and his forces felt in no way daunted; one of those brought in as a character witness was Kissinger, but the paper was already among those who distrusted the White House and its doings: "The decent man's distaste for vindictiveness to which Mr Kissinger gave expression is neither here nor there. What matters is whether the presidential election of 1976 is to be permitted to be rigged and bought as the election of 1972 was: for by that the legitimacy, and therefore the continuity, of future American government may be decided."

The administration looked even more vulnerable when doubts surfaced about the vice-president, Spiro Agnew, under investigation for taking bribes when governor of Maryland. To have both the chief executive of the United States and his deputy in deepening trouble presented a freakish dilemma. If it came to the bit, which should be the first to be dropped? The paper thought Nixon still had a function to serve in international relations. Besides, he had not yet been cornered over Watergate: "On balance, it seems better that Mr Nixon should stay: unless what is now only hearsay becomes damning evidence, or unless the cost of continued uncertainty comes to seem too great. Mr Nixon's foreign policy has been damaged, but it may still be possible to limit the damage, and it is still his policy."

The paper's American Survey had a good understanding of the man's psychology: "Mr Nixon and his associates came to Washington in 1969 as if to a hostile town, uncomfortable in their surroundings, suspicious and fearful of the press and the media, suspicious and contemptuous of the huge body of regular government servants whom they still call 'the bureaucracy', unfamiliar with Congress, and uneasy at the narrowness of their electoral victory in 1968."

It explained Nixon's insecurity and his devious way of working, his belief that he was the one being plotted against and that, even at the worst, he had done nothing that previous presidents, like Johnson and Roosevelt, had done when they thought it necessary. But the revelations that came out at the Senate inquiry hearings chaired by Senator Sam Ervin surprised even a cynical public. Bribery and perjury were uncovered relentlessly close to the Oval Office itself. John Wesley Dean III, counsel to the president, admitted conspiring to conceal the Watergate truth: "The public had been prepared for a lightweight glamour boy with a flashing smile, stepping nattily dressed out of his purple Porsche with his striking blonde wife.... What the public got was a small, bespectacled, carefully spoken, earnest young lawyer, in whom neither the facile charmer nor the self-seeking, unprincipled deserter from a sinking ship was at all easy to discern."

Within a month it became the turn of Alexander Butterfield, former assistant to Nixon's chief adviser, H.R. Haldeman. What he had to tell turned out to be momentous: "When asked in a private meeting with the committee staff whether Mr John Dean could have been right in thinking that one of his crucial conversations with President Nixon was being recorded, Mr Butterfield said, 'Oh, yes', and proceeded to explain the whole secret system, which, he said, Mr Dean and most of the White House staff probably knew nothing about."

Nixon's accusers had always doubted if they could find a smoking gun which would confirm Nixon's knowledge of what was going on in his name; now the taping system, installed to record all his conversations for history, seemed bound to settle the issue. If he were guilty the proof would be there; if he were innocent the tapes would demonstrate it. But Nixon was tenacious; he refused to hand the tapes over and when the special prosecutor, Archibald Cox, went to court for them he had Cox dismissed.

Agnew's time was up. He pleaded no contest on a tax evasion charge. The paper called it a warning to the parties to take the choice of vice-presidential candidates more seriously than the usual hasty deal at the end of the convention. It blamed Nixon for this fiasco: "It was not Mr Agnew who picked Mr Nixon, but the other way around, and ... it will be on Mr Nixon that the important share of the blame falls."

Nixon named the Republican minority leader in the House to succeed Agnew. Gerald R. Ford was a faithful party workhorse, no threat to the president, and known to be an honest man. Nixon fought on. When he had to surrender tapes to Judge Sirica, one of them was found to have been edited on the tape recorder used by Nixon's secretary, Rose Mary Woods. The paper's report delighted in the detail: "A hand had operated Miss Woods's tape recorder, and almost certainly no other machine, to erase and rerecord the $18\frac{1}{2}$ minutes on the tape in at least five distinct segments. Starting and stopping the 'record' head and the 'erase' head leaves magnetic marks on the tape which, though invisible, can be made visible by rubbing on a magnetic fluid.... The experts have not only established beyond any reasonable doubt that the erasure of the President's talk with Mr Haldeman three days after the Watergate burglary was not accidental, they have also narrowed

down the number of persons who might have done it to those who had access to Miss Woods's machine at the time the tape was out of the storeroom. Three such persons are known."

They were: Miss Woods, Stephen Bull the appointments secretary, and Nixon himself. Inside Fort Nixon the president had not quite despaired, but he was heard to talk that January of, the paper recounted, "the point at which he could do one last thing for his country and, in doing it, help himself: step down". But it was still talk; there were more twists and turns to come. By April 1974 the paper noted: "By now the leading men of both parties in both houses of Congress have accustomed themselves to planning their calendars this year with a view to the impeachment, the biggest piece of political business they will have to deal with in their lives."

At the end of the month Nixon did submit a bulky volume of recorded presidential conversations to the House committee, although it was found to be neither complete nor trustworthy. He also spoke to the country on television: "He did it well: here, after a year of floundering and false notes, was a strong, skilful politician at work. The speech was carefully constructed and economically written, its delivery grave and calm."

The volume, however, was unpersuasive: "Passages are omitted as irrelevant, rude words are mostly cut out with an indication to that effect, and damaging descriptions of third persons, or most of them, have been deleted too.... Mr Nixon might have cut it all short 12 or, better, 22 months ago, but his disclosures now lose conclusiveness by being so late."

A week later the paper concluded that nothing had changed, no satisfactory answers had been given: "Mr Nixon is back in his laager with the gates shut and the look-outs posted. His sortie was a public relations skirmish, not an effort to meet the investigating bodies on the questions of law and fact that are at issue."

By July the Supreme Court ruled that Nixon must surrender the tapes and documents he was trying to retain. The House Judiciary Committee voted to proceed on three articles of impeachment. It was time to end the long, stubborn, rearguard resistance: "The truth is—as Mr Nixon must have known above all men—that without the White House taping system he would probably never have come near to impeachment, he would not have had to fire Mr Cox, or fight the judge, or reject wholesale the subpoenas of the judiciary committee, or publish the mendacious but still humiliating White House transcripts.... The essentials are known and the Nixon matter needs to be got over and done with."

By August the paper had composed its farewell assessment. There had been much in the doomed presidency that the paper agreed with, and even traits that it had come to admire. It singled out two achievements in particular: "He extracted the American army from the Vietnam war on better terms than the communists ever offered to Lyndon Johnson, even if those terms were still highly unsatisfactory.... He has also extricated the United States from the intolerable burden of an overvalued fixed-rate dollar, and thereby given America more freedom of action in the present worldwide economic crisis than it would otherwise have had. Neither of those decisions could have been taken by anyone other than a president of intellectual courage."

From the complicated and lengthy process that had eventually succeeded in bringing Nixon down, it drew only one, brief conclusion: "Impeachment will not worry presidents for a long time to come. What the fall of Mr Nixon shows is not how easy impeachment is, but how difficult."

It did not expect much from Ford's presidency except decency and probity, qualities which, it thought, would allow Americans to respect the man and his office in a way that had been denied to his two predecessors. It quite approved of Ford's making Nelson Rockefeller his vice-president. If the United States, for the first time, was not to be governed by men it had elected, the choice was commendable: "Mr Rockefeller's experience is vast, the list of his successful public enterprises is long, and he is never without the stable of first-class advisers that an intelligent man of wealth and position can assure himself."

Ford kept Kissinger on as secretary of state, and seemed to have settled into what the paper called his "refreshing, reassuring presidential honeymoon" when, acting as he thought decently, he surprised everyone by pardoning Nixon: "The President is said to have acted out of humanitarian feelings for the Nixon family. If so, the feelings do him credit, but not the manner of their expression. It is an unsatisfactory story."

In the end it was the Republican Party that paid the political price for Watergate that November. The Democrats won two-thirds of the house, their biggest success since Johnson's sweep in 1964. There could be

only one reason: "True, the economy is in an unhappy state. President Ford's economic proposals have caused more uneasiness than reassurance.... There still has to be another explanation for the unusual scale of the party's defeat; guiltless as they mostly were, its senators, representatives, governors, state legislators and county officers were punished for the Watergate scandals."

THE NIXON INSTINCT
A political operator at work; and he was
lucky in his enemies

Nixon's conduct of his presidency, the political instinct that prompted the conception and timing of his moves, the celerity with which he saw an advantage to be exploited, the exercise of those professional abilities fascinated *The Economist*. With a theme and an opening to exploit, Nixon was an operator. He was also, in the calibre, personality and objectives of his Democratic Party opponents, decidedly lucky.

Nixon inherited an economy beset by inflation because of the Vietnam war's demands. Prices continued to rise through his first year and, as the war effort slowed down, so did unemployment. Conventional remedies did not help. By May 1970 Wall Street took fright. The paper did not; it understood its Nixon: "The bull points are that Mr Nixon's recession still has not gone so far as either of Mr Eisenhower's (a maximum annual rate drop of 3 per cent in real GNP in the first quarter of 1970, against much more worrying drops of 6% and 9% in successive quarters at the turn of 1957–58), and that Mr Nixon will be even more determined to win the 1972 presidential election for himself than Eisenhower was to win the 1960 one for Mr Nixon."

Still, early action was needed: "Since President Nixon's election Americans who hold stock exchange securities have seen a third of their wealth disappear; an enormous relative impoverishment which really must be expected to have some deflationary impact on both consumers' expenditure and eventual business investment. There are grounds for suspecting that this impact may be being underestimated by the Administration."

Among the first to pay the penalty for business fears were the Japanese textile exporters. Nixon put quotas on; it was to be a regular American reaction across the board, either voluntary or involuntary quotas, but the

*Before the fall. At their re-inauguration in 1973 Nixon
and Vice-President Agnew shake hands. Both were driven from office, Nixon over Watergate and its
aftermath, and Agnew for taking bribes.*

Japanese could not deny they had been warned by the president: "Nor could he have guessed what a sly game would be played by the Japanese. He gave them back Okinawa last November and was certain they would 'play ball'—to use a term from baseball, which seems now to be one of the few things common to these two nations of wholly different mentalities—on textiles. The Japanese prime minister, Mr Sato, encouraged this belief. But the extent of the Japanese offers to restrain exports, when finally made last winter, could only be called insulting."

To that point it was just another anecdote to support the contention that Japan was innately an unfair trader, but the Japanese idea of a compromise left no American doubts: "Mr Miyazawa, the suave minister of trade and industry, arrived in Washington early last week ... when the offer turned out to be as limited and unacceptable as before, it was really the final insult."

It was far from a solution to America's problems. The richest country had its first trade deficit for 78 years; prices went on rising; Nixon faced another close-run election. What he did was produce the unexpected; he floated the dollar and he froze wages: "President Nixon's new economic policy has been cobbled together principally as part of his election campaign. He has long had his eyes on target rates to which he hoped that America's unemployment and inflation would have fallen by the middle of the presidential election year of 1972, but forecasts coming to him in early August were gloomily united in saying that he would not hit them."

The paper approved of most of the economic programme of August 1971, the sign of praise being that it should all have been done long before. Incomes policy was still then one of the paper's basic beliefs: "Under modern conditions of trade union monopoly bargaining power, all advanced countries need to bring an incomes policy into effect.... Now the most advanced country in the world has resorted to an incomes policy. It has done so with the clumsiest possible device of a total but far too short-term freeze, in an electorally-motivated package largely thought up by a handful of men in a single weekend, on the eve of an election year into which any extension of the freeze would become politically unpopular."

Floating the dollar was good, but with two caveats. First: "The devaluation of the dollar was welcome and overdue, but it will have been dearly bought if one of the prices turns out to be another devaluation of the idea that a sensible incomes policy really can be made to work." Second, the dollar had been unpegged under cover of a 10% tariff surcharge, which was illegal under GATT rules, meant to curb directly Japanese exports to the United States. But America had imposed it "on most of its dutiable imports, and thus on about 8 per cent of all the world's exports". It was not a free-trading paper's favourite remedy.

Still, it much preferred floating with the dollar to putting up with what it suspected would otherwise turn out to be another round of pointless international conferences whose eventual proposals, if any, the paper would probably have despised. For Nixon's political purposes in the 1972 election it did the trick: "The pleasant state of the American economy can be summarised in two figures. In October industry production was 9.3 per cent above a year earlier, while in the same period consumer prices rose only 3.4 per cent. In the international league tables this is the year when the United States moves not only into the first division but into first place."

It was after Nixon had gone that Norman Macrae set out his fear of what would be most likely to curb American prosperity in the future; the new, restrictive society that opposed growth, developments like nuclear energy, and exploiting natural resources, all in the name of conservation and the environment: "The United States has joined the Fabian Society of about 1903. Many of the new Democrat members of Congress, including some presidential aspirants, would find that Fabian Society their most natural home, militant middle-class feminism and all, but plus the old American disease. When upper-class Americans impose snob values on emotional populists, they often think they have gotten religion—and catch the lynching spirit."

There was, he thought, worse to come: "On campuses across the continent, a peculiarly innumerate anti-growth cult is being taught to a generation of idealistic kids as if it was high moral philosophy, or even a religion."

It seemed an early preview of aspects of the Carter

presidency, but the Nixon one was, after all, the age of space missions and the first moon landing when it was permissible to wonder at man's grasp and ingenuity. It was not Nixon but Kennedy who had committed America to the moon race, but he took the opportunity to ride the success with eager hands. The paper, which had had its doubts about whether or not the effort was worthwhile, went along with the exploratory interest and hopes: "The Eagle has landed. There is life on the moon at last. And space itself seems friendlier."

Once the excitement was over, however, it forecast harder times and falling interest. In the week of the landing its scientific assessment was cool: "This is where men come down to earth. In particular, the American people may come down with a bump when they discover how little the Apollo pioneers can really do now. The Americans have not spent beyond their means. To get to the moon has cost no more than the equal of nearly 3 per cent of one year's gross national product, spent over a decade, but earth taxpayers will expect more for that than a bag of rocks. They will want their crock of gold."

That was July; by November Nixon had lost interest and the doubts for the space agency were coming true: "The Administration apparently thinks Nasa should be satisfied with the moon, and not cry for a space shuttle to go with it. There just is not the same political bonus in a space shuttle when the Russians are not breathing down your neck."

The paper's attention and sense of occasion returned seven years later in July 1976 with the first live picture from Mars: "A momentous picture, the first ever transmitted from the surface of another planet, built up slowly from the left side of the television screen, displaying Martian rocks in crisp focus and minute detail. Then, when the picture was half complete, an advertisement for Jello took over the screen. American television networks have an uncanny feel for the lowest common denominator."

When proper account is taken of the Democratic politicians that Nixon faced after 1968, and the parlous state of the party, it becomes even harder to account for the methods he was ready to countenance in 1972 and the sink of Watergate. In the very week that the paper covered Neil Armstrong and Buzz Aldrin on the moon it reported a lesser event from Cape Cod: "Until July 18th Senator Edward Kennedy of Massachusetts was first in the field of probable Democratic candidates for the presidential nomination in 1972. Things changed for him on the night of the 18th to 19th, when his car went off the road into a tidal pond on Chappaquiddick Island, which adjoins the Edgartown end of Martha's Vineyard."

The paper was less concerned with the young woman, Mary Jo Kopechne, who was drowned than with the young senator whose career and promise had been blown away by his own weakness and by the inflated expectations of his family and friends: "Whether or not Senator Kennedy is ambitious for himself, it was not his ambition, but the ambitions of others that forced him, a man of moderate talents, so precociously into the forefront of national political life. For himself he might perfectly well have been, and so far as anybody knows he may still be, content to wait another seven, or 11 or 15 years to reach for the Presidency. But it is natural that the people who rather arbitrarily pinned their hopes on him for 1972 should blame him when he showed himself unready."

A week later it turned on the Kennedy establishment, its ambitions and its standards, now so damagingly revealed to the common gaze: "Nor do people like the way in which his wealthy family and his influential friends (including such international figures as Mr Robert McNamara) rallied round almost conspiratorially, as it seemed, to protect him and maybe even to take or share the blame. Once nothing more could be done for Miss Kopechne, human feelings appear to have been subordinated ruthlessly to political considerations, candour and sympathy to Mr Kennedy's career and the allied interests of his associates."

Human frailty struck twice at the more elderly, conservative wing of the Democratic Party in Washington when powerful committee chairmen whom placemen and supplicants held in awe were found to be foolishly and fleshly fallible. In October 1974 Wilbur Mills, chairman of the House Ways and Means Committee, who had held the power of life and death over legislation, especially liberal legislation, which he disagreed with was found in a midnight misadventure: "A Washington news cameraman came upon Mr Mills walking away from his car, policemen fishing a hysterical woman out of a tidal basin not far from the Jefferson Memorial, and spots of blood on Mr Mills's face. The woman turned out to be an Argentine strip-tease artist recently retired from a Washington 'go-go' bar, and more recently a valued customer at that and similar establishments, often in the company of a free-spending Congressman Mills." Mills had been accountable to no one, except to his own alcoholic self. Even the party that had toadied to him could take no more.

In May 1976 another Democratic patriarch, Wayne Hays of Ohio, chairman of the House Administration Committee, said to be the most feared and hated man in the Congress, found that his secretary and mistress had taken it into her head to write a book and promote it: "Miss Elizabeth Ray, the staff secretary, once runner-up in a beauty contest in her home state of North Carolina, once briefly a starlet in Hollywood, told the Washington Post that she could not type, file documents, or even take telephone calls and did none of these, but was paid $14,000 a year out of committee funds to fornicate with Mr Hays when he required it; which, she said, he did regularly and in a businesslike manner, keeping his eye on the digital clock. Becoming uneasy and depressed, she decided to tell all."

The ogre had to make a swift departure from Capitol Hill where he had been so accustomed to domineer. A Nixon on the hunt would not have missed his opportunities. In the 1972 campaign he was lucky from the start. First, the Democratic front-runner and eventual candidate was the inoffensive, naive, liberal Senator George McGovern. McGovern's blunders, his original choice for vice-president, his ignorance of the media, his preference for radical groups, views and follies, made him easy game for Nixon's professionalism.

Second, the candidate who did worry Nixon and had cut into the rightward-leaning, ethnic, blue-collar vote in 1968, George Wallace, was shot in mid-May, and although he survived he was removed from the campaign. With that populist out of the way—the paper called his assailant "just another unstable, unsuccessful, uninteresting, unemployed young man, fortunately white"—the highway was open for Nixon and middle America to march down. After the election the paper chose to explain the result less tellingly by Nixon's virtues than by McGovern's failings. It was the public mood: "They were frightened of Mr McGovern, feeling that he lacked the competence, decisiveness and judgment that are essential for a President.... The change Mr McGovern proposed might have upset the comfortable lives that the great majority of citizens were leading and revived the fires of social disruption that had been banked down by Mr Nixon. So only the blacks and the Mexicans, the poorer whites, the students, the committed liberals and the hard-core Democrats—and by no means all of them—voted for Mr McGovern."

THE KISSINGER STRATEGY

How America was meant to recover its
confidence and forget its self-inflicted wounds

Nixon had a grasp and a dexterity in international relations that belied his hardline reputation. He counted on the intellectual support and the negotiating diligence of Henry Kissinger, but he knew what he was doing and where he wanted to get to. Experience, foresight and a knowledge of duplicity are not handicaps in diplomacy. Nixon's greatest coup, perhaps because it was the most unexpected, was his approach to communist China which showed the Soviet Union that a new adroitness had come into the cold war competition. Besides playing that card, it had been his intention to use the opportunity to put relations with the Russians, too, on a better basis. Kissinger shared, encouraged, laboured for, implemented and—on Nixon's disgrace—continued the policy.

Moreover, western Europe came into the equation, almost for the first time, as a factor whose role was no longer just to be propped up or rescued or even merely patronised, but a force with growing resources and a mind of its own on aims and intentions. Kissinger's mind delighted in the complications and difficulties which this required him to solve until, towards the end of his responsibility, his thoughts began to seem oppressed by the years and what they required of him. It was a notable era in American policy-making. The paper appreciated much of it.

It believed Nixon was right not to make too much of the tactic of splitting China and the Soviet Union. It noted in October 1971: "It is always possible that Mr Nixon will never actually reach Moscow; two of his predecessors, General Eisenhower and Mr Johnson, thought they were going but never got to board their planes. But just by announcing his Chinese and Russian travel plans, Mr Nixon has surprised and delighted American public opinion and reminded the world that conservatives are often very good at pursuing flexible foreign relations."

By negotiating the first Strategic Arms Limitation Treaty (SALT 1) Nixon put limits on part, at least, of the missile race. The time was well chosen. The Soviet

Communist Party leadership in Leonid Brezhnev's hands had wide ambitions, not least in expanding its naval power, but it was cautious enough not to press the cold war too far or too openly. The paper also felt that Brezhnev's Soviet Union was more shaky than it or its friends pretended; the sense of confidence about Soviet economic growth had not been sustained: "The probability is that in many fields of economic activity the gap between the Soviet Union and the advanced capitalist countries is getting wider, not narrower. Mr Brezhnev, unlike Khrushchev, seems to be willing to recognise this economic weakness as a fact of life."

It did not mean that the Soviet Union was about to collapse or even thought it should offer any concession. But it wanted to keep up the exchange; even when Nixon seemed to be without a friend in the world, Brezhnev turned up on Kissinger's instructions: "Mr Kissinger must sometimes feel like a mountain goat leaping from billiard ball to billiard ball."

The paper was suspicious about this relationship and wondered who was, in fact, getting most advantage from it: "Mr Kissinger, who can see the difficulties his Russian policy is running into as clearly as the next man, tries to defend it by arguing that the Soviet government will gradually become so dependent on his envisaged network of agreements that it will in the end change its whole attitude towards the west. That is not the way it is going now, and history does not lend much support to Mr Kissinger's theory: some of the biggest wars have been between countries that had signed a mountain of pieces of paper."

Nixon's expulsion from the White House was distinctly unhelpful to Kissinger's design: to stabilise America's reputation and increase its influence again after the demoralisation caused by the Vietnam war and its consequences. In October 1974 the paper analysed the Kissinger programme: "The core of the Kissinger policy was the decision to make use of the quarrel between Russia and China in order to create a three-sided balance of power between the west and the two communist giants that would keep the world more or less stable until the second half of the 1970s.... Its purpose was to get the United States through the aftermath of the storms of the 1960s—the Vietnam war, the race crisis, the loss of American self-confidence—until what was assumed to be the natural vitality of the American people and the American economy brought the west back into smoother waters."

These sentiments, which would have graced the planning of a Metternich, were now put under strain. The Vietnam war had not ended; the settlement was not holding; the North Vietnamese army, helped by "the constancy of its foreign backers", had returned to claim the full spoils of victory over the South Vietnamese. The policy of shifting responsibility was breaking down before America's eyes. In April 1975 the paper recorded sadly: "While the Senators and Representatives were at home for their Easter recess, the newspapers were filled with vivid tales of the South Vietnamese rout. Their constituents can hardly have been enthusiastic about the value of reinforcing an army that left millions of dollars worth of American-supplied equipment behind for the communists as it fled, or about the valour of soldiers who shot their way on to an escape plane out of Da Nang to take seats that might otherwise be occupied by desperate women and children."

The paper did not harp on it; it tried to remind Americans and others of what Vietnam had been meant to be about before the collapse: "The bungled and lost war in Indochina is not the only cause of the

present diminution of American influence, but it is one cause. But, even in the moment of reckoning of full defeat, it may help the Americans to remember that this lost war was not in its origins a purposeless war. It was a conflict about a matter of substance; and the matter of substance is closely related to what people still hope the United States can do in the world."

Any excuse to find a success for American power had to be seized. It came a month later when the *Mayaguez*, an American container ship, was boarded and captured by the Cambodians and then retaken by the United States marines. Ford and Kissinger basked for a moment in a triumph. The Washington report was complimentary: "It all went more crisply than the war of Jenkins' ear. The way it went tells something of the American president that he had not previously taken the opportunity to show. Not a wide or deep thinker, he has shown himself as a man who can take hasty decisions swiftly with a spectacular calm."

London was less effusive: "That small American victory ... was greeted on both sides of the Atlantic with an overblown exhilaration that reveals more about the

Diplomatic duo. Nixon and his secretary of state, Henry Kissinger (with Austrian chancellor Kreisky), set American foreign policy on a new tack of co-existence while America recovered from Vietnam.

state of mind of anxious Americans than about the balance of power in the Gulf of Siam."

The American mood, like the State Department's, had wished for some time to transfer part of the burden and the responsibility for defence in western Europe to the local powers, as in Indochina. The paper understood why. But, as ever, it was apprehensive that American contracting out in Europe would bring its own dangers: "It is easier to plant an American flag on the moon than it will be ... to restore many people's belief in the solidity of an American guarantee."

Its own prognosis for the Europe of the 1970s was of little change: "The western part will probably go on consisting of three beta-minus-sized powers, and a collection of gammas and deltas, so preoccupied with their own status game that they can play no effective part in the rest of the world. The eastern half may be stuck in a cycle of repression and near explosion."

If the Americans inferred from this that Europe was a "selfish and incurable mess" they could not be blamed. The paper thought the Americans, indeed, had a case against all their allies, who were growing rich but not increasing their defence spending in anything like the same proportion. It took ten countries, the six in the European common market, Britain, Japan, Australia and New Zealand, and contrasted their record with the American one: "Between 1950 and 1968 the combined gross national products of these ten allies of the United States rose from less than a half of that of the Americans to virtually three-quarters. Over the same period their combined spending on defence only rose from 34 per cent of the American figure in 1950 to 39 per cent in 1965, and then fell back to 29 per cent when the Americans were fighting against the Tet offensive in Vietnam in 1968."

The United States had to pursue a policy of retrenchment that would not slip into a new isolationism. It ought to be practicable, but the Europeans kept on making life hard. In March 1974 Kissinger had experienced so much hassle that he suddenly erupted: "One thing one must say for Mr Kissinger is that when his feelings are aroused he does not deceitfully keep them to himself. An audience of Congressional wives, assembled at the State Department for God knows what reason, heard all about it on Monday. The biggest American foreign policy problem at the moment, Mr Kissinger told them, was not to regulate the competition with its enemies, it was a problem with friends: 'How to bring our friends to a realisation that there are greater common interests than simply self-assertiveness.' "

Whether Britain was in, half in, or out of Europe made little difference. Once the United States felt sure that Franco-German rivalry had been ended by the common market its policy had been to encourage British entry, and acceptance, as a means of ensuring the continued transatlantic connection. In September 1975 the paper noted: "France goes its own way; southern Europe is in its well-known state; Germany is still solidly in place, but who is there for a dependable European associate? When the prompter calls for Britain, once cast for second lead, it turns out that Britain has chosen to play the mendicant at the gate."

By May 1976 the paper was forced to recognise what British opinion still did not accept. An old relationship was acquiring a new face: "Germany is much the most important country in western Europe. It has therefore begun to develop a special relationship with the United States not quite like the one Britain used to have, with the British-American ties of language and alliance in two world wars; but close enough to reflect Germany's economic strength and military power, and its pre-eminence in both the EEC and Nato Europe."

For those who felt the future in their bones—one of Kissinger's definitions of a statesman—this had the ring of truth. The more American policy-makers reflected on the future of the western alliance, the more attractive the German effort in the 1970s became. It was the paper's view, too: "For America the modern Bundeswehr is a model of value for (a lot of) money—just the example the administration can point to if congress becomes restive about defending allies apparently not ready to make the effort to defend themselves. Politically, Germany increasingly seems, to Americans, the only Nato ally on which they can rely."

Faced by the choice between Gerald Ford and Jimmy Carter, the American voter decided, hesitantly, for Carter. As Kissinger was leaving the State Department the paper gave him a friendly farewell: "In these past two years Mr Kissinger has avoided the failure which he once levelled, as a professor, at Bismarck: that of leaving 'a heritage of unassimilated greatness'. Though there will be rejoicing among those ... who were not among his highly-gifted chosen elect, the purposes of his diplomacy, if not his methods, have been assimilated into the department very thoroughly."

It had been a highly formative time.

Carter the peacemaker managed to talk Israel's Menachem Begin (left) and Egypt's Anwar Sadat into an agreement at Camp David, 1978. For recreation he took them to the Gettysburg civil war battlefield.

13

AMERICA THE REPENTANT

1976–1980

HE MEANT WELL

*The man of principle who found the real
world unforgiving*

The new president, Jimmy Carter, though well-meaning, turned out to have illusions which the country now had to live through.

Carter naturally sought better relations with the Soviet Union and he believed they were possible, an attribute of a non-imperial outlook. He was not starry-eyed; he had been trained, after all, by the nuclear admiral, Hyman Rickover, and there was, disconcertingly for radicals, a conservative streak in him. But his natural humanitarianism was not reflected in the Kremlin, and it was even resented; yet it was a distinctive part of what he wanted to achieve. Human rights was a popular theme with western liberals and with the idealistic constituency in the third world. The preoccupation of the visibly ageing Leonid Brezhnev was to consolidate, and use, the strategic military advantage which had been built up over the years of America's long diversion into Vietnam and racial disturbance. In the contest between the two countries' priorities, it was Carter who was eventually to be disabused.

Carter began hopefully: "Mr Carter wants to do business with Russia. He is looking for a major reduction in the two superpowers' nuclear armouries in the 1980s, and he would like to foster the sort of economic relationship between Russia and the west which might eventually help to civilise Soviet behaviour."

Even so, human rights had to come first. That was his global priority: "The president knows that his own public opinion may not allow him to pursue these policies unless it is satisfied that he has got the measure of the darker side of Russia, and is prepared to criticise what Americans want to hear criticised."

Missiles soon came up. Carter tried to persuade Brezhnev not to put his multiple-warhead ss-18s into service; that would be a serious contribution to co-existence; Brezhnev rejected it. *The Economist* was adamant that the Americans must even the missile odds by deploying enough of their new cruise missiles: "This too the Russians are still trying to prevent. The cruise missile is far from an ideal answer to the ss-18. It is astonishingly accurate, but it is also very slow, and in the hours while it was lumbering towards Russia on its counter-attack the Russians could have reloaded their

---

CHRONOLOGY

1977	Jimmy Carter becomes president
	Vietnam draft evaders pardoned
	Congress rejects Carter's higher gasoline tax
	Egypt's Anwar Sadat visits Jerusalem
1978	California voters adopt Proposition 13, reducing property taxes
	Carter, Sadat and Israel's Menachem Begin at Camp David
1979	Canal Zone treaty with Panama

Three Mile Island nuclear shutdown
Margaret Thatcher prime minister in Britain
Carter meets Brezhnev in Vienna
Somoza government falls in Nicaragua
American diplomats held hostage in Tehran
Soviet troops invade Afghanistan

1980 Zimbabwe (formerly Rhodesia) independent
US attempt to rescue hostages aborted
Solidarity union leads strikes in Poland

---

silos and fired a second broadside. But it is the only counterbalance to the ss-18s available in the near future."

Carter appeared diffident about going directly and quickly to a breakdown. The paper's Washington correspondent spelled out his continuing hopes after six months: "He wants a comprehensive nuclear test ban, he wants an agreement about the Indian Ocean, and if he is resigned to the next Salt agreement taking a little longer than might have been hoped, that is because he wants it to be more ambitious than was intended when Mr Brezhnev met Mr Ford at Vladivostok. All the same, and most of all, the Carter administration wants to be seen to be pursuing a world policy that is appropriate to the day and age."

It might be estimable, but it did not amount to what the paper thought a proper policy to cover the West's glaring weakness. The Americans were being too soft: "For the United States to accept any limits at all on cruise missiles would be a large concession. Certainly its present willingness to offer a three-year moratorium on deployment, while development of this complex piece of technology continues, is the farthest its allies should agree to its going, and even that requires a matching moratorium on Russia's deployment of its huge new ss-18 missile."

The paper was concerned: it was even alarmed. It believed Carter was in danger of making an historic misjudgment: "The United States is in the position of many great powers before it: it has to choose between an accommodation with its adversary and the confidence of its allies. It can stand ready to share the cruise missile, or it can run a very real risk of damaging the alliance on which its own security, as well as Europe's, depends."

A month later, in October 1977, the paper accused the Carter administration of withholding information on the missile issue from its European allies. The administration had replied that it was all right: "It is not all right. What the Americans now propose is to agree not to transfer the information to their allies during the first three years of their new arrangement with Russia, when they themselves would accept limits on their deployment of cruise missiles. They are adamant that they will be free to share the information after that. Maybe."

The paper's scepticism contrasted with the favourable opinions Carter was getting in the Ameri-

can media and elsewhere in his first year, and even in his second. It sensed there was a weakness in the man and in the policy which it did not forget. When Carter went to see Brezhnev in Vienna in July 1979 it was contemptuous of the very concept, let alone the outcome: "President Carter has been wasting Christian kisses on a heathen idol's foot. Except for the Salt-2 treaty ... Mr Carter flew home on Monday from his weekend with President Brezhnev in Vienna with a virtually empty briefcase."

When that September Henry Kissinger re-emerged to call for western rearmament, for a survival plan against the Soviet advantage, the paper was enthusiastic about his demand: "It is designed to get the non-communist world safely through the tricky next few years, in the hope that after that the constraints on Russia will start to bite, and Russia's pressure on the west will therefore start to ease. The western world's time of troubles is now; the Soviet world's begins some time in the 1980s."

This was, as it proved, perspicacious. The paper pointed to the falling Soviet growth rate, the apparent shortage of oil, the rapid increase in the Muslim population. It was evident that there were rocks ahead. The West must persevere and its opportunity would come. The Russians had enjoyed "a dozen years of rearming while the west has dozed". The paper had no confidence in Carter doing what was required.

The outstanding diplomatic success of the Carter administration and the president's personal style came in the Middle East. It had not been expected. In December 1977 there was a major opportunity to be grasped. Egypt's president, Anwar Sadat, had gone to Jerusalem, the first head of an Arab state to signify that it was time to face the reality of Israel's survival. Now Menachem Begin, the Israeli prime minister, had arrived in Washington: "The administration has see-sawed recently about a new role in the Middle East. Tepid and cautious at first, it has now caught the sense of excitement generated by the Israel-Egypt breakthrough. It welcomed Mr Begin's proposals on Israeli-occupied Sinai and praised him for his 'flexibility'. Still, the administration wants to be a broker in the middle at this stage, not a spokesman for either side."

There were complaints about inertia and delay in exploiting the chance. It was not until September 1978 that Carter brought Sadat and Begin together at Camp David, and the paper was sceptical of his success, even when the three had said they had agreed in principle: "If Egypt forswears war there will be a Middle East peace of a kind, for a time. And that is good. A peace that tries to meet the Soviet-led threat to the region's south in the Horn of Africa may be preventive medicine against that illness too. But a peace that ignores the central injustice done the Palestinians carries a cancer."

The cancer was to last. The paper did remember to give credit where it was thought to be due, but it kept its reservations: "This may sound a carping comment on the triumphant conclusion to a fortnight of splendid effort by Mr Carter and his men. The degree of involvement and the patience deserve unstinted admiration.... If only...."

The paper was right: it was not to be easy. But it gave Carter his moment of glory when he reported to Congress, a revived and invigorated president: "He spoke with a confidence that had deserted him in recent months. An indifferent speaker at the best of times, Mr Carter felt sure enough of himself to depart

from his prepared text. As is his habit, he wore his religious feelings on his sleeve. Describing the Camp David agreements, he said the world's prayers had been answered, ending by quoting from the Psalms and smiled up often at Messrs Begin and Sadat in the gallery."

Sadat was shot at an army parade by Muslim extremists. It was a major setback.

PILLAR TO POST
How not to deal with fundamentalists

The issue that became integral to the failure of the Carter years surfaced in November 1979 when Iranian fundamentalists, having expelled the shah, took hostage all the Americans they found in the Tehran embassy. It was a humiliation for American influence and power, and Carter seemed unable to find an effective response. The paper suggested the Americans should take three small islands—Abu Musa and the

A friend for Brezhnev. Carter sought amity and arms cuts with the Soviet president, Leonid Brezhnev, in Vienna, 1979. Carter tested the Soviets on human rights. They invaded Afghanistan.

Tumbs—at the entrance to the Gulf, which had been occupied by Iran as recently as 1971: "The taking of Abu Musa and the Tumbs would be an entirely permissible response to the damage Ayatollah Khomeini has done to the United States and to the principles of international diplomacy."

That was not the Carter approach. The paper recognised that it was difficult to advise the Americans "in their hideous predicament", but it counselled a strong line: "No Queensberry rules apply in this particular dirty game. It is the right of the blackmailed to respond with low blows, cunning and deceit; promises gouged out under pressure, for example, are not promises to be kept.... The affair is a matter of terrorism, not of religion, culture or anything else."

One handicap to determined action was that the United States was, or believed itself to be, on its own. The paper wanted to see some allied unity: "The absence of loud and clear support from America's friends has for some weeks been a shaming counterpoint to the shrill cries from Teheran." It suggested a trade embargo: "Real hardship could be caused to Iran by a widely supported trade embargo, especially in food."

It did not believe in Carter's strategy; nor did it suppose that American inaction could be prolonged, as he seemed to suppose, indefinitely: "The United States cannot maintain indefinitely a policy of patience and rather lonely hopefulness as the ordeal of its hostages continues. It needs the support of its friends in words and actions. Those actions cannot start to be planned until America's allies make it clear that they are ready to co-operate. The alternative, if nothing else works, is sooner or later going to be military action."

In December the Russians went into Afghanistan. To the paper it was the ultimate demonstration of American indecision. The Soviet Union plainly felt there was no limit to what it could do without retaliation: "Who invited 40,000 Russian soldiers complete with their Quisling into Afghanistan? Answer: President Carter, the American congress and American opinion—and those American allies who have dared not believe, and have done little to remedy or reverse the crumbling of America's willingness to exercise its power."

It listed the humiliations and failures of the Ford and Carter years, reflecting its own disappointment at American inertia: "The Cuban adventure in Angola went off with neither Cuba nor its forces in Africa much molested; congress cut off the administration from its Nato ally, Turkey, and the political damage there has never been fully reversed; Ethiopia is in the Cuban/East German maw, Somalia has been let down; South Yemen has gone Marxist, North Yemen is under threat; Saudi Arabia's ruling family is understandably nervous, and now less than half in America's pocket; the Shah of Iran, chided too little by Mr Nixon and Mr Kissinger, has been nudged and undermined into self-defeat by their successors."

The paper was hard on Carter; he was the man who had inherited the responsibility. But it was now convinced that he was presiding over a disaster. It did not even think his attempt to arrange a western boycott of the Moscow Olympics was sensible or would be successful: "The number of people uplifted by the Olympics in most societies is greater than the 2% or so of articulate people passionately interested in politics. That is why politicians should not talk about boycotts as President Carter is doing, but about switching sites." What would be better than one site, it thought, would be televising separate events from around the world.

By April the paper was counselling the Americans to worry about Afghanistan and its meaning more, and about Iran less: "A great power does not shape its strategy around the release of 50 POWs in a minor theatre of war."

It was questionable if Afghanistan were as major or Iran as minor as the paper believed, but Carter seemed hypnotised by the hostage issue. His diplomatic efforts had been repeatedly rebuffed by the ayatollah, he sensed American opinion was growing impatient with his lack of any result, and he authorised a rescue attempt. It failed, famously. The paper was scathing about the debacle in the desert: "Although one can now believe practically anything of America's present ungovernment, it is almost inconceivable that the president was not warned of the risks he ran.... One can only conclude that Mr Carter's re-election prospects weighed more heavily in his mind than they should have done."

Any regret was for the American military reputation: "America does not need cowboy escapades its superpower armed forces are not made for and should not have to be judged by."

To its disappointment the new Conservative government in Britain refused to join full trade sanctions against Iran, as other allies had failed American hopes: "That the Americans still often look almost without thinking to the British for support simply made it worse. The turnabout has ended with a bump the administration's extended public honeymoon with Mrs Thatcher's government."

It was only a minor blow. Carter had got used to those.

MISREADING THE SIGNS
Out on your own on the economy cycle

It was Carter's misfortune that he and his political advisers misread the American economy. Liberal panaceas were unfashionable. Carter himself seemed unable to decide which priorities he should follow. It did not help confidence. After his first year *The Economist* reported that America was going cheap; both the dollar and Wall Street had fallen rapidly. Sensible British firms should be taking the opportunity to buy in at bargain prices: "Foreign investors should remember that the United States is not the Cannibal Islands. Its trade unions are moderate (ie, they concede the bosses a good profit on their members' labour), the market is huge, capitalism is uncontroversial, foreign exchange controls non-existent and the growth outlook better than for most other economies."

The energy problem and the trade deficit went hand in hand. The paper regularly advocated duties to reduce petrol consumption; politicians and Detroit regularly decided they were politically impossible: "The United States will continue to run a petrosaurus-sized deficit on its current balance of payments so long as it forks out $45 billion a year to pay for imported oil and gas. While this oil deficit lasts, or grows, any sizeable intervention by the Federal Reserve to support the dollar will be throwing good money after bad."

It did not encourage deflation: "Makeshift measures to cut the country's $30 billion trade deficit in the meantime, by domestic deflation or trade protectionism, will prove foolish. They will lead to the export of recession by the United States, to higher unemployment everywhere, and to still greater budget deficits as today's taxpayers become tomorrow's unemployed and treasuries try to spend economies out of a slump."

What Carter, like other politicians in other countries, did find baffling was the conjunction of inflation,

recession and unemployment. The paper blamed him for indecision and political incapacity: "He has jammed congress with half-baked legislation at a time when his non-exercise of party patronage has gained him few friends in the Democratic party. Little time or direction has therefore been left to pull America's economy away from the threats of another recession, higher inflation and a weaker dollar, all at the same time."

The president's efforts on energy prices, substitutes and consumption were countered by the environment lobby, with which he found it impolitic to disagree. The paper was not so squeamish: "Tightened air quality standards alone have increased America's daily use of oil and gas by an amount equal to two thirds of all the oil and gas used daily in Britain. The reductions in America's planned nuclear and coal capacity by other environmental controls since 1974, and the price controls that keep down domestic production from existing American wells and keep up American consumption, are bigger gifts to Opec still."

It was not until 1979 that Carter made a significant appointment, which the radical Democrats did not like, but which the paper approved: "Mr Paul Volcker, the new chairman of the Federal Reserve Board, this week sounded like the hard-nosed east-coast banker he is when he blamed inflation on excessive monetary growth and said at senate confirmation hearings 'there is no substitute for monetary discipline'.... All had been looking for signs of leadership from someone in Washington with strong, coherent views. Mr Volcker filled the vacuum."

Beginning when it did, it was unlikely to be an election-winning programme. Gross national product was still falling and prices were still rising when the 1981 budget was sent to Congress: "Incumbent presidents do not usually win votes by promising higher unemployment and an inflation rate more usually associated with South than North America."

In March 1980 with the primary campaigning going strong, the paper had to commiserate with Carter and Volcker: "They face an American inflation rate too high at around 14%; a savings rate too low at about 3% of disposable personal income; a fiscal 1981 budget deficit too large at the $34 billion (including off-budget items) it was estimated at in President Carter's budget proposals in January."

The levers had been switched, but too late. It was the irony of the Carter presidency that its priorities were meant to be at home, where it was supposed to have good ideas and competence but showed very little of either. Everything seemed to conspire to disillusion its supporters. There had been no reason except misguided local loyalty for Carter to have appointed his friend, Bert Lance, an Atlanta banker, to head the Bureau of the Budget in Washington. Lance was soon hounded by the media. The paper was almost incredulous that the appointment had been allowed to go through in the first place; it was not all Lance's fault: "A close look puts much of the blame elsewhere; on Senator Ribicoff's committee, for recommending Mr Lance's confirmation last January with no more than the most perfunctory glance at his record; and on President Carter, for pitchforking an easy-going small town banker, merely because he was his friend, to the summit of a government for which at the same time the president announced personal financial standards of unprecedented rigour."

Lance had to go. Much though the president might have liked to disown his own brother, Billy Carter, or at least confine his commercial activities to Plains, Georgia, it was Billy who kept on capturing the headlines, and the paper's fascinated attention: "It's been one crisis after another for Mr Billy Carter, the president's beer-drinking brother. First, the tourist traffic pushed him out of his home town. Then he had to quit as manager of the family peanut business. And now the state of Virginia, exercising its rule against celebrity endorsements of strong drink, refuses to allow the sale of 'Billy' beer."

This product was an enterprise of a small brewing company fighting back against the major firms' grip of the market, but the celebrity's endorsement was less than helpful to the White House: "The beer isn't actually of Mr Billy Carter's own making, although the label does say, over his signature: 'I had this beer brewed just for me. I think it's the best beer I ever tasted. And I've tasted a lot.' "

And that was one of the more pleasant stories.

ENTER REAGAN

The elderly, conservative populist who knew his own mind, and reminded Americans of what they really wanted

It was unusual for incumbent presidents to be defeated when they ran for re-election. It had happened only twice in living memory: in 1912 and 1932. For all its disparagement and fault-finding, the paper began 1980 believing that Carter had a good chance of re-election, and all the more so when Ronald Reagan, the neo-conservative former movie actor whose political experience had been confined to the governorship of California, appeared to be the leading Republican challenger. When Reagan won the Republican vote in New Hampshire it commented, crassly: "This is good news for Mr Carter, who looks rather more likely as a consequence to be re-elected."

The correspondent on the ground in Manchester, New Hampshire, concurred: "It is no secret that Mr Reagan is the Republican the president's men are most confident of beating in the presidential election in November."

This discounted the shift in the American mood towards a new populism, one informed not only by market economics but by deeply held views on social issues; for example, being for school prayers and against abortion. It was tired of American humiliation and perceived weakness. As it had once voted Carter in because he ran against Washington, now he represented the unpopular bureaucracy and centralism. The word had gone around that there was a different way. Although Reagan had actually put up state spending in California, the frame of mind there was epitomised by the success of Proposition 13, by which voters had taken it on themselves to resist liberal prodigality by refusing to pay for it: "In the 18 months since California's voters passed proposition 13, and thereby slashed $7 billion, or about 55% off their property taxes, the state's economy has boomed. There is now widespread agreement among economists, academics, financial experts, corporate leaders and even government officials that proposition 13 has been resoundingly good for the state, and a stimulus to its economy—so far."

The prophet of the times was Arthur Laffer, advocate of supply-side economics, who argued that the best thing to do for the poor was to make the economy grow more strongly, not smother them in welfare, so that jobs were there for them to get. This message was getting across. By the end of March the paper had swiftly reassessed Reagan's strength in the primaries: "Mr Reagan, who just a few weeks ago looked unelectable, suddenly looms as a possible president.... Most Californians did not find him too right-wing; on the contrary, they felt they had to turn to proposition 13 to get their taxes cut."

The Washington correspondent found him still superficial: "Mr Reagan is shrewd without being knowledgeable. He talks, but does not appear to act, impetuously. Although he often speaks about crusades, he seems too relaxed to lead one. His simplicities are down-to-earth. He has little time for higher learning."

His verdict was precisely the one that led liberals to deride Reagan and prompted ordinary people to vote for him: "He evokes a simpler, imaginary world, in which the United States was unchallenged abroad and without serious problems at home."

As Carter struggled with the problems of Afghanistan, Iran and Nicaragua that summer Reagan's steady avowal that America should not be discomfited or embarrassed won new support, and the paper's sympathy: "Ronald Reagan is an implausible choice to preside over such a reassertion of American strength.... Harry Truman was an implausible choice in his day, and he turned out well enough. It could happen again."

It still found Carter implausible on his record, but it appreciated the plight of a man in an impossible position where too much had been expected of him: "He was just like you and me except that he didn't have our short-comings. In consequence he has been too much like you and me to make a good president. The blemishes that his critics now bemoan are the qualities many admirers applauded in him four years ago, or at least they are close relations. The honesty that post-Watergate voters sought in the God-fearing boy from Plains never looked very different from unsophistication."

The paper seemed to have made its mind up. By mid-October it had. It accepted that to support Reagan was a gamble, but it had begun to seem worth it: "Mr Reagan ... holds out the promise of a firmer line abroad, based on a sounder structure of advice. He would almost certainly bring in more new ideas, for the Republican party now shows more signs of intellectual vitality than the Democrats."

When Reagan won comfortably the Washington man was percipient: "This election may be seen, in time, to have been the turning point that many political scientists have judged overdue. If it is, and the Republicans emerge as a new governing majority, the Democrats will be in for a long wait."

THE SEVENTIES SCENE
Some Economist *discoveries*

The Economist kept its eyes open for the particular and the peculiar, the trends and the trendsetters of the 1970s.

Women at work and their rights were now integral to the economy, but equality was, if anything, more distant than had been expected: "Women workers are by no means out to get pin money, or happy to sit in a low-paid clerical job simply to escape the housework. Four out of every ten working women are alone and supporting themselves. One in eight is the head of a family. Despite their responsibilities, recent studies by the department of labour show that the average income for women is now only 57% that of men; 20 years ago, it was 64%. Despite the greater numbers of women entering the labour force, the greater openness of law and medical schools and the much-publicised promotions of a handful of women in high places, most women still take menial jobs for unequal rates of pay. In part the fault is theirs."

Hispanics settle in The rise in the Hispanic population was significant, both politically and economically. It was estimated there were 12m of them, plus 7m in the country illegally, plus 3.5m Puerto Ricans. Their birth rate was double that of whites and 60% higher than that of blacks: "Los Angeles now has a Mexican population second only to Mexico City's, while Miami's is two-thirds Cuban. Both cities, behind their superstructure of skyscrapers and concrete freeways, are Spanish rather than American. Spanish is the language of the streets, the buses and the restaurants; the smells are of burritos and fried pork rind; and there is small-scale enterprise visible everywhere, content to go along at its own pace."

A new society had established itself at the bottom of the social scale, distinctive and often impoverished, for whom the great majority of the country felt little or no responsibility: "There are now few large cities in the nation which do not have a *barrio*, a ghetto area which both whites and the better-off blacks have abandoned for the suburbs. Murals flower on the sides of the buildings; the poor houses are gaudily patched up; the repair-shops and second-hand car lots multiply overnight and so, it seems, do the people.... The blacks, whose progress in political and economic life the Hispanics take as a model, were understood to have been systematically enslaved and oppressed. But whatever the present-day hardship of the migrant farmworker or the man who washes plates in a restaurant, it is not a predicament for which the nation as a whole can easily be made to feel responsible."

The Medicaid rip-off Medical health care still revealed its inadequacies, not only for the poor but for those who could afford the insurance. Senator Frank Moss, a Utah Democrat, tried out Medicaid, disguised as a workman, to see how the government-sponsored system worked: "The senator, armed with a Medicaid card, complained of a cold. He got only a few minutes of a doctor's time, but batteries of expensive tests, a whole bundle of prescriptions, X-rays, massage for a non-existent muscle spasm, and instructions to return the next day without fail. This was one of New York's notorious Medicaid mills, which are accused of providing slipshod and extravagant treatment, 'ping-ponging' patients from one specialist or laboratory to another, with the government paying the bill. As there is no limit on the treatment that can be ordered, the system invites frauds and rewards greed: more than 100 doctors in the New York city area received over $100,000 each in 1975 and one took nearly $800,000 from Medicaid at his clinics (admittedly part of this went to pay other doctors and staff)."

The Hilltopper cannonball The railroads joined in a new system which it was hoped would continue mainline services and stave off bankruptcy with public money's help. It was called Amtrak, and the paper chose to be skittish about it: "Amtrak: not a deodorant or a detective agency, but the new American national passenger-carrying railway system.... Amtrak is operated by the quasi-public National Railroad Passenger Corporation, created last year by Congress. It was originally to be called Railpax."

Some famous trains had to be axed from the outset, among them the Wabash Cannon Ball between St Louis and Detroit, and a city the size of Cleveland, "incred-

Another humiliation: Soviet forces north of Kabul, Afghanistan. Carter's term ended with the Soviet occupation continuing and his own failure to rescue the Americans taken hostage in the embassy in Tehran.

ibly", got no passenger service at all. Amtrak was soon back asking Congress for a quick $250m: the passengers were just staying away. The disappearing railroad blues echoed around the country.

The paper took a particular interest in the last run of the Hilltopper on its route from Boston to Catlettsburg, Kentucky, in September 1979. Surviving over the years only by senatorial protection the Hilltopper carried just 18 ordinary passengers in two coaches on its last run: "In 1978 it carried, on average, 38 passengers on the Washington-to-Kentucky run, sometimes as few as two. Run is perhaps not the *mot juste*; it moved along at a stately 37mph in the Appalachians, allowing the driver to stop for the occasional passenger, who had to flag the train down at unstaffed stops. On the Amtrak system as a whole, the taxpayer forks out two thirds of the cost of each ride."

Victory for the snail-darter   The protection of the environment was the great cause that made its breakthrough in the decade, much as the paper deplored its absurdities. It found that what it thought of as mere foolishness had even reached the top of the judiciary in June 1977: "The triumph of the three-inch, impassive-featured fish, the snail darter, in the Supreme Court on June 15th, against the virtues of a $120m federal dam which is almost completed on the Little Tennessee river, might have seemed outrageous to many; but the ruling majority of the justices themselves were suitably poker-faced about it. Congress, said Chief Justice Warren Burger, has obviously passed the Endangered Species Act of 1973 to give the highest priority to just such a fish. What was more, it had declared the value of snail darters and others as 'incalculable'. The court, he said in essence, could not begin to weigh up the costs and benefits of fish or snails against hydro-electric power; a dam might cost $100m and heat 20,000 homes, but the evolutionary importance of a small and slimy obstacle could not be costed at all."

Woodstock in the rain   The definitive musical event was Woodstock, properly called the Woodstock Music and Art Fair, up in the Catskill mountains in August 1969, where 120,000 people had been expected and, the report in the paper confided, rather more turned up: "The roads were blocked for miles around by cars, motorbikes and pilgrims on foot; any attempt to demand tickets had to be abandoned. Some $1.3m

worth of tickets had been sold in advance but even so $1m may have been lost. Food and water ran out, lavatories were inadequate, performers had to be brought in (and the sick taken out) by helicopter, medical services had to be improvised. Worst of all the weather broke and the 600-acre farm which had been hired turned into a sea of mud."

The paper could not help admiring the spirit of the occasion: "That the festival survived was a miracle. That there was not a single fight struck the outnumbered police as more remarkable. So did the extraordinary kindness and good behaviour under adversity of these mostly middle-class youngsters.... Marijuana was smoked almost universally; hashish and heroin and LSD and barbiturates were hawked openly (with occasional warnings from the platform about bad LSD which provided some of the 5,000 casualties). Those who wanted to went naked."

Stigwood's amazing empire   Discos were an invariable centre of attention for the young. The paper reckoned that 10,000 were operating in July 1978, the most famous of them being Studio 54 on New York city's 54th Street. It surmised that "satiety may be approaching": "Disco fever is running high in the United States. After the phenomenal success of the film 'Saturday Night Fever' about the fun and futility of disco dancing, which has so far sold 15m soundtrack records in America and is expected to sell 23m worldwide by the end of the year, its star, John Travolta, has returned to the screen this month with more of the same. His new film, 'Grease', is an adaptation of a successful Broadway musical but with new music; the jazz and rock blend of the disco theatres that are packing in capacity crowds across the land."

A new musical empire was expanding: "'Saturday Night Fever' and 'Grease' are both offerings from Mr Robert Stigwood, an Australian-born and Bermudan-based impresario who is credited with one of the best tin ears in the business. It was Mr Stigwood who made 'Jesus Christ, Superstar' a worldwide stage success. He is hoping for an encore with 'Evita', a musical about the career of Eva Peron, produced by Harold Prince, which has just opened in London to ecstatic reviews, and should, he hopes, find the same reception on Broadway."

Superlative Disney World   The other growth empire,

for all ages, was the twin states of Disneyland and Disney World. The paper succumbed to statistics and superlatives: "When Walt Disney, who is now dead, and Mickey Mouse, whose life expectancy is infinite, created Disneyland in California, they transformed Anaheim, previously a railway whistlestop, into a city of about 165,000. Disney World is nearly 172 times as large as Disneyland. Its effects will be felt far beyond the limits of Orlando, most immediately in Orange and Osceola counties, whose boundary the development straddles. It will also be a boon to the once booming but now depressed area around the Kennedy Space Centre, 40 miles away on the Atlantic coast."

European holidaymakers should put Florida on their unmissable list: "Disney World has an $80m hotel with a monorail train running through its lobby. It has two golf courses, a transport system including two steamboats, two railways, five monorail trains and several hundred small vehicles. It has a 'theme park' with 40 attractions including Main Street, USA, Liberty Square, Frontierland, Tomorrowland and Fantasyland. Featured are more than 1,000 'audioanimatronic' figures that move, speak and play musical instruments. Its waterways are edged with six miles of white sand beaches. It has 7,500 acres of wilderness. Disney World means money."

Remembering Elvis The showbusiness funeral was that of Elvis Presley in August 1977. The paper duly acknowledged the occasion's importance: "'An unspeakably untalented and vulgar young entertainer' was how one well-known and otherwise sophisticated critic of popular culture tried to dismiss Elvis Presley on the eve of his extraordinarily rapid success more than 20 years ago. When Presley died on Tuesday at the age of 42 in Memphis, the town where he grew up, he was safely enough part of the mainstream to be awarded a fulsome presidential tribute; and the scenes of hysteria at the gates of his mansion, where he lay in

state, surpassed any mourning seen in the South since the death of Martin Luther King ten years ago."

In the blue grass country The 100th running of the Kentucky Derby at Churchill Downs, Louisville, in May 1974 in the presence of Princess Margaret, Lord Snowdon and 163,000 others got appropriate coverage: "There was a record crowd, a record field of 23 horses and record prize money of $274,000 for the winner." Cannonade was the horse that won it for its owner. The paper felt, though, that the occasion deserved a more distinguished victor: "It was a pity that last year's race was not the centenary, for then Secretariat broke the Derby record and went on to win the Preakness and Belmont stakes, the two other gems in the American horse-racing triple crown."

Secretariats do not come along every year. The paper then gave American racing its normal industrial treatment, starting with the Derby: "It was started to restore the prestige of the south's racing and breeding centres, left in shambles after the Civil War, and it was very consciously modelled on the Epsom Derby. Fittingly, 51 of the first 62 winners were lineal descendants of Diomed, the first Epsom Derby winner."

Kentucky, it reported, had no fewer than 350 horse studs, where the foals were "nurtured on the 'blue grass' which is said to be so tinged because of the high phosphate and calcium content of the soil". The commercial basis of most racing is betting. The paper looked into the finances of the Off-track Betting Corporation in New York state: "In its last fiscal year OTB handled $558m, paid $42m in state and city taxes and returned only $14m to the race courses themselves. Unlike British racing, American horse racing has hitherto been blessed with adequate prize money and low race entry fees. But that has largely been due to the race-going punter, who can now bet loyally without going to the track."

That was the bottom line that mattered.

Ending the cold war—and Soviet communism too. The paper praised Reagan for his political strategy, and for creating the incentives for Mikhail Gorbachev to invent himself.

14

THE GREAT COMMUNICATOR

1981–1989

THE REAGAN RECORD

A president with objectives, successes,
popularity; and, later, flaws

Ronald Reagan's presidency was strong in concept and practised in performance. The United States wanted a popular president, one who would restore America's pride in itself and its place in the world, a man they could admire and like. Reagan had readied himself for the chance over the years. He had taken up new ideas such as supply-side economics and he stood by old virtues: love of country, the flag, self-reliance, school prayers. He had great outward self-confidence and, valuably, a sense of self-deprecation.

He was amiable, a communicator markedly adept at the use of television. However, he had thought deeply through his career about what he wanted to achieve and believed fully in those objectives. He was not a compulsive worker and, especially in his second term, had difficulty with his concentration and hearing. The crude European image of him and his failures was resented by many Americans and by *The Economist*. Although critical of lapses like the Iran-Contra

affair, the paper did not underestimate him or the central part he played in the revelation of the Soviet Union's terminal weakness.

Decisions were needed, but two months into the presidency Reagan was shot in the street. His imperturbability on the way to hospital made him even more popular: "Most Americans this week can enjoy the exhilaration of treating a president with simple and unifying affection after 15 years of too often treating three of his four predecessors with sophisticated and divisive contempt. Ever since the botches in Vietnam and Watergate inclined America to retreat from an over-imperial presidency, it has sat snared under an overmocked and ineffective one."

There were the customary calls for the reform of the gun laws: "The usual underestimates say there are about 55m handguns lying around in American homes." The paper pointed to the sad contrast in society: "America presents the chequered spectacle of so much gentle churchgoing and so much blood."

Too many precautions, it thought, might even be counter-productive: "The kind of leadership that Mr Reagan is trying to bring to the country probably

---

CHRONOLOGY

1981	Ronald Reagan becomes president	Cruise missiles endorsed
	Reagan injured by gunman	Reagan announces strategic defence initiative (star
	François Mitterrand president of France	wars)
	Striking US air traffic controllers sacked	US forces land in Grenada
	Military clampdown in Poland	1985 First Reagan summit with Mikhail Gorbachev at
1982	Argentine forces surrender to the British in Falkland	Geneva
	Islands	1986 US bombs Libya
	Israelis invade southern Lebanon	Irangate affair surfaces
	Socialist Felipe Gonzales elected in Spain	1987 Black Monday on Wall Street
1983	Helmut Kohl's coalition elected in West Germany	Washington summit cuts missile strengths

---

requires him to mingle with people and to make things hard for those whose job it is to protect him from bullets. He could more safely leave a hotel through the underground garage than by the door, and perhaps in future he will, sometimes; but a really screened-off way of life would not suit him."

Reagan quickly returned, a winning figure apparently accustomed to success and expecting it even in a House of Representatives dominated by Democrats. By July the paper took its hat off to him: "The Reagan revolution is under way. Wednesday night's stunning victory in Congress for the president's tax plan means that the two major planks of his economic programme—big cuts in both federal spending and taxes—are now in place.... It suggests that, even though he does not enjoy a Republican majority in the house of representatives as he does in the senate, he does have a majority in the lower chamber for most of his conservative manifesto.... A last-minute surge to the president (48 Democrats came over, though he needed only 27 to win) gave Mr Reagan a surprisingly easy victory."

These were heady days for conservatives. They thought anything was possible. The Reagan presidency was not an aberration but the reality of how America was thinking: "America has been growing more conservative since the 1960s, when it became apparent that much of the Great Society was an expensive failure, that wars could be lost as well as won and certainly had to be paid for, and that the New Deal prescriptions of problem-solving by spending that had prevailed for a generation were no longer grounded in fertile intellectual soil."

In August Reagan surprised both his friends and his opponents by sacking 11,000 air-traffic controllers who had gone on illegal strike for more pay and refused to go back to work. Despite the experts' forecasts of crashes and calamities in the army's hands, the paper applauded him loudly: "He will now come under pressure from all sorts of affected interests to edge back into appeasement, so this is the week for ordinary people to call to him a clear 'bravo'. The president has set an example to timid governments around the world on how to deal with small groups of industrially muscular workers who make outrageous demands."

The union was soundly beaten; from then on others were reluctant to challenge the White House. But a year later Reaganomics was not doing the business its inventors had promised. Taxes had had to be raised, government spending was up, the economy had shrunk and 3m more people had joined the unemployment lines. In the mid-term elections in November 1982 the voters made their disappointment plain. The president retained control of the Senate, but 24 seats in the House and seven state governorships were lost: "They gave the president a rebuff, but had he been on the ballot they would probably have re-elected him. They gave no ringing endorsement to the Democrats."

It seemed a signal to him to be more flexible in his conservatism; when doctrinaire policies did not bring early success the public lost patience with them. But there was no turning to the Democrats' old policies and they ought to be worried: "He must still be disappointed that he has failed to infect America with the optimism he brought to office two years ago. The 1982 election seems not to be the second marker of a new era as much as a return to the confused, pessimistic politics of the past."

That was important to a man who had admired Roosevelt and had tried to emulate him in keeping open his personal line to the public, talking regularly on radio and using his television set-pieces to lift issues out of the other politicians' hands. But the paper felt he should not be despondent about a second term: "Viewed in the context of party politics, that may be considered good or bad, depending on your point of view. Viewed in the context of the presidency, it can only be good. The American electorate is not, after all, a praying mantis destined always to consume its chosen one after a single mating."

The president's natural allies, the blue-collar workers, many of them conservative by religion or ethnic origin, were not disaffected and would return: "The natural blue-collar attitude is (like Mr Reagan) to be against the handout aspects of the welfare state, and to be in favour (like Mr Reagan) of the family and neighbourhood values rather than an all-pervading government."

It was these voters who had developed a clear contempt for Carter's feebleness and irresolution. They responded to every sign of strong leadership in the White House: "Riven though America is over such questions as policy towards Russia or central America, each time the president campaigns for support on them he seems to get a bit or a lot of it. In the same way he seems to profit each time he socks it to congress for running an overspent budget for which Mr Reagan himself is at least as responsible as it is."

When 1984 arrived the paper's only worry was about the president's age: he would be nearly 78 at the end of a second term. Infirmity had played its part in dimming some reputations, and it wondered if Reagan might not be wise to recognise the danger: "By hanging on in old age, Mr Reagan might undermine his legacy more than if he leaves it persuasively behind him now."

There was little likelihood anyway of Reagan stepping down, and even less, in the paper's view, when the voters looked at the Democratic alternatives. It thought little of any of them. The obvious choice was the former vice-president, Walter Mondale, whom the paper thought worthy but a party man and tarred with Carter's brush: "He, in common with so many other Democrats, is unpersuasive as a deficit-cutter, productivity-raiser or economy-galvaniser."

It accepted the Reverend Jesse Jackson's assertion that it was not necessary to be a white man to survive the pace of a presidential race, but it was condescending about his contribution to the campaign: "the preacher-politician" interlacing his thoughts on issues "with breaks for chants, rhymes, folklore and unfunny jokes". When it was known that the eventual candidate, Mondale, was thinking of adding to his own charisma by selecting a woman vice-presidential candidate it declared there was no superwoman in the party but the possibles were "a fine bunch whom it should be nobody's business to patronise". When Mondale's choice fell on Geraldine Ferraro, a three-term congresswoman from Queens, New York, it was not exactly enthusiastic: "She is attractive, quick in mind and tongue, and a hard worker who is acceptable to women's groups but has placed herself in the disciplined mainstream of the party. Nobody's perfect and Mrs Ferraro has yet to learn of foreign policy."

It duly reported that Ferraro had failed to make full disclosure of her finances or adhere to the limit of $1,000 for legal individual contributions to her campaign funds. Further disclosures about the business dealings of her husband, John Zaccaro (he later pleaded guilty to falsifying figures on a property contract and an application for a loan), did not encourage further pioneering but ill-judged candidatures.

Free from worries about the women's vote, Reagan faced his final electoral trial by television in which the great communicator, for once, failed to satisfy the crit-

ics. This was news: "Time and again, since 1960, those in office have been found wanting as their failings were encapsulated by the clumsiness (Gerald Ford), or the whimsy (Jimmy Carter) or the five o'clock shadow (Richard Nixon) revealed on the screen.... On Sunday he looked, and sounded, a bit confused. Which he probably was: the White House explanation of his poor performance was not that the old slugger had tired but that he had been 'over-coached'—his head so filled with facts that he was unable to enjoy himself."

He recovered, of course, in the second encounter. The polls were unerringly for him. The paper recounted his achievements: "He has helped to persuade Americans that greater government spending is not the solution to all problems; no administration, Republican or Democratic, is likely soon to think it is. He has helped to promote an economic and fiscal climate in which entrepreneurs spring up like seedlings. He has pursued a foreign policy which has made the west's adversaries think twice before they do anything to affront the United States." Reagan won by the length of a street.

The victory ought to have cowed the Congress again, as in Reagan's early days, but it did not. He had ridden the trade cycle to success, his own success, but it did not pull the party along with him, just as Eisenhower's and Nixon's second sweeps had neither helped the Republican party nor their own prospects of organising the Congress their way. In retrospect, the paper blamed the man himself: "Had Mr Reagan been less interested in scoring a first by carrying every single state, he might have had time to campaign for more congressmen and so won a more pliant House of Representatives. More important, had he chosen to campaign not just on his record but on a programme, as he did in 1980, he could thereafter have claimed some degree of endorsement for his policies.... Instead, he steadfastly refused to commit himself to anything more explicit than 'You ain't seen nothin' yet'."

That was pertinent. By September 1987 the paper felt it right to set out what, beyond everyday party politics, was going wrong. America was sour, and the Reagan policies had not helped. First, his own state, California, on which so many hopes had depended: "For years, California has led America—not just in cults, riots, triple garages and topless shoeshines, but in scientific research, educational excellence and enlightened state government. At its apex, California's education is as sharp as ever. But lower down, it is suffering from the pinchpenny consequences of taxpayer revolts and the lacklustre outlook of those who run the Golden State. Proposition 13 and its 1979 successor, both limiting public spending, threaten to institutionalise mediocrity in state government."

So much for the birthplace of Reaganism. Second, the paper condemned American opinion's wish to withdraw from the world, to renounce two generations' effort to enthuse over internationalism: "This year has seen the 40th anniversary of the Marshall Plan, perhaps the greatest example of national generosity in history.... And America's lead in international affairs after the second world war was not confined to rebuilding Europe; it encompassed the setting up of the United Nations, NATO, the Bretton Woods monetary system and a network of alliances across the globe. For good reasons as well as bad, Americans are now more inclined to thumb their noses at internationalism."

Third, it discerned again what it had hoped had gone with Carter, a sense of reverting to defeatism, no longer on international authority or ranking, but on matters close to home: "This is true not just of drugs and crime, but of one problem in particular: poverty. After decades of experiment, more than 32m Americans, 13.6% of the population (and nearly 20% of children), still live below the poverty line. An underclass, isolated from mainstream America and stubbornly resistant to incorporation within it, is now accepted by many as a fact that society can hope only to recognise, not change."

Increasing America's pessimism had not been Reagan's objective.

His own well-wishers were feeling particularly let down. He had done what he had said he would do in international affairs and on the economy, but in social policy he had not attempted to give them what he had promised: "The true believers have been disappointed. They have not seen the social change they wanted; no big rolling-back of the preferment programmes for blacks and other minorities and women; no new opportunities for prayers in schools; no sweeping bans on abortion. Congress would not oblige and nor would the Supreme Court."

Presidents are said to use their appointments to the Supreme Court to ensure that their own concept of America survives and even prospers when they have left the White House. Reagan's first nomination to the court, Sandra Day O'Connor, the first woman member, had dissatisfied the Moral Majority who thought her unreliable on abortion. In 1987 he had the chance to satisfy them by submitting Robert Bork, a conservative intellectual. This was duly challenged. The paper thought Bork "a classy man, intelligent and scholarly", but it was not happy either: "Mr Bork interprets the constitution narrowly, determined not to read into it more than is there, or was intended by its authors. This is a defensible approach.... But Mr Bork has carried this challenge to an extreme: the rigour of his legal reasoning has landed him on the wrong side of every major ruling by the Supreme Court on civil-rights issues over the past quarter of a century."

The president stuck by his man, insisting that political bias was the only reason for the opposition, but he did not have the votes any more. It was a defeat; there followed a humiliation. It turned out that Bork's replacement, Douglas Ginsberg, despite his qualities, was known to have smoked marijuana in the past and he was disqualified too. The third choice, Anthony Kennedy, was found to be impeccable, but not the reactionary the diehards had wanted.

Few, if any, presidents, achieve all that they wanted; few, if any, end on the high note they would wish for themselves. It was Reagan's misfortune to spend much of his last two years not only conscious of deteriorating hopes but caught up in a tussle with Congress which threatened to diminish his own reputation calamitously. This was variously known as Irangate or the Iran-Contra affair.

THE TAMING OF THE SOVIET UNION
How Ronald Reagan dared to rearm
America—to the paper's great peace of mind—
and found everything going for him

The development of President Reagan's diplomatic policy from 1981 onwards was much in keeping with *The Economist*'s view of the world. The paper was indignant at America's missile inferiority, and welcomed his intention to rearm after the weakness of the Carter years. It was sceptical of the possibility of negotiation with the elderly Brezhnev. It saw no option but the installation of cruise missiles in western Europe, and had scant regard for the anti-American opposition to them.

However, it also sensed that the Soviet Union was beginning to run out of superpower resources and the initiatives it could afford, that it was virtually a satisfied power wishing to retain what it held and aware that its economy could gradually erode in a military spending competition. It did not expect the Soviet system to fall apart, nor did it see in Reagan's strategic defence initiative the instrument of communism's downfall. It came to recognise that Mikhail Gorbachev was a Soviet leader with a difference, but it expected him to negotiate throughout with an overriding policy of Soviet advantage, and it suspected tricks. It had no sympathy throughout the decade with what it thought were the illusions of most American and European liberal pursuers of detente or a nuclear freeze, far less of concessions to Soviet rapacity.

The paper began 1981 unhappy with the balance of forces in Europe. NATO could not hold the line conventionally, and the United States had lost its old nuclear superiority. The Americans no longer led in intercontinental missiles; in medium-range and battlefield ones the Russians were streets ahead. Cruise was not available yet: "Even NATO's new missiles-in-Europe plan, which will only half-solve the problem (if its opponents do not scupper it before the missiles are deployed), is more than two years away from starting."

Yet there were latent opportunities in Reagan's policy once his rearmament took effect and the vulnerability of the American counter-attack missiles sitting in their silos in mainland America was diminished: "Like a cold dawn, the realisation of what a Reagan administration means for Russia is slowly breaking over Moscow.... Mr Reagan is prepared to question the whole concept of what came to be called detente—the summitry, the SALT-2 treaty, the growth of east-west trade—and to take his time over the answers. Mr Brezhnev feels the chill but has to wait."

Reagan could find the resources for a renewed arms race: confidence in supply-side economics and a willingness, as it turned out, to run a substantial deficit saw to that. The Soviet economy could not: "The Soviet Union's GNP is little more than half of America's, but the Russians already spend 11-13% of theirs on defence. By 1986, even with President Reagan's new defence programme, America should still be spending little more than 7%. So Mr Brezhnev needs arms control."

In any future arms talks the paper much preferred the zero option: "The rule is that zero should mean zero for the same kinds of weapons on both sides; that, where exceptions are allowed, they should be equal exceptions for both sides; and that the net result should be as close to zero as possible."

The paper was distinctly unhappy at the signs of disagreement between the State Department and the Pentagon, and the welling-up among Reagan's Californians of the notion of forgetting Europe and disagreeable Europeans and concentrating on an American Pacific connection. Nor did it like the superior European way of deriding Reagan, the B-picture actor, and his objectives. By February 1982 it thought it time to examine the western alliance and diagnose its ailments as "a mid-Atlantic newspaper" (as it called itself) should.

The reality was that the United States and Europe needed each other when they looked at the Soviet Union. It was still armed to the teeth even if it might be decaying inside its armour. But Americans and Europeans had different styles and reactions: "When Americans are nervous, they tend to get pugnacious; they look for quick solutions to problems, and expect others to agree with them, and they prefer strength to subtlety. When Europeans are nervous, they slide towards caution, and call for patience and compromise. Neither reaction is necessarily superior to the other; the point is that they are different."

A first test of rival tempers came when the United States ordered west European firms not to supply turbines for the pipeline to carry Siberian natural gas westwards. This was resented by depressed engineering firms, especially as American farmers were allowed to sell 6m tonnes of grain to the Russians each year. The paper was derisive: "The governments of the United States and the European community are creating a fiasco about a pipeline from Siberia that must be amusing the ghosts of both Groucho and Karl Marx."

It was a sensible approach. Within three months Reagan had lifted the sanctions put on the European firms.

The paper continued to brood about the American strategic vulnerability to Soviet accurate, land-based intercontinental missiles. It did not consider the B-1 bomber an answer, nor the MX missiles in their dense-pack deployment. It welcomed the development of the Trident-2, said to have the precise accuracy to hit individual Soviet silos, so that the American deterrent could be moved gradually out to sea: "The objection to stopping MX is that it would be giving up something without obtaining a Russian concession in return. The obvious answer is to build more Trident-2 submarines. They would be both a better deterrent and a better bargaining chip."

It was taken, like everyone, wholly by surprise when Reagan went on television in March 1983 with a novel idea: "Mr Reagan appealed to the nation's scientists, some of whom he had invited to the White House, to undertake over the next two decades a search for a workable defence against nuclear missiles."

Initially the paper was wary. It thought Reagan was trying to recover some of the moral high ground lost when the Roman Catholic bishops joined the peace movement in opposing the deterrent. The anti-ballistic missile (ABM) treaty in 1972 had allowed both sides to deploy one ABM system, as the Russians had done, but scientists were sceptical about its efficacy: "The particle beams, microwaves and lasers mentioned by the president's advisers as possible means of destroying Soviet missiles go well beyond current ABM ideas. Scientists who have worked on ABMS dismiss some of the ideas out of hand, but they say that lasers might some day work as ABM weapons."

The elegant simplicity of the Reagan idea and its impact on the conservative minds in the Kremlin (Yuri Andropov, said to be the sharpest among them, was in charge at the time) had sunk in a week later. The Washington correspondent emphasised what had happened: "Mr Reagan's ability to cut through the worst-looking complications and come up with something attractively simple is often seen as one of his best qualities by Americans. Not by Mr Andropov. He called the anti-missile concept insane.... Russia would have to find ways to beat it to maintain military credibility."

Six months later the Russians weakened their standpoint further by shooting down Korean Air Lines flight 007 and trying, with the help of western sympathisers, to tough it out. The paper was hopeful: "There is a good chance that, because Russia has once again been unable to avoid showing what it is, Americans will be reinforced in their commitment to defence expenditure, to an active foreign policy to deter and contain Russian aims, and to arms-control deals with Russia based on realism, not hope."

Reagan spoke strongly about barbarism and savagery but his reactions were moderate: "Since his response in deeds to the Soviet act has fallen well short

of the severity of his words—he would more or less settle, it seems, for a genuine apology, compensation for the victims and guarantees that attacks on stray commercial flights will never recur—he has made himself immune to criticism from American moderates. Some of them in fact were initially yelling for more punitive action than he has judged wise."

The Reagan policies were showing results elsewhere. In November 1983 the first American cruise missile arrived in Europe, "and Europe," the paper declared, "is a slightly safer place as a result". Even his visit to Peking, largely irrelevant to his policy, turned out to his advantage because of Chinese clumsiness: "The smiles for Mr Reagan in Peking were genuine enough. They faded a little when, true to his principles, Mr Reagan slipped in some public remarks about God, democracy and the Russian threat, and, true to theirs, his hosts censored them."

In Moscow Andropov died and was succeeded by the ineffectual Konstantin Chernenko and his young lieutenant, Mikhail Gorbachev. The cruise missiles were set up in Britain and West Germany despite the socialist and pacifist protesters. The military balance was moving the West's way: "The resolute rearming of Mr Reagan, the new ebullience of America and last year's narrow victory by Europe's pro-missile-deployers over its anti-deployers have, between them, changed the terms of the argument. For the time being, Russia may have to accept that the bear can neither hibernate nor dominate."

The influence of Reagan's strategic defence initiative (SDI), or star wars, as it was easier, and more derisive, to call it, gladdened the paper's heart: "It was the announcement of the Strategic Defence Initiative that brought the Russians back to the negotiating table. The programme is also the best way of keeping them there, and getting them to accept lower levels of missile armament than they have so far been willing to contemplate. This is leverage, and public opinion in the west should welcome it."

The paper was dismissive of claims that the SDI might be beyond financing and technology. A missile-proof roof was one thing; a feasible defence of the strategic missile system was another: "A more modest version, protecting the American missile silos, is almost certainly workable. There is nothing wicked about the concept: an ability to ward off attacking missiles is a better form of deterrent than the threat to slaughter millions of Russians in retaliation."

The paper, inured to decades of the cold war, was mistrustful of the idea of a summit meeting between Reagan and the newly instated Gorbachev at Geneva in November 1985: "That President Reagan harbours any illusions about finding common ground with Mr Gorbachev does not seem likely. Nor is it apparent what, in the way of substance, he may hope to achieve by going to Geneva at all."

As for the consequences of SDI on Soviet defence, they were so threatening that the paper could not conceive of agreement: "The Russians would not only refuse to sign a missile-cutting agreement without some limits on SDI; they would be right to refuse."

Even so, it thought a deal could be done, a trifle artlessly: "Let Mr Reagan privately tell Mr Gorbachev that the Americans will commit themselves by treaty not to deploy an anti-missile system with less than, say, four years' notice, provided Russia in return drops the unreasonable conditions it has attached to a deep cut in missile numbers (its definition of 'strategic' missiles, its attempted monopoly of new missiles, and its reluctance to discuss equal megatonnage). The way could then be open to a serious negotiation."

It was sure that both Reagan and Gorbachev were being propelled to a meeting, and whatever it might bring, by economic forces. They both faced difficulties; they both had reason to try to capitalise on what they had: "The long Reagan boom is fading in America (though growth was still running at over 4% in the autumn), and budget-cutting may check the amount of money Mr Reagan can spend on star wars. But the wind blowing on Mr Gorbachev is much keener. He is already offering, to a Soviet people with a standard of life well below half of America's, an improvement of little more than 1% a year above recent performance in the rest of the century."

Reagan insisted on personal conversation, on talking about aims and objectives, on making it clear to Gorbachev what he intended to happen. He had his way: "The week since his first summit meeting with Mr Mikhail Gorbachev has seen a welcome dent kicked into the ignorance about what this long-thinking American president is actually about; in Europe where, for the umpteenth time, underestimation of Mr Reagan was proved gorgeously wrong; and in the mind of Mr Gorbachev, who returned to Moscow obviously perplexed by an American president so singularly unsci-

entific in his mastery of detail but so clear, unbudgeable and somehow reasonable in his strategic aim."

European condescension was not stilled, it never was, but the negotiating process was going on and was getting somewhere. This was not what the liberals and pacifists had predicted: "The doomsters' predictions that Mr Reagan's renunciation of SALT-2 would ruin the negotiation has proved spectacularly wrong. Since then, the Russians have offered better terms on star wars, on medium-range missiles, on the what-counts-where question and ... on chemical weapons too. The threat of a new arms race implicit in the abandonment of SALT may or may not have caused these concessions, but it did not prevent them."

The paper was rather doubtful about the Reagan-Gorbachev meeting arranged for Reykjavik, Iceland, in October 1986. Negotiations on arms control bored the public and it paid scant attention: "When the two great leaders meet at the summit, however, the effect is that of a large whisky: a warm glow, a relaxed feeling, a tendency to put the slippers on. Look, the superpowers are getting on fine with each other, there's no need to worry. This is often inconvenient for the West."

The failure did not worry it much, despite the instinctive media reaction to blame Reagan for not conceding on SDI. Europeans had not been persuaded that it was worth losing an agreement on nuclear weapons, but the loss was not disastrous: "If Mr Gorbachev returns to the search for a deal with America ... he knows that he can at least delay the arrival of the anti-missile era, and so spread out the extra spending these weapons require. He is likelier to stick to this sensible line if people in America and Western Europe do not let themselves be panicked by the failure in Reykjavik. And public opinion in the West will be less likely to panic if the Reagan administration will at last explain what the point of the Strategic Defence Initiative is."

What was possible was that if the SDI stopped a third or a even a quarter of the incoming missiles it would start to change the whole uncomfortable theory of deterrence. That was worthwhile. Nor was Reagan behaving precipitately: "Mr Reagan has said he will not deploy anti-missile weapons for ten years, and he can probably be persuaded not to manufacture any during that time (if they can be manufactured at all); but he will insist on doing a certain amount of testing.... Hints are already coming from Moscow that a deal on this can be worked out."

By early 1987 the concession came from Moscow: Gorbachev accepted what the paper called a semi-denuclearised continent of Europe. This was widely represented in the media as a Soviet offer. *The Economist* was not going to allow that: "Most of them seem to think that this happy possibility is the result of a 'Gorbachev initiative'; whereas in fact the zero-option proposal that Mr Gorbachev embraced on February 28th was put forward by Mr Ronald Reagan in 1981."

It meant a substantial NATO success. The Soviet missile superiority secured by the arrival of the SS-20s in central Europe had been met by the counter-deployment of the cruise forces. Now Gorbachev was admitting it. When the Washington summit to confirm the arms cuts was being arranged the paper said it was satisfied, provided the agreements served the West's interests. It felt sure that Gorbachev was prompted by economic pressure. He wanted to give the Soviet Union a necessary, and unpopular, jolt of market forces. The Americans were satisfied that they should let him try: "The United States has been carried as far as it is likely to be by the Reagan resurgence of military spending and American assertiveness.... Now is the time for America to start enjoying the fruits of what it worked for in the earlier Reagan years."

The summit agreed to the abolition of shorter-range missiles within 18 months, and medium-range ones in two phases over three years. In total, 859 American and 1,752 Soviet weapons were to be dismantled. It was greeted on both sides as a great success, a sign of the new relationship, although the paper felt it was not unanimous: "Outside Washington, the enthusiasm was less extravagant."

The doubters may have agreed with an earlier Reagan that the Soviet Union was an evil empire. Looking ahead, the paper advised against an "amateurishly hasty agreement" on long-range weapons. It still disliked the concentration of diplomatic effort on missiles: "The current preoccupation with arms control ... tends to obscure the many other big issues in relations between communist East and pluralist West: Afghanistan; Nicaragua; the Gulf; Kampuchea: human rights, you name it. Arms control is widely seen as the factor which dominates all the rest, and can miraculously pull them along with it. It is the other way round: they are the horse, arms control is the cart." It was a turning-point.

The paper's judgment on the Reagan years was not unjust: "For leading the advance, Mr Reagan deserves much credit. So does Mr Mikhail Gorbachev, for leading the retreat. Mr Reagan did not invent Mr Gorbachev, but he did create the right incentives for Mr Gorbachev to invent himself."

HOW TO DEAL WITH THE BRITS
The Falklands, Grenada, Qaddafi: what a superpower learns to do

The three critical moments in the Anglo-American connection during the Reagan years—the Falklands war, the invasion of Grenada and the bombing of Tripoli—were resolved as *The Economist* wished and had advocated. This was not done without grave doubts, uncertainties and divergences among the politicians. The paper's part, on both sides of the Atlantic, was its customary one: to explain, ameliorate and persuade, but also to give clear and consistent advice. Twice, on Grenada and the Libya bombing, it was not popular advice in Britain. On the Falklands it was not popular with a significant section of American opinion.

The paper appreciated from the outset that the Reagan administration itself was divided and unclear about what it should do when the British task force sailed from Portsmouth towards the South Atlantic in April 1982. Whatever the instinctive personal sympathies for Britain, the policy pressed strongly and persistently by the ambassador to the United Nations, Jeane Kirkpatrick, emphasised the necessity of conforming to South American sympathies. The paper believed that in the negotiating for a peaceful settlement American influence would be paramount: "It will argue that concession by Argentina will threaten President Galtieri's government and that the most likely alternative after so many failed generals in office will be a return of the Peronistas, possibly looking to Russia for succour. To such arguments Britain should not bend. The incentive will then be the greater for the United States to push Argentina towards compromise."

It also recognised that Britain would have to pay a price for assistance of any kind to the task force: "The Americans may extract a price from Britain for any logistic or other support they give to its fleet—requests, for example, that Britain should re-examine its naval cuts. This pressure Britain need not resist. It would strengthen the alliance."

The paper advanced all the arguments of a smaller power, uncertain then of the precise capability of its forces. It was political blackmail: "Under this or any future British government, have-it-both-ways irresolution on the part of the United States will lose Britain's popular support for America's nuclear policies and deployment, and for its European, its NATO and its Soviet policies. The tendencies towards neutralism in west Germany and the low countries, and towards belligerent abstention from the alliance in France, will be vindicated."

It was very much the test for the paper's own arguments for the alliance over the years. Even when the president and official policy were known to have decided the British way, even when British troops were on shore in East Falkland, it sensed there were still serious American doubts. It declared at the end of May: "The United States should recognise that it would lose more friends than it would gain by equivocation."

It repeated its admonition: "In Britain and elsewhere in western Europe the damage could be very large. There, American ambivalence would be a signal that the United States was a fair-weather friend whose commitment to a European ally fighting a difficult war for a principle the United States shares could be tailored to mere tactical convenience. This would undermine the Atlantic alliance and give proof to many in Europe (there are, at the moment, relatively few in Britain) who believe that the right path between the United States and the Soviet Union is unarmed neutrality."

The paper, like the remainder of Britain, was unaware then of the full extent of the American logistical help, which proved decisive. When the campaign was over and the islands had been recovered, it was still unforgiving: "Of Britain's NATO allies, only four, France, Greece, Canada and Norway, backed Britain's 8,000-mile expedition with steady conviction. West Germany backed it wearily, the United States tardily."

It had been doubtful of the connection for a moment, and its tone was reproving: "The United States will have, as time goes by, many chances to twist Britain's arm. It will be right to do that.... It will be wrong, however, if it yet again prefers the very American desire to be liked to its much greater need to be respected."

It was an inaccurate criticism. The paper pursued the Falklands issues with as many participants as it could. In November 1983 it got the views of Sir Nicholas Henderson, who had been ambassador in Washington during the weeks of the crisis. He believed the Argentines should have accepted the proposals offered them before the fighting started. He believed the sinking of the Argentine cruiser *Belgrano* had not thwarted any such negotiations. He was definite about the value of American support: "American support was not something that was inevitable: it could not have been taken for granted and could have been lost at any time had we shown complete intransigence in negotiation." He gave credit to Reagan and to Alexander Haig, when Haig had been convinced that the Argentines were not negotiating seriously.

Within three months the paper had been given an account of the Falklands which clearly indicated that the campaign, whatever anyone else said, had been a victory for the defence secretary, Caspar Weinberger, and the US navy, besides those who had actually fought. From the start, theirs had had to be a secret war: "Given the Reagan administration's carefully nurtured rapprochement with Latin America, there was a clear foreign policy motive for neutrality—overriding any historical special relationship with Britain. Any military help had to be in defiance of this policy."

This help was extensive: missiles, particularly the Sidewinders, fuel and the Ascension fuelling bridge, and especially communications. The Americans were even persuaded to move the orbit of a military satellite watching the Soviet Union to cover the Falklands. None of this could have been done without the political backing that mattered: "It was in effect Mr Weinberger's own foreign policy, and it was strongly conditioned by his concern at the consequences of a British failure."

Weinberger was more than anglophile, he was concerned about the military effectiveness and morale of NATO and the other alliances. Had the British force sustained a calamitous loss, like the sinking of either of the aircraft carriers *Hermes* and *Invincible*, he was prepared to offer an immediate replacement, however impracticable it might seem: "It was proposed that an amphibious assault ship of about the same size, USS *Guam*, with capacity to handle helicopters and Harriers would simply be turned over to the Royal Navy. Given the political explosion this would have caused both in Latin America and from the war's opponents in Washington, the ship would have had to be staffed entirely by British sailors, only a handful of whom would have seen such a ship, a risky and bizarre idea."

The paper's conclusion was candid: "Not for the first time, America was trapped by the obligations of superpower status. Britain's military victory that June was not a particular triumph for any special relationship. It merely showed how easily America's allies can involve it in conflicts not of its own choosing."

The British task force had been ordered to sail without consulting Washington. Not all that much had changed since Suez.

When American forces landed in the east Caribbean island of Grenada in October 1983 to expel the government, they did so without notifying, far less consulting, No. 10 Downing Street. The Thatcher government dissociated itself from the invasion: the French and others in Europe condemned it. The paper was unimpressed by the anti-American abuse, or by the intelligentsia's refusal to accept that there was any incipient danger to democracy: "If, as the Americans have promised, the invasion enables the Grenadians to restore their democratic institutions and freely choose who shall govern them, that will provide a stronger justification than is likely to be found in any other quarter. It may also make some of this week's shouting sound far too shrill."

Official Britain was vexed that it had not been told and that, unlike six small Caribbean states, it was not invited to join in, even though Grenada was a Commonwealth country. The paper was not bothered; what it thought more important was the warning it gave to putative communist satellites: "If they cannot fear the certainty of brutal retaliation, then the adversaries of the west should live in a state of uncertainty, even anxiety, as to whether and where America and its allies are going to topple undemocratic dictators (of left or right) or resist communist—or merely illegal—expansion. This sense of uncertainty needs to be periodically nourished by unpredictable actions such as that in Grenada."

The controversy quickly hardened the paper's opinion that Reagan was right, and his critics were merely ineffectual in their notions of how the world worked: "Only one form of deterrence does not work, and that is the one that Europe's intellectual demi-monde and America's decent liberal tradition constantly wish on the United States: the absolute, destructive certainty

that America will do either nothing or the decent thing—clothed, it goes without saying, in resolutions of the United Nations or whatever other cloak for inaction is to hand."

Americans were puzzled for months afterwards at Mrs Thatcher's continuing, particular and lasting exception to the invasion. Her popularity in the United States had been based precisely on her willingness to act and take risks in the democratic cause. They did not believe her assertions that the invasion had been an insult to the queen, or had let the Russians off the Afghanistan hook; they put it down to pique. The paper did not dissent. The so-called relationship did not matter anyway. America's casualness towards Britain was simply a function of overwhelming American power in the hemisphere: "Superpowers do not need allies, only cheerleaders."

It saw a cheerless future for British pretensions, especially if and when American attention turned away from NATO and its purposes: "Britain treated Washington, during both the Falklands and the Grenada crises, with a spirited independence. It was largely bravado. American foreign policy-makers are increasingly gazing south and east, away from Europe. When they can no longer be bothered to consult their friends, it is the friends who need to worry."

The paper did not hesitate, though others did, to support the American bombing of Libya in retaliation for terrorist attacks over the years. The aircraft took off from bases in Britain in April 1986. The raid was condemned almost universally on television and in the newspapers; only three governments, those of Britain, Canada and Israel, supported the United States. Even Mrs Thatcher had been reluctant to give the planes permission to go, and did so chiefly to show adherence to the Atlantic alliance. The paper was clear: "A government's first duty is to protect the lives of its citizens, and the evidence has damningly piled up over the years that Mr Qaddafi has paid for, housed, trained and directed terrorists whose business it is to murder Americans (and Europeans)."

True to its conviction that retaliation was the one way to deter errant governments and instil uncertainty and fear into their calculations, it approved the message that had been delivered in Tripoli: "The physical safety of the West ten years from now depends on its setting clear rules today which tell state backers of terrorism that they will be stopped."

It believed Qaddafi would take the meaning: "better behaviour by Libya is not out of the question". But if he did not he would need to be visited again: "Unless this week's bombing causes him to stop sponsoring terrorism, the time will come when it will be right to use more force and, if necessary, to overthrow him."

It suggested a start could be made by mining Libya's oil-exporting ports. This sense of purpose was contrary to most British opinion; from Washington the paper reported that "most Americans loved it". The frustration that had been building up since the slaughter of the marines in Beirut had suddenly been released and, up to a point, endorsement was widespread. The doubters were worried about the Libyan casualties, and among the doubters, it said, was America's "softhearted president (who is better equipped to accept anonymous distress than individual sad stories)". This insight into Reagan's feelings was not shared by the critics. The paper understood that many Americans had been disappointed by the lack of what they thought should be a proper gratitude in Europe. It spelled the realities of life out again: "The Americans are not just the people who have twice this century marched into Europe to end its civil wars (in their own interest, to be sure, but also to the huge relief of most Europeans). They are also the people without whom today Europe would not be within a mile of a balance of power against Russia, either nuclear or non-nuclear. In an ideal world, gentlemen would not mention that. In the real world the Americans inhabit, they do."

Europe could not replace the Americans if the Americans went home: not in NATO manpower, not in nuclear weapons, not in reinforcements, not in money. In truth, "Europe needs the help of sensible Americans, because it needs America." It was convinced that there was an increasingly broad spectrum of American opinion which was tired of European thanklessness, broader than Europeans supposed. Americans had the "to-hell-with-it" feeling as well and sensible policy-makers knew it: "They know that the popular pressures that would say 'sod 'em' to ungrateful Europeans can also be found among bright young men in right-wing think-tanks, who ask, in these budget-clipping days, why a Western Europe that is richer and more technologically advanced than Russia should depend on America for its defence."

At least nothing more was heard from Libya for an appropriate time.

THE TOILS OF IRANGATE
What a superpower should never be caught doing

The first word about the United States breaking its own previous rule and paying a ransom to Iran for the release of the remaining American hostages in Lebanon came in November 1986, just as the administration was losing control of the Senate in the mid-term elections. *The Economist* did not like the sound of it at all. It went directly against everything it had said about hostage-taking in the Middle East; it also happened to be against the Thatcher government's consistent policy. The paper tried to put the best face on it that it could. It would make sense, it thought, if the Americans put it this way: "Yes, we have decided to supply arms to the Iranians because we believe it is in our interest to use this method of influencing the shape of the Iranian regime that will follow Ayatollah Khomeini's death."

Then came the tricky bit: "But we also have a duty to try to release our hostages in Lebanon. We are not swapping the hostages for weapons; we are making a release of the hostages a condition for giving Iran the weapons it needs, something we wanted to do anyway to create a friendlier future Iran."

The paper's Washington correspondent was not concerned to offer ideas on a cover-up: "The White House protests that its covert dealings with Iran were neither illegal nor immoral. Hard to be sure about that, until the administration reveals what precisely those dealings were."

The more that emerged, the worse it looked for Reagan. By the end of the month the scales had fallen from the paper's eyes: "The comparisons with Lincoln and Roosevelt suddenly seem phoney. Hostage-dealing with Iran has echoes of Carter, secret bank accounts stir memories of Nixon. The president whose simple charm and simpler views worked magic to make America stand tall is now caught looking muddled and shifty."

The Washington man said he was not imputing "self-serving illegality" to the president but he was no less scathing: "Call it a scandal, a crisis or merely a mess, the hostage-ransoming, money-laundering arms trade with Iran now ranks among the great presidential follies of modern times."

That profits from the arms sales had been siphoned

off to help the Contras in Nicaragua might have seemed ingenious, but nothing could have been better calculated to rile the Congress that had insisted on cutting the Contras' aid. Some show of contrition from the White House was necessary: "President Reagan is not under pressure to admit to breaking the law, hazy as he seems to be about what it requires of him. An admission of error about his arms-for-hostages policy is the priority.... If the Reagan presidency is to be restored, the bond with the people needs to be repaired. That means admitting that mistakes were made, and reassuring them that laws are not there for presidents or their subordinates to break."

When the Tower report on the imbroglio came out in March 1987, four months after the scandal first broke, Reagan had to admit that it was indeed an arms-for-hostages deal. It was a test of dexterity: "His speechwriter, who had the exacting task of squaring this admission with the president's earlier statements to the contrary, without confessing to a lie, reconciled the irreconcilable with wondrous subtlety."

It was, of course, far from the end of the affair. In July the remarkable Lieutenant-Colonel Oliver North gave his testimony to Congress's interrogators and to the whole of the country on television. North's display of patriotic commitment was a bravado effort but the

Oliver tells them. Accused for his part in the Iran-Contra affair, Lieut-Colonel Oliver North told his congressional interrogators persistently that he had only done his duty.

The paper was clear that it was the president's personal fault, however much or little it turned out that he knew. He was 76. The only charitable explanations were laziness or ignorance: "Mr Reagan thought, because he was so popular, that he could ignore the need to account to Congress. He may have been lulled into thinking that he would simply dispatch servants to do his bidding, explicit or implicit, across the world."

paper was not impressed. What North's account amounted to, it said, was to aver that the end justifies the means. There was more to the United States than that: "The American way of putting a legal check on the powerful has led to better government, freer people, greater prosperity than any yet known to man. Even as the United States fetes a new television star, this old truth is the main lesson to be drawn from the Iran-contra affair. The congressmen and the lawyers may be fat and verbose; but the system they are operating, to seek out the truth, is the real hero of this extraordinary hour."

The details of the testimony pointed, the paper thought, to nothing less than a conspiracy to act outside the authority and workings of the proper government, and to do so systematically: "A tight handful of Mr Reagan's advisers, suspicious even of their colleagues, had been exploring the possibility of a free-wheeling covert operation, built on the Iran-contra foundations but stretching beyond. This self-sustaining off-the-shelf slush fund for secret activities ... would have been outside the framework of government, far beyond any notion of accountability."

It was not until the Bush presidency in 1989 that the affair was effectively ended by George Bush's own intervention to save North from going to jail. As North had got Reagan off the hook the paper assumed that this was the pay-off. It had been an elaborate and skilful business: "It now appears beyond question that Mr Reagan knew all about efforts to help the contras—indeed, that most of his administration, possibly not even excepting the upright Mr George Shultz, was up to its neck in knowing. What emerges is a saga of cover-ups and half-dissemblings on a Watergate scale, but so nicely timed that nobody of note will get hurt."

The misdirection was adroit: "Not only the press but two investigating committees were inveigled by the administration—indeed, steered—on to the wrong trail. They decided that the relatively minor diversion of Iranian arms money to the contras, and whether Mr Reagan knew about that single detail, was what they were mainly concerned with. Conveniently, it seems that Mr Reagan really did not know about that."

That outcome, in fact, was what most Americans had come to want. They liked Reagan and did not wish to see his presidency end in ignominy. Many, right up to the end, did not believe he had done anything blameworthy.

SORTING OUT CENTRAL AMERICA
Did the Reagan line work? The paper thought
it would. But was it worth it anyway?

The confused, and confusing, struggle for influence in Central America found *The Economist* persisting in its advocacy of a firm line against communist coups and infiltration. It did not like many of America's clients and friends but thought that wherever they could show more than a semblance of democratic support they were preferable to guerrillas, however fashionable the insurgent causes might be in Europe. President Reagan's advent was therefore welcome, and the paper hastened forward with its advice: "American arms will be required in El Salvador and Guatemala if Cuban or other outside support tilts the wars there revolution's way. If the Cubans sent in ground troops, President Reagan should jog his Latin American neighbours into joining an inter-American force to help the Salvadoreans, or find a way of cutting off Cuba's ability to export revolution."

Nor did it think Nicaragua, in the Sandinists' hands, was wholly lost; there was work for pro-American partisans to do: "In revolutionary Nicaragua, the Americans might legitimately help local fighters for democracy to resist the imposition of a collectivist dictatorship there; but they should not send soldiers in unless the Cubans do."

This caution was wise. However, the American reputation among liberal reporters and commentators was almost beyond recovery. The paper had to insist that the United States was "a belated do-gooder, not a bloodthirsty meddler". It was sure the rebels in El Salvador lacked popular support and survived on the arms channelled there from eastern Europe, Vietnam and Ethiopia, mostly through Cuba and Nicaragua: "The United States would be supine indeed if it refused to arm its friends, albeit unattractive, against an even more unpopular bunch brandishing Russian-supplied weapons."

The test was a democratic one: the willingness to hold popular, plausibly clean elections and hold them regularly. It was not an easy test to apply, but it should be attempted: "The United States should be prepared to live peacefully alongside a southern neighbour whose people have chosen socialism, just as the Soviet Union should let live a western neighbour whose people have chosen a form of pluralism. But the United States is under no obligation to watch Russia and Cuba help an election-rejecting minority impose its will upon the rest of the population." The paper felt that applied to Nicaragua.

For the remainder of the decade it settled down to monitor how its rules worked out. Elections, difficult as they were to hold, were never exactly reliable in allowing the paper's favoured parties to win. In March 1982 El Salvador voted, throwing out President Napoleon Duarte's passable Christian Democrat government and giving a clear majority to the hard-featured right. It was inconvenient: "The United States loaded, primed and fired El Salvador's election.... It went off with a splendid roar. El Salvador has never had a more popular election. But the relief that the election did not turn out a dud is now being tempered by the realisation that it hit the wrong target."

The paper was the more anxious to have the arms conduit through Nicaragua cut, so that the Salvadorean army could cope with the guerrillas and Reagan could distance himself from "the unsavoury far right". However, when the guerrillas said they would talk about a cease-fire if they could be left in control of a strip of "liberated" territory, the paper would have nothing to do with it: "Partition of a country the size of Wales is unrealistic, and would give the guerrillas time to dig in and reinforce themselves for the next offensive. Another guerrilla suggestion—that they be given a share in the government—is equally unacceptable. The United States is trying to push El Salvador towards democracy, not towards power-sharing at the point of a gun."

It had even fewer hopes of Nicaragua that summer, where the Sandinists were "digging themselves in against the sullen resentment of many of their people". Their methods were thorough: "The Sandinist apparatus of 'people's' army, 'people's' militias and neighbourhood spies, copied from Cuba, will be hard to dislodge. With success there so unlikely, President Reagan should be careful not to let his support of 'our' guerrillas in Nicaragua confuse congress into denying aid for the fight against 'their' guerrillas in El Salvador."

By March 1984 it was the actual turnout in the presidential election in El Salvador as much as the result which showed how weak the insurgents were, and how justified American patience had been. To critical outsiders the first round seemed a shambles, but the people there were determined to vote, whatever the difficulties put in their path: "Many waited for hours, or tramped from polling station to polling station. The 65–70% turnout was not bad at all, considering the difficulties involved. In the United States, only around half the voters usually cast votes, even in presidential elections."

Duarte had taken 43% and duly won the run-off; the

right wing Roberto d'Aubuisson took 29%. It seemed as if El Salvador was on a hopeful road. Nicaragua was finding it harder. In April 1985 the paper returned to the pro-Contra argument: "The contras deserve help because they are trying to hold the Sandinists to their 1979 promise of replacing Somoza's tyranny with a pluralist democracy, and because their struggle helps to dissuade the Sandinists from promoting anti-democratic revolution in El Salvador and elsewhere.... American meddling in El Salvador to ensure that Mr Duarte held the furies of the far right at bay has been correctly, if belatedly, applauded."

It was one thing to argue that the Contras were useful in preventing the Sandinists from taking the final steps to state control of industry and the imprisonment of free-thinkers; it was another to persuade Congress that the Contras had played a part in changing Central America from the mess it had been five years before. The House was suspicious; it had been disconcerted to learn that the CIA had been organising mine-laying off Nicaragua's harbours. Congress was uncertain in its own mind: "It does not really know whether the Sandinists are enough of a threat to their own people, or to the rest of Central America, to warrant sponsoring a war against them; but if it does not keep the contras alive now it may, if things go badly, have no instrument short of its own army to put a stop to the advance of communism in Central America."

The revelation that money paid by the Iranians was being used to supply the Contras pushed congressional support down to a new low. The policy seemed doomed to be abandoned when in March 1988 the Sandinists became overconfident and invaded Honduras to try to destroy the Contras' arms supplies. This promptly brought 3,200 American troops down to confront them, and it angered the Congress. The paper felt encouraged: "The United States has to do two things. The first is to give consistent backing to the contras until the Sandinists are either forced out or forced to be the pluralists they do not want to be. The second is to recognise that even Mr Gorbachev's Russia is happy to finance Marxist revolutionaries until the United States shows it will not work. A big stick still helps to keep the peace."

It turned out to be the paper's last effort to push that policy. By November, and Bush's election, it recognised that the Reagan military pressure was deemed to have failed: Congress had cut off the military aid and would not resume it; the new policy to be followed depended on the conciliatory efforts of President Oscar Arias of Costa Rica. American aid might play a part; the Nicaraguans were increasingly impoverished and friendless: "Until the Sandinists prove their willingness to tolerate dissent and move to regular free elections, they deserve no help. But the United States could propose an end to its trade embargo, and a renewal of international loans, in return for a precise and supervised programme of Nicaraguan democratisation. It might not work, but it is better than doing nothing."

The paper seemed discouraged. It had reason to be. The Central Americans insisted on pleasing themselves. By March 1989 another election in El Salvador brought Roberto d'Aubuisson and his Arena Party back to power: a reign of right-wing terror was expected. The paper declared the election had "far too much killing and not nearly enough voting", partly because of the continuing efforts of the communists. It now disparaged American aid: "The economic results of its efforts have been feeble. Some $3.7 billion over nine years have made the tiny country not a whit better off: natural disasters and terrorism have kept Salvadorans as poor as their Nicaraguan neighbours, ruled by the incompetent Sandinists whom the Americans despise."

Despised or not, the Sandinists had survived. Seven months into his presidency Bush was taking the credit for having extricated the United States from the imbroglio: "He may have shared Mr Reagan's visceral support for the contra rebels, but that became more of a cause than a policy once it was clear he could not persuade Congress to help them."

Things duly began to go from bad to worse again in El Salvador. A sudden left-wing uprising was beaten back but left its mark throughout the country. Uniformed men, believed to be from the president's Arena Party, murdered six professor-priests at the Jesuit university: "The country's present real rulers have spurned the conditions the Americans sought to impose. If the United States wishes its terms to be taken seriously on other occasions, it has no choice now but to withdraw its patronage."

The paper's new policy seemed to be a washing of hands: "One great lesson of post-colonial times is that people dominated from outside do not learn to govern by themselves. It is time to let the Salvadorans make their mistakes unaided."

The Bush administration had had its eye on General Manuel Noriega in Panama. Noriega, a former American client, was an illegal ruler wanted for trial on drug-dealing charges in Florida. An attempted coup against him in October 1989 was bungled and Bush himself was accused of succumbing to overcaution. This embarrassment was mastered by Christmas when American troops were sent in: "The strike was surgical but the knife was not quite sharp enough. Yet, if Panama were to be invaded, Christmas 1989 was the perfect moment. The attack could be legally justified, with a reasonably straight face. It released swelling American frustration with a tiresome foreign despot and, much less, an over-prudent president."

A legal reason made the timing vital. On New Year's Day the United States had to hand over to Panama the preponderant share of control over the Panama Canal and the military bases around it, and it was not going to hand it to an illegal regime run by a crook. Noriega was eventually found and rounded up, but not before the world had enjoyed some broad comedy at the American military's expense. The paper certainly found it funny: "The Pentagon is treating Panama as a playground in which to practise its new arts—high tech and low farce, and not much in between."

The clinching surprise came in 1990. The Sandinists in Nicaragua, having been persuaded to call an election and having persuaded themselves and their foreign sympathisers that they would win it, contrived to lose it to Violeta Chamorro's underestimated United National Opposition: "With luck, Sandinism can now pass peacefully into history as a mutant of communism, less virulent than most but no more satisfactory as a means of running society."

The paper, carefully, did not determine where the credit lay.

REAGANOMICS: PROMISE AND PERFORMANCE

Supply-side economics, tax cutting, the Reaganauts' programme ended up in massive deficit financing

The Reaganauts set off on their voyage of economic discovery in 1981 brimful of confidence and ideas. They ended it eight years later in many ways sadder and wiser. A great deal was expected of them at the outset to restore America's fortunes, as Reagan the candidate had promised. *The Economist* was guarded. The economic record was not greatly encouraging: "The brave American clout of which he dreams was created by a small lead in productivity growth in the Grant-to-Truman years, and it has been eroding in a big relative productivity lag in the Eisenhower-to-Carter ones. There is likely to be a crash during the Reagan presidency unless he changes economic policy in some of the ways he says he will."

The budget director, David Stockman, won the paper's early approval by envisaging $54 billion of tax cuts: "It is a measure of the intellectual disarray in the Democratic party these days that it has stumbled back towards the orthodox economics of Herbert Hoover, while allowing the Republicans to don the tax-cutting mantle of John Kennedy."

Carter had certainly mistimed his pre-election boom. He left a legacy of 12% inflation and a productivity rise of around nought. By contrast, as early as the end of May Reaganomics seemed to be paying off: "Ronald Reagan swept into the White House forecasting 4% economic growth by 1982 and a decline in American inflation to 5% by 1986 even with no direct restraints on wages or prices. His critics sneered that a promise of faster growth with slower inflation was 'novel and controversial', but the president has had the first laugh. He has overachieved each of these long-term objectives within four months."

That was when Reagan could do no wrong. By the end of the year things were not so bright. Recession, with high interest rates, was still the problem. The Federal Reserve had not been enamoured of the new policy: "The battle between the Reagan administration's optimistic supply-siders and the Volcker Fed's sound-money men could ... have been settled in a way that rang true on Wall Street. The administration might have trimmed its planned budget deficit for fiscal 1982, the Fed might have slackened the monetary reins a fraction—and interest rates could then have come down without a massacre."

At the centre of the battleground was Stockman, an intelligent, hard-working young conservative from Michigan who had given up his seat in Congress to take charge of the Reagan effort to reform and reduce the federal budget. The scheme was not going as well as he had hoped: "The move involved an intellectual transition by which he accepted along with his own budget-cutting principle the supply-side theory of fiscal policy, according to which large cuts in direct taxes

will so stimulate the economy that public revenue will actually increase."

He had not reckoned on the natural instincts of congressmen of both parties: "So Mr Stockman soon saw the attempt to use the tax cut with discrimination for economic effect swamped in a wave of greed (his word). His programme of spending cuts, by contrast, tended naturally to wither, every attempt at a real cut producing an equal and opposite reaction."

The traditionalists on Wall Street, used to America's 40 years of effortless superiority, did not take to the new approach, even though it was the policy of a Republican president: "Because Wall Street is mesmerised by the government's growing fiscal deficit (even though it will be equivalent this year to only about 3% of American GNP), interest rates are rising at a time when the economy is in full recession."

Reagan pushed ahead. The budget for fiscal 1983 cut programmes for the poor and unemployed by 14% and federal government purchases, including the civil service's payroll, by 12%. No new taxes were proposed, but collection was tightened up. It got the thumbs-down: "So long as Wall Street believes that big deficits will lead to higher inflation and higher interest rates in the years to come, there will be higher interest rates in the here and now."

The test in Washington was to see which side was going to blink first. The president and his men were determined not to: "President Reagan has convinced himself that his deficit is a chance not to be missed to force Democrat congressmen to cut spending. The thousands of Republicans on Wall Street and in corporate boardrooms, who would raise taxes now to reduce the deficit, are becoming inconvenient allies to the Democrats."

The paper fathomed the strategy, but while Reagan had won much of the argument it thought him too doctrinaire: "That defence spending should be increased is scarcely challenged nowadays; the question is by how much. Similarly, that non-defence spending should be controlled is widely accepted; the question is how. But the president must also take the blame for the size of the current recession; it is a direct consequence of his belief that it is possible simultaneously to cut taxes, increase defence spending and balance the federal budget. Mr Reagan's stubbornness in persistence in this belief could yet undo his presidency."

By the end of August 1982 the president had to admit to defeat, or at least to compromise. He agreed to two bills: to increase the revenue by some $98 billion over three years; and to reduce spending by some $31 billion in the same time. Whatever sound financiers thought it put the congressional Republicans in a spin: "It was the tax increases that set Mr Reagan's party in an uproar. They went flat against the theory which he first chose as his economic doctrine. They flouted another principle long cherished by Mr Reagan, that government needs to be cut down to size by being starved of money."

Paul Volcker, the Fed's chairman, had, in fact, already altered his policy. He had changed, as the paper put it, from tough to permissive monetarism. The effects began to show sooner, it seemed, than was comfortable politically if not economically. Four months later in July 1983 the paper became nervous over the figures coming in showing what had happened over the previous year: "The narrow M1 money supply has increased by 13.3% while the federal budget deficit is running at a record 6½% of gross national product. Reaganomics in the past year has been more reflationarily Keynesian than was Franklin Roosevelt's New Deal."

By November the reflation was fully visible: "America's gross national product has grown in real terms at an annual rate of 6% in the first nine months of this year. Consumer prices have risen at only 4%. Some 2.8m more Americans have got jobs. On Wall Street, the Dow Jones industrial average has risen from below 800 to over 1,200 in the past 15 months."

It was a political gamble and it worked.

The president's overwhelming victory in November 1984 emboldened the paper to suppose he might do something about the trade deficit. It would not be popular but he no longer needed popularity: "He could ask Congress to impose a federal tax of 30 cents on a gallon of petrol (gasoline) and one of 20 cents on cheaper diesel and promise two more such increases in the next two years."

It was one of those political improbabilities but the paper insisted it made sense: "The federal government could therefore raise an extra $37 billion a year.... Repeated for three years in a row, and assuming no change in fuel consumption, the taxes would eventually be bringing in about $110 billion a year. That is more than any of the deficit-cutting schemes now being proposed in Washington."

The paper opened 1985 with a warning. Something had to give: "The United States is borrowing heavily from abroad and running down its overseas assets. This year it will become—or may already be—a net debtor for the first time since 1918. It would not be able to borrow so easily and cheaply unless lenders thought the dollar was going to rise. Once they think it will fall, higher interest rates will be needed to persuade them to keep lending to America."

It was Stockman who gave way first. He said he was not fooled by supply-side economics any more. If spending were not cut, taxes must rise. He had his list of politically improbable cuts to hand: "The more sacred the cow, the more gleefully he brandished his axe. Shut down Amtrak, the subsidised rail network, immediately. Let the farmers go bust. Cut social security. There was an outburst of senatorial fury after he told a congressional committee that, in his experience, the top brass at the Pentagon were always ready to sacrifice national security if that was the only way to protect military pensions."

The administration's inability or unwillingness to cut the deficit brought Congress back into play. The Gramm-Rudman Act, passed in December, was meant to bring financial discipline to their discussions with the executive on pain of it being done for them automatically. Budgets would be cut, however crudely, to end the federal deficit by 1991: "The Gramm-Rudman legislation is one of the most desperate acts ever to have come out of Washington. It is like a girl who can't say no, so she puts on a chastity belt and throws away the key."

The paper was convinced that the Reagan administration had virtually abandoned monetarism by now, even though it had cut inflation from 14% to 4% in six years. What cheered it up by July 1986 were the indications that the administration meant to carry through a radical reform of the tax system, simplifying rates, ending "the lobby-driven system" of investment and other tax credits, and closing loopholes and wangles: "A tax revolution is about to stalk through the West because politicians in America have suddenly seen that the money wasted by these systems can be redistributed in more popular as well as clearly more efficient ways."

Its enthusiasm was persuasive: "Because so much money can be saved by closing such loopholes, America seems quite likely to emerge with only two federal income-tax rates called 15% and 27%, although phase-out complications may mean that the top marginal rate is around 32% really. Whatever happens, the world's wealthiest country will then have the industrial world's lowest top tax rate."

Corporation tax, it thought, would be cut from 46% to 33% or 36%. Encouraged by this realism, it insisted that what America thought difficult was indeed relatively easy. Tax hikes and spending cuts amounting to no more than 3% of present plans would end the deficit difficulty: "It defies belief that the world may have a trade war—and thus a slump—because the political leaders of a great and free country are incapable of making a 3% shift in their plans."

It was pleased to see American companies slimming down their staff, learning more about foreign markets and improving the quality of their design: "Too many American companies are still determinedly turning out goods that look as though they were designed in the 1960s, and probably were."

They would go on looking that way if the appeals for protection were listened to. But Reagan had to do what only he could: "In most circumstances, Mr Reagan's aversion to raising taxes is simple: higher taxes can often make it easier for an irresponsible Congress to spend more. But not in this case. His willingness to put the no-tax-hike principle to one side would open the door for the budget deficit to shrink faster (which he says he wants)—not just because higher revenues will cut the deficit directly, but also because that tactical withdrawal would strip Congress of its last excuse for doing so little to cut spending."

The president was not anxious to oblige. By June 1987 the decision he had to take was whether or not to continue with Volcker as chairman of the Fed. Alan Greenspan got the job. The paper naturally told him what it wanted him to do; he must cut the budget deficit: "Mr Greenspan's role is to lash Congress and the White House when they make their excuses for failing to, and to make it clear that he will not allow a collapsing dollar followed by higher inflation to take the strain of their fiscal recklessness."

Warnings and worries duly came true. In October Black Monday hit Wall Street and stockmarkets around the world. The paper's instant view was that it was because the deficit had not been tackled, the central banks had run out of money to support the dollar, and now private investors insisted they would need a good

old capitalist incentive to buy more dollar assets. The central bankers' decision at a meeting in Paris that the dollar had actually fallen far enough had not helped: "To America's policy-makers, that insistence translated into a choice between lowering the dollar again or raising interest rates. Since the tryst at the Louvre had ruled out a lower dollar, higher interest rates it had to be."

That was what set it off: "It was not long before American investors started fearing that dearer money would push the economy into recession. When, last week, the trade figures for August appeared to suggest that the deficit would never come down, fear turned to panic: if the Fed was going to support the dollar at this level, interest rates would have to go higher, the threat of recession would grow, and profits would then start to shrink.... Crash."

When the official report, the Brady report, came out in January 1988 there was another factor to emphasise, "the shortcomings of the financial fad of the moment", as the paper put it, "portfolio insurance": "The report establishes beyond doubt that a cluster of powerful investment funds were relying upon a computerised hocus-pocus that promised, in effect, to relieve them profitably of their stock without a buyer being in sight. These 'insured' funds dropped the equivalent of almost $30 billion of shares onto the market only to find that their benefactor in the futures market wasn't there."

That was technology. But the paper thought the report wrong in trying to hark back to old trading practices: "Nostalgia for a golden age of calm share markets is understandable but fruitless. When markets are close to a turning point, share prices often move abruptly, and new technologies of information and trading have merely exaggerated this trait."

In January 1989 the paper considered Greenspan's contribution to Black Monday, and what he had learned from it. Volcker's successor had to be clearly against inflation: "He needed to prove his hatred to the world, so one of his early decisions was to raise the discount rate. Sixteen months later, all the members of that overcrowded club, the Hindsight Forecasters, agree that the rise in the discount rate tipped an overvalued stock market into the plunge of October 1987. For Mr Greenspan inflation has become a scourge to be hunted with stealth."

Back in 1987 the paper did not look for much from the "dilly-dallying" over the federal budget; a November summit between the White House and Congress produced an "underwhelming" solution. It was plainly designed "not to ensure prosperity but re-electability in 1988". In fact, the paper suggested, the dollar was now recovering at last. Compared with 1985 the labour costs of American manufacturing were below those of the Germans and on a par with the Japanese. However, as always when a currency was on the run, recovery was late and slow to be recognised. It would, of course, help Bush, but the paper did not think anything of the budget that emerged in December. It had "the usual missed opportunities (no extra taxes on petrol or pensions) and conjurer's sleights of hand (one-off asset sales, phoney extra revenues)".

It was simply the child of indecision and cowardice: "The best informed, best staffed, best educated politicians in the world are, it seems, either ignorant of the need to react decisively to events or practically powerless to do so."

FALLING OUT WITH JAPAN
Faltering America, having picked a scapegoat
for its worries, set out on a pointless vendetta

Main Street America's growing economic nervousness in the Reagan and Bush years set off a national search for a scapegoat. It did not last long. Japan was nominated and promptly adopted. The Japanese were capturing American markets, cutting American profits and costing Americans their jobs. It was not, the story went, because they were efficient and hard-working, but because they did not trade fairly; their own market was closed to competition. The cries for protection and retaliation were lengthy and loud. *The Economist* was scornful but it was also worried. The last thing the democratic, industrialised world needed was the mutilation of a trade war between its two strongest economies. It was appalled by the language of politicians who, it thought, ought to know better: "The Democrats used to be the free-trading party. Yet both Mr Ted Kennedy and Mr Walter Mondale are spouting rhetoric against Japanese goods that approaches the verge of racism."

The automobile industry and its union workers were at one in their demands: "The campaign has developed into base sloganeering at times. In Detroit, bumper stickers commanding drivers to 'Remember Pearl Harbor' are the rage. At UAW headquarters, peo-

ple insensitive enough to drive imported cars are not allowed to park in the official lot."

There were millions of insensitive buyers. The mounting trade deficit, naturally, was blamed less on them than on discriminatory Japanese practice. The administration was exhorted to do something about it: "Any honest president will have to report that Japan is playing fair. Its tariffs are low and its non-tariff barriers are mostly cultural—a Japanese preference for Japanese goods that international rules will not change. Unfortunately, any such truthful presidential response could provoke congress to demand the toughest protectionism: a 25% tax on imports from Japan."

The paper felt it was time to read Americans a lecture: "Truman's and Eisenhower's America was a pioneer of free trade, ranting against countries that discriminated against its imports. That ranting served everybody well. Between 1948 and 1973, real gross world product grew by 5% a year, world trade by 7% and America's gross national product by 4%. That period of ever-freer trade helped the United States become the world's first trillion-dollar-a-year economy, benefiting from imports because the most efficiently produced goods and services create new markets and free capital to be invested elsewhere."

What mattered, it believed, was not so much the size of Japan's countervailing surplus to America's deficit as the way it was used: "Protectionism against Japan is the least efficient way of curbing that surplus; it cuts everybody's real income by increasing everybody's inflation, and might quickly cause Japanese institutions to stop lending so much money to a falling-dollar America. If they do stop, America's interest rates will rise and America's trade deficit will be 'cured' by recession."

By early 1988 the paper felt it right to assert that Japanese-American tensions were those of a growing intimacy, not a breakdown: "The surprise is that they are not worse, Japan and America are running the most unbalanced bilateral trade account the world has ever known." It had amounted to $60 billion in the first ten months of 1987. But then it was an unusual relationship in every way. The United States spent 7% of its GNP on defence, a fair amount of it on defending Japan. The Japanese spent 1.5% of their GNP on defence, all of it on themselves: "America and Japan are strenuously competitive economic great powers, one of which (Japan) may by the end of the century be ahead of the other in both economic and technological strength but which nonetheless depends absolutely on the other for its military security."

The paper accepted that there was a danger of mutual incomprehension because the two did not share the common cultural heritage that helped Americans and Europeans to understand each other even when they were quarrelling. But they did share values and interests that made them natural allies: "Both are strenuously capitalist, both are devoted to success.... Their interests are so congruent as to be identical. Both countries have a huge stake in the free-trading system. Both want the free market principle of economic organisation to spread. Both are antagonistic to any geopolitical advance by Russia."

It thought that, among the answers to the problem, the yen should become a reserve currency, Japan should become more prominent in the IMF and the World Bank, and it should become a leading economic and financial patron of the developing countries. The essence remained the retention of the free-trade system. It was assumed in the General Agreement on Tariffs and Trade that governments did believe in it, even though they faced political difficulties in bringing it about. However, when Bush entered the White House in 1989 the paper was not at all sure what he stood for: "The Bush administration, despite its avowals to the contrary, evidently does not believe in free trade.... Whereas the GATT approach, at worst, tolerates the present level of protection, Mr Bush is teaching his electorate that protection confers an economic advantage; unless the foreigners restrain themselves, he will make sure America has a lot more."

Americans and Japanese were not fated to hate each other, but it was right to recognise that there were cultural differences. Some of them, however, rankled: "To Americans, the obsession with racial purity, contempt for foreigners, sexism and conformity of life in Japan are repellent. To Japanese, the self-righteous obsession with 'rights', the disorder, the profligacy and the self-indulgence of Americans are just as bad."

If the Americans were really worried about their trade deficit the solution was in their own hands: "The real problem is that Americans spend more than they save and that most American companies do not make things that Japanese consumers want: try fitting the average American fridge into a Tokyo kitchen or driving an Oldsmobile around Japan's narrow streets. Over the past three years Japan's imports of manufac-

tures have soared by 30% a year; America's share of those imports has slumped from over one-third to one-quarter."

The Americans had to be reminded that Japan's economy was barely half the size of America's. Americans had an average income 7% higher than that of their nearest large rivals who were not the Japanese but the Canadians, who were accepting free trade: "As for Japan's legendary productivity, it has indeed been growing faster than America's. But the average Japanese worker still takes one hour to produce what his American counterpart can rattle off in just 31 minutes."

By preaching the free-trade doctrine, and by trying to talk up American self-confidence, the paper plainly believed the argument could be swung decisively its way. No line of reasoning, no helpful insult was ignored. When the Japanese stockmarket slumped by more than 23% it drew the convenient moral: "For an economy that is supposedly manipulated to make it impervious to market forces, Japan has moved remarkably rapidly from joy to gloom."

When the day of the 50th anniversary of the Japanese attack on Pearl Harbor approached the paper was ready to sermonise: "What both ought to want most is the rescue of multilateral free trade from the dangers of trading blocs, quotas and the other wealth-destroying apparatus of control now closing in on it."

The old champion of free trade in one group of industrial islands, anxious to keep the United States in the system, knew the script: "The free-trade system brought Japan its post-war miracle. It also allowed ... the near doubling (unprecedented for a rich country) of America's manufactured exports in the years 1986–91 from what was already the highest level of manufactured exports in the world."

The paper simply thought it ludicrous that Bush should take the trouble to go to Japan, with American auto manufacturers in his train, to complain about Japan's closed markets in the reality of 1992. It thought few ambassadors could be less persuasive: "Many are yesterday's men, such as Lee Iacocca of Chrysler, from yesterday's companies (the other two heads of Detroit's Big Three are also present). Most pay themselves munificently—on average, six times more than their Japanese equivalents and 100-plus times more than their own employees—come good times or bad."

If Japan's surplus were to be challenged it should be done properly: in the market itself.

THE AGE OF AIDS

And of much else

Among events and matters that caught *The Economist*'s attention in the 1980s were the following, thought worthy of a report or a sermon.

Discovering Aids   The first considered mention of AIDS was in October 1982 in an article on sexual diseases, especially genital herpes, which continued: "And, worse though much rarer, a lethal disease of obscure origin that causes its victims' immune systems to fail and strikes most heavily at promiscuous homosexual men. It is called acquired immune deficiency syndrome (AIDS).

"AIDS seems to have been around only since about 1978. By September 22nd the Centers for Disease Control had counted 608 cases of it in America: there are about two new cases each day.

"Most of the sufferers, 457 at last count, have been young homosexual or bisexual men (another name for the disease is Grid, ie, gay-related immune deficiency). This may be a statistical oddity, as the number of reported cases rises, the proportion of heterosexuals increases and is now 20%, up from 5% earlier this year.

"Most doctors studying the disease think it is caused by a new virus, or a new type of old virus, and that it is probably sexually transmitted (though among heterosexuals intravenous drug users seem to be most affected).

"It is hard to know whether the sexual behaviour of young Americans is actually changing because of this; but there is certainly much more anxiety than there was only a year or two ago."

The paper took the problem seriously and reported regularly. Typical coverage (from September 1985) included concern about prejudice: "The fearfulness of this plague is beyond question. To begin with, it is a death sentence. At the last count 13,074 American cases of AIDS had been reported; of these half are now dead and the rest are dying. No cure or vaccine is in sight, and the numbers, in the United States, double each year. Further, the people dead or dying of AIDS are the tip of an epidemic iceberg: underneath are up to 1m people who carry the AIDS virus, some of whom may, after an unknown period of incubation, develop the disease and all of whom may, according to the Centers for Disease Control, be rather more contagious than the

disease sufferers."

The carriers, it said, "are not, the alarm of parents notwithstanding, all that contagious. The virus is not airborne and has never been passed on by ordinary social contact".

Dealing with insiders   Insider dealing in the markets and the exploits of Ivan Boesky provoked another address from the pulpit in November 1986: "What matters is the gut instincts of millions of ordinary people whose savings fuel the markets and whose votes can turf out of office politicians who favour free markets and private property. People who are lucky enough to live in capitalist democracies can easily forget that open markets and property rights have been the exception in man's history. They are there conditionally, the main condition being that they are seen to serve the interests of the many, not the greed of the few."

Their kind of gospel   The ambitious plans of Jim and Tammy Bakker of PTL (Praise the Lord) television near Charlotte, North Carolina, to build a "Christian Disneyland" were covered in October 1985. Their theme park was to have kiddies' rides such as "The Shipwreck of the Apostle Paul" and "Jonah in the Belly of the Whale" besides the existing attractions: "The resort has a luxurious 504-room hotel, camping grounds, restaurants, an enclosed shopping mall, a theatre, three swimming pools (used for weekly baptisms as well as splashing), lakes for boating, a miniature golf course, floodlit tennis courts and a roller-skating rink.

"The ministry facilities include a home for unmarried mothers, a licensed adoption agency, a halfway house for newly-released prisoners, centres for daily Bible seminars and marriage counselling, and an Upper Room, a supposedly exact replica of the room where Christ conducted the Last Supper."

The paper reported that whenever money ran short Bakker merely went on air declaring that he needed another miracle and donations poured in. PTL itself had just been saved by such a marvel. But there seemed to be a few dissenters: "Some viewers express dismay that during last year's money crisis Jim and Tammy bought a holiday home in Palm Springs for $449,000, a Mercedes-Benz and an antique Rolls-Royce costing about $100,000. During the current crisis, PTL officials announced that they were beginning renovations of the Bakkers' house near Charlotte, bought by PTL for

$340,000 in 1981."

Dutifully the paper stayed in touch with the story, and was rewarded in March 1987: "Mr Bakker resigned from the whole enterprise and his membership of the Assemblies of God (the Pentecostal sect that ordained him), confessing that he had been 'betrayed' into a 'sexual encounter' with a young woman, Miss Jessica Hahn, seven years ago and had since succumbed to blackmail."

Persevering, it was there for the dénouement too; it reported in October 1989: "'I have sinned,' said Mr James Bakker, as he stood before stern Judge Robert Potter convicted of defrauding his television flock of millions of dollars. The judge, known as 'Maximum Bob', sentenced him to 45 years in prison (he will be eligible for parole after ten years) and fined him $500,000."

Rake-offs, OK Wholesale wrongdoing in the state of Oklahoma came to the paper's attention in November 1981 when the Inland Revenue Service employed a Mrs Dorothy Griffin, "just a dumb old country woman standing out here in my bare feet", to get to work with a bugging device. "Little that happens down the farm roads of Oklahoma has ever hit the national headlines; in truth, there is not much to tell. Occasionally a bridge falls down, or a pick-up truck founders up to its axles in mud. Whenever this happens, the county commissioner in charge of the subdivision takes in bids for road repairs, concrete, asphalt and timber. His office requires him to take the bid that is 'lowest and best'; but since a low bid cannot ipso facto be a good one, he takes, naturally, the highest. When the supplier delivers, the commissioner also takes a little rake-off of about 10%. Nothing wrong with that; as one commissioner has explained, 'If the supplier wants to share it with you and you don't take it, he keeps it all.' He certainly does.

"Most Oklahomans are only now realising that this system, as painless and regular to them as the sun coming up in the morning, is considered an offence by the federal government.

"Fifty-seven commissioners in 29 counties were

Unbanning the Beach Boys. The inoffensive rock group found themselves in the limelight when told they were not wholesome enough to play at the White House. Two fans, name of Reagan and Bush, then rallied round.

caught in that particular net. Since then the haul has multiplied. No fewer than 120 of Oklahoma's 231 county commissioners have now pleaded guilty to taking kickbacks; their misdemeanours account for $25m in misspent funds."

Conservative groupies Culture invaded politics in Washington in April 1983: "A nice little storm has blown up ... over whether the Beach Boys, whose surfin' sound is approaching respectable middle age, should be invited by the administration to perform on the Washington Mall on the Fourth of July. The Beach Boys count as hard rock to Mr James Watt, the secretary of the interior. 'We're trying to have an impact for wholesomeness,' he explained to the press, and told them that the Las Vegas lounge lizard Mr Wayne Newton (of 'Red Roses for a Blue Lady') would be invited instead.

"But President Reagan overruled him at once. He likes the Beach Boys. His wife thinks they are 'fine upstanding people'. The vice-president, Mr George Bush, counts them as friends; they gave a fund-raising concert for him when he was running for president. This makes the Beach Boys almost presidential protégés, along with such Reagan stalwarts as Frank Sinatra, Pat Boone, Donny and Marie Osmond and other far-west conservative crooners."

Afternoon torpor The sporting prowess or, more often, lack of it in the Chicago Cubs baseball team caught the paper's eye in October 1984 as the season reached its climax in excitement that rarely reached the Cubs. Players and supporters shared a bond of mutual despair: "The arena for their commiseration is Chicago's Wrigley Field, an antique vine-draped stadium which alone in major league baseball spurns artificial lighting that would allow evening games.

"Wrigley Field has been called a cross between a temple and a torture chamber. Its afternoon congregation consists mainly of Chicagoans stricken by unemployment or sloth. Their fidelity has always been heavily laced with scorn, which caused one tormented Cubs manager of the past, his logic deserting him, to denounce them as lazy bums who had nothing better to do than waste an afternoon watching the Cubs. The last time the club won the World Series was in 1908; the last time it even qualified to take part in this summit battle against the champions of the rival American League was in 1945, a couple of months after Hiroshima. The Cubs have been waiting for the earth to move ever since."

On Champ's pond And the brute creation found its way into the pages too. In July 1981 the paper gave an update on Champ, and his mysterious survival: "Somewhere in the 400-foot depths of Lake Champlain, the 100-mile long lake which separates Vermont and New York, lives Champ, America's answer to the Loch Ness Monster. First sighted by Samuel de Champlain, the French explorer who discovered the lake in 1609, Champ has since been seen on more than 100 occasions: by fishermen, a county sheriff, a school principal, a newspaper publisher and many tourists, most of them sober. The latest sightings were in April and May, 1981.

"The monster, described by de Champlain as a serpent-like creature with the thickness of a barrel, is assumed to be male. He is 15–30 feet long and allegedly good natured, although his sudden appearance did scatter a United States Canoe Association flotilla in 1892.

"Zoologists suggest that Champ may be a zeuglodon, a snake-like ancestor of whales which inhabited the Louisiana swamps until 25m–30m years ago. How he got to New England is not known."

The brief triumph of George Bush. Bush presided over the collapse of the Soviet empire and threw Iraq's Saddam Hussein out of Kuwait. But he chose to know nothing about the economy and lost the voters.

15

THE HARD-UP SUPERPOWER

1989–1993

THE JITTERY PRESIDENT

*The paper did not know what he was about
from the beginning. The less he said about
economics, the better*

The conservative, internationalist Republican wave
that carried Ronald Reagan to the presidency and sustained him there had enough momentum to make
George Bush his successor. But it was an uncertain
country that voted for him. Bush had to run America
without his own party controlling either the Senate or
the House of Representatives. His success was eminently unconvincing. *The Economist* thought the 1988
campaign "brought new depth to the meaning of shal-
low" and the outcome "more of a mudslide than a
landslide". From the beginning it was doubtful about
what Bush stood for: "He has given few signs of thinking deeply, let alone thinking hard, about the great
questions of governance. Mr Bush entered politics, at
best, out of a sense of noblesse oblige; at worst, out of
the kind of empty ambition that leads somebody to
run for president of his high-school class."

It suspected he knew nothing about finance and
would not be the man to rectify the deficit financing
Reagan had bequeathed to him. He had assiduously
told the electorate: "Read my lips; no new taxes." The
paper thought him foolish, "unilaterally disarming
himself in the greatest battle he may have to fight". It
believed the best advice he could be given was to leave
it to the chairman of the Fed and the professionals to
keep him out of trouble.

He had promised to be the "education president".
But the small print in his first budget showed him
proposing to spend less than Reagan in real terms. He
encouraged the Poles to strike away from communism
but he could only offer them $119m over several years:
"the deficit still meant he could not afford it". Unlike
Reagan he was poor at handling Congress and the
Democrats saw no reason why they should help him
to keep his tax promise. By June 1990 he was forced to
make his U-turn: "President Bush took the inevitable
plunge. After meeting congressional leaders from both
parties, he issued a statement saying that a budget
package needed to include domestic and defence
spending cuts; reforms in budget procedure; and 'tax
revenue increases'."

CHRONOLOGY

1989	George Bush becomes president
	Exxon Valdez pollution in Alaska
	Thrift industry crisis
	Contras in Honduras to be disbanded
	Tiananmen Square crackdown in Peking
	Berlin wall pulled down
1990	General Noriega captured in Panama
	Sandinists defeated in Nicaraguan election
	Bush agrees to increased taxes
	Unification of Germany

	Iraq invades Kuwait
1991	Saddam Hussein's forces defeated
	Mikhail Gorbachev arrested; the coup fails; Boris Yeltsin takes over Russia
1992	Bush attacks Japanese protected market; taken ill at banquet
	Civil wars in Yugoslavia
	War in El Salvador ends
	Los Angeles riots after policemen acquitted
	Bill Clinton elected president

Even so, the paper thought he would not be hurt too much politically because the American public had not really believed him anyway: "by three to one they have consistently said they expected he would break his pledge". Shortly thereafter they had something else to think about. Saddam Hussein invaded Kuwait. Even the budget, when produced, was not fearsome. There was a rise, though smaller than first proposed, in petrol taxes and top-rate income tax went up from 28% to 31%; there was even a smaller bite than expected out of Medicare.

The paper accepted that he was a prudent man: that he had served his time diligently and successfully in the oil industry, in politics, as an ambassador and in the Reagan administration. He was adaptable and flexible, a man accustomed to compromise. But he was not the leader that Americans, sensing and exaggerating wherever they were no longer effortlessly superior in the world, seemed to need: "Mr Bush's central problem is that, for many in America, the times do not call for such cool common sense. This is not just because there is a recession. It is much more because Americans know in their bones that an era has ended. The old enemy is dead, the old certainties of the cold war lie shattered. The easy hegemony and easy wealth which Americans came to regard as their birthright are gone for good, as they were bound to go one day."

If too many Americans were becoming paranoid, however, Bush seemed to be among them. By early January 1992 the paper thought his re-election was "by no means a sure thing", something the primaries duly began to confirm. The trip to Japan with the Detroit industrialists was a disaster at more than the dinner-table: "America needs a president who can respond to misguided gloom with calm proposals to promote long-term growth. Instead it has Mr Bush, who has surrendered to panic and is making things worse."

It thought his package for fiscal 1993 was "a wimp of a budget" dominated by electioneering gimmickry. It recognised in him a man who largely deserved "the gratitude of the rest of the world for managing an internationally difficult time", but who did not have the courage to stick his neck out in giving domestic leadership and, were he to be given a second term, "will, in the end, neither deserve nor win gratitude at home". Although the economy had actually begun to recover, the second term never looked like being given—and was withheld.

INTERNATIONAL MANAGEMENT
Dealing with the dwindling Soviet Union was easy; Saddam Hussein was tougher than it seemed afterwards

Bush the international manager had begun well. It was not, of course, an especially difficult start. It was more a lap of honour for what the Reagan administration had achieved. When Bush met Mikhail Gorbachev at a floating summit in the Mediterranean *The Economist* was suitably approving: "Having ended the cold war over a weekend in a Maltese storm, President Bush can bask in his popularity for a while."

He was not tempted to throw money in the direction of the struggling Soviet economy, even if there were money to throw. He was not the man to call American troops home from western Europe; America had, the paper said, "woven itself into the fabric of European stability". He found it easier than Reagan did to accept that Congress had shut down the Contra rebels in Nicaragua. The individual test for Bush himself came in the Gulf in August 1990. The paper saw it as an opportunity: "The ending of the cold war has left America not in the position of a diminished superpower but with its freedom of regional manoeuvre greatly enhanced."

That was the assumption. It was not, at first, widely shared in Washington. To evict the Iraqis from Kuwait, by force if necessary, was not instantly popular, especially in the Senate. The paper had no doubts: "Fear, cynicism, greed: they make a powerful case for appeasement. The big job for the western powers is to recall for themselves the lesson of the 1930s, and to persuade the other Arabs of it too. In the long run, appeasing a dictator is far more dangerous than standing up to him."

It believed that to keep Saddam Hussein's ambitions in check he must not only be prised out of Kuwait, he must be visibly defeated there. If it came to a choice between fudge without war and victory with war "Mr Bush should go to war". When Bush and Margaret Thatcher met at the Woody Creek summit in Colorado, the paper accepted the American insistence that he had not needed her hectoring: "Americans present at the meeting deny that Mrs Thatcher needed to stiffen Mr Bush's spine over Iraq; they insist the president's steely determination in this matter has not been sufficiently understood."

Subsequently, the paper concluded that Bush's decision to risk war and then wage it "was not so much the hallmark of his presidency as an aberration in it". In deserting his natural caution and his instinct to search for compromise he was, it thought, responding to the same principle he had once obeyed as a young pilot in the Pacific war: "a moral responsibility to deter aggression". The paper approved: "George Bush offers the world its one chance of bringing to an early end a dangerous prospect—that a military machine, which other countries foolishly built, run by a man of proven ruthlessness, will refuel itself with Kuwaiti oil, and launch a series of invasions culminating in an Arab-

ambassador in Baghdad, who appeared to be out of her diplomatic depth in her interview with Saddam Hussein: "Ms Glaspie knew the threat of invasion was still there. Even so, she—that is, the United States—did not warn the Iraqi president of what could happen, and has, if he put it into effect: that America would send a mighty army ready to hit back."

That army would take some time to assemble. While everyone waited, the paper's concern was to contradict the several arguments of the compromisers. The United States was making a fuss, it was said, only because of the oil industry: "Oil is not just any commodity, it is the fuel on which every country's hopes for growth and

Stormin' Norman's war. General Schwarzkopf commanded the allied forces in the Gulf in the expulsion of the Iraqis. The paper thought it "horribly one-sided, which is excellent".

Israeli war."

It disregarded everyone who thought differently: "The weasel chorus has already begun. Mr Edward Heath, a former prime minister of Britain, says that Mr Hussein is no Hitler, and should therefore be allowed to hold on to some if not all of his ill-gotten gains. Kuwait, say America's new isolationists, was a faraway country about which Americans should care little."

It derided April Glaspie, the luckless American

prosperity rest."

Kuwait, it was said, was not much of a country to go to war over. It was feudal, avaricious, intractable over women's rights and penal reform, and the reverse of democratic: "Kuwait was no democracy. But by the standards of the Arab world it was a decent place, tolerantly run, with a freeish press and livelier politics than any Mr Hussein would ever countenance."

By January 1991, as Bush's deadline approached and

the Iraqi Republican Guard showed no sign of moving out, the paper reiterated that Saddam Hussein must not be allowed to stay in even a part of Kuwait or to turn the international debate into one on the Israeli occupation of Arab Palestine: "It would be a tragic error to buy this man out of Kuwait by awarding him the starring role in Arab dealings with Israel."

That applied especially to Kennedy-inspired efforts to allow nothing to be done until a further six months of economic sanctions were applied, and the effects evaluated. All the paper would countenance was a strict application of the United Nations requirement that military action should be confined to securing the liberation of Kuwait. "Letting Mr Hussein stay in power after leaving Kuwait may stick in the throat, but it would be a lesser evil" to turning the war to free Kuwait into one to subjugate Iraq: "When the war is over, the West cannot impose peace, order and democracy at the point of a gun. That is colonialism, and it doesn't work."

It was a spirited thing to say before the start of the land war, for which there had been many forecasts of high allied casualties which western opinion might soon find unacceptable. Others were to contest its wisdom—once the fighting was over. For this campaign the pacifists and protesters were numerous (100,000 outside the White House, 50,000 in San Francisco) but mannerly; the paper was able to be indulgent: "The protesters now take pains to show their love of country. So many flags were held aloft on Pennsylvania Avenue that the Washington demo could almost have been mistaken for an Independence Day parade. The troops are not reviled as baby-killers; the enemy's leader is not honoured; the war is portrayed as a mistake, not a crime."

When the land fighting began it lasted 100 hours: "It all seems horribly one-sided, which is excellent."

While Bush and his people began to talk of ushering in a new world order, however, the paper was more impressed by how difficult and exceptional it had been to put the operation together at all: "America could not possibly have blockaded Iraq, let alone fought it, without the wide support of allies. It could not have won the support of its own Senate without the sanction of the UN Security Council. That sanction could not have been won without the assent of the Soviet Union. The United States could barely have afforded the battle without plentiful free oil, yen and D-marks."

To beat a country of the status of Portugal the United States had had to deploy 75% of its tactical aircraft and 40% of its tanks. The country was still in recession; the government was still borrowing nearly 6% of GNP to fund its budget. It was all a long way from a world order: "In such conditions, illusions of omnipotence will not persist."

Whether or not the United States had a moral imperative to help the Russian people, as liberals demanded, or ought to act in sheer self-interest, the paper doubted if the last superpower could muster the resources to do so. The total figure of Marshall aid delivered to western Europe by 1950 had been $12.5 billion, worth $70 billion in 1991 terms; that had been 4.4% of American GDP, or only 1.5% of 1991's GDP: "But America's public finances have since been transformed for the worse. The Truman administration was able to finance the Marshall plan without running a budget deficit. For the Bush administration, finding $70 billion would mean a gross expansion of the budget deficit, which is unthinkable."

Compassionate Americans, however, had no call to be embarrassed. The effort would not be worth it because it would not work: "The Marshall plan worked because it helped to repair a West Europe-wide economic system that was horribly damaged, but had worked in the past…. The Soviet Union does not have a workable economic system. It has therefore excluded itself from world trade. It has never had world-class industries, which could be revived and integrated into the world economy. Unlike Western Europe 44 years ago, it has to change itself fundamentally before it can be helped."

Nor was Mr Gorbachev the right man to help. He had not changed Russia's politics and economics "radically enough to create a better life for the people who live in it". His usefulness to the West "is getting steadily smaller, and will soon no longer justify any attempt at closed eyes". If the United States government could not pay its way, neither could too many of the country's small banks. Their mounting deficits overhung the industry, or rather, overhung the minds of the taxpayers who understood the massive bill they would have to settle one day. The extravagances and the incompetence, to put it mildly, of the savings and loan ("thrift") industry had become a national scandal by the time Bush entered the White House.

THE WORRIES OF DECADENCE
How the victors of the cold war found themselves with new problems: the banks, the environment. And old ones: the blacks, health, poverty. And worries about worries

The paper had long thought that the system of federal insurance of thrift deposits was an unequal bargain. The private owners of the thrifts could follow their own investment policy, taking foolhardy risks in search of profit, and the taxpayers could only lose. The Bush plan would cost $285 billion over 30 years: "This is only the cost of paying back depositors and paying the interest on bonds. And it assumes that things do not get worse."

A year later, in 1990, the thrifts were back again. The problem of deposit insurance was causing worse headaches: "The Treasury is rightly alarmed by the contingent liability posed by the $2.9 trillion of insured deposits in America's banks and thrifts, plus about a further $1 trillion on uninsured deposits at America's banks."

The moral hazard in deposit insurance had not been tackled yet. It was the continuing story: "Because taxpayers foot the bill for losses, depositors do not stay away from cavalier banks. If a deal pays off, banks keep the profit; if it fails horribly, the helping hand is there. Deregulation has increased the range of risks that banks can take. The result is systematic financial rot, and loss of control by the Fed."

The paper believed the limit on federally insured deposits should be lowered from $100,000 to $30,000. It agreed with the Bush proposals to restore banks' profits by letting them spread their risks geographically, by getting rid of the barriers to interstate banking, and by letting them into other business such as securities. Excess capital needed to be stripped out by mergers; if not, bank failures would do it: "The truth is painful, and plain: most banks are sick. New competition has eaten away at commercial banks' businesses, pushing them to take bigger risks in the vain hope of profit. Banks now account for less than one-third of all financial assets held by American financial institutions. They are short on capital, long on red ink."

Rediscovering class The problems of poverty and race persisted. There were still many winners on the escalators of class and desegregation, but the plight of the losers seemed to be getting worse. The paper thought the numbers were grim in 1990: "Blacks are over twice as likely as whites to be jobless. The median black family income is 56% of a white family's. Nearly a third of all blacks, as against 10% of whites, live below what is officially reckoned as the poverty level; among them 45% of all black children, as against 15% of white ones.... The 31m or so blacks are 12% of America's population but supply nearly half its prison population."

Most immigrant groups had taken the traditional way out: education. Many young black men were taking a shorter one: crime. Although the college enrolment of black women had held steady in the past decade, that of black men had fallen. Analysing New York's underclass of all races, the paper still felt education remained the answer, but better-run schools would be needed if the next generation were to be lifted out of it: "Repair and clean the schools. Make them smaller: 600 pupils is too many for elementary schools, 2,000–3,000 far too many for high schools. Shift power away from the city's 32 politicised and often corrupt community school boards to the staff and parents of each school."

There had been a substantial growth in middle-class suburban blacks, the beneficiaries of the civil rights movement: "One example; Prince George's county, outside Washington, DC, now has a black majority. It may neither look nor be as prosperous as neighbouring (and overwhelmingly white) Montgomery county, Maryland; but it resembles Montgomery county more than it does the slums of south-east Washington, DC. In those slums the increasing concentration of low-skilled, jobless people has contributed to a vicious spiral of illegitimacy, crime and drug-taking."

What was happening was that Americans were rediscovering class as the gap between the comfortable and the poor widened. The paper could find no simple cause of this divergence: "A large part of it is explained by the movement to the south and west, to the suburbs, and by the worship of the car. This Holy Trinity of America has made life immeasurably more comfortable for most, but awful for some."

It thought federal dollars should be spent, preferably by a Republican president, to get poverty traps out of the tax structure, reinvigorate public transport, train people for jobs and start to control crime, by which it did not mean more concentration on punishment.

Health care was still a sore point. It was hugely expensive, yet the system still left some 37m people uninsured, including 12m children. Medicaid, the government programme that reimbursed poor people's health-care costs, reached fewer than two-fifths of them: "The cost of long-term care forces old people into poverty, after which the state picks up the bill. Although most doctors still make money, many honest hospitals border on bankruptcy. America's fee-for-service system creates an incentive to treat patients in the most expensive possible way after they become ill."

The paper advocated the scrapping of the tax exemption that individuals got for health-insurance premiums paid by their companies; it cost $50 billion a year. Instead people should get a tax credit but only for approved managed-care plans. Basic health care insurance should be made compulsory. And awards in medical malpractice suits should be limited.

The costs of an American hospital bed or college place had been rising far faster than productivity, the average American's ability to add value: "So either productivity must rise by more, or the cost of college and hospital must rise by less. Both goals require changes in health care and education, so that children are taught the skills that make them productive, while doctors and professors deliver their services at prices ordinary people can afford."

General Motors, posting record losses, had actually begun to spend more on health care than on steel.

Coping with the polluters The environment had already become an instinctive issue among much of the middle class. The pollution of the Alaskan coast by 11m gallons of oil from the stricken tanker *Exxon Valdez* in 1989 got saturation media coverage. The paper thought the outcry was out of proportion to the facts: "Some 8,700 loaded tankers have made the trip from Valdez since the Alaska pipeline began disgorging oil in 1977. They have spilt 0.00004% of their load (including the latest spill). Indeed the amount of oil spilt worldwide has fallen since the 1970s while the volume shipped has grown. The oil-shipping system is basically safe—so safe that men forget that they are still required to run it properly."

So directors and employees alike should lose their jobs when disasters did happen, just as the president of Japan Air Lines had quit when an ageing airliner crashed: "The sense of personal responsibility would do much to keep the safety drills slick, the captain sober, the otters swimming."

The pollution produced by automobiles was an issue that divided many families, though American politicians of all tendencies were chary of stringent increases in gasoline taxes. The paper was not courting voters. It thought regulation should be swept aside. The market, reinforced by taxation, would work much better: "Car exhaust makes ozone (which damages lungs) and kills trees (far more than does power-station smoke). Cars demand the drilling for oil in wildernesses; they dictate a growing dependence on imports of oil (about half of America's oil comes from abroad). Roads swallow up land and reduce people to traffic-jammers. Cars make much of the carbon dioxide that may overheat the global greenhouse."

But no solution would work effectively that did not get, however unpopular it was, to the heart of the matter: "Instead of dealing with each of these problems piecemeal—with emissions standards, fuel-efficiency averages, car-pooling laws, oil-drilling bans, domestic oil production subsidies (all with their own bureaucracies)—a bold president would attack the main problem through the market. He would put a ten-cent-a-gallon tax on petrol."

The paper refined this to a carbon tax, to tax the carbon content of fuels as they left the mine, dock and wellhead. Naturally, it would help the budget deficit too: "A tax of roughly $28 per ton of carbon content of coal, oil and gas would raise $22.5 billion revenue in 1991 and $163 billion over five years: enough to make a big hole in the budget deficit. Such a tax would also allow America, the world's biggest puffer of greenhouse gases, to stabilise carbon-dioxide emissions by the end of the century."

Into the twenty-first The twentieth century had been indisputably the American century, and the paper showed no doubt that the remaining superpower would have a decisive, and positive, part to play in the twenty-first. As the early *Economist* would not believe that the United States would refuse to see the common sense of free trade until the late 1940s, so the modern one insists that America's present difficulties and deficits are susceptible to no more than common-sense measures that future Americans will not believe were resisted for so long by a country still with unbounded aspirations, energies and resources.

The coming of Clinton The paper did find some

Bill takes over. He brought the Democrats back, inherited overseas worries and a reviving economy at home.
What mattered to Europeans was that the remaining superpower should keep its world responsibilities.

reassurance at the end of 1992 in the manner of George Bush's defeat by Bill Clinton, and in an apparent consistency of fundamental American attitudes. The election's outcome was entirely understandable, had been readily forecast and owed nothing to any unexpected shift in the American psyche. The suburbs voted as the remainder of the country did: because they thought that "the economy was in a mess". The young voted for Clinton and Al Gore, "two rather stiff, unhip, middle-aged men", because they put being hip second to getting a job. What were called the social issues, like abortion and fear of crime, "played virtually no part in the campaign, except possibly in California".

In fact, the moment the votes had been counted, the Bush people appeared to have been doing perfectly reasonable things about the economy, without troubling to persuade anyone they were. Both output and spending had been rising, even if sluggishly; the statistics were now widely adjudged to be encouraging. So recovery could be "stronger (and less inflationary) for coming slowly". But no one had bothered to sell this policy to the public.

So the paper told Clinton that the challenge to the modern state would be to meet the popular demand for action to revive the economy "without delivering, as bold interventionist governments have in the past, a crushing disappointment". His first goal must be to reduce the budget deficit. There must be "radical surgery" on non-discretionary federal spending, which would be "a bloody business" because it would mean disappointing friends. On public education, the cost of health care, investment in the infrastructure and tax reform, success would depend not on killing market capitalism but giving it a new lease of life.

The departing Bush, the paper said, deserved the credit he had been given for his successes abroad. In a world turned upside down, the United States had become "a steadying and collegial force". Bush's management of the Gulf war, the Middle East peace efforts and the free-trade agreement with Mexico should all be emulated. America, it transpired, had a continuing common purpose. Even though the intervention in

Somalia was a Bush initiative, "there can be no doubt it is also Mr Clinton's cause". A new foreign policy philosophy, "call it neo-Wilsonism", would have a strong moral dimension to it.

Still, the world which America found in its lap was a heavy responsibility. There were growing concerns that the country risked overextending itself on humanitarian missions to the detriment of its national security. To spread itself farther ("Liberia? South Africa? Azerbaijan?") would be better done within, and by, the United Nations. But was the United States, and the America-firsters especially, ready to put on the blue helmets and even pay the membership dues "in full and on time"? It would be wise to do so. Being the "world cop" might mean finding itself "in the worst mess of all".

The new order, such as it was, was perilously fragile. In all the real problems that would beset Clinton and post-cold war America—budgets, trade, Russian instability, Japan, Islam, the Balkans, poverty, AIDS, drugs—all the second-rank problems that success had inherited, the paper saw a continuing purpose in reminding Americans: "Yes, you are the superpower." With the experience of 150 years it settled down to go on nudging them in the direction a superpower should correctly wish to go.

INDEX

Acknowledgements

The photographs in this book are from the Hulton Deutsch Collection, except for those on:

page 13, which comes from The Economist Newspaper;
pages 256, 259, 263, which are credited to Consolidated/Hulton;
pages 223 and 228, which are from Camera Press.